6/02

REGULATING INTIMACY

Regulating Intimacy

A NEW LEGAL PARADIGM

Jean L. Cohen

PRINCETON UNIVERSITY PRESS
PRINCETON AND OXFORD

Copyright © 2002 by Princeton University Press
Published by Princeton University Press, 41 William Street,
Princeton, New Jersey 08540
In the United Kingdom: Princeton University Press,
3 Market Place, Woodstock, Oxfordshire OX20 1SY

All Rights Reserved.

Library of Congress Cataloging-in-Publication Data

Cohen, Jean L., 1946–
Regulating intimacy : a new legal paradigm
p.   cm.
Includes bibliographical references and index.
ISBN 0-691-05740-0 (cloth : alk. paper)
1. Sex and Law—United States. 2. Privacy, Right of—United States.
KF9325 .C64 2002
342.73′0858—dc21   2001027844

This book has been composed in Galliard

Printed on acid-free paper. ∞

www.pup.princeton.edu

Printed in the United States of America

10 9 8 7 6 5 4 3 2 1

Contents

Acknowledgments

◆ This book has been long in the making. My initial interest in the regulation of intimacy was triggered by an invitation to participate in a conference organized by Professor Martha Fineman at the Columbia University School of Law in the fall of 1991 entitled "Reproductive Rights in a Post-*Roe* World." At the time, many feared that the Supreme Court was about to overturn *Roe v. Wade* in *Planned Parenthood v. Casey* (finally decided in 1992). My defense of the privacy justification for abortion rights was first developed in the paper prepared for that conference, which subsequently appeared in the *Columbia Journal of Gender and Law* (1992). At the 1993 CSPT conference, "Democracy and Difference," co-sponsored by the Yale Program on Social Thought and Ethics, I presented another version of my privacy analysis in a paper entitled "Democracy, Difference, and the Right of Privacy," which appeared in the volume *Democracy and Difference*, edited by Seyla Benhabib, in 1996. Chapter 1 of the present book is adapted from these articles, and incorporates the feedback I received at these and other conferences.

I would like to thank the Institute für die Wissenschaften vom Menschen for funding the next stage in my research on gender, privacy, and the law in the spring of 1994. My stay in Vienna gave me the time to develop the main ideas of what became the second chapter of this book. A version of this chapter was first published in the *Texas Journal of Gender and Law* in 1996. A different version was developed for a paper presented to the 1995 CSPT conference, "Private Virtues and Public Life," co-sponsored by the Yale Program in Ethics, Politics, and Economics, organized by Alan Ryan. There I explored the relation between law and the construction of gendered identity as well as the neocommunitarian approach to the regulation of "minority sexual orientations." A version of this paper appeared in the volume *Public and Private*, edited by Maurizio Passerin d'Entreves and Ursula Vogel, in 2000. Chapter 2 synthesizes the ideas presented and discussed in these conferences.

The main thesis of Chapter 3 on sexual harassment was first presented to the feminist reading group at Columbia University's Institute for Research on Women and Gender in 1998. The feedback from this session was very helpful, and I would especially like to thank Dorothea von Mucke of the German department and Carole Sanger of the law school. They both read several versions of this chapter and offered very good advice. I would also like to thank Gertrud Koch and the Kulturwissenschaftliches

Institut in Essen, Germany, for inviting me to be a fellow in 1998. There I had the leisure to further develop and then present the rough draft of what became Chapter 3. Matthias Kettner and Maeve Cooke gave especially helpful comments. Pierre Rosanvallon, of the Ecoles des hautes Etudes en Sciences Sociales, deserves very special thanks for inviting me to lecture on this topic at the Centre Saint Simon in Paris in May 1999. A first-rate discussion occurred at the Centre, for which I am very grateful. Irene Thery and Monique Cantos Sperber deserve special thanks. I am also indebted to Denis Lacorne of Sciences Politiques at the University of Paris for inviting me to the international conference also held in Paris in December 1999 on privacy and intimate life. Beate Roessler deserves thanks for inviting me to present my work on privacy and sexual harassment at the Amsterdam conference she organized, "Private and Public," in May 2000. Her comments and the discussions with Anita Allen and, again, Maeve Cooke were very helpful. Finally, Jeff Weintraub deserves thanks for having invited me to present my work on sexual harassment at an NEH seminar at Dartmouth in August 2000. Each of these conferences afforded the opportunity to further develop my ideas and generated important discussion. Chapter 3 is adapted from my essays on sexual harassment prepared for these conferences. The essays appeared in slightly different versions: *Constellations* 4, no. 4 (December 1999) and subsequently in *La Revue Tocqueville* 21, no. 2 (2000) and in the superb issue edited by Irene Thery of *Esprit* on "l'un et l'autre sex" (mars-avril 2001).

I cannot omit thanking my co-organizers of the yearly seminar on philosophy and the social sciences, for they have heard and discussed versions of these initial three chapters. They include Hubertus Buchstein, Peter Dews, Alessandro Ferrara, Axel Honneth, and Frank Michelman. Frank Michelman deserves special thanks for his extraordinarily helpful suggestions on my first two chapters. Participants in these seminars, too numerous to mention here, provided extremely insightful and helpful commentary. In particular, I would like to thank Jodi Dean for her helpful criticisms.

The most insightful comments on Chapter 4 came from William E. Scheuerman and Gunther Teubner. Both these colleagues were extraordinarily generous with their time and gave me very helpful suggestions on the reflexive law discussion, albeit from opposite points of view.

I would like to thank Ute Gerhard and Cristel Eckart for inviting me to the conference "Public and Private," sponsored by the Graduiertenkollege at the Johann Wolfgang Goethe–Universität, Frankfurt-am-Main, in the spring of 2001. There I had the chance to present a version of the final chapter of this text and received very thoughtful and helpful comments.

In addition to those already mentioned, I would like to thank the following friends and colleagues for their help and support: Alan Ryan, Seyla

Benhabib, Martha Fineman, Rainer Forst, Morris Kaplan, Kendall Thomas, Bob Shapiro (in his capacity as chair of the political science department), and, last in the sense of most recent, Susan Sturm.

Special thanks go to my editor, Ian Malcolm, for his great patience and help with seeing this book through. Allison Dawe has my gratitude for very helpful suggestions regarding Chapter 1. Eric Schramm did an excellent copyediting job, for which I am grateful. I would also like to thank my research assistant, Mona Krook, for her invaluable assistance on the footnotes and for her overall helpfulness and generosity. I thank James Turner as well, for his diligence in the preparation of the bibliography.

Last but most important of all, I want to thank Andrew Arato for his intellectual support, his willingness to discuss all aspects of this manuscript, and his encouragement of my project. Without his support this book would not have been written.

REGULATING INTIMACY

Introduction

◆ There have been remarkable changes in the "domain of intimacy" over the past four decades.[1] The massive entry of women (married, single, with and without young children) into the labor force and into public life, the declining importance of marriage with regard to the onset and pursuit of intimate relationships, and the shift in society's view of reproductive sex from a moral imperative to an ethical choice are some of the relevant processes at work here.[2] For the first time in history, women are coming to be recognized as full legal persons and as equal citizens—a change in status of epochal importance. They are also beginning to insist publicly upon their own agency and happiness in the domain of intimacy and elsewhere. Profound shifts in the cultural meaning of sexuality and gender inform and follow from these developments. So does contestation over the forms and ethics of intimate relationships and over the gendered division of labor.

Conventional attempts to determine the appropriate relation between the state, law, and intimate relationships have been undermined by these developments. It is no longer possible to ignore issues of justice arising in "legitimate" intimate association by relegating them to the domestic sphere of the "private" conjugal family, deemed off-limits to legal intrusion. Nor has the corollary of this approach remained acceptable: that state "morals" legislation should control non- or extramarital intimacies through direct regulation or outright prohibition on the assumption that they are, by definition, immoral. The naturalness of the old public/private dichotomy along with the gender assumptions that informed previous strategies of juridification have largely collapsed.

Indeed, the rights revolution that began in the 1960s to address issues of race and class has also had a major impact in the area of sex/gender and intimate association.[3] Controversial national legislation and the much-debated constitutionalization of key rights protecting privacy and equality in that domain are an expression of this trend.[4] Just how intimate relationships (at home, at work, and elsewhere) are to be regulated by law has become a key stake in America's infamous culture wars. Reconceiving the purpose and appropriate form of juridification in this domain is thus a pressing theoretical and political concern.

The two dominant approaches to this issue leave us with a dilemma. The classical liberal insists that nothing is more personal, more central to the pursuit of happiness, more intrinsic to individuals' conception of the good, of who they are and how they want to live, than intimate relationships involving sex.[5] Surely this should be a matter of personal choice, protected by basic privacy rights. Libertarians agree with the substance of this assessment, although some argue against constitutional privacy protection for intimate association, preferring that traditional status-based regulations be replaced by contractual arrangements—in other words, a shift from public to private ordering.[6] According to this approach, provided there is no force or fraud, the less state regulation and legal interference in this domain, the better.

Yet we know, thanks to feminist interventions, that intimacy can involve gendered power relations and that sexuality can be a medium of injustice. The personal is also political. Many feminist egalitarians thus argue that direct, substantive legal regulation in a domain once considered off-limits to state intrusion—the private family—is indispensable to justice between genders.[7] They also call for legal regulation of sexual expression and intimate relationships in the workplace, in order to address the shifting boundaries between private and public, to undo gender hierarchies, and to prevent sexual harassment and related forms of injustice.[8]

This sort of juridification, however, can pose serious threats to personal privacy, autonomy, and freedom of expression and association. It is apparent that both regulation and nonregulation of intimacy creates normative dilemmas. The principle of equal liberty at the center of modern constitutional democracies seems to disintegrate into its component parts in this domain. We are confronted with the following paradox: legal regulation of sexual expression and intimate personal decisions in the name of justice seem to undermine the personal autonomy and privacy crucial to intimate relationships and to interfere with the pursuit of happiness that is, after all, their purpose. Yet nonregulation permits injustice to go undeterred and unpunished.

This paradox has appeared irresolvable in two key areas of innovative juridification: the development of constitutional privacy rights covering certain intimate personal decisions and relationships, and the creation of sexual harassment law out of civil rights legislation aimed at deterring discrimination on the basis of sex. In both these areas, liberty and equality values seem to clash, and an unattractive choice between legal regulation and nonregulation seems unavoidable.

By bringing together feminist theory, political philosophy, and legal analysis, this book attempts to clarify these dilemmas and provide some tentative solutions. I attempt to show that it is possible to avoid some of the most intractable paradoxes involved in the legal regulation of intimacy by shifting to a new theoretical framework. In particular I argue, first, that despite the demise of the old public/private dichotomy, we still need a normatively compelling and analytically cogent conception of privacy and of privacy rights. Otherwise, the issues involved in the regulation of intimate relationships cannot be addressed fruitfully because privacy is an enabling condition of intimacy. I argue that it is only one certain conception of privacy that puts personal autonomy, equality, and community in an antinomic relationship. That conception, together with flawed justifications of privacy rights and a cavalier attitude toward privacy by its critics, is partly responsible for the unattractive choices apparently facing those striving for gender justice in the domain of intimacy.

But I also defend a second thesis: that these choices are dictated by a deeper problematic. I have in mind the tendency to approach the issue of regulation from within either of two competing paradigms of law—the liberal model and the welfare model—that structure the possible responses in ways that are one-sided and reciprocally blind. Only if we explore this deeper problem will we be able to grasp the dynamics behind the paradoxes in regulating intimacy. Indeed, I argue that the paradoxes arise in large part from anachronistic paradigmatic conceptions of law, of the relation between state and society, and of the forms legal regulation must take. I argue that what has come to be called the "reflexive" legal paradigm is a much better framework within which to conceptualize the normative choices, political stakes, and appropriate legal forms involved in the regulation of intimacy.

It may be helpful to give a working definition of a legal paradigm before I proceed. A paradigm of law is not a scientific theory or a legal doctrine, but an integrated set of cognitive and normative background assumptions informing legislative and juridical interpretations both of the relationship the law should establish between state and society and of the appropriate forms of legal regulation.[9] Legal paradigms can harden into ideologies if these assumptions blind us to the emergence of new facts or situations and, in doing so, screen out innovative interpretations of rights and principles.

I believe this has occurred with the two legal paradigms that dominate discussion of the juridification of intimacy today. Both are guided by the principle of equal liberty, although they construe it differently. Briefly, the liberal paradigm sees threats to liberty from the state. Accordingly, the state should restrict itself to formally guaranteeing the equal liberty of everyone to pursue in the private sphere their particular conceptions of the good. The private sphere, off-limits to state intervention, is construed as the terrain of freedom. Provided there is no force or fraud, what sorts of relationships people create with each other is not the law's business. To be sure, personal freedoms must be secured by a set of basic rights that construct people as legal persons. To accomplish this and prevent arbitrariness and unfair privilege, the law must be formal—rule bound, general, and concise—and limited to the function of defining the abstract spheres of action, or liberties, for the autonomous pursuit of personal interests. This form of juridification allegedly establishes a structure for fair interpersonal and contractual relations, acknowledging private orderings established by autonomous legal subjects.

Although it operates with a similar conception of personal autonomy, theorists and advocates of the welfare paradigm reject the core premise of the liberal model: that the universal principle of equal liberty can be guaranteed through the status of the legal subject, formal law, and constitutionalized autonomy rights. On the assumption that state and society are inextricably fused, juridification in the welfare model is regulatory, interventionist, and direct. Law based on the welfare paradigm is materialized—substantive, particularized, and goal-directed. Unlike formal law, it does not take prior distributions of wealth, power, and status as given. Rather, substantive materialized law, especially when it intends to equalize, does so by dictating outcomes.

It should be obvious from this brief description that within both of these legal paradigms, trade-offs appear necessary between state action and individual agency, between formal and material law, and between personal autonomy/privacy and equality. As my analysis of three case studies shows, this conundrum creates problems for legal opinions and political-theoretical debates in very diverse contexts.

But recently influential theorists have begun to articulate the rudiments of a third paradigm of law that enables one to rethink problems in the domain of intimacy. Indeed, a major thesis of this book is that from the perspective of an emergent reflexive paradigm of law, one can reframe the relevant conflicts and discover that other alternatives are available. Using the reflexive paradigm, I attempt to show that it is possible at least to diminish, if not to fully resolve, the conflict among the warring gods in this domain. In particular I argue that the reflexive paradigm leads to a new understanding of legal regulation and of state/society relations, allowing one to see how state regulation can foster autonomy and recognize plurality while still satisfying the demands of justice.

Gleaning insights from the best available sources on the reflexive/procedural paradigm, I try to develop a conception of a specific type of law: reflexive law as a "postregulatory" mode of regulation.[10] Reflexive law applies procedures to procedures (hence its reflexivity), steering and fostering self-regulation within social institutions. Guided by the principle of equal liberty, reflexive law echoes formal law in its support for social autonomy. Unlike formal law, however, it does not simply adapt to "natural private orderings" or "prior distributions," or posit "natural liberty." Instead, it creates and protects "regulated autonomy," ensuring that the bargaining power, voice, and standing of the interacting individuals in the relevant domain are equalized and oriented by the appropriate principles. Provided certain procedural norms and principles of justice are respected, the relevant parties are free to strike whatever substantive agreements they wish. Thus unlike material law, reflexive regulation does not entail dictating particular substantive outcomes. Accordingly, juridification on this approach can reduce the tension between autonomy and equality that seems so obdurate from the perspective of the other two legal paradigms and their corresponding forms of law. I attempt to show that there are important elements of this mode of juridification already at work in the domain of intimacy and that they should be fostered when appropriate.

But the reflexive procedural paradigm can also be construed as a "meta-paradigm" allowing for a flexible use or combination of the various forms of law in the appropriate circumstances.[11] It thus allows for a new form of law and a new framework within which the choice among all available forms of juridification can be made. My argument is for legal pluralism and cogent choice among legal forms within a coherent paradigmatic framework. This is important because the state and regulatory regimes are indeed always involved in the domain of intimate association even when the autonomy of the individual is acknowledged. Even where constitutional privacy rights are concerned, one must recognize that they do not only protect personal interests of individuals against the state but also actualize a state interest: the interest in fostering responsible ethical choice and equality of personal autonomy.

The book thus operates on two levels simultaneously. The first addresses the normative, political, and legal debates over privacy rights, equality concerns, and the regulation of intimacy (decisions and relationships) in three specific contexts: reproduction (contraceptive and abortion rights), same-sex relationships, and sexual harassment in the workplace. My focus is on reconceptualizing constitutional privacy rights and demonstrating their importance for each domain, although I acknowledge the relevance, indeed indispensability, of equal protection in each case as well.

The second level of analysis discusses the more fundamental assumptions and issues involved in the choice of paradigmatic approaches to legal regulation of intimacy in each context. A great deal hinges on the mode of legal regulation of a particular intimate matter. Superimposing this perspective on the first allows one to develop convincing justifications for existing rights and to envision a new set of alternatives that, as already indicated, mitigates what otherwise appears as an irreconcilable clash of values when it comes to the freedom for and within intimate relationships and the necessary regulation of intimate association.

OVERVIEW

Initiated by the landmark 1965 decision in *Griswold v. Connecticut,* in which the Supreme Court explicitly recognized a constitutional right to privacy for the first time (covering the use of contraception), what is commonly referred to as the "new privacy jurisprudence" has developed around matters of reproductive rights, sexuality, and intimate personal relationships.[12] What was new in this jurisprudence was not the application of the concept of privacy to the marital relationship or to the family construed as an entity. Rather, the innovation lay in the Court's attempt to articulate constitutional grounds for directly protecting the personal privacy and decisional autonomy of individuals in relation to "intimate" personal concerns, whether these arise within the family setting or outside it.[13]

Prior to *Griswold*, the common law doctrine of family privacy protected the authority and prerogatives of the male head of household over everyone within the family unit against outside interference.[14] Accordingly, statutes challenging family autonomy or family privacy in derogation of common law were narrowly construed, while those reinforcing common law by protecting morals throughout civil society were given a wide latitude.[15] Two assumptions underlay this jurisprudence: state legislation could not violate "natural orderings" of intimate relationships in the private sphere; and the regulatory police powers of the states were limited to matters involving an accepted public purpose and what was in the public interest.[16]

This mode of regulating intimacy had a clear logic: the states' public purpose was to promote heterosexual marriage and, within that institution, to support reproductive sexuality and shield the family unit. The states' privileging of heterosexual monogamous marriage and the "natural" patriarchal gender order it institutionalized meant that privacy protection was limited to the nuclear family unit. The "civil death" of the married woman—her lack of legal personality and civic equality—fit this model perfectly.[17] Correspondingly, states had considerable freedom to regulate non- or extramarital intimacies or "public morals."

The new constitutional privacy analysis turns this approach on its head. It articulates the concept of a right to personal privacy as an individual right of ethical decisional autonomy (to pursue one's conception of the good), control over access and personal information, and a new conception of the scope of individual privacy that now applies to important aspects of the domain of morals, formerly the special preserve (along with health and safety) of state regulation.[18] The Supreme Court's decisions overturning state laws on reproductive rights and other aspects of intimate association rest on the relatively recent assumption (since the New Deal) that the federal government has wide regulatory powers, and that constitutional amendments articulating fundamental rights apply to the states as well as to the federal government.[19] Previously it was assumed that government should leave individuals alone unless the exercise of state power advanced a valid public purpose. Now the prevailing premise is that the government's power should be left undisturbed unless it can be shown that the law infringes upon a discrete fundamental right.[20] Accordingly, the Court's new task has become the specification of those discrete "fundamental," "preferred" liberties that deserve to be protected both from unjust state legislation and against an ever-expanding regulatory federal government.[21] Hence the discourse of fundamental rights.

As juridification of important aspects of the domain of intimacy has begun to shift to the national level, tracking deep cultural and social transformations, a trend has emerged toward the individualization and constitutionalization of matters that in the past had been dealt with under the rubric of family law and states' morals legislation. The recognition of claims to full legal personality and civic equality of women informs this trend. Pluralization of the forms of legitimate intimate association is one of its effects. The assumption that there is one morally correct way to form intimate relationships has been undermined along with the raison d'être of a large part of the states' morals legislation. The constitutionalization of individualized privacy rights that are construed as fundamental in the domain of intimacy ascribes to the intimate associates themselves the competence to choose both how to pursue happiness and how to realize their conceptions of the good life. This in turn implies that moral monism (based mostly on religious foundations) has essentially given way to ethical pluralism regarding sex and the forms that intimate relationships may take. At the very least, a new rationale for regulation and juridification in this domain is now called for.

The discovery of fundamental privacy rights in the domain of intimacy, however, raises important philosophical and legal/constitutional issues, and it certainly has not gone uncontested. Indeed, it seems paradoxical that privacy and autonomy rights are being asserted as fundamental in American jurisprudence just when their supporting philosophical arguments seem no longer convincing.[22] Notions of natural rights or natural liberty antecedent to and limiting government have an almost quaint air to them after the linguistic turn in philosophy.[23] The argument that there are essentially private, purely individual matters that concern no one else and hence deserve to be shielded from public scrutiny appears antiquated and difficult to defend. So is the sociological image of the natural, private, prepolitical sphere in the epoch of the interventionist state. Many argue that since the state legally constitutes the domains of action subject to its regulatory power, even the decision not to regulate a particular activity is a political decision rather than the expression of a prior fundamental right. The autonomy or privacy that the law claims to recognize is its own creation. The whole discourse of fundamental privacy rights protecting the individual and her negative liberty against state intervention seems anachronistic.

So does the Court's talk about "substantive due process" privacy rights covering intimate association. Since there is no mention of a right to privacy in the Constitution, the Court's revival of substantive due process analysis seems suspect: it appears to be a strategy to regain the jurisdictional power the Court lost over the economy, in a new area.[24] The constitutionalization and individualization of privacy rights in the domain of intimacy simultaneously constructs new legal persons and a new role for the Courts: the protection of each person's equal liberty regarding intensely personal matters through judicial review of legislation. The growth of the Court's power with respect to the states and other branches of the federal government has not gone unnoticed or uncontested. Indeed, some have come to see the Supreme Court's new role in the intimate domain as yet another lamentable example of "government by the judiciary" to the detriment of democratic representative institutions.[25] Others decry the Court's discretionary power over intimate concerns, arguing that it establishes a new, national form of judicial patriarchy.[26]

This book is not about judicial review. While I believe the issue of judicial power is very serious for constitutional democrats, I bracket this problem and focus instead on the forms of legal regulation and the types of reasoning that should orient courts and legislatures actually engaged in the regulation of intimacy. I try, in short, to present a constructive agenda for such regulation by focusing on the substantive assumptions and legal paradigms that should orient the new approach to privacy rights and to the regulation of intimacy generally.[27]

In political philosophy, two theoretical traditions have stressed the importance of privacy, albeit for different reasons: republicanism and liberalism. The former, primarily concerned with public freedom and active citizenship, argues the importance of protecting a sphere of personal liberty and privacy on *instrumental* grounds: without such protection, democratic citizenship would be insecure and the public space for the exercise of political freedom would tend to become both overextended and undermined.[28]

Liberals, by contrast, insist on the *intrinsic* value of a protected sphere of personal privacy and liberty. They do so usually by invoking the centrality of individual choice and judgment to moral autonomy and/or self-realization. They stress the importance of freedom from intrusion and state regulation when moral deliberation and ethical judgment of personal matters are at stake and when no direct harm to others ensues from one's choices.[29]

But both traditions have relied on a set of core assumptions, ranging from foundationalist and metaphysical arguments for personal autonomy associated with the philosophy of the subject and/or natural rights theory, to a stereotypical conception of gender roles and natural orderings, often mapped onto an understanding of the private (especially the domestic sphere of the family) as a prepolitical sphere of life. These underlying assumptions determined what each deemed to be essentially private and essentially public. For both, the sanctity of private property (attached to the private family) symbolizes the meaning of privacy and what shields it in the domain of intimacy.[30]

Today, however, such anachronistic theoretical presuppositions have been abandoned by most serious philosophers. Few believe it is possible to find an ultimate ground for norms; the sociohistorical construction of gender roles and identities is widely acknowledged, as is the cultural and social meaning of private and intimate matters and relationships. The idea of natural orderings, or that there is one right way to form and conduct intimate relationships, is no longer convincing. Consequently, neither the boundary between public and private nor any particular conception of the core of personal privacy can be determined or justified by invoking their natural or intrinsic character or by gesturing to what is innate, logically speaking, to the concept of the moral person. In short, the philosophical rug has been pulled out from under the two most important political theoretical defenses of fundamental privacy rights. There no longer exists a knock-down theoretical argument that can ground such rights or supply a principle for determining precisely what they cover.

It is nevertheless my thesis that the new discourse of constitutional privacy rights constitutes an important normative advance and can yield indispensable protection to citizens living in globalized societies. By construing privacy in the domain of intimacy as a matter of individual decisional autonomy (already very different from the "right to be let alone"), the relevant Supreme Court decisions have taken an important if inadequate first step in that direction. However, much of the reasoning involved in privacy jurisprudence is deeply flawed.

In Chapters 1 and 2 I take up the theoretical challenge to articulate a coherent conception of privacy and personal autonomy that I believe is implicit in the Court's new privacy jurisprudence. I also attempt to develop a constructivist justification of this new conception, free of the baggage of anachronistic philosophical and social assumptions often adduced by the Court to justify its decisions. My purpose is to replace the quasi-metaphysical and foundationalist reasoning presupposed both by the defenders and critics of privacy jurisprudence.

Although important changes have certainly undermined the old boundaries, the public/private distinction has not been abolished. Instead, it is being reconstructed around new, highly contested boundaries in relation to and within intimacy: personal intimate relationships and personal intimate decisions. Indeed, the idea of a right to the privacy of intimate relationships and all that this entails is replacing private property as the cardinal symbol of personal freedom, symbolizing the boundary of the legitimate scope of governmental authority and of appropriate concern by third parties.

That intimacy requires privacy is obvious: all the main dimensions of privacy, from the informational to issues of access and expressive concerns, are, along with autonomy interests, evoked by this idea. Conversely, if a privacy right is to have any meaning at all, it must at the very least shield intimacy. Thus it is well worth the effort to develop a convincing justification for contemporary privacy rights in this domain.

Nevertheless, the revival of the discourse of privacy and of fundamental liberties in the domain of intimacy appears paradoxical. It looks as if the new constitutional right of privacy devoted to marking off a protected sphere of personal autonomy, personal expression, and control—deemed fundamental and construed as a form of negative liberty—simply transfers an older, now defunct property rhetoric along with the anachronistic assumptions of the liberal paradigm into a new area.[31] Even if we can develop a normatively compelling conception of personal privacy that fits "our" intuitions regarding intimate relationships, reviving the discourse of privacy vis-à-vis a doctrine of fundamental rights on the constitutional level may be wrongheaded. How can the charge of archaism or arbitrariness be avoided when there are no agreed upon criteria to determine just what is fundamental to personhood or just which intimate choices, relationships, and modes of expression are to be covered?

Chapter 1 takes up these questions. There I address the controversy over constitutionalized privacy rights triggered by the Supreme Court decisions in *Griswold v. Connecticut, Eisenstadt v. Baird,* and especially *Roe v. Wade.* Through the prism of the debates in political and legal theory over the privacy justification for reproductive rights, and by looking at the relevant Court opinions, I attempt to clarify the theoretical issues at stake here.

I focus in particular on two recent challenges to the privacy justification for reproductive rights, both of which target what are taken to be its conceptual and normative presuppositions, albeit from opposite points of view: one articulated by neocommunitarian critics of liberalism, the other by feminist legal theorists favoring equality jurisprudence. Shifts and instabilities in the concept of privacy and privacy rights become apparent in my discussion of the paradoxes of privacy analysis in this context. The main work of this chapter is to explicate the new conception of privacy implicit in the Court's constitutionalization of individual privacy rights in this area and to provide a constructivist justification for it that does not rely on anachronistic assumptions. Indeed, I argue that the use of a broad concept of privacy by the Court is not just an imprecise, arbitrary, or merely strategic way of establishing a right to sexual autonomy.[32] Rather,

I maintain that the concept of a right to privacy in relation to intimacy is felicitous and hermeneutically cogent precisely because of its diffuseness and breadth: it does indeed ascribe decisional autonomy and control over access and information to the individual regarding certain intimate matters, but it also speaks to our contemporary cultural imaginary about personal identity and the importance of being able to creatively shape and reshape oneself through intimate relations shielded from the conformist pressures and intrusions of public judgment.

While the criticisms of constitutional privacy analysis are certainly not frivolous, I attempt to demonstrate that most derive from a misunderstanding of what the concept of a right to privacy entails regarding the nature of the private sphere and the notion of the individual it allegedly presupposes. In short, the criticisms succeed only against anachronistic justifications for such a right, but not against my constructivist approach.

I attempt to prove that it is possible to acknowledge the (socially and legally) constructed and historically specific dimensions of a conception of privacy, as well as the relational and situated dimensions of personal autonomy, and nonetheless present convincing arguments for privacy rights on the basis of the reflexive and linguistic turn in law and philosophy. In short, one goal of Chapters 1 and 2 is to redeem the insights of republican and liberal theorists regarding the intrinsic and instrumental importance of privacy on a different theoretical terrain than what such arguments have in the past presupposed. We can develop a cogent constructivist concept of privacy without relying on an individualist ontology, without resurrecting philosophical foundationalist arguments, and without resorting to essentialist presuppositions about gender to justify its scope. This, however, requires shifting to the perspective of the paradigm of reflexive law.

Even a theoretically defensible concept/conception of privacy and personal autonomy in relation to intimacy remains vulnerable to the charge of being sociologically obsolete. On this argument, the twentieth-century institutional realities of complex, differentiated, yet quite interdependent features of a modern social structure make any conception of a private sphere of life that is off-limits to state regulation naive and anachronistic. Even the articulation (by the Supreme Court or by Congress) of individual rights concerning intimate matters and protected by the Constitution or by national statute, can be construed as a form of juridification that shifts regulatory power from one level (states) to another (federal courts, legislators, administrators).

Critics of privacy discourse (often drawing on social construction theory) take this to mean that since "the private" is legally and politically constructed, any discourse of privacy rights securing fundamental liberties against the state is meaningless. In this view, the notion of a prepolitical, naturally private sphere was always a myth, but it took a vast increase in direct and open state intervention and juridification to dispel it. However, the discourse of intervention and nonintervention, of protecting the individual and her freedom (negative liberty) against the state and its regulatory scope, especially with regard to the domain of intimacy, was always ideological.[33]

The new forms of juridification in the intimate domain have indeed shifted the locus of regulation of intimacy. But the fusion of state and society that this shift allegedly entails is itself a myth. The reasoning of both critics and defenders of privacy analysis in the relevant cases is flawed because both operate with the assumptions of the liberal paradigm of law, although they assess them differently and, in some cases, advocate shifting to direct substantive regulation. I argue that the type of juridification developed within that paradigm (formal rules protecting negative liberty) can be defended on new grounds, free of anachronistic presuppositions regarding a prepolitical private sphere or natural liberty.

Absent the defunct theoretical baggage of the liberal paradigm, moreover, I also attempt to show that some of the paradoxes apparently inherent in this line of privacy analysis dissolve. I have in mind in particular the understanding of the state action doctrine that implies that protection of a negative liberty absolves the state from the responsibility of ensuring the worth of that liberty on the grounds that the state is not responsible for inequalities that arise in the prepolitical private sphere.[34] After deciding *Roe v. Wade*, the Court declared that states have no obligation to provide funding for indigent women who exercise their right to choose, invoking the state action doctrine. I maintain that nothing in the first decision compels the second. Rather, the flawed assumptions about state action, about a prepolitical private sphere composed of equally autonomous individuals, and about the limits to state regulation allegedly entailed by negative liberty informing the Court's decision are the artifacts of an inappropriate paradigmatic understanding of law.

Important forms of regulation intrinsic to the welfare paradigm aimed at ensuring the equal worth of negative liberties can and must supplement liberal privacy rights and present no justification problem once one shifts to the perspective of the third theoretical paradigm. From the standpoint of the reflexive paradigm, it becomes possible to relativize both approaches and, as already indicated, to select cogently among the three types of regulation. And from this perspective, the discourse of fundamentality (justifying constitutional privacy rights as liberties against the state) would not involve the absence of regulation or the hopeless task of determining the scope of an individual right of privacy by discovering what is intrinsic to personhood or essential to an identity. Rather, the task would shift to providing a constructivist articulation of the grounds and acceptable modes of public regulation of intimacy that everyone could accept in a society committed to personal liberty, gender equality, and ethical pluralism. Moreover, on the reflexive paradigm, fundamental rights would not refer to natural but to constructed autonomy: to the legally recognized discretion and competence imputed to adults to devise and pursue their chosen types of intimate relationships provided certain principles of justice and certain procedures are respected. The relational autonomy that is at stake here need not be construed as natural or somehow inherent in the atomistic individual—it is in part constructed by law (the state). In so constructing and shielding personal autonomy, the law does not thereby protect a stereotypical naturalized gender order regulating intimate relations as private. Rather, my thesis provides a way to consider the appropriate forms of regulation of intimate association on the assumption that the state interest in this domain is not to impose one form of intimacy on everyone; it is to foster civic equality, personal autonomy, and responsibility and to acknowledge what Rawls has called the fact of pluralism and the burdens of judgment in this particular domain of ethical life.

The limits of the liberal form of juridification and the paradoxes of privacy analysis seem incontrovertible, however, when it comes to the issues of group difference that emerge with regard to minority sexual orientations and identities. How can negative liberty and personal privacy protect gays and lesbians from being discriminated against because of their intimate choices or sexual identities? How can privacy rights provide public recognition of the ethical integrity of gay and lesbian relationships?

Indeed, many fear that the strategy of privatization as a mode of juridifying tolerance is dangerous. It risks reinforcing the stigma attached to minority sexual identities and exacerbating discrimination against public displays of disdained forms of life. Moreover, the assumption that sexuality defines identity and is fundamental to personhood, underlying many justifications of privacy analysis in this domain, is a double-edged sword. It can be used to reify group identities and impose them on individuals regardless of their own sense of themselves, thereby undermining personal autonomy.

I take up these issues in Chapter 2. I address the argument that gays and lesbians who invoke privacy rights to secure legal protection against persecution trap themselves in what Eve Sedgwick has called the "epistemology of the closet."[35] The privacy afforded by such a right appears equivocal, for it seems to presuppose that there is something shameful about one's sexual desires and intimate relationships that should be kept secret. On this terrain, privacy discourse can turn into a Faustian bargain: a duty of privacy (secrecy, concealment, silence, shame) in exchange for benign treatment (being let alone).

The Supreme Court's privacy analysis in the infamous *Bowers v. Hard-wick* case and the first Clinton administration's policy on gays in the military—the subject matter of Chapter 2—substantiate such fears.[36] In *Bowers* the Court invoked a traditional conception of privacy in order to deny claims to include same-sex relationships under its protective shield. The new military policy imposed a duty of privacy, of silence regarding gays' and lesbians' sexual orientation in exchange for tolerating their presence in the armed forces.

By analyzing these instances of juridification of "minority" intimate sexuality, relationships, and identities, and the debates they have generated, I show how, on a particular understanding, legal privacy analysis can indeed serve to undermine personal autonomy, ethical pluralism, and civic equality.

But conceptions of privacy, fundamentality, and personhood vary with the mode of incorporation of difference and the relative thickness (or thinness) of our ethical understanding of national identity. Constitutional regimes and legal paradigms influence and are affected by these conceptions.

Accordingly, I attempt to show that when properly conceptualized, constitutional privacy rights could provide an indispensable shield for "difference" and help protect against the inequality and oppression that result from harsh sex laws. Indeed, I argue that the *denial* of privacy protection for same-sex relationships in *Bowers* fostered oppressive privatization, and the epistemology of the closet in the new military policy. But I also show that while the privacy rights are necessary, they are not sufficient. Regulations enforcing equality principles are indispensable when stigmatized forms of intimate association linked to a particular minority are at issue. In the epoch of multiculturalism, it is no longer justifiable to construe a single model of intimate association as intrinsic to our national identity nor to assume that there is only one morally right way to conduct intimate relationships. There is disagreement over how best to realize the general values appropriate to intimacy: love, care, happiness, pleasure, loyalty, mutuality, trust, responsibility, reciprocity. Decoupling these from one ethical model of intimate relations means that they may be realized in a variety of ways. Everyone's equal liberty, everyone's personal autonomy and privacy, must be respected in this domain. Appropriately construed, privacy and equality rights acknowledge that a plurality of types of intimate association can realize the relevant values as long as they do not violate the moral principles that regulate interaction generally. But one must also beware of reifying or essentializing group identities under the guise of protecting their rights. It is thus necessary to develop a complex regulatory regime that can accommodate ethical plurality. Again we come up against the issue of legal paradigms. Clearly a plural approach regarding legal forms is required here, and the reflexive paradigm permits us to develop precisely that. In other words, the dilemmas of privacy analysis and the false choice between it and equality analysis dissolve from that perspective, allowing for an innovative combination of regulation and autonomy that can provide for both personal autonomy/privacy and civic equality.

A somewhat different set of problems besets the use of equality principles established in national civil rights laws and in the Fourteenth Amendment, to regulate intimate expression (sexual harassment) in the workplace. The same cultural transformations in sexuality and gender are at issue here as in the new privacy jurisprudence. But unlike the concept of a privacy right, the principles of equality and anti-discrimination are clearly present in the Constitution and in federal statute law. Indeed, it seems that the equality approach would avoid the worst difficulties of privacy analysis, for instead of having to discover unenumerated, discrete fundamental rights, the courts need only establish discrimination on the basis of sex, outlawed by Congress and in violation of the Fourteenth Amendment.

But there's the rub. It is by no means obvious which sexual expression in the workplace constitutes harassment and why any of it should be construed as gender discrimination instead of, say, as the individualized abuse of supervisory power actionable as a tort. Intense debates have erupted over just what the harm of harassment is, over the reasoning behind recent Court rulings that construe even same-sex harassment as discrimination on the basis of sex, and over the more general issue of equality analysis in this area.

I address these debates in Chapter 3. The clash between liberty, privacy, and equality values appears especially intense in the arena of sexual harassment law. Here, too, deep cultural conflict and normative disagreements over gender and sexuality call for renewed reflection and justification of legal regulation. Accordingly, in this chapter I provide a brief overview of the development of sexual harassment law in the United States and a discussion of the various positions in the new debate it has triggered. Feminist philosophers and legal theorists now disagree about how to characterize the harm of sexual harassment. Most want to revise the hegemonic "sex-desire/subordination" model informing legal and corporate regulation, because it tends to confuse sex with sexism and to cast women as victims in need of protection with no sexual agency of their own. It thus leads, paradoxically, both to over- and underregulation.

Yet neither the liberal objections to this model that inspire some feminist proposals nor the postmodern theoretical approach that informs others, each of which I analyze, has led to a satisfactory alternative. Instead, the new debate has spawned a set of antinomic positions, each offering remedies to one redescription of the harm while screening out the others.

Part of the problem lies in the monistic character of each approach. But not even the most comprehensive construal of the harms of harassment will resolve the dilemmas of regulation unless the effects of particular legal forms on the relevant domain of action are also addressed. Law has its own efficacy and the mode of legal regulation matters very much indeed. I thus shift perspective and discuss the paradigmatic conceptions of law presupposed by the various approaches and informing much legal interpretation. The tendency to over- or underregulate, and to turn equality (secured by regulation) and liberty (secured by nonregulation?) into a zero-sum game can be traced back to these sets of background assumptions. I show that on a different understanding of the harms of harassment and of the actual structure of harassment law, creative reforms that could minimize the conflict between equality and liberty values are quite conceivable.

The three substantive case studies point to the necessity to rethink legal regulation not only in light of new cultural orientations and social practices of intimate association and gender, but also from the standpoint of the paradigmatic assumptions informing legal regulation in this domain. There are serious problems and dilemmas plaguing attempts to regulate intimacy that do not stem from conceptual confusion over the meaning of privacy or equality. Nor can they be attributed to the political and strategic discourses deployed by those defending pluralization of forms of intimate association against those seeking to privilege traditional heterosexual marriage as morally best, once again. For even if one gets the normative principles of justice right regarding what equal liberty must entail in this domain, even if the lawmaker's or interpreter's understanding of public purpose is informed by feminist rather than traditional/stereotypical gender expectations, even if tolerant and solidary attitudes toward diversity prevail, the mode of legal regulation itself can nevertheless have negative consequences.

I address this problematic indirectly in the first two chapters, more explicitly in the third. As noted, I seek to show that dichotomies taken to be unavoidable in the regulation of intimacy—liberty versus equality, regulation versus nonregulation, public versus private orderings, status versus contract, diversity and autonomy versus responsibility—do not derive from the intrinsic nature of intimacy or law. Rather, they must be attributed to assumptions about the appropriate relation between state and society and about the forms that legal regulation must take, inherent in certain legal paradigms. Of course, this raises issues that go well beyond the regulation of intimacy. Indeed, the paradigm problematic was first articulated with regard to dilemmas that arose in the areas of economic regulation, labor, and environmental law.[37] It pertains, in my view, to every legally regulated domain. It is thus necessary to consider the concept of a legal paradigm directly. Accordingly, in Chapter 4 I address the theoretical and normative issues involved in the debate over legal paradigms in general and over the reflexive paradigm of law in particular. Legal theorists, among them Gunther Teubner, Jürgen Habermas, and Philip Selznick, have argued that a new paradigmatic approach involving "reflexive," "procedural," and/or "responsive" law, respectively, offers a way to reframe and even resolve many of the old dichotomies and regulatory paradoxes. Recently, however, the "reflexive/procedural" paradigm has itself become the target of criticism. Three charges in particular have been raised: first, that reflexive law is simply a new form of privatization and/or neocorporatism involving the delegation of authority and decision making to ultimately irresponsible powers; second, that the reflexive/procedural paradigm undermines either the rule of law or democracy or both; and third, that the theory of legal paradigms is itself unconvincing because it rests on an untenable evolutionism.[38]

There is also a debate about whether reflexive law is simply a "context-sensitive" form of central political steering (thus, not so new), or a distinct and innovative form of contextualized political law. On the latter approach, local organizations "make law" and literally develop the content of legal norms in response to outside stimuli (legislation, liability, adjudication) instead of applying norms whose content is developed in the political and legal systems, as the former approach implies.[39] These two competing models of the third paradigm rest on distinct conceptions of society and its relation to regulation: the context-sensitive approach still privileges political steering while the "contextualized law" approach sees society as composed of a multiplicity of equal subsystems, each of which can generate internal norms but none of which can steer the others.

In Chapter 4 I revisit the various approaches to the theory of legal paradigms and reflexive/procedural/responsive law in order to parry these charges and clarify my own conception. I argue that the reflexive form of law is not a panacea but one useful type of regulation in certain circumstances. As to the question whether reflexive law is best described as context-sensitive central steering or as the contextual genesis of legal norms, my position is somewhere in between. I construe society as decentered but argue for stronger possibilities of communication between the various subsystems than what the second approach admits to. I favor publicly articulated general legal norms whose content, however, is developed on the local level through institutional (substantive and procedural) innovation oriented toward effective, fair problem solving. Through the help of mediators, recursive learning within and across organizations on the part of the judiciary, and ultimately by political lawmakers (legislators), becomes possible.[40] Accordingly, the judiciary should be seen as a catalyst for innovation, learning, and communication within and between subsystems. The Court's regulatory purpose should be to guide and supplement local bases of norm generation and local efforts to change behavior, by creating incentives for compliance with general constitutional principles. However, as Chapter 3 makes clear, a great deal depends upon how the regulation of self-regulation, how reflexive law, is institutionalized. I also argue that it is necessary to shift to the general standpoint of the reflexive legal paradigm suitably reinterpreted: this provides a meta-perspective that allows one to reframe choices and alternatives among legal forms and to resolve regulatory dilemmas in the domain of intimacy, in a fruitful and productive way.

I was thus delighted to come across a first-rate article on employment discrimination and sexual harassment that develops a similar approach, just published by Susan Sturm.[41] While I encountered this piece too late to address it in depth in this book, I mention it here to indicate that work similar in approach to mine is being done by American legal theorists. Although it employs a different language and uses a two-part rather than a three-part framework, this work is focused on developing the new regulatory legal paradigm with which I am concerned. For example, Sturm distinguishes between a "rule-based enforcement" model and a "dynamic structural" approach to regulation. The latter is exactly parallel to the model of reflexive law that I use.[42] Her article analyzes in wonderful detail how what I call the reflexive form of legal regulation already works and could work better with regard to "second generation" sex discrimination, including sexual harassment, in the workplace. Sturm not only makes a very strong case for this form of regulation in such contexts; she also grants that in different areas and for different problems, other forms of regulation remain appropriate. I bring this intuition to the level of theory: reflexive regulation of self-regulation is a particular legal form that suits some aspects of intimate association, while the reflexive paradigm permits reflection on reflexivity and on legal forms generally, enabling one to select other types of regulation, including nonregulation, when appropriate.

Chapter 5 applies the perspective of my revised conception of the reflexive paradigm to the issues raised in the first three chapters. It shows how this approach resolves these and many other problems that arise regarding the regulation of intimacy under the contemporary presumption of gender equality. Indeed, I am not alone in noting the transformation of intimacy and the changes in the legal regimes that regulate intimate association. Many have registered the decline of the old status regime and the profound cultural and social change that the premise of gender equality has performed. The value of personal autonomy to intimate association has been acknowledged, as has the necessity of fostering and shielding the diverse purposes of intimacy: happiness and experimentation on the one side, with solidarity, mutual care, and responsibility on the other.

Yet the debate over how to respond legally to the changes in this domain remains mired in categories and conceptions that preclude adequate responses and unnecessarily dichotomize choices and values. The concluding chapter takes up this problem from the optic of the increasingly shrill debate over contractualist versus status-based models of intimate association. Although it partly overlaps with the privacy versus equality dichotomy discussed in the first three chapters, this controversy raises distinct issues. Protagonists in this debate assume that we must choose between private ordering or, alternatively, a reconstructed status regime attuned to contemporary conditions, but one that seeks nonetheless to protect marriage, the family, and vulnerable family members from "disintegrative forces" through direct substantive public ordering of intimate association. From this perspective, the dilemma appears as the tension between letting intimate associates choose their forms of intimacy, including entry and exit conditions (the contractual model), or legally imposing a nationally articulated status regime that ensures responsibility within intimate association and hence restricts choice regarding the relational dynamics, dependencies, and issues of care and solidarity that such association entails. In other words, once again the choice appears to be between contract and status, private and public, deregulation and heavy-handed, intrusive state regulation (to ensure relational responsibility and to protect community). Theoretically, this is expressed in the debates between the law and economics school (the contractualists) and neocommunitarians (the regulators).[43]

The tendency to construe recent trends toward the constitutionalization and individualization of key aspects of intimate association as a wholesale switch from status to contract is indicative of the problem.[44] The shift of large areas of what was once the province of state-controlled family law over to private ordering seems to indicate that the contractualists have won. But the communitarian critique invited by this empirical and conceptual shift is gaining ground, as the discourse of family values and pleas for the revival of status to protect marriage reveal.[45] Even feminist critics of privatization seem forced to deploy the language of status, although they of course assume that its revival along with renewed state regulation will occur on the terrain of gender equality.[46] Their hope is that it is possible to sever status from connotations of gender hierarchy, male dominance, and moralism regarding sex.

Because it structures the contemporary debate over how to regulate intimacy, I discuss the arguments and assumptions of the contractualist and the status-oriented communitarian approach in some detail in Chapter 5. I argue that neither the constitutionalization or individualization of family law nor constitutional privacy analysis need entail a wholesale shift to contractual private orderings. This would be unavoidable only on the premises of the liberal legal paradigm construed as the only alternative to the welfare model. My goal is, once again, to shift the terms of the debate and to show that the reflexive paradigm offers a way to recast the entire problematic and to construct more appropriate responses then either approach has to offer. Postregulatory regulation, as we shall see, provides for regulated autonomy and regulated privacy—each an oxymoron in the other two paradigmatic approaches. On the meta-paradigm level, the reflexive framework allows one to thematize the likely effects of different modes of regulation. In short, it facilitates a flexible combination of the various forms of law in the appropriate circumstances.[47]

This is important since the domain of intimacy is no longer localizable in the domestic sphere of the private family, partly because women have entered the public spheres of work and politics. Intimate relationships now openly form in a multiplicity of sites, from the workplace and the school to the home, and require different forms of regulation. These can range from outright prohibitions (in criminal and civil law, such as rape laws, laws against spousal violence, and laws against quid pro quo harassment), to constitutional guarantees of personal privacy in the form of negative liberties (protection of decisional autonomy regarding contraception, abortion, sexual history of rape victims, wanted consensual adult sex, and so on), to substantive regulations (such as child-support requirements upon divorce and visitation rights), to reflexive laws fostering collective self-regulation when appropriate (as in the case of sexual harassment in the workplace, divorce mediation procedures, and domestic partnerships and marriage). Just which mode of juridification is the most appropriate to the issue at hand has to be determined contextually, but in a principled manner, guided by norms of civic equality, personal autonomy and democratic citizenship.

In sum, the reflexive paradigm would allow us to shift attention away from the fruitless debate over regulation versus deregulation of intimate relationships, and it would suggest possibilities other than the unattractive choice between privacy or equality, autonomy or responsibility.

We should all be aware of how high the stakes really are in the culture and gender wars being fought on the terrain of law and intimate association. If concerns for due process and personal autonomy are not attended to, if wanted consensual intimate relationships are not shielded from intrusion and unwarranted regulation by the state or third parties, if in the name of justice the personal life of even the most powerful figure in the country can be exposed in court and the mass media, if law intended to secure gender equality can be misused in the politics of scandal, then no one's privacy or liberty is safe. On the other side, if the equal citizenship of all women (including the poor) and "sexual minorities" is not vigorously protected so that their liberties have some value and discriminatory practices are deterred or punished, the law will not function justly. The need for a new approach to the regulation of intimacy should be clear.

Needless to say, my project should be seen as an intervention in what has become a highly politicized field. I am convinced that it is now urgent for political as well as theoretical reasons that the reflexive paradigm of law inform legal regulation of intimate relationships. Otherwise, I fear that the hand of those who want to remoralize and retraditionalize the domain of intimacy through the use of law (threatening plurality, equality, *and* personal autonomy) will be strengthened. The 1990s has seen the emergence of a highly active, well-organized, well-funded brand of conservatism, focused squarely on the domain of intimacy, deploying the rhetoric of moral, religious, and cultural decline. The aim of this movement is to remoralize this domain, by imposing ethical uniformity and conventional gender distinctions masked as family values on everyone, everywhere.

The new social conservatives are more than willing to use the central government and direct substantive regulations to accomplish their purposes. In this they mirror feminist egalitarians enamored with the welfare paradigm, even if the substantive values and goals of the former have little to do with gender equality. Surely this accounts for the bizarre alliances between radical feminists and puritanical cultural conservatives on a number of issues in the domain of intimacy (ranging from pornography regulation and censorship to sexual harassment and even divorce law). Indeed, the former's lack of concern for personal privacy and autonomy plays right into the latter's hands: for those focused on eradicating immorality, privacy is immaterial. Yet reversion to the liberal paradigm, the discourse of privacy, and negative liberty will not help here because it is too vulnerable to the charges of ethical blindness and unable to provide adequate guidelines when regulation really is required. Thus, unless we fully embrace and help develop a paradigm shift, I fear that the fundamentalist minority in the culture wars will succeed in using the regulatory state and law to undermine the personal autonomy, equal citizenship, and voice not only of sexual minorities or nontraditional women, but of everyone. If the politicization of intimacy leads to the remoralization of politics, leaving sex cops at liberty to invade home, schools, and the workplace, the future of our secular, relatively tolerant democracy will be uncertain indeed.

CHAPTER ONE

Constitutional Privacy in the Domain of Intimacy: The Battle over Reproductive Rights

> "A well-protected private autonomy helps secure the generation of public autonomy just as much as, conversely, the appropriate exercise of public autonomy helps secure the genesis of private autonomy."
> —Jürgen Habermas, "Paradigms of Law"

> "[The point is] . . . to affirm the moral judgment that women are entitled to be treated as individuals rather than restricted because of their sex, but also the moral judgment that the group to which they belong may no longer be relegated to an inferior position."
> —Nadine Taub and Wendy Williams, "*Will Equality Require More Than Assimilation, Accommodation, or Separation from the Existing Social Structure?*"

◆ Reproductive sexuality within monogamous heterosexual marriage is no longer a legally sanctioned moral imperative. The link between sex, marriage, and childbearing has at last been loosened for women, as has the once compulsory symbolic link between being a woman and being a mother.[1] Women's presumptive equality has replaced their once self-evident inferior and subordinate social status in law and public political discourse in the United States. Accordingly, choices must be made regarding the form, onset, goal, and content of intimate sexual relationships, including whether or not to reproduce; these choices are increasingly being construed as personal matters.

Indeed, the right to make such decisions is deemed especially important to the individual because intimate relationships and decisions now appear to be entwined with one's strong evaluations regarding the good: with reflection on who one is and wants to be, and how to lead one's life.[2] Individual decisional autonomy in this domain of intimacy has come to be linked to a claim to personal freedom and ethical competence. Women as well as men now claim the right to lead a personal life in tune with one's values and judgments, to pursue happiness through intimate choices, and not to have a personal identity that one can neither affirm nor embrace (such as mother) imposed through unfair or unacceptable legal restrictions of intimate decisions.

The need to reconceptualize the purpose and appropriate form of legal regulation in this domain, along with the boundary between public and private, follows from these developments. As already indicated, the old approach to drawing this boundary was premised on gender inequality, on legally entrenched gendered social hierarchies, on essentialist conceptions of gender roles, and on the assumption that nonreproductive sex (particularly for women) is immoral.[3] Once the premise underlying regulation becomes the full legal and moral personhood of women as well as their civic equality, the conventional ascription of privacy to the family unit (granting decisional autonomy/control to the male head of household), and of legitimate regulation (repressive/punitive) of nonmarital, nonreproductive sex to the state, is undermined. The appropriate referent and scope of legally protected personal privacy, as well as the line demarcating the community's and the individual's province of ethical decision making, must be rethought.

To be sure, feminist theory has hardly ignored the private: rather, it has for some time been engaged in critical and genealogical investigations of the power strategies subtending privacy discourse. Feminist theorists have long argued that the personal is political, meaning that the apparently natural private domain of intimacy (the family and sexuality) is legally and socially constructed, culturally defined, and the site of power relations, including oppression and gendered violence. For the most part, the emphasis has been on the critical deconstruction of privacy rhetoric as part of a discourse of domination that legitimizes women's oppression.

But unmasking (or, in more contemporary jargon, deconstructing) the deployment of concepts that serve the ends of domination is only one half of the task of critique. It is also important to move beyond the hermeneutics of suspicion and to redescribe the good that privacy rights can and should protect for all of us. Otherwise, important shifts in the interpretation of privacy and innovations in law will be misconstrued. This chapter, by examining developments on the level on constitutional jurisprudence, demonstrates that it is possible to redescribe personal privacy rights covering intimate concerns—in ways that are women-friendly.[4]

The old certainties are gone, as the heated debate over the very meaning of privacy reveals. But once we reject one particular conception, the question of how to articulate and gain acceptance of a different conception of personal privacy, and why this is important, remains on the agenda. I see the debate over the meaning of the right to privacy in the domain of intimacy as part of an ongoing battle over the vocabularies, idioms, and cultural codes available for allocating control and agency, for pressing claims, for attributing ethical competence, for constituting identity, for asserting difference, and for gaining recognition. Thus the demise of the old public/private dichotomy makes the need for a normatively compelling and analytically cogent conception of privacy rights all the more urgent. Legal, social, and jurisdictional boundaries between private and public are, at least since the 1960s, being redrawn: we should attempt to influence this process.[5]

I address these issues in this chapter through the prism of the debate in American legal and political theory over the privacy justification for certain reproductive rights in the United States. This controversy provides an illuminating context for rethinking the significance of privacy because it reveals both the importance of privacy rights to women and the paradoxes that such rights entail. Indeed, it was women's struggle to get reproductive freedom that propelled the right to privacy to a constitutional doctrine.[6] Initiated by the landmark decision in *Griswold v. Connecticut* (1965), in which the Supreme Court first recognized a constitutional right to privacy (covering the use of contraception for married couples), and, in a follow-up case, *Eisenstadt v. Baird* (1972), which extended it to unmarried individuals, what is commonly referred to as the "new privacy jurisprudence" has developed around matters of reproductive rights and intimate concerns generally.[7] As is well known, a woman's right to decide upon an abortion was constitutionally protected as part of her fundamental "right to privacy," by the Court in *Roe v. Wade* (1973).[8] Both abortion rights and the idea of a constitutional right to privacy involving decisional autonomy and covering intimate personal decisions and relationships have been challenged ever since.

I argue that a constitutionally protected right to personal privacy is indispensable to any modern conception of freedom, and that without the corresponding reproductive and sexual freedom, women are deprived of the good that privacy rights are meant to protect. In the present context, where many feel that reproductive rights have been eviscerated, not a few are tempted to lay the blame at the door of the privacy justification underlying the Court's decision of 1973.[9] Yet I remain unconvinced that this is due to the alleged intrinsic flaws of privacy analysis. I am also unconvinced that some other justification, be it an equal protection argument, one appealing solely to First Amendment principles (invoking expressive freedom or the freedom of conscience), or one based exclusively on the idea of bodily integrity, could serve as an adequate normative substitute for privacy rights in this domain. Nor do I believe that the normal political process would serve women better then the principle of a constitutional right to personal privacy.[10] I argue to the contrary that if women do not receive adequate protection of their intimate decisions and reproductive freedom, it is not because they have been granted privacy rights, as some argue, but because these rights are misinterpreted and/or willfully restricted. I seek to demonstrate that a right to personal privacy/autonomy covering key aspects of the domain of intimacy should be seen as part of the basic system of rights that every modern constitution should acknowledge.

In what follows I consider two recent challenges to the privacy justification for reproductive rights (in particular abortion), both of which target what are taken to be its conceptual and normative presuppositions, albeit from opposite points of view. The first of these critiques, articulated by feminist legal theorists who favor grounding abortion rights in equal protection arguments, charges that privacy analysis reinforces an ideological, liberal model of the public/private dichotomy that has long been used to justify gender inequality and private male power within the patriarchal family, along with exclusionary and discriminatory treatment of women outside the domestic sphere. The Court's new privacy analysis allegedly revives this anachronistic model and consequently disadvantages women.

The second, articulated by communitarian critics of liberalism, argues that constitutionalized individual privacy rights undermine community values and solidarity while blocking needed public policies that would advance the public good. This, they claim, is due to the atomistic, self-centered, and autarkic conception of the sovereign individual that allegedly underlies these rights. Individualized rights talk, in particular talk about a fundamental right to privacy, apparently resurrects a now untenable property-paradigm of rights with all its misleading assumptions. These include a flawed conception of the relation of the individual to herself (possessive individualism), to her identity or core commitments (voluntarism), and to moral concerns (contractualism). While the first critique offers an alternative justification for abortion rights, the second challenges rights talk in this domain altogether.

We seem to be facing different forms of what I shall call the "paradox of privacy rights." According to the first argument, the attempt to correct the flaws of domestic privacy with more privacy seems quixotic: how can private power (over women) be undermined by privacy rights? From the communitarian perspective, on the other hand, to accord decisional autonomy to individuals (women) in family matters through the vehicle of privacy rights is to purchase individual choice at the price of community solidarity.[11] And there is yet a third dimension to the paradox of privacy pointed out by critics in both camps: while privacy rights purport to be the means for protecting individuals from state power, they also reinforce the disintegrative, atomizing, and leveling tendencies in modern society, thereby exposing people to increased regulation by state agencies, and in the process destroying both the solidarity of the family community and the autonomy of the individual.

It is my claim that the paradoxes of privacy are not unavoidable—they stem from the trap of ideology into which both critiques fall. In short, both approaches assume that what they take to be the paradigmatic liberal interpretation of privacy rights is definitive of such rights, and thus both propose to abandon the discourse of privacy altogether. Both critiques are consequently rather one-sided: the first, because it considers only the subordination of juridical practice to the preservation of a system of domination; the second, because it confuses the formal with a particular substantive meaning of individuality attached to privacy rights.[12] The first approach misses the normative, symbolic, and empowering dimensions of privacy rights because it is preoccupied with unmasking the functional role they can play in preserving inequality and hierarchy. The second is distracted by the old atomistic assumptions subtending many liberal justifications of privacy (and other) rights. Thus, it fails to grasp the moral importance of rights guaranteeing decisional autonomy and ascribing ethical competence and a sense of control over one's identity needs in the domain of intimacy to socialized, solidary, individuals—a complex of rights for which *privacy* has increasingly become the umbrella term.

The task before us is to break with functionalist and anachronistic interpretations of privacy without jettisoning the valid principles protected by privacy rights. I argue that a constitutionally protected right to personal privacy covering key issues that arise in the domain of intimacy is indispensable to any modern conception of freedom, and that without reproductive and sexual freedom secured in part by such a right, women suffer great injustice. Indeed, I maintain that one of the most important examples of normative learning in the twentieth century is the recognition that personal privacy involving decisional autonomy and control of certain intimate decisions and relationships is a good for every individual that deserves to be protected in its own right, on grounds that ought to be differentiated—legally and morally—from those pertaining to private property, freedom of contract, or "entity" privacy (attached to the family as a unit).[13] This is the great achievement of the new privacy jurisprudence developed by the Supreme Court. Many of us intuitively acknowledge the importance of this development, despite the confusion and controversy over the very meaning of privacy—a confusion that derives in part from the old associations of privacy with property and the patriarchal family, in part from flawed reasoning in the Court's privacy jurisprudence. As I show, the flaws in the Court's justifications of its privacy analysis are attributable to anachronistic assumptions deriving from the liberal paradigm of law. This feeds the criticisms from both sides.

But these old associations and paradigmatic assumptions are not essential to the justification of privacy rights. It is true that the notion of private property used to serve as the symbolic center of the personal rights complex, but it neither can nor should do so any longer.[14] Instead, the privacy justification for a constitutional right protecting intimate decisions and relationships has to be reflexively reconstrued, as already indicated. It is no accident that, over the course of the past forty years, there have been increasing efforts to reorganize the personal rights complex around the principle of personal privacy. In the process, constitutional privacy jurisprudence has become a key symbolic shield for individual ethical autonomy and the freedom of one's personal imaginary domain against majoritarian intolerance.[15] As we shall see, it is precisely this new thrust in privacy doctrine that the critics challenge. Thus, the stakes are very high indeed.

I proceed in the following steps. A new conception of privacy, which I embrace, has made its way, albeit imperfectly, into law. After providing a working definition of the concept of the right to privacy entailed in the Court's new privacy jurisprudence (to be fleshed out in the course of the chapter), I turn to the feminist and communitarian criticisms of this jurisprudence and attempt to defend it against the various charges. I grant that much in the Court's justifications of the new right to privacy invites these criticisms, but I try to show that other justifications of privacy analysis are possible and that these are implicit in or mesh well with the thrust of this jurisprudence. In other words, I provide a constructivist justification of such a right in lieu of the quasi-metaphysical, essentialist, and anachronistic (in relation to the model of the social structure) justifications that tend to accompany the Court's discourse of fundamentality regarding privacy in the intimate domain. I shall also try to provide an argument for what the scope of such a right to privacy should be and discuss which forms of legal regulation are appropriate to it, based on my constructivist understanding of privacy and on the perspective afforded by the reflexive paradigm of law.

What does the constitutional right to personal privacy entail? Among the dimensions of personal privacy recognized by the Supreme Court today in its new privacy jurisprudence, the "right to be let alone" (freedom from unwarranted intrusion or surveillance) and "decisional privacy" (freedom from undue regulation or control) in the domain of intimacy are central. Of the two, the first, especially as concerns the most intimate details of one's personal life, is far less contested than the second. The right to be let alone emphasizes informational privacy—control over the acquisition, possession, and spread of information about oneself, along with control over access or attention by others, be they private individuals, organizations, or public officials. This principle, if not its applications, is widely accepted today. The debates are over the extent, rather than the very idea, of our right to be let alone.[16]

The controversy on which I focus revolves primarily around the second prong of the new privacy doctrine, namely, privacy construed as involving decisional autonomy in the zone of intimacy—marriage, divorce, sexual relations, sexual identity and expression, procreation, abortion, and so forth.[17] At issue is the ascription to the individual of the ethical competence to make certain intimate decisions, including the choice of one's intimate associates. Control over access and informational privacy regarding one's personal decisions are, to be sure, also relevant here. Autonomy and informational privacy are inextricably linked but they are not identical. Privacy as decisional autonomy protects the freedom of choice of and within intimate association and all that it entails. Conceptually, it references the interest in acting on one's own personal reasons in the pursuit of happiness, in forging personal ties, in testing and developing ways of living with and relating to intimate others without government or third parties dictating how we conduct our personal intimate affairs.[18] As such, the concept of the right to privacy informing the Court's jurisprudence in this area has a relatively wide range of symbolic meanings including agency, autonomy, responsibility, ethical competence, and independent judgment. Because it provides a shield for personal paths to happiness, for imaginative experimentation with intimates, and for the special and personal experience of relating to oneself and to intimate others freed from the pressures of public judgment, a right to privacy as decisional autonomy does entail some of the usual aspects of informational privacy as well as one peculiar to autonomous judgment or decision making: one cannot be forced to justify one's intimate life choices publicly or in terms that everyone else would agree to.[19] The symbolic meaning of such a broadly construed right to privacy is, of course, open to reinterpretation, to efforts at reconceptualization. The relatively indeterminate concept of a right to privacy developed by the Court allows for challenges to any specific conception or formulation by a particular power constellation. This is one of its strengths. But this is also the arena where the battle rages today and why the very principle, rather than the reach, of an individual constitutional right to privacy can and is being contested.[20]

THE FEMINIST EGALITARIAN CRITIQUE OF PRIVACY ANALYSIS

Feminist scholars have long argued that more is at stake in the struggle for reproductive freedom than the right to choose an abortion. This struggle also involves a challenge to the unequal and often oppressive social, gendered, and material conditions under which women make such decisions. Often the very need for abortion can be attributed to these factors. Thus, as Rosalind Petchesky argued in her classic work on the subject, any attempt to interpret reproductive freedom simply as a matter of privacy rights is reductive.[21]

On the other hand, Petchesky also insisted that rights which ensure individual self-determination are indispensable for women. She thus rejected the opposite sort of reductionism, which assumes that women need abortion rights only because of the hegemonic and repressive cultural equation of "woman" with "mother" and the gendered division of labor that ascribes to women the sole responsibility for the consequences of pregnancy—the care and rearing of children—while denying to them the economic means and community support to carry out these tasks.[22] Accordingly, she argued for a double agenda for reproductive freedom: one insisting on the importance of rights protecting a woman's autonomy, and another emphasizing desirable changes in the social, economic, and gender relations of reproduction.

Recently, however, an important group of feminist legal theorists have argued for abandoning the privacy justification for reproductive rights (preferring some version of the equal protection doctrine). They claim that privacy discourse reinforces a misleading liberal model of society/ state relations that conceals gender hierarchies and obscures the social reality it helps to constitute, instead of opening it up to public scrutiny.[23] On this model, the state is construed as the public sphere—the locus of power—while all that is nonstate is construed as the private sphere—the realm of freedom—in an undifferentiated manner. Accordingly, the right to privacy "is based on the assumption that as long as the state does not interfere with private life, autonomous individuals will interact freely and equally."[24] Liberty protected by privacy rights is understood as negative liberty: noninterference. Legal regulation and personal autonomy are placed in a zero-sum relationship. Privacy rights so construed allegedly presuppose and construct an ideological notion of a "natural," prepolitical sphere of life where relations are based on consent between free and equal adults and which is off-limits to legal regulation or state intervention.

But this dualistic model is superimposed in liberal privacy doctrine upon another model—the boundary between domestic life and the rest of society.[25] When the private means the home, however, it is construed as the sphere of dependency, of hierarchical relationships and particularistic bonds, not as the locus of equal rights–bearing autonomous individuals. Here, of course, women have been positioned, like children, as dependents. Yet their subordinate status within the family is considered to have been voluntarily assumed, just as their entry into and chance to exit from the so-called marriage contract is considered to be voluntary.[26] On this model, then, privacy attaches to an entity—the family unit—shielding its internal (and presumed natural) intimate relations from public intervention and scrutiny.[27]

Although they are not always clear about the distinction between these two conceptions of privacy, feminist critics of privacy rights argue that both models inform and distort the reasoning in privacy doctrine even when privacy rights are being accorded to women. First they show that there are fundamental inequalities between the sexes in the private sphere with regard to control over the decision to have sex, and in relation to the degree to which one's sexuality and reproductive capacities are instrumentalized by others or by the state.[28] Second, they argue that under the guise of privacy rights, relations of domination and exploitation are fostered, protected, and to some extent created by the state.[29] Thus women are simultaneously deprived of the autonomy and equality that is ascribed to individuals on the first model of the public/private dichotomy, while they do not benefit from the protection offered to dependents by the second model (entity privacy).

Indeed, in her classic critique of *Roe v. Wade*, Catharine MacKinnon has argued that "the legal concept of privacy can and has shielded the place of battery, marital rape, and women's exploited labor."[30] Cass Sunstein maintains that privacy doctrine posits a natural, prepolitical sphere of sexuality and reproduction that is used as the baseline for distinguishing between government action and inaction in the distribution of benefits and burdens, including constitutional protection. Whatever inequalities may exist in private life, if the state is not their source, if it has not intervened to take away equality, then no constitutional right can be invoked as the vehicle of regulation in the private domestic sphere:[31] "Decisions that upset existing distributions are treated as 'action,' decisions that do not are perceived to stay close to nature and thus to amount to no action at all."[32] The former are often construed as partisan and interventionist, the latter as neutral and facilitative of independent private relations.[33] Sunstein's point is that nonintervention by the state is neither impartial nor inaction, but rather a form of state action that reproduces the status quo of inegalitarian gender relations. He concurs with Frances Olsen's challenge to the innocence and coherence of the distinction between state intervention and nonintervention as a liberal myth. Accordingly, the private/public split allegedly presupposed by the concept of privacy rights constructs an entire arena of social relations and issues as off-limits to the demands of justice through the conceptual sleight of hand that construes them as natural, nonpolitical, and the domain of voluntary association, consent, and freedom. The critics seek to show, however, that the private is neither natural nor apolitical—it is culturally (and socially) constituted and permeated by power relations—perpetuated, directly and indirectly, by the state.[34]

Thus, even though the privacy right articulated in *Roe* was framed as an individual right, in MacKinnon's view it nonetheless shores up the negative aspects of entity privacy. Accordingly, the state secures privacy by centering its self-restraint on the home and the bedroom, by staying out of marriage and the family, by not intervening. Ever since *Griswold*, doctrinal constitutional privacy rights have allegedly been rooted in traditional morality (keeping the cops out of marital bedrooms) and have reinforced the gender hierarchies that such morality has always entailed. Privacy doctrine so understood means that no act of the state contributes to—hence should properly participate in—shaping the internal alignments of the private domain or distributing its internal forces. Injuries arise in violating the private sphere, not within it.

To the privacy critics, this conceals the fact that even when they are construed as rights-bearing individuals, women have no control over the social conditions of their existence and do not enjoy substantive equality with men in matters of reproduction, sexuality, child care, or economic wherewithal. And the privacy justification for reproductive rights does not give it to them, for it abstracts away from the social conditions under which sexual relations, reproduction, and child care take place.

MacKinnon, Sunstein, and Olsen each maintain that unlike the privacy justification for reproductive rights, an approach based on a revised interpretation of the equal protection clause would highlight the issue of gender inequality and allow one to confront the significance that gendered social, sexual, and economic inequalities between men and women have for abortion law in particular and sex law in general.[35] Their arguments for the sex-equality approach draw on the claim that in criminalizing abortion, the state unfairly limits the efforts of women to control their reproductive freedom, but not of men.[36] Such laws turn a biological capacity to bear children into a source of social disadvantage, unduly burdening women with the difficulties of pregnancy, parenthood, and child care, while denigrating their status as moral agents and impairing their capacity for self-determination and equal citizenship.[37]

But it will not do to supplement privacy with equality arguments according to these theorists. The heart of the radical critique of the privacy justification is the charge that it individualizes and depoliticizes the issue, concealing the power relations subtending the abortion debate and struggles over reproductive rights generally: "One should recognize that anti-abortion laws are part of the systematic oppression and devaluation of women. . . . [They] are a *result* of the devaluation of women, not just a *cause* of women's inequality."[38]

In other words, anti-abortion laws are the product of, and reproduce, inegalitarian gender relations. Privacy analysis must be abandoned so that attention can be shifted from the individual woman isolated in her right to privacy to the broader context of sexual politics: the relations of inequality and domination between the sexes and the disparate impact of a given law on the different genders.

Several post-*Roe* Supreme Court decisions lend support to this critique of privacy analysis. MacKinnon, for example, attributes to the privacy rationale of *Roe* the decisions in the series of abortion funding cases that denied a right to public funding even of medically necessary abortions.[39] And indeed, the reasoning in these cases was disturbing, for the Court clearly relied on the anachronistic liberal paradigmatic understanding of the public/private dichotomy and of negative liberty in its reasoning. The Court argued that since the state is not the cause of the economic inability of poor women to obtain abortions through their own means, it does not impose new burdens on women or violate their constitutional rights in denying them a right to state funding in this domain. By implication, the state renounced responsibility for redressing inequalities in the private sphere that are not of its own making, that is, that are not due to state action.[40] Reasoning back to *Roe* from *Harris v. McRae*, critics have accordingly argued that the public/private distinction presupposed by privacy doctrine turns abortion into a private right to be exercised only by those women rich enough to buy the medical care they need, leaving others in the lurch.

But as the dissents of Justice Brennan in *Maher v. Roe* and Justices Brennan and Stevens in *Harris* show, the new doctrinal constitutional privacy analysis need not have led in that direction. In *Maher*, Brennan argued that the withholding of financial benefits had already been held to constitute an invalid burden on fundamental rights in other contexts.[41] Moreover, as Justice Marshall argued in his dissent in the same case, the provision of state funding for childbirth and not for abortion violates the privacy principle according to which the woman's decision may not be interfered with by the state, because such regulations are "in reality intended to impose a moral viewpoint that no state may constitutionally enforce."[42] Nonfunding thus appears as an impermissible form of discriminatory state action after all. In the abortion funding cases, the state imposed its view only onto pregnant women who are too poor to afford a privately funded abortion.

Like the dissenters, I do not believe that this was due to intrinsic flaws in the new constitutional privacy analysis but to a non-neutral and restrictive application of this analysis.[43] I argue that the restrictive conception of constitutional privacy rights used to justify this application derives from the hegemony of the liberal paradigm of law in this area that collapses two different meanings of privacy, not from the concept of a constitutional right to privacy, nor from the fact that it takes the form of a negative liberty. The dissents target one conception while defending the other.

There are at least two different ways in constitutional law to distinguish private from public actions and the relevant role of the state (its regulatory scope and its obligations).[44] The first refers to a strong conception of privacy as decisional autonomy accorded to individuals as a matter of basic constitutional right, and thus beyond government's discretion or control. The right to privacy protected in cases like *Eisenstadt v. Baird* and *Roe v. Wade* that accord decisional autonomy to the individual woman is an example. This does not preclude government facilitating the exercise of the right or the Court from regulating it to ensure fairness and justice, but it does preclude unduly burdening its exercise by state regulations.[45]

The second refers to actions construed as private in the more modest sense that they are simply not regulated by the Constitution. Privacy in this second, weaker sense accords no basic rights, but rather is the negative implication of clauses that impose constitutional duties on public authorities but not on other people. This aspect of privacy, textually and historically very different from the first, implies that some parts of the Constitution regulate only the action of the state.[46] In other words, it implies that private actors can treat each other in ways the state cannot. It also implies that where there is no state action, the Constitution is silent.[47] On the other hand, it does not preclude state legislation or regulation of such private action. Constitutional privacy rights in the strong, first sense, however, prohibit just that.

With this analytic distinction in mind, it is ludicrous to blame the privacy justification of constitutional rights to decisional autonomy regarding reproduction, for the Court's refusal to find an affirmative obligation in the Constitution for state funding. The state-action doctrine long predates the new line of privacy analysis. It is this doctrine, not the new constitutional privacy analysis, that is intrinsically bound up with the liberal paradigm of law, insofar as it posits a private sphere beyond the reach of the state. Indeed, one would have to look to the peculiar features of the American welfare state, and the fact that we have never constitutionalized welfare rights, for an explanation of the refusal to fund abortions for poor women as standard medical care.[48] Very few of our established rights have so far been construed to yield constitutional grounds for requiring states to provide economic support for the poor.[49] This also holds for the right to equality articulated in the Fourteenth Amendment's equal protection clause.[50] Thus, if the state did not fund either childbirth or abortions, one would be hard put to extract from the Constitution a requirement for funding on the basis of privacy or equality analysis. There is nothing that constitutionally proscribes such state action, nor is there anything that demands it.

The blame for this unfortunate situation, however, cannot be placed on the concept of a privacy right, for the latter does not entail the state action doctrine—protection of decisional autonomy can go perfectly well with state support for exercising one's basic constitutional rights, even privacy rights. Moreover, this right is protected against the efforts of states to criminalize or unduly burden abortion choice and against the efforts of husbands (private persons) to control the decision. It can also entail rather hefty state intervention in the family, to secure the respect for the individual woman's autonomy rights.

Thus, much as I agree that the state should have an affirmative obligation to provide support to all women in order to make their reproductive rights effective, this argument does not have a strong foothold in the Constitution as it now stands. The reasons can be traced back to the power of market ideology and the liberal paradigm of law, but hardly to the privacy justification in *Roe*.

It is not the concept of personal privacy/autonomy rights that militates against social supports for rights, but the ways these are interpreted and justified from within the liberal paradigm of law by certain Supreme Court justices. One legacy of the liberal model of society/state relations and the market ideology that has accompanied it is that jurists tend to set up an antagonism between collective solidarity and individual autonomy (construed as negative liberty), between autonomy and state support.[51] The liberal paradigm (like its statist critics) collapses the two meanings of privacy: it is assumed that having constitutionally protected personal autonomy, construed as inherent in the individual, the state has acknowledged a nonpolitical, private sphere of liberty for which it has no responsibility and into which it must refrain from intervening.

State action and personal liberty are placed in a zero-sum game in this model. Liberty is negative liberty construed in Isaiah Berlin's, or even Thomas Hobbes's, sense: the absence of impediment, the absence of intervention.[52] The principle of equal liberty can be assured only formally: state intervention to insure the substantive equality of that liberty apparently violates the principle of autonomy and independence from regulation. Thus it seems that the constitution cannot simultaneously guarantee privacy rights, or decisional autonomy, while providing the social supports (in this case access to public funds, facilities, or medical care) that are necessary for exercising these rights.[53]

But we need not buy into anachronistic conceptions of privacy doctrine or of state/society relations. On a different paradigmatic approach to law and to state/society relations (the reflexive paradigm), and on the basis of a constructivist understanding of privacy rights, we can be aware that the liberties or rights secured by the Constitution are those that we (would) have chosen to grant one another, not those that are somehow found to be inherent in a prepolitical social sphere or in our nature.[54] We could thus easily acknowledge that in order for the liberty that we grant one another to be equal, we must provide certain supports for its exercise, as we currently do when it comes to state provision for legal defense for the poor so that their right to legal standing has meaning. This holds generally for privacy rights as it does for other liberty rights. Accordingly, nothing precludes ensuring the worth of the liberty that we grant to one another. There is no contradiction in this approach between according a right to privacy as decisional autonomy to individuals for certain concerns, and state provision for the equal opportunity to exercise those rights.

For this argument to make sense, however, one must see that the concept of personal autonomy or liberty in question cannot be grasped either as Hobbesian negative liberty, as Kantian self-determination, or Millian personal self-realization, for these approaches all cast legal regulation as interference, detracting from freedom.[55] The liberty at stake in the new privacy analysis is a form of negative liberty, but the freedom it secures should be understood in the sense of nonsubordination, nonsubjection, nondomination, security from arbitrary power, not simply as noninterference.[56] The autonomy accorded by such rights protects against being treated as merely a means and against being entirely instrumentalized to another's purposes. In other words, the decisional autonomy at stake in privacy analysis refers to relations of power. By according decisional autonomy to individuals within and for certain relationships, the point is to help turn relations of (gender) subordination and domination into nonhierarchical social relations.[57] On this model, the conceptual opposite to personal liberty is slavery, not legal regulation or intervention. Indeed, honoring the decisional autonomy of individuals and groups traditionally disfavored by the law has rightly been seen by the Supreme Court as enhancing personal freedom and promoting equality goals, as indicated by many of the subthemes in its right-to-privacy decisions.[58] But these two values are, nonetheless, irreducible to each other. Only on an ideological conception of the public/private distinction that creates a rigid dichotomy, one which collapses the two meanings of constitutional privacy and liberty and interprets them in anachronistic ways (positing prepolitical, autonomous, naturally free subjects for whom any law detracts from liberty) must a zero-sum game ensue between constitutional privacy rights and provision for their equal exercise.

This leads to the core theoretical problem raised by those who wish to substitute equality for privacy analysis. Is the good that privacy doctrine inadequately protects simply some form of substantive or relational equality with men? What if men's *and* women's reproductive capacities were turned into something for the use and control of others—say, by the state—for purposes of population policy?[59] Imagine a world of sex equality, without gender hierarchies, without unequal functionalization of women's bodies, and with adequate social supports via public policy for childbearing and care. Would this mean that women would no longer have the right to terminate unwanted pregnancies or that they would not need privacy rights protecting their personal decisional autonomy in this domain? Sunstein[60] and MacKinnon[61] imply as much.

But why? While greater gender equality in substantive and distributional terms may decrease the incidence of abortion, I fail to see why it would weaken the normative case for choice. Should women have to relinquish their rights to personal autonomy in exchange for governmental benefits or for equal treatment? In the world of sex equality, who decides? Would women have to reveal their personal reasons for wanting an abortion in such a world? To whom would they have to show that they have just cause? Whose permission would they have to get? To whose judgment would they have to defer? In short, is a woman's right not to be used as a mere means by others contingent on the degree to which men are or are not so used? Is her ethical autonomy regarding the intimately personal decision of whether to bring a child into the world dependent on how men would make such decisions?

This line of reasoning confuses two distinct levels of analysis: explanation and justification. While gender inequality and disdain of women as a group may be why their reproductive rights are unduly restricted, and why their sexuality is controlled, it does not follow that the main fault with such restrictions is that they violate principles of nondiscrimination or have a disparate impact on women. An independent argument is needed to show why it is important to protect personal decisional autonomy over intimate decisions of this sort, concerning reproduction and sexual choice, for men and for women. Normative argumentation, in short, is required to show that such restrictions constitute a real harm and violate basic moral and constitutional principles for everyone. Only then can one shift to the second level of analysis, namely issues of fairness and impartiality. The privacy justification for reproductive rights and for other dimensions of intimate association does just that: it brings the normative principles and symbolic meanings associated with privacy in the domain of intimacy—personal autonomy, freedom as nondomination, ethical self-determination, agency, the pursuit of happiness—into play in ascribing decisional autonomy to the individual rather than to the family unit, the state, or third parties. The claim, in short, is that a woman's moral autonomy and ethical competence and agency are denied in laws criminalizing abortion.

Sunstein acknowledges as much when he insists that what is at stake in the right to abortion is "the interest in ensuring that women's sexuality and reproductive functions are not turned into something for the use and control of others."[62] What is this interest, if not an interest in personal autonomy and freedom from domination? To be sure, it is an additional and important argument in favor of abortion rights that men's reproductive functions are not so instrumentalized. No one's sexual life, reproductive functions, and intimate relationships should be instrumentalized by the state or third parties without very compelling reasons indeed.[63] That is the principle which should be impartially applied to all. Privacy analysis supplies the necessary protection and justification. Thus it is doubly unjust to functionalize the reproductive capacities of women. But let us be clear—the wrong here is first and foremost the refusal to ascribe ethical competence and agency to women to pursue their own conception of the good by denying them decisional autonomy over intimate matters—in this case, abortion. Instead of undermining privacy analysis, the presumption of gender equality should reinforce it by stressing the principle of equal liberty and stripping away the legitimacy from anachronistic arguments for denying decisional autonomy over intimate concerns to women. By "anachronistic" I mean arguments based on a conception of privacy that is no longer meaningful today, and on gender assumptions and views regarding sexual intimacy that are no longer valid, and which those concerned—namely, women—could very reasonably reject.

The privacy critics share the biases of the liberal legal paradigm while evaluating them negatively, as it were. They too assume that privacy discourse entails a rigid dichotomy between public and private spheres and a zero-sum game between decisional autonomy ascribed to the individual and state action. State regulation oriented to redressing unequal background conditions or aimed at ensuring, to paraphrase Rawls, the worth of liberty seems to undermine privacy. That is why the critics urge abandonment of privacy analysis altogether. To be sure, they reject what they take to be the central premise of the liberal legal paradigm: the sociological image of a natural, private, prepolitical sphere immune to the regulatory powers of the interventionist state, because it is the domain of individual (negative) liberty. But their alternative is to abandon any distinction between state intervention/nonintervention, public and private, on the assumption of the omnipresence of the political, and to focus only on the substantive equality effects of state regulation. Their aim is to finesse the thorny issue of the reach of personal autonomy (and the moral status of the fetus in the abortion decisions) by focusing on nondiscrimination.[64] But it is equally misleading to pretend that the state is everywhere because power is everywhere, as it is to posit a power-free prepolitical natural sphere that is beyond justice.[65] Such an approach screens out the possible negative effects of certain forms of regulation on personal autonomy, and deprives us of the possibility of invoking the symbolic and normative surplus of privacy discourse to protect against overregulation and paternalism.[66] In short, it throws out the baby with the bath water, restricting the concept of privacy rights to one particular outmoded conception. This blinds the critics to important new dimensions of current privacy analysis that can be justified without anachronism or metaphysics.

For example, the least convincing part of the analysis (adopted by Sunstein and Olsen) is the charge that the privacy justification in *Griswold, Eisenstadt, Roe,* and their progeny reinforces the old ideology of entity privacy regarding the family, by resting on a conception of a sacrosanct private sphere identified with marriage and the home. Indeed, this is an odd interpretation of *Roe,* the very decision that guaranteed a right of decisional autonomy regarding abortion to women as individuals, not as wives; securing the privacy of a woman's communication with her doctor, not with her spouse; about a procedure that does not take place in the home, but in hospitals and clinics! Moreover, the Court has consistently overturned husband notification provisions in state law, thereby challenging the patriarchal model of the family along with gender stereotypes. The strong argument against husband notification rules made by the plurality in the 1992 decision on abortion rights in *Planned Parenthood of Southeastern Pennsylvania v. Casey*, which cites family violence including battery and rape of wives by their husbands, supports my point.[67] The decision notes the role secrecy plays in shrouding abusive families and explicitly rejects the old common-law understanding of a woman's role in the family, along with the view that entity privacy trumps individual privacy within the marital unit.[68] One would think that with her nondomination frame for equality analysis, MacKinnon would be quick to acknowledge the thrust of these arguments. But her wholesale rejection of autonomy/privacy discourse precludes this. MacKinnon and the others are thus mistaken in interpreting the legal concept of privacy simply as a vehicle that "has preserved the central institutions whereby women are deprived of identity, autonomy, control, and self-definition."[69] Rather, the recent developments in privacy law have begun to secure precisely these goods to women—which is why they are so hotly contested.

To be sure, what I have called entity privacy has had the negative effects on women that many have described. The old entity approach to privacy, found in the common law, protected privacy for the family unit. It is incontestable that deploying the term *private* to designate institutions and spheres of life as off-limits to the principles of justice (be it the factory or the family) is indefensible. This ideology has most certainly played a role in preventing the democratization of the family and in keeping important issues out of the public sphere.

But what the critics of the new privacy analysis fail to note is that while the old legal regime governing family relations and family privacy shielded certain sorts of decisions and activities from public oversight, this did not entail a commitment to the private ordering of family behavior, or to individual autonomy. Instead, it constructed the patriarchal family as an important source for public norms. While according decisional autonomy to the family unit (and hence to the male head of household) over what occurred within it, the traditional notion of family privacy nonetheless reinforced a high degree of state control over the institution of marriage and reproduction.[70] Marriage and the family were deemed of great importance, but the importance was to society, insofar as it allegedly preserved morals and stability. Traditional constitutional doctrine regulating marriage and family privacy construed marriage as a key public institution carrying out vital social functions.[71]

Indeed, the power exercised by husbands and fathers (over *femmes-couvertes* and children) should be understood as a set of legal immunities granted (delegated) to them in their capacity as "private office holders" heading the household. Courts traditionally justified their refusal to intervene in intrafamily disputes by invoking the family as a private domain "into which the King's writ does not run and to which his officers do not seek to be admitted."[72] The point was that the jurisdiction of legally acknowledged "private officers," namely husband/father heads of households, as well as masters and employers, should not be violated by public officers.

In a fascinating article, Karen Orren has recently argued that the image of society as a great system of officers, public (the president, legislators, judges) and private (employers, masters, husbands, parents), with specific jurisdictional authority over their respective domains, inherited from England and in particular from Blackstone's *Commentaries*, has informed American legal and constitutional interpretation of private relations well into the twentieth century.[73] The powers, immunities, and controls exercised by some private citizens over those subordinate to them and respected by judges adjudicating the common law made perfect sense in terms of an image of society as an overarching hierarchical status order. Indeed, there was a real continuity in legal discourse between public and private hierarchies. The discourse of family privacy/autonomy secured the jurisdictional powers of husband/fathers in the domain of intimacy as inherent in a publicly ascribed and legally acknowledged status. Although husbands/fathers were private citizens, their legally constituted rights as private officers over subordinate persons (wives/children) were not available to citizens who did not have these statuses.

Notwithstanding conventional social science talk of the shift from status to contract with the emergence of "modernity," status hierarchies and private officers' rights remained legally entrenched until rather recently, and still are in some areas.[74] Not until the 1960s were legal private gender hierarchies and private officers' powers successfully challenged in the name of uniform personal and citizen rights and an image of society based on the principle of gender (and racial) equality rather than social hierarchy.[75] The new privacy jurisprudence is part and parcel of the gradual elimination, in favor of individualized citizenship rights, of legalized hierarchies and officers, powers in private relations.[76] While the courts' privacy jurisprudence since the 1960s did pick up on the traditional notion of family privacy, it transposed it into a doctrine singling out the individual, not the family unit, as the bearer of autonomy insulated from publicly created norms.[77] The new approach still considers marriage and family of fundamental importance, but now the focus is on their importance primarily to individual happiness. This purpose is invoked to limit collective constraints on individual decisions regarding marriage and family.[78]

Thus, to construe the personal privacy rights protected by *Roe* as continuous with the old assumptions of common law entity privacy is absurd.[79] The grant of privacy rights to women as individuals (married or not) with respect to reproductive decisions and intimate relationships explodes the ideology of family privacy that had been used to justify rigid gender norms and patriarchal forms of subordination, predicated on the denial of full legal personhood to women. Indeed, by gaining individualized privacy rights, women can at last accede to the status of full legal personhood and begin to demand both protection and autonomy, both rights and legal benefits, within, as well as for, intimate relationships. They can also demand state action in the form of protection of their rights as persons within the family, while retaining control over the intimate decisions that individual privacy rights afford. This provides the answer to the first paradox of privacy mentioned above. By acknowledging women as full legal persons whatever their marital status and wherever they are, personal privacy rights bring the demands of justice right into the home, forcing a reevaluation of the goals of family policy as well. The new privacy rights operate on the "social imaginary" terrain of social equality, not social hierarchy.[80]

Going one step further, one can argue that both sorts of privacy rights involve important protection. While entity privacy has shielded the patriarchal marital family unit and all its disturbing practices from the demands of justice, this need not be the case.

The ideological conception of the patriarchal family has been traditionally presupposed by entity privacy, but it is not logically entailed by it. Other family forms and other intimate relationships could all benefit from entity privacy—that is, from protection against unfair and unwarranted state regulations.[81] Yet legal regulation can provide a protective shield as well as a structure of justice for a range of intimate relationships.[82] Once we acknowledge that the family is not a natural but a conventional civil association; that what counts as a family varies over cultures and over time; that law plays an important role in constituting families—we can ask what, if anything, about the nature of the protected relationship is worth protecting. In other words, once we abandon the old ways of construing intimate associations and their relation to state power and law, once we shift over to the perspective of the reflexive legal paradigm, we must still address the question of whether and how to draw a boundary within the terrain of the social, and how law can be used to protect as well as regulate intimate associations for appropriate purposes.[83] But we can do so freed of anachronistic assumptions and justifications.

If we redescribe entity privacy as the privacy of intimate relationships, the answer will be evident. In short, I wish to invoke the notion of relational privacy to cover what entity privacy covered without its patriarchal baggage. As such, relational privacy protects the intensely personal communicative interaction among intimates (including the choice of adult intimates and intimacies) from unwarranted control or intervention by the state or third parties, with one key proviso: that the demands of justice are not violated within the relationship.

Intimate relationships are characterized by a particularly vulnerable, fragile sort of interpersonal communication that would fall apart or become seriously distorted if the principles of publicity (open access, inclusion, availability of information) were applied to them. In other words, information, access, and internal communication, crucial for the special trust involved in intimate relationships, must be under the control of the intimate associates themselves. Intimacy requires privacy: a special boundary vis-à-vis the outside, protective of the special bonds inside. This is what relational or associational privacy rights secure.[84] Thus, even if we acknowledge all the criticisms of the ideological versions of the public/ private dichotomy, we still need the concepts of privacy and privacy rights.

However, any type of intimate association can involve power domination and exploitation. Individuals need protection within and not only for intimacy. Thus while entity privacy ought to serve as the protective shield for the fragile communicative relationships that constitute intimacy, individual privacy rights securing each individual's decisional and ethical autonomy ought to serve as protection for the personal and bodily integrity of family members, should these relationships become distorted or break down.[85]

In sum, I see no good reason for refusing to rethink privacy analysis, by developing a serviceable theoretical conception of personal privacy/ autonomy appropriate to current conditions, needs, and understandings. Why not do the same favor for privacy that the critics have done for equality analysis? After all, the equal protection clause of the Fourteenth Amendment has also served to justify some rather unsavory practices in the past: these include segregation, differential (worse) treatment, and lower pay for women at work, "protective" labor legislation that defined women out of the best jobs, and a rigid formalism entailing such things as denial of basic benefits to women when their needs differ from men's, such as the need for pregnancy leaves or child-care provision. MacKinnon, among others, has subjected equal protection analysis to a withering critique, showing that on its standard interpretation (the discrimination frame), women are subjected to a male standard and tend to be disadvantaged whether they are similarly situated or not similarly situated to men.[86] Some feminists have concluded from this that equality discourse, like privacy discourse, must be abandoned in favor of a "post-egalitarian" feminism.[87]

MacKinnon, Sunstein, and Olsen, however, have not taken that route. They have instead expended much effort, along with others, to reconceptualize equality analysis in ways that are women-friendly, in ways that do not penalize them (or others) for their difference and that address structures of domination and exploitation. MacKinnon in particular has helped deconstruct the resultant equality/difference dichotomy apparently inherent in equality analysis in order to reappropriate it, by resituating it within an anti-subordination frame.[88] As a consequence, it became clear that it was only on a particular conception of equal protection that the distinction between equality/inequality is mapped onto the distinction between sameness/difference, yielding a dichotomy that installs a male standard and systematically disadvantages women. Unwilling to abandon the concept of equality (and rightly so), MacKinnon and others attempted instead to develop a better conception of it, severing it from the liberal legal paradigm and shifting over to the welfare model (the anti-subordination, nondomination frame). Considerations of fairness and impartiality must, in short, address asymmetrical relations of power and subjugation.

I argue that the same service (reconceptualization and a paradigm shift) should be done for privacy analysis. Privacy and liberty values are well worth preserving. Instead of losing concepts and principles that we need— such as privacy, equality, liberty, autonomy—we should expend the intellectual effort and reconfigure them so that they no longer work against us. The new privacy jurisprudence allows us to do just that: it provides the occasion for rethinking privacy outside both the liberal and the welfare paradigms of law. The constitutionalization and individualization of privacy rights in the domain of intimacy involves an important shift and break with the old public/private dichotomy, which we would do well to theorize. Indeed, a key goal of this book is to develop a conceptual and legal framework within which convincing justifications for privacy rights (which can replace anachronistic ones) can be developed.

In this regard, it seems that the communitarian critics of "the new privacy" are closer to the truth when they argue that *Roe* abandoned the traditional conception of family privacy. They at least acknowledge openly what is new in this jurisprudence. But this is precisely what they object to. Let us turn to their analysis.

THE COMMUNITARIAN CRITIQUE

Two influential communitarian critiques of the right to privacy as it is applied to the zone of intimacy are provided by Michael Sandel and Mary Ann Glendon.[89] Both argue against the new developments in constitutional privacy doctrine in this domain, because these allegedly privilege individualistic over community values. Both reject the landmark case of *Roe v. Wade* on these grounds.[90]

Sandel and Glendon each note, with dismay, the development of privacy doctrine from a traditional concern to keep certain personal, intimate facts from public view—informational privacy—to a contemporary right to engage in certain conduct without governmental restraint, in the name of individual choice.[91] For both thinkers, the important change is not the application of the notion of privacy to the zone of intimacy but rather the shift within the intimate zone, from informational privacy to decisional autonomy, and from substantive justifications appealing to communal values and prized traditions or practices, to voluntarist, individualist justifications.

Because Sandel and Glendon, like so many communitarians, are enamored with the family and "family values," they do not object to the reasoning in the landmark case of *Griswold v. Connecticut* where the Court, for the first time, explicitly recognized a constitutional right to privacy and found it to apply to the right of married couples to use contraceptives.[92] Both agree that the Court justified the privacy right it proclaimed in *Griswold* on teleological rather than on voluntarist grounds: the right to privacy was defended not for the sake of letting people lead their sexual lives as they choose, but rather for the sake of affirming and protecting the social institution of marriage, and the human goods realized in it (intimacy, harmony in living, bilateral loyalty, a sacred association). *Griswold*, in short, affirmed a social practice and tradition valued by the community.[93] The violation of privacy consisted in the intrusion required to enforce the law, not in the restriction on the freedom to use contraceptives. Moreover, the decision allegedly remained true to the traditional doctrine of privacy as the interest in keeping intimate marital affairs from public view (unseemliness). As such, *Griswold*'s privacy protected the family as a unit against intrusion.[94]

The shift within the intimate sphere to voluntarist and individualist arguments began, according to Glendon and Sandel, with *Eisenstadt v. Baird* (1972), which involved a law restricting the distribution of contraceptives to unmarried persons.[95] Here the Court struck down the law through the explicit innovation that "redescribed the bearers of privacy rights from persons qua participants in the social institution of marriage to persons qua individuals, *independent of their roles or attachments.*"[96] Moreover, privacy was no longer conceived as freedom from surveillance or disclosure of intimate affairs, but rather as protecting the freedom to engage in certain activities without governmental restriction. Sandel cites the now famous statement in *Eisenstadt* as proof of these "invidious" innovations: "If the right of privacy means anything, it is the right of the *individual*, married or single, to be free from unwarranted governmental intrusion into matters so fundamentally affecting a person as the decision whether to bear or beget a child."[97]

One year later this reasoning was applied in *Roe*, where the privacy right was extended to "encompass a woman's decision whether or not to terminate her pregnancy." Moreover, the language of decisional autonomy was made quite explicit in the 1977 majority opinion in *Carey v. Population Services International*, where Justice Brennan argued that the constitutional protection of individual autonomy in matters of childbearing is not dependent on the element in *Griswold* that forbade the restriction on the use of contraceptives because it would bring police into marital bedrooms.[98] Rather, Justice Brennan maintained that the autonomy rights of individuals were really at the core of what even *Griswold* protected. Indeed, Brennan maintained that the lesson of *Griswold*, *Eisenstadt*, and *Roe* is that the Constitution protects individual decisions in matters of childbearing from unjustified intrusion by the state. Later decisions upholding abortion rights also used the language of decisional autonomy to describe the privacy interest at stake. And in his important dissent in *Bowers v. Hardwick*, Justice Blackmun summarized what was at issue in the Court's previous privacy decisions: "We protect those rights not because they contribute . . . to the general public welfare, but because they form so central a part of an individual's life. 'The concept of privacy embodies the "moral fact that a person belongs to himself and not to others nor to society as a whole."' . . . We protect the decision whether to have a child because parenthood alters so dramatically an individual's self-definition."[99] The Court thus clearly construed the new privacy as securing decisional autonomy to individuals over certain intensely personal concerns.

What is so objectionable about this development? Here I can only take up one set of criticisms: the objection to the conception of the self allegedly underlying the very idea that privacy rights secure decisional autonomy to the individual with respect to personal matters.[100]

PRIVACY AS DECISIONAL AUTONOMY: THE ISOLATED, DISEMBEDDED SELF?

The communitarian argument leveled against the principle of an individual constitutional right to personal privacy protecting decisional autonomy over intimate concerns is that such a right presupposes an atomistic (Glendon) or voluntarist (Sandel) concept of the individual and a philosophical anthropology of the self that is both incoherent and incompatible with moral responsibility. Glendon and Sandel each make this charge, albeit with differing degrees of sophistication. Glendon argues that the Court's rulings protecting decisional autonomy embody a view of society as a collection of separate, self-involved, self-sufficient individuals.[101] This "flaw" in privacy doctrine is, according to Glendon, distinctively and deplorably American.[102] In short, she construes the right to privacy in American constitutional law simply as the right to be let alone, which in turn presupposes a conception of the individual as autarkic, isolated, and sovereign. It is the atomism of the concept of the individual presupposed by the new privacy doctrine that she dislikes.

Sandel's critique of the principle of privacy as autonomy goes even deeper, to challenge the disembedded conception of the self and the voluntarist conception of individual moral agency that it allegedly presupposes. Recall his argument against Rawls, contending that the liberal conception of justice, which privileges the idea of equal rights over substantive conceptions of the good, rests upon an anthropological concept of the self that is not only isolated, atomistic, and autonomous, but also radically unsituated.[103] The essentially unencumbered self is a "a subject . . . of possession, individuated in advance and given prior to [its] ends."[104] This self adopts a distanced attitude toward all possible life goals and voluntaristically chooses its own conception of the good as if this were one among many dispensable preferences. Accordingly, the autonomous unencumbered self is construed as external to its own identity. It has no constitutive attachments, but merely a set of preferences from which it can pick and choose.

It is this self that is allegedly presupposed by the new privacy doctrine. Thus, in its privacy cases, it is the Court's expressive and voluntarist individualism that Sandel abhors, for the Court seems to conceive intimate relationships as entirely the product of trivial personal choices about lifestyle, instead of as constitutive of the persons who participate in them. Sandel echoes the fears articulated by Robert Bellah in *Habits of the Heart*, that expressive individualism, rampant since the 1960s, leads people to view intimate relationships solely as contexts for self-fulfillment and hence as temporary or endlessly renegotiable, entailing no real commitment, sense of duty, or responsibility.[105]

The Court's privacy jurisprudence is allegedly guilty of turning this cultural orientation of a relatively small minority into a valid norm and spreading it to the population at large. Post-1950s liberal jurisprudence generalized the expressivist, egoistic conception of the self along with the contractualist model of obligation, to society.[106] The rights revolution in family law thus introduces a destructive atomization and an adversarial relationship into otherwise solidary family communities pitting one member's rights against another's. In short, the new privacy rights undermine ethical community (in this case, family) and concrete identity (the charge of fragmentation) because they rest on a disembedded conception of the self that is in turn subsumed under abstract universalist principles (rights) that deny and even undermine the particular communal identities of situated individuals.[107]

Against this conception of the self, Sandel insists that everyone is radically situated—their identities, self-understandings, and values are shaped through community-mediated communicative processes of socialization. Thus, on theoretical grounds, the liberal conception of the self as a solipsistic presocietal being presupposed by the new privacy rights is impossible. Moreover, our moral experience belies voluntarism, or the view allegedly inherent in the new privacy jurisprudence that sovereign authentic selves need recognize obligations only if they are voluntarily assumed by the moral agent.[108] For Sandel, this misconstrues the moral fabric of that all-important community—the family—with important negative consequences for the rest of civic life.

Indeed, he insists that in order to have moral intuitions, we must view ourselves as particular persons situated within this family, this community, this nation or people, as bearers of this history and this particular identity. We are not separate from but tied to and defined by our attachments and aims, and these flow from our embeddedness in a specific context and community which is constitutive of who we are and to which we owe duties of loyalty. We also owe particular duties of responsibility to the concrete specific people with whom we have special relationships. If we assume that subjects are socialized through communication, we must see them as members of communities, sharing community values and traditions and having concrete identities and relationships. Individuals do not create their moral vocabulary ex nihilo; it is inherited from the traditional understandings into which they are socialized and which, in turn, nourish their capacity to be moral agents, providing the content of their particular identities. Sandel thus sees us as particular, albeit self-interpreting beings, able to reflect on our history and to revise to some extent our identities, but situated nonetheless.

Now if he and Glendon were correct about the conception of the self that they impute to the new privacy doctrine, they would have a strong case. But they are not correct. There is no obvious connection between either the atomist or the voluntarist conception of the self articulated above and the general notion of the rights-bearing individual. Nor does the new privacy doctrine entail the particular version of liberalism targeted by this critique. In short, there is no necessary conceptual connection between privacy rights that secure personal decisional autonomy in certain domains and the ideological version of the self just described. If it has been so interpreted in the past, or if some of the language of the Court's rulings rely on anachronistic dimensions of the liberal paradigm, then it is time to change the interpretation, to come up with different justifications, not to jettison the principle of individual privacy rights.[109]

The argument of both Glendon and Sandel is based on a category error: abstract concepts such as legal personality, fundamental individual rights, privacy, or decisional autonomy are not equivalent to an ontological description of the self or a particular concept of agency.[110] The principle that individual privacy rights protect decisional autonomy (choice) regarding certain personal or intimate concerns can go quite well with a recognition of the intersubjective character of processes of personal identity formation, and an awareness of the historical, contextual sources of our values. None of this obviates the need for privacy as decisional autonomy when it comes to certain choices that the relational, embedded, interdependent, communicative individual may have to make in modern societies. We do not initially choose the communities we are born or socialized into, or the strong evaluations and commitments these generate; but surely as adults we must have the opportunity to affirm and embrace some of these communities and commitments and abandon those which, upon reflection, we cannot. Only if decisional autonomy in this sense is respected in every person, however situated, only if the individual's capacity for moral deliberation and justification, on the one side, and for ethical judgment and self-reflection (involving the possibility of partial revision of identities and conceptions of the good on the basis of new insights), on the other, are protected against coercion by the state or the majority of the community, can the individual function as a moral agent at all. Ascribing a right to privacy as decisional autonomy to individuals over their forms of intimate life does not hypostatize the will or entail a voluntarist approach to obligation. Rather, it ascribes to individuals the competence to ethically shape their will and to make the relevant ethical and moral choices on the basis of insight into what is good for them as particular individuals without violating what is right for all.

To be sure, there have been rather controversial attempts to justify the personal rights complex recently secured by the new privacy doctrine that appeal to a comprehensive conception of the autonomous individual typical of a liberal worldview. But one could accept the critique of the Kantian or Millian concept of autonomy without assuming that privacy rights have to entail this sort of justification or, for that matter, any comprehensive conception of the person or any overarching substantive moral worldview.[111] One could, in other words, argue that the principle of privacy rights rests on the abandonment of "the cult of wholeness" presupposed by general philosophies of man. Indeed, it rests on and secures (along with other sets of rights) the differentiation between our status as legal persons and our functioning as concrete unique individuals involved in specific relationships and particular communities, where we may indeed be quite engaged with others and deeply involved in the pursuit of substantive communal ideals of the good. Sandel's critique, in short, mistakenly conflates the legal with the natural person. Legal personhood ascribing decisional autonomy over certain matters attaches to individuals, of course, but it does not presuppose a conception of the natural individual as atomist, autarkic, or disembedded or of the self as voluntarist vis-à-vis her identity or moral commitments.

In sum, personal privacy rights protect one's decisional autonomy in relation to certain crucially personal concerns;[112] they do not dictate the kinds of reasons one gives for ethical decisions or the reflective processes informing the decision. Thus, on the privacy justification for reproductive choice, a woman may decide for or against abortion on the basis of her community's values, her religious worldview, or her discussions with "significant others"—her relation to tradition, community, or loved ones are not in question here. Her right to decide does not dictate the basis of her decision. Decisional privacy rights designate the individual as the locus of decision making when certain kinds of moral dilemmas or ethical issues about the good, or about personal happiness, are involved—they do not dictate to whom one must justify one's ethical choices, nor the kinds of reasons one must give. As Hannah Arendt argued long ago, such rights ascribe a legal persona to the individual that serves as a protective shield for her concrete unique identity, particular motives, and personal choices, but do not prescribe these. Rather, they provide the formal enabling conditions for her to pursue her conception of the good without unjust interference by the state or by others.[113]

Therefore, when the language of autonomy or choice appears in its opinions, there is no reason to automatically impute to the Court a voluntarist ideal of the person.[114] Ascribing decisional autonomy to individuals over certain issues does not commit the concept of privacy rights to a conception of the disembedded individual; it simply militates against state paternalism, whether in the guise of community norms or majority will.[115] There are times when the Court does seem to invoke voluntarist arguments. However, it is my thesis that these do not derive from the concept of privacy rights granting decisional autonomy to the individual over certain matters: rather, such justifications are attributable to anachronistic assumptions stemming from the liberal legal paradigm that insinuate themselves into the opinions of various justices at various times. My point is that privacy as decisional autonomy can be defended on other than voluntarist grounds. Furthermore, the new privacy rights in the domain of intimacy, with the contemporary pluralization of forms of intimate association, necessarily involve far more than the right to be left alone: by protecting their decisional autonomy, they secure to intimate associates the possibility of constructing wanted and shared forms of life—the building blocks, as it were, of community in diversity.

PRIVACY AND IDENTITY

Even though this interpretation of the new privacy right to decisional autonomy in the domain of intimacy can be defended against the above criticisms, it is not sufficient to account for the issue of identity raised by the communitarian intervention. According to Sandel, we must proceed in our moral and legal reasoning on the assumption that we are dealing with concrete selves, not abstract persons, with individuals defined in and through their ends, for whom attachments and beliefs are constitutive of who they are, and whose identity is formative of their ethical reasoning.

Thus, when Sandel and Glendon speak of the community's conception of the good, of the "right" of the community to institutionalize its values, of the "duty" of the individual to the well-being of the community, they have apparently shifted terrain from issues of autonomy/justice to concern with identity/the good.[116] But they are wrong to restrict the issue of the good to the integrity of community values or common identity, as if there were, in highly differentiated, pluralist, and multicultural civil societies, a single overarching conception of the good, or a single substantive collective identity upon which we all agree.[117]

It also seems as if these theorists assume that the individual and the common good, as well as individual and group identities, completely overlap. If certain versions of liberal theory have operated with a controversial notion of autonomy, the communitarians suffer from the opposite difficulty. They have not only tended to abandon the principle of autonomy altogether, but also to suppress the problem posed by the difference and potential conflict between individual and group identity, individual and group conceptions of the good, and minority and majority forms of intimate life. Group identity is, of course, part of the identity of the members of the group. But in modern pluralist, differentiated, civil societies, individuals belong to many different groups, play a variety of social roles, and have communal identifications that are operative on different levels of the social structure. The sources and inputs into individual identity are multiple and heterogeneous. Indeed, the fact that one is situated within a plurality of communities, that one must act out a number of often conflicting roles, ought to lead back to the acknowledgment of the centrality of individual agency and ethical choice in the shaping of a life.[118] The personal dynamics of shifting involvements among separate spheres, roles, and commitments required by life in a highly differentiated modern society create the need and the possibility for each individual to develop a strong sense of self, along with the ability to form, self-reflectively affirm, and express her unique identity in an open multiplicity of contexts.

While people do not invent the traditions, patterns, or norms into which they are at first socialized, as they become individualized they do invent and reinvent the unity of their lives and their unique identities (of course in interactive, communicative processes).[119] They do so in part by making ethical decisions that involve selecting among and ordering value commitments and making choices about how they want to live. They also contribute to reinterpreting and reinventing meanings, norms, traditions, and narratives. Today, personal decisions regarding the shape of one's intimate associations, sexuality, and reproduction are considered to be among the most important in this regard.

The identity of the concrete individual is not just a set of preferences among which one can pick and choose as if they were clothes. Rather, as already indicated, what Taylor has called "strong evaluations" are at stake especially regarding the domain of intimacy.[120] But this does not mean that individual identity is simply the product of the community's values, social embeddedness, shared traditions, or a set of social roles. Indeed, all these are open to conflicting interpretations on the part of individuals and subgroups within a particular society. Precisely because it is the task of individuals to develop and express their self-conceptions out of (and within) the multiplicity of memberships, affiliations, commitments, roles, and structures they are involved in, and precisely because they require recognition for their concrete personalities, their opportunity for self-development and experimental self-presentation, along with solitude and withdrawal, requires protection. Privacy protection affords to the individual a sense of control over the personal space in which she experiments with her self-definitions. It shields the self-creative synthesis that only she can fashion out of her various locations and backgrounds, in part through communicative interaction with others.[121] This communicative interaction must also be under her own control—privacy rights leave it up to the individual to decide with whom, when, and if to discuss her most personal intimate concerns. Privacy rights, in short, shield communicative liberty.[122]

It is my claim that by narrowing privacy rights to the right to be let alone, by assuming that decisional autonomy has to entail an arbitrary relation between the individual and her ends, by saddling the new privacy with a voluntarist and abstract conception of the self that allegedly ignores the real individuality of members of concrete communities, and by trivializing personal ethical and aesthetic decision making as a mere lifestyle choice, the communitarian critics abandon an important source of protection for the integrity of concrete individuals as well as group identities, which may differ from those the state at any time seeks to promote.[123]

In short, I contend that we can take up the concern for the ethical and situated dimensions of identity and argue that the new privacy rights protect both agency *and* personal identity, autonomy *and* "authenticity," without prescribing a particular concept of the self on either level. By "authentic" I do not refer to a deep self to which one has to be true, nor do I mean that sex, sexuality, or reproductive decisions define the core of who one is. Rather, I mean that only an identity or a form of life that one can affirm and embrace can be considered "authentic" instead of imposed, and that the right to privacy as decisional autonomy in the domain of intimacy gives the individual the opportunity to reflectively rediscover/construct who she is and how she wants to, or must, according to her own lights, live her life.

If not a right to personal privacy covering the domain of intimacy (securing control over access and decision making to the individual), what protects the identity-shaping ethical decisions of individuals and groups from leveling in the name of some vague idea of community values or the majority's conception of the common good?[124] Here, too, privacy as autonomy protects against domination. To be sure, provision for the participation of every group on equal terms in the public spaces of civil and political society, such that no perspective is excluded, is an important way to empower people (through voice) to assert, protect, and further develop their different individual and collective identities in public. Voice and participation in democratic public spaces certainly help protect difference. But individual personal privacy rights are nonetheless indispensable. Personal privacy rights construed to entail decisional autonomy protect the constitutive minimal preconditions for forming an identity of one's own because they ascribe ethical competence to the individual to form and pursue their conception of the good, their happiness, and their form of life in relation to intimate concerns.

Nothing is implied about the sources of values or the attitude of individuals regarding the traditions and memberships to which they are attached. Privacy rights shielding personal intimacies do not prescribe what identities should be like; they secure to every individual the preconditions for developing intact identities that they can embrace as their own.[125] On the one side, by acknowledging decisional autonomy over what are considered important personal matters, privacy rights protect every concrete individual's claim, no matter how different or odd, to be treated as a person by members of the community. On the other side, privacy rights shield the personal dimensions of one's life from undue scrutiny or interference. As such, they protect experimental, creative processes of personal identity formation. The principle that first articulated this idea in American privacy doctrine is that of *inviolate personality*.[126]

The standard that underlies this aspect of privacy may be formulated as the right not to have one's intimate decisions and associations unduly restricted/supervised by the state or third parties without very compelling reasons indeed. This standard militates against the imposition of an identity that one does not freely affirm and embrace.

A CONSTRUCTIVIST JUSTIFICATION OF
THE NEW PRIVACY RIGHTS

Of course, the crucial question of which personal matters should be covered by the new privacy right and what the community may legitimately regulate through law and public policy remains to be answered. We cannot avoid the issue of where to draw the boundary between public and private: indeed, it runs right through intimate associations. As we have seen, feminists have convincingly challenged appeals to naturalistic or essentialist arguments to determine what is intrinsically private. If we are not prepared to jettison privacy analysis altogether, then we must come up with an alternative way to justify the new privacy rights and their scope.

A constructivist justification of the concept of a right to privacy (and its reach) would proceed by posing the following question: What basic privacy rights must we concede to one another as free and equal persons and as equal citizens in a constitutional democracy that governs itself through the medium of positive and coercive law?[127] One can put this question another way. Assuming that everyone involved has equally the status of a bearer of subjective rights and is an equal member (citizen) of the political community (both of which have only recently been true of women), which categories of constitutional rights should we as "founders" grant to one another (assuming ethical pluralism and deep disagreement), and how should we fill in their content?

There is no necessity to resort to natural rights theory or to the unconvincing premises of subject philosophy to answer these questions. All that is required is that people are presumed able to engage in practical discourse, and that in the process of reason-giving they could come to accept a set of abstract, relatively indeterminant, but core principles for regulating their interaction.[128] On this approach, one can be perfectly aware of the ways in which past conceptions (of privacy rights, for example) have perpetuated instead of undermining illegitimate (gender) hierarchies. But that is precisely why a constructivist approach is needed: to correct anachronistic and unjustifiable conceptions on the basis of social transformation and historical learning.

Jürgen Habermas has framed the constructivist approach to justifying basic constitutional rights in terms of a two-tiered practice of reflection: 1. Reflection on the performative meaning of the historically contingent communicative practices (and their presuppositions) of constitution making—contingent in the sense of such a practice being an "event," a new beginning, and an incomplete project; and 2. Reflection on the continuous communicative practices involved in contesting and elaborating (amending and interpreting) the meaning and content given to basic constitutional rights, old and new, within the constituted polity, over time.[129]

Accordingly, the first level of reflection shows that a self-governing community of free and equal citizens under law requires four categories of rights:

1. Basic rights elaborating the fundamental right to equal liberties;
2. Basic (citizenship) rights elaborating the status of an equal member of an association of legal persons;
3. Basic rights to equal protection elaborating the actionability of rights; and
4. Basic rights to political participation elaborating and preserving the practice of self-governance.[130]

In a constitutional democracy, such rights must protect the public and private autonomy of all persons equally. Both forms of autonomy are ends in themselves: neither can be construed as simply of instrumental value for the other, and neither is normatively prior.

The principle of equal liberty is what concerns us here in particular, for privacy rights shielding personal liberty would have to come under this heading. On the second level of reflection, one could justify the principle of a core set of basic constitutional rights protecting individual privacy/autonomy in the domain of intimacy as an elaboration of the idea of equal personal liberty—involving, of course, equal protection of the law. I do not mean that one could derive such rights from the concept of personal autonomy or from the principle of equal liberty, each of which are presupposed by the enterprise itself. Rather, I argue that on the constructivist approach, we can show that they are now required by the historically new presupposition of gender equality and the transformation of intimacy discussed above. In short, on the basis of historical contextual learning, new content can be given to universalistic principles and basic rights, appropriate to contemporary understanding.[131] It is assumed that all those affected would, as equal participants in the constituting process, be able to give and be given reasons that none could reasonably reject for whatever basic privacy/autonomy rights are acknowledged. The justification of the specific reach of such rights and of their interpretation in public discourses could thus proceed on the basis of the linguistic and reflexive turn in philosophy. It need only involve the criterion of reasonable nonrejectability and the principle of equal liberty. One would not need to invoke naturalistic or essentialistic arguments.[132]

I argue that the justification of what should fall under the protective cover of privacy rights, and what should not, must be made from this constructivist point of view, informed by actual public discourses and claims on the part of ordinary citizens.[133] We must proceed in our constructivist justifications on the basis of reflection on what has already been achieved, taking into account new developments and needs. We must interpret the content of basic principles (equal liberty) and rights in light of important learning processes: in this case regarding gender equality. This involves drawing new lines between the moral and the ethical—between what violates universal principles that no one could reasonably reject, and hence is a question of justice, and what is a matter of a particular individual or group's conception of the good.[134] But it also involves distinguishing between what ethical understandings the community can legislate or foster and which ethical decisions should be left to the individual.

The battle over a right to privacy covering the intimate domain involves, as I have already indicated, important shifts in the status of sex and sexuality (from the moral to the ethical) as well as shifts in the status of women (presumptive gender equality). These are two empirical developments that have normative implications. One can no longer regulate nonreproductive or extramarital sex on the grounds that it is immoral or remain innocent of the negative impact such regulation has on gender equality. The community, of course, may and does legitimately legislate morality, in part by criminalizing violations to the moral code (such as murder and rape). Such regulations are justifiable by arguments that presumably no one could reasonably reject. But these sorts of arguments no longer are available to justify criminalizing or restrictively regulating a wide range of intimate decisions regarding sex, reproduction, and choice of adult intimate associates.

Indeed, the overall trend of decisions in American family law over the past four decades registers these shifts. There has been a marked change in the law's discourse about acceptable relations between family members, partly involving the transfer of many moral decisions from the law to the people the law once regulated.[135] In particular, moral discourse regarding sexual relations has tended to disappear from the law. State involvement in family life and in intimacy generally is increasingly oriented to the need to protect endangered family members or intimate associates rather than to efforts to steer intimate behavior in a particular morally sanctified sexual or reproductive direction (or monogamy).[136]

To be sure, a society may legitimately institutionalize shared ethical conceptions of the good and develop public policy on pragmatic grounds, even regarding certain intimate choices.[137] The moral/ethical divide is not equivalent to a public/private distinction or to a line separating what can or cannot be legally regulated. But if the individual's moral claims to respect, personhood, and civic equality are at stake, if regulations are made that those affected could not reasonably accept, then the presumption in favor of personal autonomy should prevail, unless the state has compelling reasons for restricting it. In other words, the moral criteria undergirding the regulation of adult intimacy should be whether adult intimacies are wanted, consensual, reciprocal (mutual recognition of rights), and responsive to the obligations that intimacy incurs, or whether they are imposed, abusive, or involve force, domination, or exploitation. Certainly law can and does intervene to offer protection to individuals against the latter.

Today, the importance of the individual right to make (and control access to) intimate personal decisions about the content and form of sexual relationships and reproduction is widely acknowledged. This reflects a cultural shift, which, together with the premise of gender equality, supplies moral reasons against regulating for the purpose (or with the effect) of reimposing marital reproductive sex, or maternal identity onto women, all of which functionalize their bodies and their life choices, denying them ethical self-determination of their personal intimate relationships. Thus it is possible to argue for a right to privacy shielding individual ethical self-determination in this domain for everyone on moral grounds that trump the ethical predilections of political majorities.

Including a right to privacy covering certain intimate decisions and relationships within the overall system of constitutional rights thus involves a moral claim: everyone should have such a right because their personhood, equal status as ethically competent individuals, happiness, moral agency, and civic equality are all at stake. What that right protects is the individual's ethical autonomy in certain areas of decision making. In other words, it ascribes ethical competence to the rights-bearer, construing her as a strong evaluator capable of affirming, devising, and even revising (if desired) her own conception of the good (i.e., her second-order desires).

Moreover, having a right to privacy as decisional autonomy means that one cannot be obliged either to reveal one's personal motives for one's choices or to accept, as one's own, any particular group's reasons or evaluations. Neither the source nor the particular content of the individual's motives for action can be imposed by the state in this domain. In other words, a right to personal privacy involves precisely the liberation from the obligation to justify one's actions by giving reasons that everyone could accept as their own (the moral). It frees one from the pressure to adopt, as one's own reasons, the reasons that everyone (in a given group) accepts (i.e., the community's ethics). Such a *telos* toward consensus holds for moral discourse and matters of justice, strictly speaking, but it is not required for individual ethical or aesthetic decisions covered by personal privacy rights. In other words, a privacy right entitles one to choose with whom one will attempt to justify one's ethical decisions, with whom one will communicatively rethink conceptions of the good, whose recognition matters, and, indeed, whether one will discuss certain matters with anyone at all. For with respect to personal decisions shielded by the protective cover of a right to decisional privacy, it does not matter whether the reasons decisive for me could also be accepted by everyone else.[138] The state may not require me to reveal my reasons for acting in the domain in which I have the right to act on my own reasons. This means that one has the liberty to withdraw certain concerns, motives, and aspects of the self from public scrutiny and control: therein lies the link between informational and decisional privacy.[139]

Thus, as Glendon has noted, privacy rights do indeed mark off a protected domain constituting an invisible shield around the person.[140] But this is not a separate institutional sphere: the spatial metaphor is misleading. Individuals carry their legal persona, their protective shields, with them wherever they go, in public and in private. This shield protects the autonomy, judgment, creative imagination, and inviolability of the concrete (situated, socialized) individual in ways that society deems crucial. Legal personhood is abstract; what it protects is the concrete individual's personal integrity.

It is by now a commonplace that although the practices and rituals of privacy vary across cultures, every society acknowledges the normative importance of privacy in some form.[141] Every society establishes what Robert Post has recently called "rules of civility" that safeguard respect for individual personal privacy and which are, in a sense, constitutive of both individuals and community.[142] Echoing Erving Goffman, Post argues that the integrity of individual personality is dependent in part upon the observance of social rules of deference and demeanor that bind the actor and recipient together. In following these "rules of civility," individuals establish and affirm ritual and sacred aspects of their own and the other's identities while confirming the social order.[143] The violation of these rules indicates a lack of recognition for personal dignity and can damage a person by discrediting her identity and injuring her personality, thereby disconfirming her sense of self. Thus, the reciprocal recognition of privacy is the condition of possibility of successful social interaction based on mutual recognition of the integrity of the participants.

Indeed, the normative nature of privacy lies precisely in the protection of what Goffman has called "the territories of the self"—a preserve to which an individual can claim "entitlement to possess, control, use, dispose of."[144] Defined by normative and social factors, these territories are a vehicle for the exchange of meaning: they serve as a kind of language through which persons communicate with each other.[145] But they are also central to the subjective sense that the individual has concerning her selfhood. What counts is not whether a preserve is exclusively maintained or shared, or given up entirely,

> but rather the role that the individual is allowed in determining what happens to his claim. . . On the issue of will and self-determination turns the whole possibility of using territories of the self in a dual way, with comings-into-touch

avoided as a means of *maintaining respect* and engaged in as a *means of establishing regard*. . . . It is no wonder that felt self-determination is crucial to one's sense of what it means to be a full-fledged person.[146]

On this normative conception of privacy, it is clearly the sense of control over dimensions of one's identity, over access to oneself, over which aspects of oneself one will present at which time and to whom, along with the ability to press or to waive territorial claims, that is crucial and empowering. Indeed, it is the sine qua non for understanding oneself to be an independent person—an individual worthy of respect and capable of establishing regard.

In our type of society, privacy rights conferring decisional autonomy over certain personal matters secure control and power to the individual. They help constitute a structure of mutual recognition and the social ritual by means of which one's identity is acknowledged, one's selfhood, integrity, and social standing guaranteed.

> Privacy is an essential part of the complex social practice by means of which the social group recognizes and communicates to the individual—that his existence is his own. . . . This is a precondition of personhood. . . . And this in turn presupposes that he believes that the concrete reality which he is . . . belongs to him in a moral sense.[147]

The language of possession here should not mislead us. What is meant is that by virtue of privacy one is able to maintain a sense of selfhood, of agency, and of personal identity, not that these are a form of alienable property. While a right to privacy is universalistic, in that it establishes every individual as a legal person with a moral claim to personal autonomy meriting equal concern and respect, what it protects is our particularity— our concrete and fragile identities.[148] It also protects the communicative infrastructure (the rules and rituals of civility) crucial to successful social interaction.

THE SCOPE OF PRIVACY: BRINGING THE BODY BACK IN

Let me return to the problem of what "personal intimate concerns" should be covered by the new privacy. Here I can only offer my own intervention in what has become a highly politicized debate on this matter. In the long run, of course, the answer depends upon the moral and cultural self-understanding of societies and on the outcome of political contestation over cultural norms, codes, and gendered social relations. These constitute the practices, domains, and understandings of privacy, personal autonomy, and appropriate intimacy at any given time.

I shall briefly address this issue by defending the extension of constitutional privacy to cover a woman's decisional autonomy in the most contested area of reproduction—abortion.[149] My interpretation does not proceed on the possessive-individualist or voluntarist conception of the person. Rather, I reason from the notion of a relational, situated, embodied individuality. Indeed, in order to understand why abortion rights—among other procreative concerns—are central to the concrete as well as the abstract (reflective) dimension of our selves, we must replace the possessive-individualist conception of the relation of self and body that has dominated our thinking for so long with something better.

Roe v. Wade holds that the right to personal privacy founded on the Fourteenth Amendment's concept of personal liberty is broad enough to encompass a woman's decision to terminate her pregnancy.[150] The majority opinion cites a line of Court decisions going back to the late nineteenth century, however, that "make it clear that only personal rights that can be deemed 'fundamental' or 'implicit in the concept of ordered liberty,' are included in this guarantee of personal privacy."[151] It then proceeds to adduce a range of reasons for considering the abortion decision to be fundamental in the appropriate sense for individual women:

> Specific and direct harm medially diagnosable even in early pregnancy may be involved. Maternity, or additional offspring, may force upon the woman a distressful life and future. Psychological harm may be imminent. Mental and physical health may be taxed by child care. There is also the distress, for all concerned, associated with the unwanted child. . . . In other cases, as in this one, the additional difficulties and continuing stigma of unwed motherhood may be involved.[152]

This list sums up the harms that state denial of choice would inflict upon the pregnant woman.

Much of this reasoning has a rather antiquated air about it today. But the decision and its progeny can be justified on general constructivist grounds more appropriate to our contemporary understanding, yet in tune with *Roe*'s essential holding. This is because the Court proceeded on the key assumption that women are persons to whom the Fourteenth Amendment's provisions against the denial of liberty without due process of the law applies. It also assumed correctly that reproductive decisions, including the decision whether or not to have a child, are of fundamental personal importance to women.[153] There is nothing anachronistic about these two assumptions.

Indeed, it should be obvious today that a woman's personhood, moral autonomy, and ethical agency are all at stake in reproductive decisions, and that she is affected by these in ways that are importantly different from men. The Court implicitly acknowledged both these propositions. One could go a step further and argue that the presupposition of gender equality (which the Court did not mention in *Roe*) and the shift in understanding of the purpose of intimacy (from a moral reproductive imperative to personal happiness related to one's conception of the good that *Roe* and *Eisenstadt* presuppose) imply that procreative freedom should now be deemed implicit in the concept of "ordered liberty" or values basic to society.

I do not believe that there are convincing countervailing moral arguments that are strong enough to override the moral claims to personhood and autonomy of a woman regarding reproductive decisions, including her right to choose an abortion.[154] Yet there are in the case of abortion important ethical considerations that weigh in on the other side regarding the value of life and the fetus. The Court's privacy analysis in *Roe* took all this into account, yielding a nuanced decision that provided protection for the decisional autonomy and privacy of the woman and also acknowledged the community's ethical values regarding the potential life of fetus.[155] It ascribed to women the moral right to choose their form of life based on their conception of the good, while ensuring that the state interest in the sanctity of life was protected by permitting restrictions on abortion in the third trimester of pregnancy.[156]

But there is another set of reasons why women in particular are the ones who should be accorded privacy and decisional autonomy for the abortion decision. Although they were implicit in *Roe*, these reasons were made explicit in the later 1992 decision in *Planned Parenthood v. Casey*, affirming *Roe*'s essential holding against criminalization of abortion.[157] They have to do with claims to bodily integrity, identity, and the implications that pregnancy carries as a form of embodiment, particularly if unwanted, for a woman.

To be sure, *Casey* also made the link between the right to choose an abortion and a woman's personhood, moral autonomy, and dignity much more explicit than it was in *Roe*:

> These matters, involving the most intimate and personal choices a person may make in a lifetime, choices central to personal dignity and autonomy, are central to the liberty protected by the Fourteenth Amendment. At the heart of liberty is the right to define one's own concept of existence, of meaning, of the universe and of the mystery of human life.[158]

It explicitly focused on the woman as the center of decision making, grounding the abortion right in the due process clause of the Fourteenth Amendment protecting liberty against both procedurally and substantively arbitrary impositions and restraints.[159] By adding to this perspective a focus on bodily integrity and a frank acknowledgment of issues of power between spouses regarding reproductive decisions, the *Casey* decision expanded a crucial dimension of privacy analysis. However, this ruling for the most part eschewed privacy talk, and in certain key respects it also eviscerated the privacy justification for decisional autonomy in this domain.[160] Let me address each innovation in turn.

In striking down husband notification provisions in the Pennsylvania law, the plurality opinion in *Planned Parenthood v. Casey* provided an innovative and important explication of privacy analysis. As already indicated, the Court roundly rejected the old common law "entity" views of marriage as inconsistent with contemporary understandings, citing the relevant language in *Eisenstadt* that individualized privacy rights.[161] Moreover, it abandoned the common law understanding of the woman's role within the family as a subordinate to her husband with no legal existence of her own.[162] Reasoning from the contemporary understanding that women and men, husbands and wives, are presumptively both individuals and legal persons, the Court declared that it is obvious that when a husband and wife disagree about abortion, the view of only one can prevail. This must be the view of the pregnant woman:

> It is an inescapable biological fact that state regulation with respect to the child a woman is carrying will have a far greater impact on the mother's liberty than on the father's. The effect of state regulation on a woman's protected liberty is doubly deserving of scrutiny in such a case, as the State has touched . . . upon the very bodily integrity of the pregnant woman.[163]

Acknowledging that women continue to live today in a social context of gender inequality and citing statistics that indicate that "there are millions of women in this country who are the victims of regular physical and psychological abuse at the hands of their husbands," the Court defended both the informational and decisional aspects of the woman's privacy with regard to her spouse. Indeed, it noted that in a well-functioning marriage, husband notification requirements would be unnecessary since spouses would be likely to discuss important intimate decisions. In failed or abusive marriages, such a requirement would be dangerous and unjust because it could expose the pregnant woman to abuse and deter her from exercising her right to choose.[164] Privacy as decisional autonomy, entailing the freedom from having to inform or give reasons for one's choice, is in this aspect of the Court's ruling doubly grounded in bodily (and psychical) integrity.

To understand this, we must, as it were, bring the body back into the theoretical analysis while avoiding the possessive individualist model that construes one's body as one's property. In short, we are all embodied selves.[165] We do not happen to have bodies or choose to take them with us, like purses; we are our bodies even if the meaning of this is a sociohistorical construction.[166] By this I mean that our bodies, our symbolic interpretation of our bodies, and our sense of control over our bodies are central to our most basic sense of self, to our identity and our personal dignity. My body is not extrinsic to who I am. Of course, this is not a simple physical fact, for we can lose some body parts without losing our identity, and the symbolic meaning we give to our bodies is communicatively mediated, varying across cultures and over time. Nevertheless, our selves, our identities, and our personal autonomy are intricately implicated in our bodies and in what we make of them—for our bodies are our mode of being in the world.

Indeed, Goffman views the body as one of the core territories of the self. He argues that a sense of control over one's own body is crucial for maintaining an intact sense of self and to the ability to interact with others.[167] Self-confidence is predicated upon the sense that one can dispose freely over one's own body: that one can coordinate its functions autonomously and regulate access to it.[168] Without recognition by others of one's autonomous control over one's body, of one's bodily integrity, without at least this most basic acknowledgment of one's dignity, the individual's self-image and self-confidence are crippled, as is the security she needs in order to interact successfully with others and to express her own needs and feelings. Thus the slogan, "our bodies, our selves," employed by women to defend their abortion rights, rings quite true—for what is at stake in the abortion controversy is precisely a woman's selfhood and identity. This is why the liberty and privacy interests in this case are deemed so personal, so intimate, so fundamental.

It should be obvious that to force a woman to endure an unwanted pregnancy is to partially impose an identity upon her—the identity of pregnant woman/mother. Clearly her bodily integrity in the physical and emotional sense are at stake in laws that criminalize abortion. But so is her gendered identity. Indeed, these are intimately interrelated. This is not because women are identical with or own their wombs, or because a woman is or owns her fetus, but because the experience of pregnancy constitutes a fundamental change in her embodiment on the physical, emotional, and symbolic levels, and thus in her identity and self-understanding. An unwanted pregnancy imposes a very powerful form of embodiment on the woman, in which she risks losing control over her bodily functions and her sense of self. It also imposes a new and undesired identity and a new intimate relationship onto the woman, requiring heavy investments of herself with implications that go well beyond the physical discomfort of pregnancy or mere lifestyle issues that anti-choice thinkers believe sum up the problem of an unwanted pregnancy and unwanted motherhood for women.

The significance of motherhood and the normative understanding of what constitutes a good mother is, in our society, profoundly different from fatherhood. It entails enormous (gendered) expectations regarding care and identity that cannot be reduced to the physical fact of pregnancy but which attach to it. Thus, at stake in the privacy right to abortion is the ability to resist being molded physically, psychologically, and socially into a mother, as that role is currently understood.[169]

To assert the importance of bodily integrity to privacy analysis is not to revive the paradigm of property, or to claim an absolute right to do with one's body as one pleases.[170] Rather, it is to argue that the bodily integrity at stake here is central to an individual's personal autonomy and sense of self and should be protected by privacy rights. In this respect I agree with Kendall Thomas's argument that the emphasis of privacy analysis on protected places, intimate associations, and autonomous choice is insufficient, for it fails to recognize "that 'privacy' is always *body-mediated*."[171] Thus when women claim the "right to control our own bodies," they are claiming the right to ethical autonomy rather than being instrumentalized to others' purposes.[172]

Nevertheless, the idea of bodily integrity, I would argue, gets at one crucial dimension of our situated identity—but not all dimensions of it. We are also situated individuals in the sense highlighted by communitarians: we develop self-definitions on the basis of culturally available resources in our life-world; we draw on our location in a specific set of institutions, relationships, and contexts; we make use (often creatively) of discourses that prestructure in part what can be said and thought; and, out of all this, we fashion our own creative contribution to our self-formative processes—our identity. Our relation to our body, our embodiment, is the crucial substratum of our identity, but not the whole of it. Once we recognize that identity-formation takes place throughout our lives, we can see that the symbolic meaning we give to our bodies and our selves has many sources and presuppositions. Respect for an individual's bodily integrity involves, as do the other components of privacy, recognition within interaction of the individual's own judgment in regulating access and information, and in making ethical decisions involving her basic identity needs. While privacy in the sense of concealment is also a component of bodily integrity, it is (again) not the whole of it. Like the other dimensions of privacy, we need bodily integrity within as well as apart from interaction with others.

Thus, procreative issues are fundamental not only because, as Ronald Dworkin has argued, the "moral" principles on which such decisions hinge are quasi-religious, touching on the ultimate point and value of human life.[173] On the constructivist approach, it becomes clear that reproductive freedom is fundamental because it involves the core of a woman's personal autonomy, bodily integrity, and identity: her embodiment, her self-formative processes, her life projects, and her self-understanding are all at stake.

This is why the plurality's abandonment of privacy analysis in the rest of the *Casey* decision and its replacement by a narrower focus on liberty, along with a lower standard of review (the undue burden standard replacing strict scrutiny), is disturbing.[174] Although the plurality in *Casey* grounded the right to choose an abortion in the due process clause of the Fourteenth Amendment, like the majority opinion in *Roe*, unlike the latter it did not invoke a general right to privacy on this basis but a more narrow right to liberty. Liberty, not privacy, was the centerpiece of the plurality opinion.

This was not an innocent change, aimed at correcting privacy analysis as a sort of misnomer for what is in reality a liberty right.[175] Rather, the plurality reduced the broad concept of privacy to the narrow dimension of decisional autonomy or liberty in order to permit the state and third parties to try to influence the pregnant woman's reasoning process and ultimately her decision, by exposing it to public pressure and scrutiny while leaving her the liberty to make the ultimate decision. Indeed, this switch enabled the *Casey* Court to uphold a number of restrictions on abortion, including an informed-consent warning requirement, a twenty-four-hour waiting period in which the woman is provided with "certain information," and a record-keeping requirement—all imposable from the onset of pregnancy! It thereby overruled previous cases (*Thornburgh* and *Akron*) that struck down such regulations on the grounds that they violated the right to privacy interpreted as involving decisional autonomy *and* informational privacy. In these cases, informational privacy involved both freedom from public pressure and intrusion into one's reasoning and freedom from having to give reasons for one's choice.[176] Indeed, the majority in *Thornburgh* characterized the decision to terminate a pregnancy as an "intensely private one" that "may be exercised without public scrutiny and in defiance of the contrary opinion of the sovereign or other third parties."[177] *Casey*, on the contrary, permits just such scrutiny and pressure:

> What is at stake is the woman's right to make the ultimate decision, not a right to be insulated from all others in doing so. Regulations which . . . create a structural mechanism by which the state . . . may express profound respect for the life of the unborn are permitted, if they are not a substantial obstacle to the woman's exercise of the right to choose . . . if they do not constitute an undue burden.[178]

As Linda McClain correctly shows, this erosion of privacy analysis exposes women to public pressure and interference and gives wide latitude to state second-guessing, imperiling their reproductive freedom.[179] It also vindicates my argument for a broadly construed right to privacy covering intimate association and intimate personal decisions. Liberty to make the ultimate decision is not enough: decisions are not autonomous unless they are free of pressure and scrutiny from powerful third parties, be they administrative officials, judges, boards of doctors, or male partners.

Casey thus leaves an ambiguous legacy: on the one hand it makes explicit the fundamental importance of reproductive freedom to women, arguing that a woman's personhood, bodily integrity, conception of the good, and deepest existential values are all at stake.[180] It even opens the way toward supplementing privacy with equality analysis because it openly rejects the old common law conception of (married) women as subordinate to men, casting them as full legal persons.[181] But the evisceration of privacy analysis in *Casey*, despite rejection of the husband notification provision on privacy grounds, does not bode well.[182]

All individuals need to have some sense of control over their bodies, their self-definitions, and the self-creative synthesis that only the individual can make out of her various locations, background, and future projects. The sense of control that privacy rights give to the person over the territories of the self, including the body, remain indispensable for any conception of freedom. In the abortion issue in particular, and in intimate decisions concerning sex and reproduction generally, both the abstract and situated dimensions of personhood are at stake.

EXCURSUS: ON PROPERTY, PRIVACY, AND LEGAL PARADIGMS

There is one remaining aspect of the new privacy jurisprudence that may give pause. As already indicated, the constitutionalization of individualized rights in the domain of intimacy has involved the transfer of many moral decisions from the law to the people the law once regulated. Family law is being infused with liberal notions of privacy, individual autonomy, and gender equality coming from constitution jurisprudence. These have radically undermined the premises of the old family law regime.[183]

This transformation appears to entail a wholesale shift from public to private ordering of intimacy. In other words, constitutional privacy analysis seems to foster privatization: the transposition of contractualist and proprietary assumptions from the market to spheres of ethical life (family) with which they are incompatible, with disintegrative (the communitarian worry) and/or unfair (the feminist egalitarian concern) consequences.[184]

Mary Ann Glendon makes a strong case for the communitarians to this effect. She is obviously wrong, as I have shown, to associate an atomistic or autarkic conception of the individual with the concept of a right to privacy protecting decisional autonomy. However, she also argues that a historical association of privacy with property tied to the possessive-individualist model of the self, continues to burden even the new privacy analysis. She reminds us that at the time our Constitution was written, private property was the cardinal symbol of individual freedom and independence in the United States and Europe. As the property paradigm developed in America, however, it acquired a rhetoric of absoluteness that allegedly persists, uniquely, in the United States due to the revival of privacy discourse.[185]

To be sure, Glendon acknowledges Jennifer Nedelsky's penetrating argument concerning the decentering of property rights in the aftermath of the New Deal, and the decline of vigorous, constitutional protection for entrepreneurial property from regulation in the wake of the development of the welfare state.[186] However, she cites the new constitutional right of privacy as evidence for the continued weight of the property paradigm in constitutional jurisprudence, albeit under a new guise:[187]

> Much of the attention the Supreme Court once lavished on a broad concept of property including the freedom of contract to acquire it, it now devotes to certain personal liberties that it has designated as "*fundamental.*" Remarkably, the property paradigm, including the old language of absoluteness, broods over this developing jurisprudence of personal rights. The new right of privacy, like the old right of property, has been imagined by the Court and lawyers generally as marking off a *protected sphere* surrounding the individual. . . . The old property rhetoric has been simply transferred to this new area.

Accordingly, the new privacy rights are heavily burdened with the legacy of the property paradigm: its rhetoric of absoluteness and the notion of sphere of individual sovereignty shielded from the community's claims.

For Glendon, the prime example of this "flaw" in American privacy doctrine is *Roe v. Wade*. Glendon traces the problem back to the influential and pathbreaking 1890 article by Warren and Brandeis, "The Right to Privacy."[188] The authors claimed to have discovered what was really being protected in a range of cases involving victims of unseemly prying, in which courts had previously rested their decisions on property rights. At stake was not property in the economic sense (nor simply the right to be let alone) but "inviolate personality." Concerned that the concept of property rights was too indirect a means of protecting something that is not an economic entity at all, Brandeis and Warren argued for protecting inviolate personality through the vehicle of a general right to privacy.

This proves to Glendon that "privacy was thus, quite literally, pulled from the hat of property."[189] It looks as if the new constitutional right of privacy devoted to marking off a protected sphere of personal autonomy and control, deemed fundamental and construed as a form of negative liberty, simply transfers the now defunct property rhetoric and anachronistic assumptions of the liberal paradigm onto a new domain.[190] Constitutional privacy analysis of intimacy, in short, entails privatization. It shifts intimate association from status to contract, from normed and regulated relationships oriented to promoting solidarity and the common good, to private ordering oriented to strategic/instrumental calculations of self-interest. The rights revolution in family law thus introduces a destructive economic logic and competitive adversarial relationships into what once were solidary family communities, pitting one member's rights against another's and undermining the bases of social trust and cohesion.[191] The shift of much of family law over to private contractualist orderings seems to support Glendon's argument.

As seductive as it is at first sight, however, this interpretation of the "new privacy" is unconvincing. It collapses two levels of analysis: constitutional protection of personal privacy in the domain of intimacy and contractualist privatization of intimate relations deemed off-limits to regulation. But as we shall see, privacy as decisional autonomy need not entail unregulated private orderings.[192] In short, the error is the assumption that there is an intrinsic rather than a merely contextual link between these. This is not the case even if constitutional privacy has been invoked by some to justify privatization in the second sense.

There is not much in *Roe* that confirms the charge that the paradigm of property or possessive individualism underlies the privacy right recognized for women with respect to abortion.[193] The Court explicitly rejected the effort made by some *amici curiae* to link the idea that one has an unlimited right to do with one's body as one pleases to the right of privacy. Repeatedly, the Court insisted that the pregnant woman cannot be isolated in her privacy and that her right to terminate her pregnancy is not absolute. Neither the rhetoric of absoluteness nor the idea that one owns oneself or one's body as property is in evidence here. Indeed, the decision was a rather nuanced combination of the ascription of decisional autonomy and personal privacy to the individual woman and a regulatory framework that protects public values.[194]

Other developments of personal rights in the domain of intimacy, ranging from the criminalization of spousal violence and marital rape to protection of decisional autonomy regarding sexual and reproductive decisions, can hardly be construed as threats to the ethical substance of the family. Rather, they protect against the terrible effects of unwarranted trust and dependency. Such forms of juridification do not turn marriage into a contractual economic exchange relationship, but instead bring moral principles of justice to bear on intimate associations by acknowledging the individuality, legal standing, personal autonomy, and civic equality of all adult family members. In the place of moralistic attitudes to sex, such rights institutionalize the basic principles of mutual respect—nonviolence, bodily integrity, nondomination, nonexploitation—in the intimate domain. They shift the ethical substance of the family from hierarchical toward egalitarian forms of reciprocity.

Glendon remains insensitive to this, in part, because she fails to take seriously the doubleness of the original paradigm of property that she is so quick to criticize and to find lurking in every attempt by the Court to protect individual privacy. It is hardly a novel argument that in the American constitutional tradition, property rights have been associated with a rhetoric of absoluteness, and have served to reinforce inequality, selfishness, and injustice. Construed as the most central of civil rights, indeed as the paradigm of such rights, property discourse, together with the overall constitutional design geared toward restricting rather than fostering popular participation in government, served to turn attention to the pursuit of private interests and to block state efforts at institutionalizing solidarity via rules of distributive justice.[195]

Property also symbolized personal autonomy and freedom. The opposite extreme to being an independent proprietor with a protected jurisdiction of decisional autonomy was to be property oneself: to be a slave or a dependent. Private property was thus a perfect candidate for playing the dual symbolic role of limiting government and protecting personal liberty.

Because of its concreteness, it also served the purpose of symbolically demarcating the boundary between public and private, central to the liberal legal paradigm. Whatever came to be construed as private property— land, capital, labor, or household—was presumptively immune to state regulation or interference. Relations among economic actors in particular were to be left to private orderings (contracts). On the legal level, the assumption of limited government came to be expressed in the doctrine that state police power could impinge on personal property and autonomy (especially freedom of contract) only to advance a valid public purpose.[196] This was interpreted to mean that state legislation must be reasonably related to legitimate public concerns about health, safety, and morals.[197] The Court could strike down legislation that did not advance a general community interest.

The danger this doctrine meant to block was special legislation privileging particular (class) interests.[198] It was assumed, in short, that individual rights and liberties are best protected by limiting the exercise of state power, protecting private orderings against force or fraud, and ensuring that the state is unresponsive to factional interests. By now the reader has certainly recognized the key features of the liberal paradigm of law.

Determination of what is in the general welfare (public health, safety, and morals), and hence within the proper scope of legislative authority, was of course filtered through the liberal paradigm and market ideology— freedom of contract and the "sacredness" of property—and in the case of "morals legislation," gendered patriarchal assumptions about the natural place of women and the proper shape and purpose of intimate relationships.[199] As previously indicated, while property symbolized autonomy, as long as marriage involved control and inheritance especially of landed property, the state was rather deeply involved in regulating it.[200] Entity privacy and the property/autonomy rights accorded to the male head of household squared the circle.

However, as Jennifer Nedelsky points out, since roughly 1937, property lost its central place in the constitutional structure and neither it nor its sister concept, freedom of contract, have been invoked by the Supreme Court to challenge legislation for many years.[201] After the New Deal, property ceased to be regarded as the first among civil rights, and it no longer plays the role of integrating the entire framework of rights against the state. Nedelsky argues that to the degree to which property has been redefined as a bundle of legal rights with no sacred or privileged status, it neither is nor can continue to be the basis on which the Court draws the line between individual rights and governmental power.[202] In this assessment, she and Glendon are in accord.

While fully acknowledging the ways in which the primacy given to property rights skewed our constitutional structure and bred injustice, Nedelsky nevertheless sees a danger in the present situation. She fears that the disintegration of the concept of property will entail the loss of tension between private rights and majority rule, and thus threaten the security of our entire panoply of personal civil rights:[203] "If property is finally perceived to be merely a legal entitlement . . . if it loses its moral force. . . . Either some other concept or value will have to replace it as a symbol of limited government, as the core of constitutionalism, or we may be facing a change in constitutionalism itself."[204]

Unlike Glendon, Nedelsky does not view the new privacy rights as a Trojan horse that smuggles the prejudices and presuppositions of the property paradigm back into our constitutional jurisprudence in a new and invidious form. Rather, she worries that neither privacy rights nor an abstract concept like autonomy could do the trick of protecting our civil liberties in the context of the regulatory welfare state, because they lack the material base and the intuitive clarity of property rights.[205] In Nedelsky's view, the problem with the new privacy is not that it has the same pretensions to absoluteness as the old property, but that it is too weak to play such a mythic role.[206]

What is most striking in this analysis is the claim that property drew its symbolic strength from its ability to embody a protected sphere of personal freedom. This implies that property was considered quasi-sacred by virtue of its association with the core values of personal liberty, personal self-relation, autonomy, agency, and inviolability. To be sure, the property paradigm fused these values with the possessive individualist model of the self and inegalitarian social structures that the closely associated freedom of contract certainly did not mitigate. But we should not misconstrue this lack of differentiation and assume that it is inevitable or persists unchallenged today.

Instead of interpreting the new constitutional privacy as burdened with the inegalitarian, possessive, individualist, contractualist legacy of property, one should see that constitutional privacy rights aim to protect important values that property can shield no longer, namely, personal liberty, privacy, and freedom from domination. Where Glendon sees a lack of differentiation,[207] Nedelsky sees the opposite: an attempt to give the constitutional values once associated with property and freedom of contract a primacy now unencumbered by the inegalitarian tradition or by the possessive individualist model of the self, and to protect them in their own right.[208]

Bruce Ackerman propounds a similar thesis. He argues that the new privacy rights, far from being an exercise in Court prophecy or arbitrariness, are really the result of a complex interpretive process whereby the Court sought to make sense of a Constitution that owes its meaning to the transformative efforts of several generations of "constitutional politics."[209] Moreover, he locates the turning point in *Griswold*, not *Eisenstadt*. The project of *Griswold*, he believes, was to detach the Founders' affirmation of personal liberty from the property/contract framework within which it had been embedded before the New Deal and to protect it under the rubric of privacy. Accordingly, *Griswold* reads the Bill of Rights to preserve the Founders' concern with personal liberty in a way that endures in a post–New Deal world of economic and social regulation.[210]

Unlike the neocommunitarians, Ackerman insists that it was individual liberty, and neither a traditional conception of entity privacy nor the sanctity of the family, that was at stake on the constitutional level in *Griswold*. The real constitutional question facing the Court was whether the post–New Deal government's authority to regulate markets and property should be interpreted as obliterating affirmations of private freedom previously expressed in the terms of freedom of contract. According to Ackerman, Justice Douglas's majority opinion faced the repudiation of *Lochner* head on and distinguished between the private ordering of economic relations that were now no longer immune to governmental regulation, and privacy in the more intimate spheres of life including bilateral loyalties, which he argued remained protected.[211] Looking at the Bill of Rights as expressive of principles that retain their constitutional meaning despite transformations of two centuries, Douglas found that privacy served as a leitmotif in modern efforts to make sense of personal liberty. Thus, according to Ackerman, *Griswold*'s reinterpretation of the Founding texts in terms of a right to privacy, rather than a right to property and contract, is a brilliant interpretive proposal: "Granted, when the Founders thought about personal freedom they used the language of property and contract;

given the New Deal repudiation of this language, doesn't the language of privacy provide *us* with the most meaningful way of preserving these Founding affirmations of liberty in an activist welfare state?"[212]

Indeed. From this perspective, the continuities rather than the discontinuities between *Griswold, Eisenstadt, Roe,* and their progeny are what is significant in constitutional jurisprudence. Moreover, it is in this respect that the Warren and Brandeis article "The Right to Privacy" has had its greatest impact. For as Ackerman argues, the point of this essay is to use the concept of privacy to carve off values previously protected by laissez-faire property doctrine, thereby ensuring their preservation in a world in which other dimensions of property would be subjected to increasing regulation by activist government.[213]

The language of boundaries attached to property has been replaced with the language of distribution and outcome-oriented state regulation in the economic field.[214] "Boundary talk" has been revived within privacy analysis in relation to the domain of intimacy, but without, pace Glendon, the baggage of possessive individualism. The abstract constitutional principle at stake is the right to protection of personal liberty and privacy from governmental regulation that is either arbitrary, unfair, or lacks a compelling purpose. This can, but need not, entail the conception of the self the communitarians so abhor.

Yet, pace Ackerman, this principle received a radically new application in *Griswold*, and a new doctrinal justification. As we have seen, *Griswold* and its progeny rested on the Court's interpretation of a change in public values regarding the status of women, the purpose of marriage, and the acceptability of sexual relations not aimed at procreation.[215] The new legal doctrine invoked in these decisions on which the right to privacy is based is the jurisprudence of "fundamental rights" and "preferred freedoms," predicated on the assumption that certain individual rights and liberties are so fundamental that they can serve as a trump against the state.[216]

As we have also seen, the old doctrine limiting the legitimate exercise of state power to a "valid public purpose" was linked to a core premise of the liberal paradigm: government should leave individuals alone unless the general welfare of the community is at stake. Liberty and freedom in the prepolitical private sphere would be secured if arbitrary or corrupt governmental intervention were prevented. Discourses invoking the sacredness of property, freedom of contract, the public/private dichotomy, and the state action doctrine were all part and parcel of this approach.

As Howard Gillman succinctly puts it, "By contrast, under the contemporary model, it has been assumed that the government's power should be left undisturbed unless an individual can convince a court that the law infringed on a discrete fundamental right."[217] On the premise of the plenipotentiary state and of wide regulatory and redistributive powers of Congress (or of administrative agencies to which they are delegated), the old rule restricting "intervention" to what could be justified in the name of "health, safety, and morals" was abandoned. The exercise of public power no longer needed special constitutional justification.

The demise of the public purpose limit on legislative power, however, seemed, as Ackerman pointed out, to leave individuals defenseless against arbitrary, unfair, or oppressive government: a perennial and valid concern not only for atavistic liberals. On the one side the old reasons for regulating sexual morals lost their justificatory power; on the other, the old limits to the state's regulatory power collapsed. The Court's new doctrinal discourse of "preferred freedoms," "fundamental rights," "suspect classifications," and its effort to maintain an "open and unprejudiced democratic process" was devised, in part, to address this paradoxical situation.[218] This discourse serves the Court's need to find some method of identifying a specific set of rights and liberties that could provide a basis for limiting the newly unrestrained power of the state—i.e. of the executive and legislative branches.

The revival of substantive due process and the discourse of fundamentality plays this role in the new privacy jurisprudence. The shift in paradigms has thus been accompanied by an unprecedented enterprise on the part of the Court: the self-appointed task of enumerating the specific "fundamental" individual rights and liberties covered by the abstract principles of the Constitution.[219] Therein lies the problem. For it is not self-evident which rights are fundamental, or just which set of liberties should be deemed "preferred" or construed as intrinsic to the principle of "ordered liberty."[220] When the Court has invoked "constitutional tradition" in its substantive due process privacy cases, it did so in a way that did not perpetuate traditionalism. Surely the decisions in *Griswold*, *Eisenstadt*, and *Roe* cannot be seen as traditionalistic. But they do raise the question of the appropriate level of generality in the resort to traditionalist justifications. At stake is the following dilemma: "If tradition is defined too narrowly, the challenged legislation will presumably conform to the relevant 'tradition' and substantive due process loses its bite; but if the tradition is defined too broadly, judges are encouraged to act as free-wheeling censors of state judgments."[221] Hence we have the charges of arbitrariness and illegitimate judicial "activism" in the new privacy cases.[222]

Moreover, the Court has often used an essentializing discourse of fundamentality, preferred freedoms, and rights as trumps, evocative of anachronistic liberal natural rights ideology.[223] This may help legitimate innovative judicial decisions by casting the basic rights at stake as inherent in the concept of the person or judicial activity as "preservationist," but it does so at certain costs. Apart from inviting the obvious communitarian critiques, it involves the Court in blatant contradictions, such as the willingness to engage in direct and detailed regulation, as in *Roe*'s trimester framework, while denying any right to funding for abortions in the name of the state action doctrine.

It is thus also this new doctrinal discourse that triggers the charge of absoluteness and anachronism on the part of Glendon and many others. I agree that this discourse is open to such charges. We should be clear, however, about where the problem lies. Talk of "fundamentality" and reference to "preferred freedoms" is an artifact of the Court's embrace, not its rejection, of the welfare paradigm's key assumptions, as Ackerman's and Nedelsky's analyses suggest. It is invoked in order to protect personal liberty against what is now presumed to be a regime of general rather than carefully circumscribed state powers. Yet the critics have a point: such talk does seem to revive the imagery of a domain of liberty antecedent to government, of a subject whose inherent autonomy and freedom has to be protected, of areas of contractual arrangements immune to regulation, of rights as trumps, along with anachronistic conceptions of state action and of the opposition between negative and positive freedom. In short, it seems to revive the core elements of the liberal paradigm of law.

Moreover, this discourse has been accompanied by what appears to be a wholesale shift from public to private ordering in many doctrinal areas in the domain of intimacy. Glendon has noted a certain "dejuridification of marriage": a trend in the United States and Western Europe toward withdrawal by the state from much that it had done to regulate marriage, and intimate association generally.[224] The rise of no-fault divorce, surrogacy contracts, market-mediated adoptions, and the honoring of prenuptial contracts are only the most obvious examples of the replacement of public by private orderings.

The penetration of economic discourse into the domain of intimacy, celebrating contractualism and delegitimating regulation, certainly should give us pause.[225] Privatization in this sense cannot be seen as an unambiguous good fostering women's autonomy and equality with no negative consequences.[226]

It is nevertheless tendentious to argue that the full legal standing and constitutional protection for intimate associates covering the right to consensually order the terms of their intimate association and reproductive decisions (constitutional privacy) ipso facto turns families into contractual business partnerships with no ethical content or bonds beyond the rights of their members. Indeed, communitarian critics of "rights talk" in the domain of intimacy conveniently forget that the old system of status-based public ordering, although justified in the name of the common good of society, was deeply sexist and unjust.[227] They carelessly imply that the choice we face regarding the domain of intimacy is between status and contract, between direct heavy-handed public regulation to force conformity to majoritarian morals and standards or no regulation at all. But this is deeply misleading.

Everything turns on how, or from which perspective, the new doctrinal discourse of fundamental, preferred freedoms and ordered liberty is interpreted. Certainly some justifications for the new privacy rights invite the interpretation Glendon has made of them. The image of rights as trumps does appear to re-create domains immune to regulation and to revive absolutist rhetoric regarding constitutional rights. Yet the discourse of fundamental rights need not lend itself to natural law revivals, libertarian contractualism, and/or too much discretion or arbitrariness by the Court in overturning legislation.

I am convinced that what is at stake is a paradigm shift—one that must get us beyond the dogmatic assumptions of both the liberal and the welfare paradigms that distort the debates over constitutional privacy rights and over regulation of the domain of intimacy in general. There are two dangers that must be avoided. First, it will not do to postulate a natural sphere of fundamental liberty (the liberal paradigm) to be delivered over to private orderings and for which the state has no responsibility. But, second, neither should the assumption of the omnipresent state and outcome-oriented analyses focused on equality (the welfare paradigm) lead us to dispense with concerns for liberty or limits to arbitrariness, or to opt for a return to heavy-handed public ordering of intimate association. Recall that equality analysis cannot tell us which liberties deserve heightened protection; it can only argue for their equal distribution across groups.

I have sought to defend a constructivist reading of constitutional privacy analysis protecting personal autonomy in the domain of intimacy that eschews essentialism and the flawed assumptions of the liberal and welfare paradigms of law. We must reason reflectively and constructively, in full awareness that it is we—not nature, tradition, or God—who give ourselves and interpret basic rights and the laws that construct and protect our autonomy. The basic rights we grant one another and to which we accord heightened protection on the constitutional level must be justifiable in (universalistic) terms of what we now think it means to be free as a person and an equal citizen. The choice among legal forms and doctrinal formulae has to be made in light of this contemporary understanding.

Constitutional rights in the domain of intimacy should protect against arbitrary and unfair government regulation. But they should also serve to protect personal liberty against injustice, domination, and subordination by third parties. Such protection is equality-reinforcing. Understood in this way, privacy analysis is not incompatible with forms of legal regulation oriented by accepted public values and protecting against injustice. Indeed, constitutional privacy rights should be seen as putting in place the basic elements without which a new and just model of regulation would be impossible. From within the perspective of the reflexive legal paradigm, in other words, it is perfectly possible to create certain formal rights against the state, which protect negative liberties without invoking the anachronistic assumptions of the liberal legal paradigm, and to supplement these with other modes of regulation when necessary. On this approach, rights are not absolute trumps; they are mechanisms that trigger inquiry into the justification for governmental decisions.

From this perspective it is also possible to see that private ordering is not the inevitable consequence of constitutional privacy analysis. The application of contractualist economic models to a new domain (family and intimacy) by many judges and legislators should be deemed transitional, as a "stepping stone to imagining and implementing a more just form of public ordering."[228] For we are now at the point where what is called for is not simply privatization (to undo the old just family law regime) but, in key areas of intimate association, the appropriate regulation of self-regulation. A nuanced and pluralistic approach that acknowledges intimate relationships as important to individual happiness and autonomy and as a locus for important public values, yet also as an arena where domination and exploitation may well exist, is required.

My point here is that constitutional privacy analysis remains in many areas the appropriate response to unfair or arbitrary public regulations and private structures of domination. Privacy rights can be empowering. This is obviously true in the case of contraception, abortion, consensual mutual choice of adult sexual intimacies, partners, and so forth. Nevertheless, a plurality of legal forms and a reflexive approach to the regulation of self-regulation in the domain of intimacy that are premised on and foster gender equality as well as personal autonomy should be developed.

CONCLUSION

In this chapter, I have tried to clarify what a constitutional right to privacy entails and to develop a normatively compelling conception of the personal concerns it should protect—one that fits our contemporary moral intuitions regarding intimate relationships and decisions and which respects the principles of gender equality.

I have argued that privacy and decisional autonomy in relation to intimate relationships and intimate (sexual) decisions deserve constitutional protection and should be covered by a reconceived right of privacy. But this is not because they have always been inherent in our tradition of ordered liberty or involve objective truths that a Court can "discover." Rather, it is because we have developed moral insight into the meaning of such a right for individual freedom and happiness today, and we have learned that we now must ascribe it equally to women and men. It is, in short, becoming part of our understanding of what ordered liberty—the liberty that any constitutional democracy should recognize—must involve. In other words, it is because we acknowledge the full personhood and citizenship of women and because we understand that these are at stake for everyone when the state seeks to regulate the domain of intimacy that we need heightened protection in this area.

Years of public discussion, political agitation, and social movements involving profound cultural change are behind this argument, and they can and should influence Court decisions.[229] Articulating such rights as negative liberties when appropriate, as rights against the state, does not lock one into the liberal legal paradigm. Rather, the choice of the liberal legal form in the case of reproductive rights (and sexuality generally) can go perfectly well with reflexive awareness about the source of all constitutional rights and principles, and about the choice of legal forms available to us today for the most appropriate regulation and/or support for self-regulation. On this approach, and given the cultural shifts I have discussed above, unless there really is a valid and compelling public purpose or moral stake that can outweigh a right to privacy covering the "domain of intimacy," which all affected could reasonably accept, then such a right should not be abridged. Regulating the exercise of such a right when there are important countervailing principles at stake, as in the abortion case, and provision for the worth of the liberty it ascribes, presents no justification problem and no paradox once one reasons from this perspective.

I maintain that we should redefine and defend all the dimensions of privacy identified by commentators: the decisional, the relational, the bodily, and entity privacy. Instead of rejecting the concept of privacy rights because of the ideological usage that has been made of it in the past, we should redescribe the principle and defend its normative content. We can, in short, show that entity privacy need not be burdened with a prepolitical conception about the naturalness of the patriarchal family; that decisional privacy need not entail the atomistic, unencumbered self or the property paradigm; that relational privacy need involve neither the construction of "normal" versus "deviant" relationships nor a wholesale shift to private ordering immune to the demands of justice; and, finally, that acknowledging our embodiment need not resuscitate biological determinism.

Everyone's moral autonomy, ethical self-determination, bodily integrity, personal happiness—the "territories of the self"—are at stake. Understood in the appropriate way, a general constitutionally protected right to personal privacy shielding intimacy is indeed a cardinal symbol and element of personal freedom. To cast the right to abortion in particular as a privacy right is to acknowledge women's "difference" while leaving it up to each individual woman how to define this difference.[230] While women thereby acquire protection for their unique capacities (ability to become pregnant), their difference need not be reified: it can be simultaneously acknowledged and left to them to construct. I take it that this, after all, is the point of asserting the right to be different yet treated with equal concern and respect.

Is There a Duty of Privacy? Law, Sexual Orientation, and the Dilemmas of Difference

◆ The limits of constitutional privacy analysis and of the liberal legal paradigm seem incontrovertible when it comes to the issues of group difference that emerge with regard to minority sexual orientations and identities. How can personal privacy and negative liberty protect gays and lesbians from discrimination and oppression based on their intimate choices or sexual identities? How can privacy rights secure respect for disdained forms of intimate association?

Indeed, many fear that the strategy of privatization as a mode of juridifying tolerance for homosexual intimacy is both ineffective and dangerous. It risks reinforcing the stigma attached to minority sexual identities and exacerbating discrimination. Moreover, the assumption that sexuality defines identity and is fundamental to personhood underlying many justifications of privacy analysis in this domain is a double-edged sword. It can be used to reify group identities and impose them on individuals, regardless of their own sense of themselves, thereby undermining personal autonomy.

Three recent developments substantiate such fears: the new privacy rhetoric of neo-republican political theorists; the new military policy on sexual orientation established under the first Clinton administration; and the Supreme Court's privacy analysis in the infamous *Bowers v. Hardwick* decision.[1] All these construe privacy as the right to be "let alone," entailing a correlative duty: secrecy and "discretion" in relation to one's sexual orientation and intimate relationships. The neo-republicans insist that the condition for toleration of "deviant" sexuality is privatization. The new military policy imposed a duty of privacy—of silence and secrecy—regarding their sexual orientation onto gays and lesbians in exchange for tolerating their presence in the armed forces. The *Bowers* Court invoked a traditionalized conception of marital privacy in order to deny claims to decisional autonomy for those involved in same-sex relationships.

It is well worth looking into these developments in theoretical and legal privacy discourse, because they reveal how a particular conception of juridical privacy can indeed serve to undermine personal autonomy and civic equality. However, I shall argue that when properly conceptualized, constitutional privacy rights provide an indispensable shield for "difference" in the domain of intimacy, helping to protect against the oppression and stigmatization that results from harsh and unjustifiable sex laws. It is patently obvious that equality—equal protection of the laws, equal citizenship—is at issue when the law punishes stigmatized forms of intimate association linked to a particular minority. But unless this involves equal privacy protection, other aspects of equal citizenship for minority sexualities will be at risk. It is thus necessary to develop a complex regulatory regime and set of justifications to accommodate ethical plurality in the domain of intimacy and to ensure appropriate protection for the personhood and equal citizenship of those who "differ."

I begin this chapter with a critical discussion of the neo-republican rhetoric of privacy as a duty of civility. I then address the most recent attempt to impose a "duty of privacy" onto gays and lesbians, namely the military policy regarding homosexuality implemented during the first Clinton administration. The following section analyzes criticisms of privacy discourse that arise from its alleged dangers for gays and lesbians. Next I turn to the legal backdrop that made such a policy plausible: the Supreme Court ruling in *Bowers v. Hardwick*. I hope in the process to provide an alternative to what I take to be the unfortunate and politically dangerous linkage of privacy rights with the obligation to conceal—a connection made both by advocates (like Jean Elshtain) and critics (especially within the gay and lesbian movement) of privacy analysis. The next section involves an analysis of the standard "personhood" approach to privacy and the paradoxes that it entails. I argue that this approach rests on two conceptual errors: the failure to distinguish between a right and a duty of privacy, and reliance on essentialist rather than a constructivist justification for the scope of privacy analysis. I also show that an inappropriate understanding of what toleration involves follows from these misconceptions. Finally, I consider the implications that the "moral indifference of sex" on the one hand, and the presumptive moral equality and equal citizenship of persons on the other, should have for the legal regulation of their intimate relationships, including those of gays and lesbians. I criticize utilitarian "law and economics" arguments for private ordering as a substitute for constitutional privacy analysis. I plead for a combination of the latter plus a more varied range of legal regulation that fosters freedom for and equality within intimate association.

THE NEO-REPUBLICAN REVIVAL OF PRIVACY DISCOURSE

Modern republican political theory has always had an ambivalent relationship to privacy. Theorists in this tradition insist on the importance of a clear demarcation between public and private. Both Tocqueville and

Arendt (the two most important nineteenth and twentieth century exemplars) argued that rights which institutionalize and protect the private sphere are a basic precondition for an adequately demarcated and autonomous public sphere. Such rights counter the danger specific to egalitarian forms of republican government, namely, the inherent tendency of public power to expand and to trespass on private interests.[2]

Nevertheless, republican theorists are far more preoccupied with the opposite risk of civil privatism. Recall Tocqueville's prescient warnings about the potential effects of an acquisitive and expanding commercialism (egoistic individualism) on civic virtue in an egalitarian democratic society. The danger of corruption of representative organs by powerful private interests was also a key concern of his. Arendt's analysis of the rise of the social sphere and her fears regarding the impact of the corresponding deepening and expansion/intrusion of intimacy on public life parallels Tocqueville's. With respect to the latter, she explicitly noted two additional dangers: First, the citizen's deepening experience of private happiness in the domain of intimacy could seduce him away from public life. Second, the preoccupations of the intimate domain could invade the public sphere, replacing interest in the res publica with personal concerns of the self, leading to general indiscretion and to the degradation of the public into a mere social space. Democratic citizenship would be insecure and civic virtue undermined, unless a sphere of personal liberty and privacy were clearly differentiated from the public sphere and protected by basic rights. Republican theory, in short, is interested less in the intrinsic goods that privacy protects than with its "external face" and instrumental value: its role in demarcating public space.

The contemporary neo-republican revival in political and legal theory has resurrected much of this rhetoric.[3] Elshtain's marriage of Arendtian republicanism with her own particular version of communitarianism in her recent book, *Democracy on Trial*, is a particularly striking case in point.[4] Elshtain marshals a discourse of public space, civic virtue, responsibility, and duty in an effort to defend the distinction between public and private against what she calls "the politics of displacement." This is a version of identity politics that makes everything private public, including one's sexual practices, and that gives precedence to one's private (group) identity and desires over public ends and purposes.[5] Echoing Arendt's critique of the rise of the social and the blurring of distinctions, Elshtain insists on the importance of maintaining clear boundaries.

Accordingly, she argues that certain issues, actions, and talk—in particular regarding sexuality, the intimate aspects of the body, and the self—are essentially private. Against the narcissism of relentless self-disclosure, she advocates silence, secrecy, discretion. Citing Arendt, she affirms the importance of shame and concealment regarding the "body's functions,

passions and desires."[6] Indeed, in the context of a discussion of "gay liberation," she insists upon a duty of privacy (that she calls civility) and the
value of shame regarding desire, intimacy, and sexuality.

She does so in order to distinguish between acceptable and unacceptable claims for gay rights. Accordingly, an acceptable civil rights agenda
would revolve around the claim that society has no business scrutinizing
or intruding on the private sexual preferences of gays and lesbians. But,
she insists, these groups would have to accept a "duty of civility" in return
for privacy protection, and refrain from "flaunting" their sexuality and
desires in public.[7] Moreover, in her view, demands for public legitimation
of a "gay lifestyle" or "homosexual ethos" (allegedly the credo of "gay
liberationists") are utterly unacceptable. No one has the right to public or
state-induced acknowledgment of the worth of their ethical values, beliefs,
or habits. Indeed, demands for public validation of minority sexual identities blur the distinction between the personal and the political, the private
and the public. They lead to "shameless," narcissistic public disclosures of
one's own orientations and sometimes forced disclosures ("outings") of
others'. These things should not intrude into civic life.

Against such a "politics of displacement," Elshtain reproduces the standard strategy for securing (reinstating) a clear and distinct boundary between the public and private: she maps an analytic distinction (public and
private) onto institutional spheres of life and/or substantive contents (do-
mestic/intimate-private sphere/political-public sphere). She thereby constructs an essentialized and rigid dichotomy that has the effect of silencing
and excluding not only issues but the people associated with them, from
the public realm even if that is not her intention.[8] Her arguments for
privacy are meant to privatize, and they do.

The neo-republican discourse of boundaries and distinctions is a response to real problems. Nevertheless, this way of reinstating the boundary between public and private is politically suspect, and deeply unjust. As
already indicated, changes in the last quarter century impacting on the
domain of intimacy make reconceptualization of the boundary between
public and private, of what it is that personal privacy rights should protect,
as well as the justification for such rights, a pressing theoretical and political issue. Shifting gender relations, processes of individualization, the demotion of reproductive and even heterosexual sex from the moral to the
ethical, the declining importance of marital status, the (partial) shift from
public to private orderings of intimacy, and the corresponding pluralization of forms of legitimate intimate association are the key processes at
work here.[9] Challenges by social groups to legal repression and stigma
because of their sexual identities or homosexual intimate relationships are
part of this conundrum.

We cannot fruitfully address the difficult conceptual and political issues regarding the appropriate types of personal autonomy/privacy today if we simply try to resurrect the myth (itself never innocent) of essentially private concerns whereby "private" means what is secret and shameful. Nor can the relevant legal issues be adjudicated justly if the classic model of tolerating minority differences, provided that they are kept private or concealed, is, without further ado, simply applied to minority sexual identities.

Indeed, the choice is not, as Elshtain assumes, between toleration on the condition of privatization, silence, and secrecy (objectionable to the minority) or state-imposed esteem of disdained forms of life (objectionable to the majority). There is another available conception of toleration and of privacy screened out by the neo-republican approach that would be far more just in this context, as I shall explain.

The model of toleration proposed by Elshtain hovers between what Rainer Forst has called the "permission conception" and a formalistic "respect conception."[10] In the permission conception, a majority lets the minority live according to their ethical beliefs on the condition that the latter accept the dominant position of the majority. The minority does not challenge its dependent, inferior position. They raise no claims for equal public or political status, and they keep their "differences" strictly within those limits specified by the majority. The ethical views of the majority are positioned as superior, authoritative, and the legitimate basis for general legislation. Toleration means simply noninterference: the minority is tolerated as different, not as political equals.

By contrast, the respect conception proceeds from the presumption that the minority and the majority are moral and political equals meriting equal legal and political status.[11] Decisions regarding the distribution of fundamental rights and resources are to be guided by norms that all parties can accept as fair or just, despite strong ethical differences about the good. Thus reciprocity and mutuality characterize the relationship of toleration between groups of citizens on this approach.

Neo-republicans interpret the respect conception as requiring formal equality based on a strict distinction between the political and the private, as we have seen. Accordingly, cultural or ethical differences among citizens should be confined to the latter while public political life should remain neutral regarding different conceptions of the good. In Elshtain's hands this seems to require that gays and lesbians conceal their sexual orientation and refrain from revealing their same-sex desires in public ("duty of civility"), although they are permitted to articulate their views on civil rights issues in (their) civil public spaces. The state, for its part, should not criminalize their private encounters.

To try to revive a strict separation between public and private on the premise that the way to be fair and avoid civil strife is to confine ethical differences (cultural, religious, and now sexual) to the private sphere, permitting only neutral civic selves and common interests into the public sphere, is, in my view, a hopeless and unjustifiable strategy today. Willingness to tolerate privatized differences because it is deemed wrong or fruitless to try to force people to give up certain deep-seated orientations or beliefs may seem principled to the majority. To the minority, however, it can appear as a lack of respect and a denial of justice because it is premised on the absence of reciprocity. The allegedly neutral civic self usually turns out to be filled with particular content determined and privileged by the majority. In other words, when it comes to differences that matter a great deal to people, that involve personal dignity, and that may require a certain form of public expression, to insist on privatization of difference is to revert back from the "respect" to the "permission" conception, with all the implications of unequal status and stigma that it entails. The reciprocity supposedly informing "secular republicanism" collapses in such cases. No one demands, for example, that heterosexuals hide their sexual orientation. This is hardly a receipt for impartiality.

Changes in the moral significance of sex and in the relation between sexuality and identity, combined with the principle of equal moral personhood and citizenship, make the classic republican way of demarcating the public and private and of tolerating difference unjustifiable when it comes to minority sexual identities. There are no convincing moral arguments to justify the conditioning of tolerance on forced privatization (secrecy, shame).

The alternative to this conception of privacy/toleration, however, is not, as neo-republicans seem to assume, state-imposed esteem.[12] Justice does not require that people consider the different beliefs and practices of others to be ethically valuable. Elshtain is correct—there is no such right to public esteem. But justice does require reciprocity among equal citizens and generality of legislation regarding basic rights. In other words, powerful groups cannot legitimately accord themselves basic rights denied to other groups, nor can laws be considered just merely because they mesh with the ethical values of the politically dominant majority. The respect conception of toleration requires that justification involve reasons that could be acceptable to all affected as equals.

Instead of invoking reifying definitions of the "intrinsically" public and private, the way we must proceed is, once again, by using the constructivist approach. We must, in short, ask what conception and scope of privacy/decisional autonomy citizens must grant one another (in the form of privacy rights) if everyone is recognized as (1) equal moral persons meriting equal concern and respect and (2) as equal citizens with equal or equivalent rights and fair opportunities for voice in the public domain.[13] Accordingly, treating a minority justly (different yet equal) requires interpreting the respect conception of toleration on the model of what Forst calls "qualitative equality."[14] Reciprocity on this approach would preclude relegating ethical differences to a private sphere sealed off under a duty to conceal. Qualitative respect for the plurality of ethical differences in domain of intimacy would mean, instead, that the same decisional autonomy enjoyed by the majority regarding their intimate choices and their freedom of intimate association, and the same right to public presentation of their "intimate" selves (ethical identities), should be accorded to minorities. Whatever principles are institutionalized in law for regulating intimacy should be based on reasons that all affected could accept or at least not reasonably reject.[15] This does not require that people esteem one another's forms of intimacy. Rather, it requires reciprocity (equal rights to participate) in the on-going process of rethinking the forms of privacy and the duties of civility needed for just and rewarding intimate relationships to flourish and for the type and scope of personal autonomy that we all want and need in and for such relations.

Thus the strategy of my privacy analysis goes in a different direction than the neo-republican approach. The attempt to restore the link between the idea of a right to privacy and notions of shame, silence, and secrecy is an example of what Tocqueville called an "improper use of the idea of privacy rights." The most serious incivilities in public life are tied to injustice, not to indiscretion. The best theorists in the republican tradition always understood this: hence their efforts to prevent domination and to control "faction" defined as the concerted action of a unified majority or minority, motivated by passion or interest, adverse to the rights of others or to the common good.[16] The injustice at issue involves the use of public power to unfairly burden or oppress particular groups. Thus I argue that, pace Elshtain, it is the injustice of denying full privacy rights, including the right to present who one is in public, to gays and lesbians for their intimate associations (along with attempts to exclude them from the public realm and denial of equal protection of the law) that ought to be our target, not the sometimes foolish and unfortunate responses (the politics of displacement) that such injustice leads to.

Privatization, as we shall see, protects neither one's privacy nor one's difference; rather, it invites intrinsically unjust and arbitrary forms of regulation that maximize surveillance and threaten punishment for one's stigmatized sexual orientation. I will try to show, however, that when properly construed, the right to privacy need not lead to privatization either in the republican sense of the abandonment of public for private happiness, or in the sense of silencing and depoliticizing the issues or bearers of such rights. On the contrary, the concept of a right to privacy militates against the imposition of a bogus "duty of privacy" on stigmatized minorities. It thus can serve as a protective cover for different forms of intimate association that do not violate any principle of justice.

It is worth stressing again that protection for personal autonomy and choice in the domain of intimacy need not be tantamount to delegalization, or the absence of governmental regulation in the intimate domain. It does or at least should shift the focus of regulation from the effort to impose a monolithic substantive moral vision onto everyone to the effort to protect against injustice in a context of pluralized forms of intimate association.[17] This, however, is hardly what the recent privacy discourse of the military regarding homosexuality accomplished.

THE "NEW MILITARY POLICY": PRIVACY PROTECTION FOR GAYS AND LESBIANS?

Almost immediately upon taking office in 1993, President Clinton announced that he would fulfill his campaign promise to lift the ban on gays and lesbians in the armed forces.[18] The president sought a policy that would end discrimination in the military based on sexual orientation. Things did not turn out quite the way the new administration had assumed, however. The heated debate that ensued within and outside the government clearly came as a surprise.[19]

Indeed, the campaign promise led to a prolonged, open controversy during the first six months of Clinton's presidency that reemerged periodically during his second term as well.[20] Once mobilization among the citizenry against lifting the ban was reinforced by criticisms from the Joint Chiefs of Staff and Senator Sam Nunn, chairman of the Senate Armed Services Committee, simply rescinding the ban by executive order became politically impossible.[21] Instead, the administration, the Joint Chiefs of Staff, and Congress reached a compromise, apparently designed to protect the privacy of gays as well as discipline and morale in the military.[22] The compromise, summed up in the phrase "Don't ask, don't tell, don't pursue," has been codified into law by Congress.[23]

The previous policy involved both a prohibition on acts of consensual sodomy and an outright ban of homosexuals from service.[24] It required the investigation and discharge of anyone evincing homosexual desire, identity, or acts.[25] Since the early 1980s, the U.S. armed services have accordingly excluded and expelled homosexuals from their ranks.[26] Standard military procedure entailed questioning recruits about their sexual preference and rejecting those who disclosed a homosexual orientation.

The new compromise policy forbade the interrogation of recruits on this matter and revoked the automatic dismissal of military personnel for alleged homosexual feelings or identity.[27] This apparently meant that gays and lesbians would no longer be subjected to discrimination and that their privacy would be respected.[28]

But only apparently. What makes the new policy a compromise is that military personnel continue to be susceptible to investigation and discharge for homosexual conduct. Instead of focusing on sexual status, orientation, or same-sex desire, the new policy merely forbids homosexual acts. A great deal hinges, of course, on just what counts as a homosexual act. The conception of such conduct in the new guidelines is rather broad: it includes not only same-sex marriage and sodomy, but also same-sex hand-holding and kissing as well as publicly stating that one is a homosexual.[29] To be sure, the new rules specify that "mere confession" of one's homosexual orientation is not sufficient grounds for drumming a service member out of the military. But such a confession is considered sufficient to begin an investigation into whether the individual engages in homosexual behavior.[30] Moreover, the military will discharge a member who makes a public statement that he or she is a practicing homosexual or bisexual. In effect, "homosexual conduct" is made so elastic a concept that it can be "stretched into virtual equivalence with homosexual status."[31]

Thus, the measure of personal freedom secured by the new rules is ambiguous. One is assured of freedom from investigation by the authorities, of privacy protection, only on the condition of silence and secrecy. That is the upshot of the "don't ask, don't tell, don't pursue" compromise. Small wonder that many have construed this policy as an alarming attempt, disclaimers notwithstanding, to force gays and lesbians back into the closet.[32]

The new policy has important implications, particularly for the theoretical understanding and normative assessment of the right to privacy, that transcend its limited application (in that it applies only to the military). It reveals quite clearly the weaknesses of the neo-republican approach as well as the inadequacies of the permissive model of liberal toleration described above. But it is also worth addressing because it seems to confirm the worst suspicions of many scholars critical of privacy analysis, regarding the dangers of invoking privacy for the purpose of securing relief to homosexuals and lesbians from surveillance, persecution, and discrimination. Surely the military's concession of privacy (don't ask, don't tell) to homosexuals—or rather, its seeming imposition of privacy upon them—reinforces the stigma attached to them without affording much protection against harassment or ultimate expulsion from its ranks. On the contrary, as report after report has indicated, it has led to even greater surveillance, harassment, and expulsions of homosexuals and lesbians from the military than ever before.[33]

Nevertheless, the new policy reveals the importance rather than the uselessness or danger of privacy rights. Far from confirming the critics' views as to its risks, the policy makes the opposite case. Despite appearances, it is predicated on denying, not granting, the most basic privacy rights to homosexuals and lesbians as a group. Indeed, the policy must be understood against the backdrop of the 1986 Supreme Court ruling in *Bowers v. Hardwick* that no fundamental privacy right attaches protectively to "homosexual sodomy."[34] The *Hardwick* ruling affirmed the constitutionality of laws criminalizing certain consensual sexual conduct among adults, thereby considerably restricting the protective reach of privacy analysis. It was this opinion that constructed the terrain on which the military's ostensible focus on homosexual conduct rather than status could make sense.[35] The shift from status to conduct, so pivotal in the new policy, is inconceivable outside a social and legal context in which the proscription of sexual conduct is made to serve as the vehicle for discrimination on the basis of sexual orientation.

Accordingly, I take the new policy and the debate it has generated as an opportunity to clarify the difference between having the legal protection afforded by constitutional privacy rights and being forced into "privacy"—into the closet—and exposed to harassment and discrimination in their absence. My thesis is that in addition to constituting a grave injustice, the denial of privacy protection for acts of "homosexual sodomy" plays a pivotal role in legitimating the legal and extralegal discriminatory and even violent practices against homosexuals and lesbians in a wide range of institutions including but hardly restricted to the military.

THE RIGHT TO PRIVACY AND THE "EPISTEMOLOGY OF THE CLOSET"

While criticism of the idea of a constitutional right to privacy has become something of a cottage industry, two arguments have emerged with respect to gay and lesbian rights that are distinctive.[36] The first maintains that by invoking privacy rights in order to secure legal protection against persecution on the basis of their sexual activity, gays and lesbians become trapped into what Eve Kosofsky Sedgwick has called the "epistemology of the closet."[37] The second argument insists that the privacy paradigm is at best incapable of securing equality or political empowerment for gays or lesbians, and at worst serves as a roadblock to such goals.[38]

Sedgwick writes, "The closet is the defining structure for gay oppression in this century."[39] In other words, given the social stigma and legal sanctions attached to gay and lesbian sexuality, its status is that of a shameful, highly significant secret even when it is revealed publicly and openly affirmed.[40] It is not possible in such a context for gays to avoid having to make (and remake) the rather unattractive choice between disclosure and secrecy regarding their sexual orientation and practices. Unfortunately, as

Sedgwick correctly notes, neither alternative breaks the oppressive construction (the epistemology of the closet) within which homosexual sexuality and/or identity is situated; rather, it places gays and lesbians in a painful and harmful double bind. In an environment saturated with homophobic attitudes and laws, one can either go public, thereby risking condemnation and discrimination, or remain private, concealing one's sexuality and thus becoming complicit with the negative evaluations attached to it.

The logic of self-disclosure inherent in the first option has, perforce, the form of an open secret: an admission or public confession that "I am one of them," a member of a despised social category. One thereby becomes visible but hardly protected, uninjured, or unburdened. Self-disclosure does little to allay the vulnerabilities attached to gay/lesbian identity. Nor does it mitigate the stress of information management that burdens gays and lesbians. Moreover, the price of "coming out" is often that one has to adopt or confess to an identity that, under other circumstances, one would not necessarily embrace as the "deep truth" of oneself.

On the other hand, the privacy afforded by remaining in the closet (the second option) is equivocal, to say the least. It seems to presuppose that there is something shameful about one's sexual desires, conduct, and intimate relationships that should be kept secret. One can pass and be treated as an equal only if one dissociates oneself from the stigmatized qualities ascribed to the social category or group to which one secretly belongs. Thus, both disclosure (confession) and silence are part of the "epistemology of the closet." Both involve strategies of adaptation to a legal and social context that makes the shameful secret, whether or not it is told, the defining feature of gay life. Both entail the obvious harms of furtiveness, shame, denial, and/or a very risky and expensive self-revelation.[41] Neither strategy can transcend the dilemmas posed by difference: going public (assertion of difference) or choosing silence (pseudo-assimilation) are two flawed alternatives constructed by a context in which a particular mode of intimate relationships and sexuality—heterosexual marriage—is (re-)centered as the norm and the standard to which one must either conform or be construed as deviant.

That is why so many legal and political theorists concerned with gay rights opt for abandoning the discourse of privacy.[42] In the best statement of this position, Kendall Thomas argues that privacy analysis reinforces the epistemology of the closet.[43] Gays and lesbians at times invoke privacy as a tactic to avoid being exposed, yet for them, "the closet is less a refuge than a prison-house."[44] If for heterosexuals the value of claiming a privacy right is that it can be used to provide a space for self-discovery and self-direction, gays and lesbians invoke it to protect against the dangers of disclosure.[45] Indeed, in Thomas's view, there is a "structural" link between privacy and secrecy, between the closet and shame, that obtains in the broader context of homophobia and marks the difference in the meaning of privacy rights for homosexuals.[46] Accordingly, Thomas concludes that the privacy paradigm is a trap, for it serves as a cornerstone of the very structure of domination it purports to protect against.[47]

The second argument invoked against the privacy paradigm is related to the first. It consists of the apparently straightforward claim that it is a strategic error to focus on gaining privacy protection for gay sex because this can yield neither equality nor power to gays and lesbians. Personal privacy rights cannot undo the stigma attached to gay identity. Nor can they end discrimination against gays and lesbians as a group. Thus, to couch the issue of gay oppression as a matter of sexual liberty, that is, as an issue of constitutional privacy rights, is to misconstrue what is at stake: "as though political empowerment were a matter of getting the cops back on the street where they belong and sexuality back into the impermeable space (the bedroom) where *it* belongs."[48]

According to the critics, this approach trivializes the issue of toleration that confronts gays and lesbians. To frame the problem of gay oppression as a privacy issue is to presume that what is at stake is forbearance for idiosyncratic personal sexual taste, rather than equality and power for gays as a group. Privacy analysis, in short, depoliticizes the problem.

Even worse, the conception of toleration that goes with privacy analysis not only does nothing to undermine the stigma associated with the tolerated group's identity or status; it seems to presuppose and reinforce it.[49] In other words, a privacy right interpreted as a liberty right to engage in various forms of consensual sex out of public view, in a homophobic context, goes hand in hand with the compulsion to secrecy and thereby reinforces individual shame along with the denigration of homosexuals as a group. It certainly does nothing to undermine the public disdain for homosexuality, in this reading: hence the charge that "liberal privacy" affords toleration of gay and lesbian individuals on the condition of privatization (the injunction and warning to be discrete about your sexual preferences in public) and depoliticization. Since prejudice against gays and lesbians is usually the motive behind laws and policies that regulate their sexual conduct, to focus on privacy is to forgo the real terrain of contestation.[50] Issues of equality, power, and respect, not personal privacy, are at stake in such laws whether or not they are articulated in neutral terms or mention sexual orientation explicitly.

I believe that these critiques of privacy analysis are convincing but only against a particular conception of privacy and the particular model of toleration that goes with it—the permission model—granting inclusion and apparent equality with the proviso that stigmatized qualities or types of relations are concealed. But this, as we have seen, is only one model of privacy and toleration. The critiques are misguided when they target the very concept of privacy rights. In my view, they are based on two conceptual mistakes: first, the confusion of a right to privacy with a duty of privacy, and, second, the failure to differentiate between the permission model and the qualitative respect-based model of toleration.

Those who assume that invoking privacy rights would lock gays into the closet mistake what it means to have a right to privacy with what I consider to be an unfair—because selectively imposed (be it through social or legal sanction)—"duty of privacy." It is the duty and not the right that is structurally linked to secrecy, shame, silencing, and depoliticization, especially when it is imposed only on particular groups, as is the case with the new military policy. Confusion over the difference between rights and duties goes hand in hand with the failure on the part of most privacy critics to distinguish between the permission and respect models of toleration. Once we develop an adequate conception of what a privacy right entails, once we justify its scope on constructivist grounds, it becomes possible to conceive of a model of toleration based on respect (as the correlate of the right to privacy) that proceeds from the basic moral-political equality of majorities and minorities and demands a certain reciprocity regarding their ethical differences. Instead of reinforcing stigma and shame, instead of privatizing and construing difference as deviance, a right to privacy (entailing freedom of intimate association) on this model could foster mutual respect for difference and equality of social status.

The new military policy is a textbook example of the conception of privacy appropriately described as the "epistemology of the closet" and of the sham of a purportedly liberal and tolerant public policy that forces privatization and shame onto certain groups. The operative conception of privacy here is that of secrecy about what one does at home and self-effacement (discretion) in public: just what the neo-republicans seem to advocate. But, as Sedgwick herself has shown, these dynamics come into play precisely in a context in which the privacy rights (along with certain speech, associational, and equality rights) of gays and lesbians have been denied constitutional protection.[51] The military policy does not concede such rights; rather, it offers an exchange: we won't pursue you into your bedrooms on the condition of silence and concealment of your sexuality. This disingenuous offer of noninterrogation and nonharassment is made conditional on acceptance of a duty of privacy; rights have nothing to do with it. Indeed, what I am calling here the "duty of privacy" is not the correlative of the right to privacy in the usual sense. Rather, the form it has taken ("don't tell") is predicated on the absence of key privacy rights for those on whom it is imposed.

Under constitutional privacy doctrine, to say that a matter is private means that it is presumptively immune from legal prohibition and that the decisional autonomy of the individual in the matter is protected.[52] This means that the decision whether or not to reveal one's private affairs in public is also protected. The concept of a right to privacy that secures decisional autonomy in the domain of intimacy thus includes—along with the right to associate intimately and sexually with adult partners of your choice—the right to say and be who you are in public without risking either your dispositional control over information—access to the self and speech—or the claim to have your individual integrity respected and recognized. *Privacy rights entail freedom from the obligation to conceal as well as informational privacy, i.e., the choice not to reveal or have revealed one's personal affairs.* The correlative duty to such a right is that others respect it.[53] It entails, in short, communicative liberty. In other words, if certain conduct, information, or relationships are constitutionally protected as private, it does not follow that society may mandate that they be kept secret. On the contrary, if homosexuals' and lesbians' relevant intimate relationships, sexual acts, object choices, bedrooms, and so on were protected by constitutionalized privacy rights, government would be powerless to impose special requirements of secrecy or silence about them.

This becomes obvious as soon as one reflects upon what is involved precisely in the obligation of privacy that is conceptualized as silence and secrecy entailed in the "don't ask, don't tell, don't pursue" policy. Let us be very clear: the duty at stake here is not that one refrain, out of mutual consideration for each other's privacy, from engaging in sexual intercourse or sexual acts visibly and openly in public. Since sex acts are coded as intimate in our society, and since we have cultural taboos on nudity, everyone is presumed to owe to everyone else a duty of civility that involves refraining from violating these taboos. That is what strictures about public decency supposedly enforce.

Whatever we might think of such rules of civility, they are not at issue here.[54] But then, what is? The obligation of privacy imposed in the "don't ask, don't tell" policy explicitly enjoins speech and expression about sex acts, and, despite disclaimers, insists upon discretion regarding sexual orientation and desire—a duty imposed exclusively on homosexuals and lesbians. To be more specific, people are required to refrain from indicating in any way that they have performed or might yet engage in homosexual acts. The duty of privacy here refers to speech about acts when linked to homosexual orientation, not to the public or private performance of the acts.

The new policy makes no distinction at all between public and private conduct, between acts engaged in on or off duty, on or off base. It is one thing to forbid genital sexual activity between any one on base or on duty, something apparently well within the province of military authority. It is quite another to attempt to regulate speech about what one does in private, off base, especially when such regulations are applied only to a particular group. No such obligation of secrecy, no such duty of privacy, is imposed on heterosexuals. So far as I am aware there has never been a case in which a legal duty to be discrete about legal action has been selectively imposed on any group.[55] The question to ask in this context is: how can the imposition of such an obviously discriminatory obligation onto a minority be legally possible? One would think that in addition to the violation of personal autonomy, there are obvious First Amendment issues involved here, not to mention anti-discrimination principles. Indeed, two relatively recent Supreme Court rulings (in the *Watkins* and *Meinhold* cases) held that homosexuals as persons—as a particular kind of person—are entitled to constitutional protection under the Equal Protection clause, and that the (former) policy of the U.S. Army and the Department of Defense of discharging service members merely for admitting that they are homosexual violates constitutional anti-discrimination principles.[56] Hence the new military policy that no longer cites homosexual status as a reason for interrogation, investigation, or discharge.

What, then, does it cite? We already have the answer: "conduct" and its voluntary disclosure. But in order to understand what that means, we must turn to another context and look at the Supreme Court decision which ruled that "homosexual conduct" could be criminalized without violating the Constitution. Only then can we begin to see what function the selective denial of privacy rights plays in the official oppression of gays and lesbians.

As indicated, I contend that the revised military policy must be understood against the historical, socio-psychological, normative, and legal context constituted by the 1986 Supreme Court decision in *Bowers v. Hardwick*.[57] In that decision, the Court ruled that the Constitution does not confer a right of privacy that extends to "homosexual sodomy" regardless of whether it is consensual or practiced in the privacy of one's home. Indeed, the Court maintained that the fundamental privacy rights of homosexuals were in no way violated by the anti-sodomy statute under consideration. It is this ruling that I contend is the condition of possibility of the new military policy. For had the Court not affirmed the constitutionality of the criminalization of "homosexual sodomy," it would hardly have been possible for the military to simultaneously accept gays and lesbians into the service and yet punish them for committing "homosexual acts" off base and in private, while exposing them to interrogation and likely dishonorable discharge should they express their sexual orientation in public or engage in speech about such acts. Unless something called "homosexual sodomy" were denied constitutional privacy protection, and unless it were legal for states to criminalize it, the military would be hard put to justify discharging only gays and lesbians for committing it or for speaking about it![58]

If one reflects that *Watkins* and *Meinhold* were decided shortly after the *Hardwick* ruling, it seems rather clear that the focus on criminalizable "homosexual acts" provided the military with a constitutionally safe route to target and regulate the behavior of a particular group without, as it were, having to name names.[59] The focus on conduct serves admirably to accomplish what the old emphasis on status can do no longer.

And yet it should be clear that the situation is somewhat complex. After all, most anti-sodomy statutes, including the one at issue in *Hardwick* and in the military code, are neutral regarding the gender of the persons committing the forbidden acts.[60] How, then, could *Hardwick* provide the implicit justification for regulating the conduct of homosexuals and lesbians exclusively?

I discuss this decision in detail in the next section. For a provisional answer to the question, let me invoke Janet Halley's suggestive analysis of the "deep equivocation" between acts and identities in statutes criminalizing sodomy.[61] This equivocation derives from the tendency, so prevalent today, to construe sodomy as a metonym for homosexual personhood. Reproduced and raised, as it were, to constitutional principle in *Hardwick*, it supplies the ground for targeting and policing the sexual behavior of gays and lesbians through gender neutral law. The trick is accomplished by articulating sexual preference (homosexuality) onto criminalized acts (sodomy), and criminalized acts onto identities (the homosexual as personage). A vicious rhetorical circle ensues that becomes the basis for the construction of an inferior group identity ("homosexual sodomites") and for the denial of basic rights to individuals associated with the respective group. This is a two-level process. The first level involves the formation (from above) of the identity category and its alleged meaning; the second level involves the process by which an individual is designated (often by others' discretionary power) as a member of the group and is assigned the relevant identity.[62]

Halley is right: the criminalization of sodomy today plays a crucial role in the generation of stigmatized sexual-orientation identities.[63] To be sure, discrimination on the basis of homosexual preference (and status) exists in places that abolished or never had anti-sodomy statutes, as in England.[64] Nevertheless, criminalization certainly makes it easier to construe those associated with the outlawed acts as unworthy of equal concern and respect. It is not only that people with a particular group identity are targeted for prejudicial and discriminatory treatment by such rhetorical means. Rather, the problem is that law—which maintains a cover of neutrality and draws on culturally available meanings—constitutes in part, while rendering visible and vulnerable, the very identity it simultaneously stigmatizes as criminal and abnormal ("homosexual sodomite") for engaging in the acts it outlaws.

Although the critics of privacy are correct to argue that what is at stake in the struggle of gays and lesbians against oppression is not "sexual liberation," they are wrong to suggest that we should jettison privacy analysis. If it is true that gaining the protective shield of privacy rights to cover gay sex will not of itself deliver full equality or power to homosexuals, the denial of this shield has played and continues to play a central role in supporting official and unofficial oppression, surveillance, and discrimination against them.

However, the critics are also wrong to belittle the importance of a privacy right protecting the freedom of intimate association among consenting adults, so long as no other principles of justice are violated. Whatever their original function, today harsh sex laws, even if unenforced, serve not only to deny certain liberties but also to construct, impose, and codify sexual identities, norms, and gender hierarchies.[65] State laws that criminalize or regulate the choice of sexual act and partner obviously restrict decisional autonomy in what many consider to be an intensely personal and ethically important domain of life. I repeat my claim that if there are no moral arguments available to support such regulation, and if regulations violate the basic moral principle of equal personhood, then they are illegitimate. But such laws also take the discretionary power of identification, of the naming and locating of individuals within group identities, out of the hands of the individuals themselves and place it into the hands of the state. The right not to have an identity imposed upon oneself that one cannot affirm and embrace—a right, in my view, that is, along with autonomy issues, at the center of contemporary privacy jurisprudence—is thereby violated. If the law constructs the subject before the law, then it is certainly worth the effort to have some input into the legal construction of sexual subjects.[66]

Insisting on privacy rights for gays and lesbians, pace Sedgwick, is thus not a matter of getting sex back into the impermeable space of the bedroom, but of challenging the role that sex law plays in regulating all individuals, in unfairly privileging certain forms of intimate association over others, and in oppressing specific categories of people without even naming the categories. The decriminalization of sodomy statutes and the extension of privacy protection in this area will not yield the full panoply of rights that gays and lesbians need, but it would pull the rug out from under the rhetorical/legal construction of gays and lesbians as a tendentially criminal population undeserving of the rights that others enjoy. The current military policy ostensibly focusing on conduct rather than status would thereby lose its raison d'être. Affording privacy protection to cover the intimate associations and choices of homosexuals and lesbians would abolish many of the inequalities established and reinforced by sex law, including rigid gender norms and hierarchies. Moreover, it would constitute an enormous symbolic victory, for it would indicate that the law no longer construes homosexuals as so different (abject and inferior) that they may be denied basic rights and be subject to a degree of surveillance and administrative/police intrusion in their personal lives that would not be tolerated if imposed on, say, heterosexual men. Indeed, securing their right to privacy is the sine qua non for shifting from the permissive to the respect model of toleration.[67]

THE CONSTRUCTION OF A STIGMATIZED IDENTITY: *BOWERS V. HARDWICK*

As many have pointed out, the *Hardwick* case seemed to be a textbook example of privacy issues.[68] Michael Hardwick was arrested for engaging in consensual sexual conduct with another (male) adult in the privacy of his own home.[69] All three of the central dimensions of constitutional privacy analysis considered standard since *Griswold* seemed to come into play here: the spatial (sanctity of the home as a protected private space), the relational (protection for consensual intimate personal relationships), and the decisional (freedom of choice as to intimate adult partners and intimacies between them).[70] That is why the case appeared to fall squarely in the line of the Court's privacy jurisprudence. And yet in a 5–4 decision, the majority denied that previous privacy cases were in any way relevant to the case at hand. Why and on what grounds?

Michael Hardwick challenged Georgia's gender-neutral sodomy statute that outlawed acts of sodomy defined as follows: "A person commits the offense of sodomy when he performs or submits to any sexual act involving the sex organs of one person and the mouth or anus of another."[71] The Court, however, maintained that "the issue presented is whether the Federal Constitution confers a fundamental right upon *homosexuals* to engage in sodomy and hence invalidates the laws of the many States that still make such conduct illegal and have done so for a very long time."[72] To the majority, the fact that Hardwick was caught engaging in sodomy with another male was the central pivot of the case.

In his vigorous dissent, Justice Blackmun radically disagreed with this characterization. He insisted that the case was not about a "fundamental right to engage in homosexual sodomy" at all.[73] Rather, it concerned a number of more general rights that had been protected under the rubric of privacy, including the right to control the nature of one's intimate associations with others, the right to conduct intimate relationships in the intimacy of one's own home, and the "right to be let alone" in order to be able to decide for oneself whether to engage in particular forms of consensual sexual activity in private.[74] As Justice Stevens also pointed out in his dissenting opinion, not only is the Georgia statute at issue not lim-

ited to homosexuals, it does not even mention them.[75] Instead, it expresses
the traditional view that sodomy is an immoral kind of conduct regardless
of the gender of those engaged in it.

Accordingly, a proper analysis of the Georgia statute's constitutionality
requires consideration of two questions: whether a state may totally prohibit the described conduct by means of a neutral law applying without
exception, and, if not, whether the State may save the statute by announc-
ing that it will only enforce the law against homosexuals.[76] Stevens be-
lieved that under *Griswold* and its progeny, states may not totally prohibit
the conduct proscribed by the Georgia criminal code.[77] Indeed, he re-
minded the Court that the Georgia attorney general conceded that Georgia's statute would be unconstitutional if applied to a married couple,
because of the "right of marital privacy" as identified by the Court in
Griswold![78]

A careful reading of the majority opinion shows that it was cleverly
designed to anticipate, finesse, and trump precisely these sorts of arguments.[79] The Court defined the issue presented by the Georgia statute
as whether the Federal Constitution confers a fundamental right upon
homosexuals to engage in sodomy, and hence invalidates the laws of many
states that still make "such conduct" illegal.[80] But it was left unclear
whether the term "such" in "such conduct" referred to sodomy or to homosexuality. This equivocation in the meaning of "homosexual sodomy"
allowed the Court to deny privacy protection in this "most private of privacy cases," in part by masking an indefensible antipathy (its own) to a
group in the form of a "moral" aversion to what the group allegedly does.[81]
The strategy of the majority opinion was to play upon the ambiguity in
the very meaning of the concept "homosexual sodomy" to "erect a wall
of difference" between the case before it and the line of earlier cases in
which certain fundamental rights in the "domain of intimacy" were
deemed to be protected under privacy jurisprudence.[82]

Justice White set aside the privacy precedents by defining the rights at
stake in earlier cases as having to do with family, marriage, and procreation.[83] He then insisted that "none of the rights announced in those cases
bears *any* resemblance to the claimed constitutional right of homosexuals
to engage in *acts* of sodomy that is asserted in this case. No connection
between family, marriage, or procreation on the one hand and homosexual
activity on the other has been demonstrated."[84]

The rhetorical function of combining the focus on identity and acts
under the rubric "homosexual sodomy" served two purposes. First, it enabled the majority to rely on the fact that the Court had not explicitly
questioned the right of states to forbid particular sexual acts. Indeed, Justice White pointed out that many forms of voluntary sexual conduct be-

tween adults are prohibited, including adultery, incest, and other "sexual crimes."[85]

Accordingly, the idea that privacy precedents "stand for the proposition that any kind of private sexual conduct between consenting adults is constitutionally insulated from state proscription is insupportable."[86] Only if the previous privacy cases were interpreted broadly would they cover Hardwick's case.[87] Speaking for the majority of the Court, White asserted, "We are unwilling to start down that road."[88]

The second purpose the focus on "homosexual conduct" served was to enable the Court to evoke disgust about particular sexual acts (sodomy) deemed immoral in the past, and then to attach this disgust to the persons who are today habitually associated with the commitment of such acts (i.e., homosexuals). Chief Justice Berger's concurring opinion devotes itself entirely to this task. Paraphrasing Blackstone, he states that sodomy has long been deemed an "infamous crime against nature," an offense of "deeper malignity" than rape, a heinous act, " 'the very mention of which is a disgrace to human nature' and 'a crime not fit to be named.' "[89] He concludes that to deem the "act" of homosexual sodomy to be a fundamental right would be to cast aside "millennia of moral teaching."[90]

The slippage of the rhetoric of acts into the rhetoric of identity thus attaches the stigma associated with allegedly immoral and hence justifiably criminalized acts onto the persona of a specific group: homosexuals. The group is thereby constructed as radically different, a criminally inclined class requiring differential treatment by the law. The homosexual sodomite is rendered visible, perpetually open to surveillance. At the same time, heterosexual sodomy is erased from view. Here is the place to locate the legal context for the epistemology of the closet. Indeed, the establishment of radical, abject difference and the reinscription of the privileged status of heterosexual marriage as the only acceptable form of intimacy is the real point of White's assertion that "no connection between family, marriage, or procreation on the one hand and homosexual activity on the other has been demonstrated."[91]

It is worth pointing out that the appeal to tradition and to historical attitudes regarding the immorality of a practice is hardly sufficient to save a law from constitutional attack, as the example of miscegenation law shows.[92] Moreover, by the time of the decision, "half of the states had repealed their sodomy laws . . . [and] in that half that retained them, the laws were no longer enforced unless there was evidence of aggravating circumstances."[93] This would seem to indicate that the alleged historical consensus regarding the immorality of sodomy had dissolved, along with the will to punish offenders as criminals.

But this has to mean that what really drives the entire argumentation is not the "ancient," "traditional," or "moral" disgust for certain sex acts, but rather an antipathy to homosexual object-preference. As Richard Posner put it, "It is the fact that some men lust after other men, rather than the form in which this lust is expressed, that in the minds of a majority of justices of the Supreme Court marks homosexuality as being profoundly different from heterosexuality."[94] This partly explains the effort by the majority to revive the privileged status of marriage and to distinguish it radically from homosexual intimate association by denying the latter the protective shield of constitutional privacy (and hence also permitting states to outlaw homosexual marriage).

The justices in *Hardwick* drew on social constructions of homosexual identity as radically different and inferior, constructions that had been readily available in psychological, medical, sociological, and moral discourses ever since the nineteenth century. But the reproduction of such constructions in the legal text was not mere mimesis. Rather, with the concept of "homosexual sodomy" we have a clear example of the legal construction of the subject before the law. The category served to create, or rather re-create, a stigmatized group identity just when those sorts of constructions were in the process of being abandoned and just when the stigma attached to homosexuality and the "deployment of sexuality" was being openly challenged.[95] It continues to provide a pretext for differential (greater surveillance and regulation, reduced rights) (mis-)treatment of individuals associated with that identity. Indeed, if "homosexual sodomy" simultaneously constitutes both criminal behavior and a criminal class, then at least on some influential interpretations, the equal protection clause must allow the states and the federal government a broad scope for treating it differently from heterosexuality even when expressed in physically similar acts.[96]

THE PERSONHOOD JUSTIFICATION: NORMATIVE PARADOXES

It was the discourse of radical difference that enabled the Court to refuse to extend constitutional privacy protection to cover acts of sodomy performed by homosexuals even if they occur in that quintessential private space, the home. It was also this reasoning that has led many legal scholars to charge that the majority opinion in *Hardwick* was "unprincipled."[97]

Apart from the obvious prejudice against homosexuals that drives the ruling, the chief jurisprudential issue had to do with the Court's treatment of the privacy precedents. Although the Court insisted, as we have seen, that "homosexual activity" has "no connection" to the previous privacy cases, it never attempted to provide a reason for this claim. Justice White simply stated that the Court has recognized three categories of activity protected by the right to privacy: "family, marriage, [and] procreation."[98]

As several critics correctly point out, the Court never articulated any unifying principle underlying these three categories that could serve as a test for new cases.[99]

The imperative to do so derives from the fact that under due process privacy claims, one must provide arguments as to why the conduct or choices at issue involve fundamental rights, fit into the privacy precedents, and thus should rise to constitutional stature as protected.[100] Indeed, the logic of due process reasoning is to articulate the principles at stake in a line of precedents and to see whether the precedents can be read at a level of generality that draws in the particular practice at issue without betraying the integrity of the legal tradition embodied in past decisions.[101] This also has direct bearing on equal protection arguments: if it can be shown that privacy protection for consensual intimacy is being granted to one group but denied unfairly to another, even via facially neutral statutes, then those laws would have to be struck down.

As indicated earlier, a framing battle over the proper level of generality was at the heart of the dispute between the dissent and the majority in *Hardwick*. Clearly, the former sought to argue that at the level of generality that best explains the previous privacy cases from *Griswold* through *Carey*, the governing tradition would require very strong justification (strict scrutiny) for criminal bans on sexual activity between consenting adults.[102] Challenging the overly literal and particularistic approach of the majority, Lawrence Tribe has maintained that the question raised by *Hardwick* is not whether sodomy "has long enjoyed a special place in the pantheon of constitutional rights, but whether private consensual adult sexual acts partake of traditionally revered liberties of intimate association and individual autonomy."[103]

But just what is the unifying principle underlying the "liberties of intimate association and individual autonomy"? The answer that most advocates of privacy analysis have given is that rights of privacy in this domain protect "personhood."[104] According to Tribe, the right to privacy protects a particular substantive vision of the needs of human personality, namely the idea that one's identity (individuality), no matter how formed or shaped by social forces and interactions, is sufficiently one's own to be deemed fundamental in confrontation with the one entity that retains a monopoly over legitimate violence—the government.[105] On the personhood conception of privacy, certain intimacies should be protected because they are crucial to individual self-definition and self-expression. Indeed, intimate relationships involving sex stand at the center of the new substantive due process privacy jurisprudence.[106]

However, many personhood theorists take an additional step and assume that they must demonstrate the fundamentality of the conduct at issue to personal identity in order to show that it has constitutional stature.

Accordingly, Lawrence Tribe, David Richards, and others have argued that sexual conduct should be protected not only because it concerns the most personal and intimate of human activities but also because it is central to individual identity.[107] *Griswold* and its progeny are interpreted by personhood theorists as involving cases that gravitated around sex and that were leading toward a constitutional right of sexual autonomy whose importance to individual personality was at last being recognized by the courts.[108] On this reading, the *Hardwick* decision was indeed "irresponsible" and "lawless."[109]

But it is precisely this version of the personhood conception of privacy that has recently led legal scholars to criticize privacy analysis on analytic and normative grounds. Analytically, the chief flaw of the personhood thesis is that it is overbroad: any activity might be deemed fundamental to one's identity. The normative objection is to the essentialistic and reified conceptions of identity that the personhood thesis fosters. On the one hand, it seems to invite, as we saw in the analysis of *Hardwick*, the imposition of ready-made identities ("homosexual" or "homosexual sodomite") onto individuals (often to mark them as different) that they may not want to embrace. On the other hand, by asserting that sexual conduct must be protected because it is definitive of who one is, it also reifies sexual acts, burdening them with an excess of significance—the very logic that informs the stigmatization of certain sexual identities in the first place. In other words, according to the personhood thesis of privacy (together with the claim of the fundamentality of sexual acts to identity), one's rights seem to hinge either on proving that certain acts are constitutive of one's particular group identity (the argument from difference) or that they are central to the identity of everyone, without exception (the argument from sameness). Either claim leads to absurdities.

For example, in a laudable attempt to extend privacy protection to homosexuals' intimate relationships, Justice Blackmun's dissent stated that "homosexual orientation may well form part of the very fiber of an individual's personality."[110] Involving much more than idiosyncratic personal taste, the criminalization of homosexual sodomy targets one's right to differ in one's identity and ethical commitments: "Freedom to differ is not limited to things that do not matter much. . . . It is precisely because the issue raised by this case touches the heart of what makes individuals what they are that we would be especially sensitive to the rights of those whose choices upset the majority."[111]

To be sure. Yet this way of emphasizing difference and stressing the constitutive importance of sexual acts to personhood is a trap because it comes at the price of reifying the very conduct and identity it seeks to destigmatize. As Jed Rubenfeld points out, to make homosexuality so essential to a person's identity is "the flip side of the same rigidification of sexual identities by which our society simultaneously inculcates sexual roles, normalizes sexual conduct and vilifies 'faggots.' "[112]

The argument from sameness falls into a similar difficulty. Tribe, Justice Blackmun, and Richards all argue that consensual sexual acts and choices should be protected because they are central to everyone's personal identity. That, allegedly, is the red thread unifying the line of privacy precedents established since *Griswold*.[113] As noted, Blackmun's dissent argued that consensual adult sex falls under the general rubric of a right to intimate association protected by constitutional privacy because of "the fact that individuals define themselves in a significant way through their intimate sexual relationships with others."[114] Homosexual sex should be protected like other consensual sexual activity because in terms of acts, it is not fundamentally different from heterosexual sex.

Here, too, sex acts are burdened with an excess of significance. Here, too, essentializing arguments regarding identity, as well as reifying arguments about sexual acts, seem to be at the heart of the personhood thesis. And here, too, the results are paradoxical: surely it is absurd to maintain that acts of sodomy are central to self-definition and therefore should be protected by the Constitution. To imply that any discrete sexual act is fundamental in that way is ridiculous. No advocates of the personhood thesis argue this, but that is where the reasoning focusing on conduct seems to lead.

To be sure, one could argue that sexuality is deemed fundamental by the personhood theorists because it can be an integral part of intimate relationships. Surely it is Blackmun's view that the consensual, wanted intimate sexual relationship is what constitutional privacy protects along with the freedom of ethical choice regarding how one conducts these relationships and with whom. Accordingly, the personhood argument could be interpreted to assume that one partially defines oneself through one's intimate sexual relationships and ethical choices, not through any particular sexual act. On this reading, one's identity and happiness are at stake in intimate sexual relationships and the freedom for adults to choose and conduct these is thus a basic value that should be protected for everyone. One could then give a constructivist justification of a broad reading of privacy analysis covering intimate association that would avoid the essentialist reading of acts or of identities. One could argue, in other words, that we have learned to understand today what the principles of equal liberty applied to all persons regardless of their gender or sexual orientation must entail: the privacy and freedom (decisional autonomy for and within) of intimate association. As already indicated, today the freedom to make ethical decisions regarding how to live one's personal life is deemed important to the "personhood" (dignity and agency) of every individual:

this must be respected in the "domain of intimacy," provided that principles of justice are not violated.

This version of the personhood argument could thus work together with an argument for protecting homosexual as well as heterosexual intimate association, which acknowledges the diversity of substantive ends for which we value intimate relationships.[115] For instead of positing a self independent of its ends or attachments, this conception construes intimate relationships as a constitutive context for the relational self to develop. Intimate relationships involving sexuality can entail trust, mutual reliance, mutual vulnerability, a special form of openness and interdependency, and special relational responsibilities and obligations (including care).[116] Since it is clearly the case that heterosexual couples enjoy constitutional protection for their intimate associations and decisions, there is no good moral reason for denying this to homosexual couples and strong moral reasons against such unequal treatment.[117]

Nevertheless, the cautionary critique of personhood arguments is well taken. Arguing the intrinsic fundamentality of sexual conduct to identity and to personhood is problematic. As I have shown, this at the very least requires justification on constructivist rather than essentialist grounds. What is at issue, as we all intuitively know, is contestation over the meaning and legitimacy of types of intimate sexual relationships, not of sex acts. The struggle is between those who wish to decenter as against those who wish to recenter one particular model of intimate association and the gender and sexual-identity hierarchies that go with it: heterosexual, monogamous, reproductive (patriarchal?) sexuality within marriage. The latter group does not deem sexual pleasure or happiness to be a "good of intimate association" and tends to construe other forms of sexual intimacy as "deviant" and unworthy of protection. Thus, what is at stake is whether or not every adult will be granted the legal status of ethically competent sexual subject, whose personal autonomy, agency, and chances for finding happiness in the domain of intimacy will be protected by constitutional privacy rights. But this would become possible only if the moral significance of reproductive heterosexual sex, and of particular sex acts, were denied rather than insisted upon. This is the crucial step that the constructivist (or any other) justification of decisional autonomy for and within intimate association must take.

THE LIBERTARIAN SOLUTION: MORALLY INDIFFERENT SEX AND THE HARM PRINCIPLE

Two things are at issue in sex laws such as the Georgia anti-sodomy statute: the moral status of the specific targeted conduct and the legitimate reach and mode of state regulation of that conduct. States have long had the prerogative to regulate morals and even to legally privilege preferred forms of intimate association—such as monogamous heterosexual marriage. The burden facing those who would challenge particular sex laws is that they must articulate why it is wrong to criminalize certain conduct and thereby to privilege some intimate relationships or decisions over others. In short, they must show that no moral principles are at stake in such conduct and thus that it is unjust, arbitrary, and/or irrational to forbid it. In order to avoid the pitfalls of the personhood thesis, however, this must be done without invoking essentialized identities or reifying and overvaluing the acts at issue.

The application of economic analysis to the domain of intimacy purports to do just that. Theorists in the law and economics school deny that decisions regarding the family or intimate matters involve a different motivational logic than other areas of human interaction. They challenge the ideology that the intimate domain is characterized by altruistic action-orientations and hence requires special protective forms of legal regulation. Instead, they insist that rational action geared to the satisfaction of preferences obtains in all spheres of life. They thus apply economic analysis to the domain of intimacy arguing for consumer sovereignty instead of status-based regulations that have no rational basis. The public interest will be served neither by direct heavy-handed legal regulation of sex, nor by the discovery of fundamental rights (liberal privacy analysis) protecting activities crucially important to personhood in the domain of intimacy. Instead, the state should get out of the morals business.[118] Reasoning from the "moral indifference of sex," this approach contests irrational regulation (based on mere prejudice) of intimate relationships as well as constitutional privacy analysis (allegedly presuming the great ethical importance of sex).

This is Richard Posner's strategy in *Sex and Reason*.[119] According to Posner, the Supreme Court decisions on sexual privacy "are not only poorly reasoned, but poorly informed."[120] He attempts to provide better grounds for the decisions he supports by avoiding privacy analysis, moral argument, and "fundamental rights" talk altogether. He relies instead on a utilitarian account of sexual conduct (regarding what influences choices) and a libertarian approach to governmental regulation. Because this approach rejects constitutional privacy analysis while providing an influential justification for private ordering (contractualism) in the domain of intimacy, it is well worth investigating.

The analysis proceeds in two steps. First, it proffers a bio-economic theory of sexual behavior to account for the principle regularities in the practice of sex. Thus sexual behavior, within certain clear limits, is amenable to the same type of economic analysis (cost/benefit calculations) as other conduct and that knowledge of this ought to guide legal regulation of sex.

The second and, for my purposes, more important step is Posner's call for a "model of morally indifferent sex" to serve as the test for rational legal regulation and reform.[121] This model undergirds Posner's libertarian arguments for sexual autonomy in a wide range of areas including homosexuality. It apparently enables him to avoid the pitfalls of constitutional privacy analysis while accomplishing many of its goals. Indeed, with the concept of moral indifference, Posner registers major cultural shifts in attitudes toward sex and takes an important step toward deconstructing what Foucault has called "the deployment of sexuality."[122]

Sex and Reason argues in favor of sexual autonomy. States should allow individuals to regulate their sexual conduct by their own choices, provided this involves consensual interaction between adults and no palpable harm to third parties. To be sure, this position in itself is hardly new. Prominent liberals, including Lawrence Tribe, David Richards, and others, have long argued that voluntary sexual conduct between consenting adults in the privacy of the home should enjoy constitutional protection against criminalization.[123] This argument has informed the new privacy analysis and was applied by critics to the sodomy statutes. The latter seemed to pose easy rather than hard questions. Because Georgia's anti-sodomy statute bans all sexual contacts of a specified kind, even if conducted out of public view and not for money, it is particularly indefensible. As Tribe argues, "It thus intrudes the grasp of the criminal law deep into an area that implicates no state interest in protecting public decency, nor in protecting vulnerable persons such as minors from coercion, nor in restricting potentially coercive commercial trade in activities offensive to public morality."[124]

What does the work here for Tribe et al., however, is a deontological interpretation of the Millian harm principle coupled with the personhood thesis. A strong presumption in favor of personal liberty in the domain of intimate association is claimed when forms of self-expression and ethical choice fundamental to one's plan of life and conception of the good (personhood) are at stake, to be outweighed only by a truly compelling state purpose or a counterpoised basic right. Criminalization is permissible in such cases only if it can be convincingly argued that moral principles and basic rights of others are violated by the practice at issue.[125]

Posner, on the contrary, eschews the discourse of fundamentality. Unlike adherents of the personhood thesis of privacy, or for that matter, their conservative, traditionalist, religiously inspired opponents, Posner does not base his arguments on the claim that sexual acts are somehow special and fundamental or that they raise basic moral questions. He does not argue that sex law ought to be liberalized because sex is central to a person's authentic self-expression or identity. Nor does he claim that intimate association involving sexuality should be regulated because of its intrinsic moral importance or value to society. On the contrary, Posner abandons the standard liberal discourse of fundamental rights, of the autonomy of individual moral judgment, and of the centrality of sexual choice (personal ethical autonomy) to the self. He appeals neither to some sort of intrinsic autonomy of the universal moral subject, nor to the idea of a fundamental constitutional right to privacy covering sexual relationships that legislation must respect because they are definitive of who we are.[126]

Instead of arguing the great significance of sex acts in order to claim sexual autonomy as a fundamental right, he insists on their moral insignificance and hence on the irrationality of prevailing sex law. We should be able to exercise sexual choice, but not because this is our moral right insofar as sex is fundamental to our personality or identity. Rather, sexual freedom should replace regulation because most laws criminalizing sex are costly and serve no rational purpose.[127] It is because they have no rational basis that many sex laws cannot pass constitutional muster, not because they violate fundamental rights. Posner is able to make this claim and to engage in a utilitarian calculus regarding much sex law because he assumes the moral indifference of sex. Moreover, he implies that the assumption of the moral irrelevance of much currently illegal sexual conduct must underlay any serious effort at decriminalization.

The thesis of morally indifferent sex accordingly serves two purposes: the first is to enable legal authorities to abstract away from the morass of prejudices and irrationalities that inform everyday (moralistic) attitudes to sex; the second is to provide a neutral criterion for drawing the line between sexual behavior that should be criminalized or regulated and that which should not.[128] Posner's point is that unless we abandon moralistic approaches to sex, we will never achieve rational legislation in this area. Before one can calmly reassess existing sex law and engage in rational policy making, it is necessary to rid the law of prejudices that derive from sheer ignorance or from moralizing views. The latter led to the over-valuation of sexual conduct, investing it with excess significance and extraordinary emotionality. This precludes a clear-headed assessment of the benefits and harms of varieties of sexual behavior. Indeed, it prevents the accumulation of needed knowledge about sex and its effects.[129] The criterion for sex regulation advocated by Posner is that it must serve a rational purpose. But the only way to know that sex law does serve such a purpose is to subject existing (and future) regulations to the test of moral indifference, an approach that treats sexual acts matter-of-factly. In other words, lawmakers must reason as if "the supposed moral aspects somehow evaporated and we treated sex with the same moral indifference with which we treat eating."[130]

Sexual choices and acts ought to be viewed as trivial in the sense that they neither define us nor carry any intrinsic moral weight. Were we to abandon our prejudices, we would be able to treat sexual preferences much like other preferences—and focus our attention on how to pursue them rationally (for our own good). Sex, like food, may be very important to us, but this does not make it a moral issue:

> Westerners do not consider eating . . . an activity charged with moral significance, but everyone recognizes that it is an activity to be conducted with due regard for considerations of health, expense, time and seemliness. Food disorders, such as bulimia and anorexia, are recognized; people are criticized for being too gluttonous or too fastidious; the gourmet is distinguished from the gourmand . . . healthy diets from unhealthy ones; there is a concept of good table manners. So while eating is not a moral subject except to vegetarians and to persons who adhere to religious dietary restrictions, neither is it a free-for-all; it is guided by *aesthetic and prudential considerations.* So would sex be in a society in which it were a morally indifferent subject.[131]

Freed of misleading moralizing approaches, we all would come to see that sexual conduct often is and should be guided by much the same considerations as other conduct. Indeed, from the economic point of view, sexual behavior, like any other behavior, involves the self-interested pursuit of preferences on the part of individuals. It is adaptive in the same way as other conduct to marketlike conditions and legal/political constraints that structure the costs and benefits of available choices.

Accordingly, legal limits on sexual conduct should be restricted to those necessary for preventing harms or extraordinarily high costs to third parties. To be sure, Posner is careful to warn that the sexual libertarian is not a libertine.[132] In his model there would still be regulation of sex, but this would be based on social attitudes founded on practical, concrete, nonmoralistic considerations regarding its external effects and whether or not force or fraud was used to gratify sexual desires.

This criterion should be applied to a wide spectrum of sex laws, including those regulating sodomy and homosexuality. With respect to the latter, Posner is quite sure that if we were to treat sex as a morally indifferent subject, it would be "hard to imagine people wanting to punish homosexual relations conducted in private between consenting adults, any more than they would want to punish people who eat with their fingers or pick their noses, when they think no one is looking."[133] Accordingly, laws criminalizing sodomy should be overturned not because they raise moral issues or concern acts fundamental to homosexual and/or heterosexual identity and hence involve fundamental rights, but because the conduct they regulate is of no moral significance whatsoever and because such laws serve no rational purpose.

But how does Posner know that sodomy is not a moral issue, and who decides what constitutes harm? To put the question slightly differently, what enables one to contest the moral significance of sodomy and to assume the stance of moral indifference regarding it? Posner answers this question in two steps. First, he shows that acts of sodomy became a moral issue historically, on the basis of the Christian worldview that deems human sexuality (including sexual desire) to be evil, sinful, and shameful, when not aimed specifically at procreation.[134] To be sure, the disgust at sodomy did become secularized, as it were, and entered into law as a general moral rather than religious precept. But—and this is the second step in the argument—Posner maintains that whether or not there once existed a consensus against sodomy in this society, today it has dissipated, along with the old fears and moral disgust associated with it.[135] "Because the requisite intensity and unanimity of feeling on these matters no longer exist—their immorality is contestable . . . and the contestants will get nowhere invoking the moral traditions of the West, whether in Catholic or Enlightenment versions."[136] Posner cites the fact that more than half the states have repealed their anti-sodomy laws, and that the existing ones were for the most part unenforced at the time of the *Hardwick* decision.[137] Therefore, sodomy is no longer considered a moral offense and there is no longer the same will to punish sodomites as criminals.

So far, so good. However, Posner does grant that the will to punish homosexual acts in order to target homosexual preference (object-choice) has not died, as the revised Georgia law and the *Hardwick* ruling clearly reveal.[138] If the majority is revolted by homosexual inclination or lifestyle and chooses to restrict its expression in acts, Posner needs additional arguments against the legitimacy of such legislation.

He offers two. First he invokes the classical Millian argument for tolerance: in the absence of direct and assignable harm, distaste for conduct in which others privately engage is a poor basis for public regulation. If an action is harmless except for the indignation it arouses, then there is no good reason to regulate it. In short, government has no business regulating beliefs, preferences, or even conduct, as long as these harm no one in particular.[139]

However, Posner admits to having no real answer to the well-known counterargument, recently articulated by Robert H. Bork, to the effect that "no activity that society thinks is immoral is victimless. Knowledge that an activity is taking place is a harm to those who find it profoundly immoral."[140] To invoke the harm principle will not help here because the meaning of harm is what is being contested. Moreover, as Ronald Dworkin has pointed out, utilitarian arguments cannot provide a way to distinguish between "external preferences" (preferences based on prejudice or moralism regarding others' enjoyment of goods and opportunities) and "personal preferences" (preference of a citizen for her own enjoyment of goods and opportunities).[141] The sort of arguments Posner wants to screen out through the criterion of "moral indifference" are "external preferences" in Dworkin's terms. But consequentialists must treat these preferences like any others.[142] However, Posner has another argument available to him: the claim that much of the revulsion that we feel about certain sexual behavior reflects an ignorance about sex and its consequences. This ignorance comes from the taboo character of the subject in our society. Posner maintains that "the history of persecution is, in general, based on ignorance. Were that ignorance removed, we might move rapidly toward the model of morally indifferent sex."[143] Obviously, the removal of ignorance is one task of Posner's erudite book. Knowledge about sex and about the effectiveness or ineffectiveness of regulation (available from the standpoint of sex's moral indifference), together with the harm principle, will provide rational criteria for legal intervention.

In the case of anti-sodomy laws targeting homosexuality, the knowledge that Posner supposes will dispel ignorance and irrational fears is the fact that homosexual preference is genetic.[144] This claim is meant to accomplish two things at once: to show the ineffectiveness of law aimed at extirpating homosexual desire, and to calm anxiety over contagion. Law cannot extirpate same-sex desire, but, never fear, it isn't catching. Thus, anti-sodomy laws targeting homosexuals serve no rational purpose.

One can only smile at the quaint enlightenment faith in the motivational power of instrumental reason and empirical knowledge. Does Posner really believe that revulsion against certain sex acts and preferences is based simply on ignorance about sex? Is homosexual desire really so easily confined to a particular group genetically destined to be homosexuals? Even if prejudice is correlated with ignorance, why assume that knowledge will dispel it? Surely there might be other investments at stake in permitting, say, the criminalization of "homosexual sodomy" or the prohibition of homosexual marriage, such as assurance as to one's own heterosexual desire and identity and the reinforcement of heterosexual norms.[145] One can only wonder what Posner is really up to with his feigned psychological naiveté.

I cannot argue these issues here. I simply want to show that on his narrow theoretical terrain, Posner is unable to provide better criteria than the privacy theorists for deciding which sexual behavior or relationships should be prohibited and/or regulated and which should not. Economic analysis offers little protection against strong majority preferences. Nor can it help remove the stigma attached to homosexuality. The genetic basis of a stigmatized quality certainly never undermined racism or sexism: why should it have such an effect on homophobia? Indeed, the claim that same-sex desire is genetic—together with the argument for toleration of sodomitical sex acts conducted in private because it is fruitless to try to extirpate such desire—does just the opposite: it tolerates private conduct of a group that it constructs as abnormal by birth and stigmatizes them as perhaps harmless but nevertheless as abject freaks of nature. As indicated, the permission model of toleration at work here perpetuates, via law, social stereotypes regarding flawed, inferior identities associated with disdained qualities.

Posner's discussion of whether homosexual marriage should be legal is a case in point. After considering the costs and benefits, he states, "The benefits of such marriage may outweigh the costs. Nonetheless, . . . the public hostility to homosexuals in this country is too widespread to make homosexual marriage a feasible proposal even if it is on balance cost-justified."[146] So much for the harm principle, the weight of the facts, the "prejudice-undermining" guidance that knowledge can give, and the probability of achieving moral indifference through such means.

I share the view that wanted, consensual sexual acts and same-sex desire are morally indifferent, and I believe Posner's thesis of morally indifferent sex to be an important contribution. But one also needs strong moral (referring to the equal worth of all persons) and political (thematizing the discriminatory harms of stigmatization) arguments to make the case against legal criminalization and unfair regulation.

Therein lies the difficulty: there is an ambiguity regarding just what kinds of moral reasoning the criterion of moral indifference about sex is intended to rule out.[147] Most of the time Posner seems to have in mind the specifically Christian attitude that construes sex as sinful and shameful. It is useful to show that the allegedly universal claims of the moral/immoral binary regarding the intrinsic nature of specific sex acts is derived from a historically specific worldview (Christianity) that no longer commands consensus and is contested as an ideology even in its secular formulations. This conception of a morally indifferent approach to sex, then, would imply that reasons based on that worldview are ruled out regarding the legitimacy of legal proscription or regulation. This would invalidate key portions of the majority and concurring opinions in *Hardwick*, for example. In addition, this constraint would constitute an important step toward the de-reification of sex acts because it would imply abandoning the privileging of "moral" (reproductive) over "immoral" (nonreproductive) sex.

"Moral indifference" would thereby undermine the old rationale for anti-sodomy laws. Moreover, it could serve as a first step toward undoing the "deployment of sexuality" described by Foucault, which involved not only the moralization of sex, but also the treatment of sexual preferences as constituting an essential core of individual personalities (their inner truth) and the persecution of categories of individuals as criminal on the basis of their immoral sexuality.[148] Yet Posner seems to think that once the moral/immoral binary regarding the intrinsic (evil) nature of (nonreproductive) sexual acts is abandoned, then matters of sex can be treated as what they really are: biological, instinctual, and/or genetic issues regarding the object of desire (sex as the object of scientific inquiry), and questions of rational choice among preferences and conduct on the other (sex as the object of economic analysis). To be sure, Posner has read Foucault and understands that both aspects are historical constructs. Indeed, in an explicit reference to Foucault, he states, "The broader point is that the Greeks did not moralize sex; the idea that sexuality is a moral category is an invention, not a discovery. Neither did they medicalize or psychologize sex; that was left for the Victorians to do."[149] Nevertheless, Posner insists on the biological basis of object choice and that homosexual and heterosexual desire are given and invariant. One is either a homosexual or not (hardly the Greek view). In short, he is, in his own words, "essentialist" regarding desire, "constructionist" regarding sexual behavior.[150] He thus inserts the biomedical model of sexuality into the place left empty by the (historicized/obsolete) moral model. Apparently willing to disregard what he has just admitted—that the scientific biomedical model of desire is also historically constructed and, by implication, not at all disinterested—he takes the knowledge it affords to be neutral.

As Foucault, Lacquer, and many others have shown, it was precisely the development in the late nineteenth century of the biomedical model of sex that allowed for the "deployment of sexuality" in the first place.[151] Hardly neutral, the biomedical model of sex introduced a new set of normative and normalizing binaries—(normal/deviant, unnatural/natural, pathological/healthy, perverse/normal)—that were deployed by psychologists, criminologists, and sociologists, among others. This enabled the authorities to construe the perpetrators of "perverse" sexual acts as deviant personality types—as identities—and to subject them to surveillance and regulation by the relevant specialists including, of course, the police. Accordingly, the sodomite could become the homosexual, the pervert, whose whole being is pervaded by his deviant, unhealthy, perverse, dangerous sexuality.[152] This in turn provided a new rationale for criminalizing sodomy and homosexuality, and for medical, psychological, administrative interventions in the lives of homosexuals.

Belief in the somatic basis of sexual orientation need not entail hierarchical distinctions or bad politics. But isn't Posner's insistence on the genetic basis of homosexuality meant to reassure the reader by locating homosexual desire securely within a category of people called homosexuals? And isn't such reassurance based on pejorative evaluations of homosexual desire either on the part of the author or attributed to the reader?

To be fair, Posner does insist that the cogency of his economic approach to sexual conduct does not depend on the truth of the biological model. Where conduct and hence choice is the issue, it is the calculation of costs and benefits, not biology, that is meant to replace moralistic prejudice.

Posner is a "social constructionist" regarding sexual behavior, albeit one who gives far more weight to incentives, opportunities, constraints (social engineering), and social function than to power, exploitation, and discourse theory.[153] He assumes that once freed from the moral frame of reference, sex acts (and choices) could and should be considered trivial, as mere matters of bodies and pleasure; they would thus be subject, like eating, only to aesthetic and prudential calculations and open to rational "environmental" influences (social policy) but with no moral weight at all.

However, this is both counterintuitive and unconvincing, as noted by Martha Nussbaum:

> He supposes, in effect, that if god is dead, . . . then all we have left, if we deny ourselves appeal to transcendent sources of authority in these matters, is a situation in which the world is a great market and individuals are simply competing to maximize the satisfaction of their subjective preferences, any one of which is as good as any other. If not the Christian explanatory theory, then no normative distinction-making at all.[154]

If society makes the cost of indulging in certain pleasures too high, rational actors will simply engage in different acts. But we can feel reassured: there is no rational basis for keeping the costs of sodomy high.

We have already adverted to the psychological naivete of such a position. Nussbaum also points out that those who, according to Posner, considered sex to be morally indifferent nevertheless held strong ethical views about which types of sexual activity and relationships are conducive to the flourishing of the individual or the good of the community, and they regulated sex on that basis.[155] Thus it hardly follows that in the absence of the Christian moral/immoral binary about the intrinsic value of specific desires and sex acts, sexual conduct would be construed as a mere matter of value-neutral, insignificant, and interchangeable personal preferences.

The political implications of the libertarian intervention in the sexuality debate are hardly inspiring. To view sex on the bio-economic model, to construe intimacy as ethically irrelevant, deprives us of compelling reasons to constitutionally protect individuals' sexual choices and intimate associations. Unless intimate relationships involving sexuality are considered special and important, there is little reason, in utilitarian analysis, to overturn legislated majority preferences on such matters. To show that some regulations censure activity that violates no secular moral principle is not enough to doom the legislation, because much of law institutionalizes and privileges the dominant ethical views of the community. There is nothing irrational in this. One would have to be able to show that such laws actually violate constitutionalized moral principles—the principle of equal liberty—in order to argue their illegitimacy. Only a prior commitment to equal individual autonomy/privacy regarding the ascription of ethical competence in intimate decision making could provide the requisite arguments against the community's tendency to legislate its ethics and against paternalistic policy makers who are all too willing to calculate costs and benefits for us regarding our welfare in the name of the welfare of the majority. But such a prior commitment would not be morally neutral, nor does it flow from economic or any other sort of consequentialist analysis.[156]

To be sure, Posner seems to believe that if the remnants of the Christian moralistic approach to sex dissolved, there would be no external majority preferences to worry about. He assumes that sex could then become the concern of a free and disinterested scientific inquiry. Absent that moralism, lawmakers could follow neutral science and accommodate self-interest and general welfare in regulating or deregulating sexuality.

Perhaps Posner should reread Foucault. Sex and sexuality retain enormous political and ethical importance despite the decline of the Christian moral model. As already indicated, Foucault argues that sexuality was constituted during the nineteenth century as the stake of a politically contested terrain, the importance of which is hardly reducible to moralistic prejudice, irrationality, or naive ideas about the sexual core of identity.[157] The expanded state interest in regulating the "health and morals" of certain populations, and the struggles over the social and political construction of sexuality, can scarcely be attributed to *pudeur* of Victorian secularized Christian values. Nor was it due to the steady progress of disinterested neutral human sciences. Rather, "if sexuality was constituted as an area of investigation, this was only because relations of power had established it as a possible object; and conversely, if power was able to take it as a target, this was because techniques of knowledge and procedures of discourse were capable of investing it."[158] The biomedical model of sex that Posner embraces was, as already indicated, the terrain on which this investment by power took place. All sorts of power relations were and still are at stake.

Nevertheless, there are signs today that the "deployment of sexuality" is becoming destabilized. Open contestation over the meaning of homosexuality is one. Shifts on the part of the medical profession in the direction of demedicalizing and destigmatizing same-sex desire is another. Battles over the legalization of same-sex unions, and over the right to marry regardless of sexual orientation, is a third.[159]

However, let me hasten to add the following claim to Foucault's perceptive analysis of the historically specific political investment of sexuality thanks to the "scientific" disciplines: even if a particular form of the "deployment of sexuality" is dissolving, even if the moral indifference of sex is acknowledged, this does not mean that sex or sexuality can now emerge in its authentic biological shape or that intimate choices become as casual as the choice of which film to see. Sexual intimacy can no more be stripped of its political significance than it can be denuded of ethical importance.[160]

Assuming that sexual desire is formed out of an open-ended drive rather than a biologically determined instinct, it should be obvious that sexuality could never be norm-free, ethically insignificant, or entirely irrelevant to one's gender identity.[161] Its link to the psyche—its involvement in fantasy, identifications, personal narratives—and its imbrication with interpersonal relationships involving issues of recognition, status, dependency, social norms, and cultural values invariably invest it with great personal, social, and cultural significance. I would even hazard the unsafe statement that sexual intimacy has always had (albeit varied forms of) ethical significance to society and to the individual. Sexuality is as much about words, images, ritual, and fantasy as it is about the body: the way we think about sex fashions the way we live it.[162]

Today, at least, freedom of intimate association has come to be closely associated with a conception of individuality, personal freedom, agency, and happiness. It is bound up with one's identity (as someone ethically competent to make intimate decisions that involve one's conception of the good and one's personal imaginary) and not only with a cost/benefit analysis of preference-satisfaction or a purely aesthetic focus on bodies and pleasures. It is this historically specific conundrum that has to be addressed instead of defined or wished away.

To sum up, Posner quite rightly rejects the proposition that sexual acts between consenting adults have an intrinsic moral significance. But the claim that an ethically neutral, rational choice calculus of pleasure and its costs can replace the emphasis on the inherent moral quality of sex acts is misguided. For even if there is no intrinsic morality to sexual acts, there certainly are ethical and moral dimensions to sexual relationships. As I see it, when the moral insignificance of sex acts is acknowledged, the importance of sexual intimacy shifts to the ethical domain; it does not become ethically neutral. This shift means that there is no longer only one right answer to the question of which types of intimate relationships can count as legitimate. But it also means that the question of what extent and type of regulation is just has to be rethought and justified to all concerned: this cannot be resolved via economic analysis. Sexual intimacy remains ethically and politically important, and some key moral issues regarding intimate association remain in play. Constitutional privacy analysis, suitably interpreted, addresses these issues in ways that the economic approach cannot.

Here we come to the heart of the matter. For even if sex acts are acknowledged to be morally neutral, even if on pragmatic grounds it makes little sense to regulate them, the community's ethical interest in forms of intimate relationships does not thereby vanish. Indeed, pragmatic and economic arguments focusing on preferences miss the point, because at stake are the values that shape preferences for forms of intimacy, along with the community's right to institutionalize through legislation its ethical views about the appropriate structure of intimate relationships.

The loosening of the medical model's normal/abnormal dichotomy regarding so-called perversions and the relative decline of belief in the intrinsic morality of sex acts and object choices among adults, together with gender equality, are what make room for new evaluations of the ethical quality of a plurality of types of intimate sexual relationships, none of which can now claim to occupy the moral high ground. Social contestation over the normative status of various forms of intimacy and over which evaluations should be expressed in law occur on this terrain. Indeed, the claim that the legitimacy of intimate relationships should not depend on the nature of the sexual act (a private matter) or on the gender of the sexual object, but on the quality of the intimate relationship (no force or fraud), is itself a moral, not a pragmatic claim.

For some, the moral indifference of sex means that intimate association should become a matter of private orderings. Economic analysis implies that contract should replace status in this domain, accompanied by no more than the usual protection against force and fraud. If intimacy was formerly regulated by an unjust and sexist status regime, it is high time, according to this approach, to complete the move from status to contract, and to shift over to the liberal legal paradigm. Regulations should no longer aim at substantive outcomes (like fostering reproductive marital intimacy via stigmatization and penalization of other forms of intimacy) but should only ensure the formal equality of the contracting intimate partners against force or fraud.

Experience with private ordering over the past decades has yielded ambivalent results, as indicated in Chapter 1.[163] The problem is not only the well-known fact that the formal equality entailed in contractual relations does little to mitigate substantive inequalities in power between partners. Casting intimate relations as a matter of preferences involving cost/benefit analyses also elides the specificities of intimate association and the ways in which what is at stake there differs from ordinary market transactions. To be sure, this point is hardly new: rejection of the applicability of contract to family is as old as Hegel's critique of Kant.[164] But it is not necessary to glorify the family as a natural love community "beyond justice" as Hegel did in order to realize that intimate personal relationships can generate special obligations and responsibilities that escape the language of contract.[165] It is worth recalling that intimate relationships often implicate personal identity, create interdependencies and vulnerabilities, and hence involve responsibilities. This is the correct intuition of the personhood theorists as well as the neocommunitarians.

Indeed, courts and legislators recognize this. The tendency to shift to private orderings in many areas within the domain of intimacy has not been equivalent to a wholesale withdrawal of the state from regulation. For example, while several states have adopted the Uniform Premarital Agreement Act and the Uniform Marital Property Act, apparently acknowledging the legality of private ordering, courts have nevertheless been unwilling to enforce marital contracts in the same way as commercial contracts.[166] This is not due to leftover anachronistic traditional views about family or gender but to the acknowledgment that intimate association generates obligations as well as inequities that require legal attention.

The problem is that the current presumption in favor of private ordering fostered by the law and economics approach, pace Posner, also tends to foster arbitrary regulation. For example, in the place of rigid status regulations, vague doctrines like "the best interests of the child" or "equitable distribution" statutes have accompanied the presumption of private ordering, vesting courts with broad discretion to decide child custody and the division of marital assets upon divorce.[167] The arbitrary and haphazard approach to the oversight of private ordering in this domain creates uncertainty (and often unfairness) rather than security. This is due in part to the hegemony of the law and economic discourse of freedom of contract, market autonomy, maximization of preferences, consumer sovereignty, and so on, all of which tend to delegitimize public restraints on private orderings. Thus, instead of a public discourse on the needed forms that the regulation of self-regulation should take and on the purposes of such regulation, we get the worst combination of unregulated private ordering together with intrusive and arbitrary regulations that seem to follow no clear rule-of-law principles.[168]

Once again we come up against the issue of legal paradigms. The above approach thoughtlessly shifts back and forth between the liberal and the welfare paradigm, between no regulation and overregulation, between anti-statism and statist intrusiveness, all in the name of preference maximization. What is needed instead is an understanding of the relevant status obligations (of parents, of spouses, and of other intimate associates) and of appropriate legal doctrines that articulate these on the terrain of gender equality and in acknowledgment of the importance of both personal happiness and responsibility in intimate associations. Constitutional privacy analysis aims to establish and protect the ethical autonomy and equal personhood of all adults regarding intimate association. It is indeed premised on the moral indifference of sex. But it does not entail the moral indifference of intimate sexual relationships and should not result in a wholesale shift over to private ordering based on economic analysis. Rather, from the perspective of the reflexive legal paradigm, determining the appropriate forms of regulating self-regulation of intimate association, and for which purpose, can become a topic of discussion.

What must replace the moral (and medical) assessment of sex acts and object choice is an egalitarian morality of intimate relationships. The criteria undergirding the regulation of adult intimacy should not be where one is touched or whom one desires, but whether adult relationships or encounters are wanted, egalitarian, reciprocal, and responsive to the obligations that intimacy incurs, or whether they are imposed, oppressive, involve domination, exploitation, and lack real, yet responsible exit opportunities. Freedom of intimate association should go together with regulations fostering equality, fairness, and responsibility.

The choice of forms of intimate relationships is an ethical choice, related to one's conception of the good and how one lives one's life. But it is a moral and constitutional claim that every adult should be construed by law to be an ethically competent legal subject whose ethical autonomy and privacy, as well as their interdependency, vulnerability, and mutual responsibility, merit respect and recognition in this domain. The burden of proof should shift to the shoulders of those who would criminalize forms of intimate association or sexual acts. They would have to show that the proscribed relationships and/or conduct fit the second rather than the first category. The right to privacy protecting ethical autonomy and the principle of equal protection of the laws should restrict the majority's desire to privilege its form of life by criminalizing or unfairly regulating the intimate relationships of the minority if it cannot provide convincing moral arguments for doing so.

One issue remains. Why not simply bypass the issue of conduct, dispense with privacy analysis, and focus directly on sexual-orientation status and the obvious discrimination issues involved in *Hardwick* and the new military policy? As indicated, discrimination against gays and lesbians is often the motive and result of anti-sodomy laws. It certainly underlies the selective imposition of the duty of privacy onto these particular groups. The "don't ask, don't tell" policy, however, should disabuse proponents of the idea that it is possible to bypass the issue of the morality of the conduct: relying on *Hardwick*, the policy was constructed precisely to block the application of equal protection principles. Facially neutral sodomy laws do not, as we have seen, trigger equal protection arguments. On the contrary, they have served to undermine them.[169] Moreover, an elaborate argument is required to overturn anti-sodomy laws that do not mention gender or sexual orientation on anti-discrimination grounds. Equal protection does not protect rights that are denied to everyone even if we suspect that the laws at issue are aimed against a specific group. So long as consensual adult sexual conduct can be criminalized without convincing arguments that it violates rights or moral principles, such laws can be used to produce stigma by associating criminality and abnormality with those who engage in the outlawed acts, indirectly justifying discriminatory regulation of the deviant group. No classifications are necessary. Such laws undermine the liberty and privacy of everyone. To be sure, the *Hardwick* ruling stigmatizes only those constructed as homosexual. But the Georgia statute it upheld is a threat to anyone who engages in sodomy—a floating signifier for non-reproductive sex.

CONCLUSION

Let us return to the opening questions of this chapter: Isn't it naive to construe intimate relations as private once one acknowledges that sexuality is socially constructed, always legally regulated in some form or other, and often politically contested? How can negative liberty and personal privacy protect people from being discriminated against because of their intimate choices or sexual identities? How can privacy rights provide public recognition of the legitimacy of a plurality of forms of intimate relationships?

We have already seen how on the personhood conception, privacy analysis can lead one to construe the choice of sexual pleasures and partners as inherently an act of self-definition. This follows from the tendency in the fundamental rights approach to posit an ever-expanding set of concerns as so central to individual self-definition that they qualify for constitutional protection. The assumption that there are pristine spheres of personal autonomy and identity that must be shielded from the otherwise all-encompassing regulatory state is thereby reinforced. So is the misleading conception that privacy rights shield what exists outside of and beyond power, politics, and law. This conception of privacy, in turn, appears to call for a wholesale shift from public (status-based) to private (contractual) ordering in the intimate domain. In short, it revives anachronistic assumptions of the liberal legal paradigm.[170] Apart from the problem of how to determine what lies in this sphere and what lies outside it, the entire construction entails a confused conception of sexual intimacy and its relation to personal identity, to law, and to power. Personhood theorists are right to insist on the close link between sexual intimacy, sexuality, and ethics, but their essentializing rhetoric revives an untenable conception of the private. It also seems to invite discrimination on the basis of status/identity (sexual orientation).

Utilitarian critics of constitutional privacy analysis like Posner take the opposite approach, insisting on the moral indifference of sex and the moral irrelevance of much currently illegal sexual conduct. The mistake in the utilitarian approach to sex law, however, is the assumption that the opening left by the de-moralizing of sex can be filled with biology and economics instead of politics and ethics. On the one hand, it seems to deliver the domain of intimacy over to private (contractual) orderings with little concern for the obligations, mutual responsibilities, dependencies, and inequities to which intimate relationships give rise. Controlling the validity of contracts only for force or fraud, however, is insufficient. Here, too, echoes of the liberal paradigm can be heard.

On the other hand, and despite its apparent libertarian intentions, this approach would place too much discretionary power in the hands of the state, providing few solid protections for individual rights. Shifts toward contractual private ordering is not equivalent to state withdrawal from regulating intimate association. Rather, as we have seen, it tends to foster arbitrary regulation. Thus intrusive direct regulation of intimacy typical of the welfare paradigm also accompanies this approach. Indeed, it shifts back and forth between the legal methods and reasoning of both paradigms without coherent justification for the decision either to regulate or not to regulate.

This chapter has argued for another solution. If we distinguish the concept of a right to privacy from a duty to privacy and provide an adequate constructivist justification of its scope, we can develop a conception that is in tune with the presupposition of gender equality and the equal moral personhood of all. It thus becomes possible to extend the protective shield of privacy analysis to previously uncovered intimate activities and relationships, regardless of sexual orientation. On this conception, constitutional privacy analysis need not lock us into essentialistic versions of the personhood thesis, and it can acknowledge the "socially constructed" aspects of sexuality. In other words, once certain assumptions inherent in the liberal paradigm of law are abandoned, many of the objections to privacy analysis registered by Posner and other critics would no longer hold.

If we reason from the meta-theoretical perspective of the reflexive legal paradigm, moreover, we can see that it is unnecessary to embrace a wholesale shift to private orderings allegedly entailed in privacy analysis and in its corrective, the utilitarian law and economics approach. As we have seen, the fundamental rights/personhood version of the liberal paradigm leads one to assume that there are pristine spheres of personal autonomy and deep sexual identities slumbering within the individual that should be liberated from repression, shielded from state intrusion, and left to private orderings. Freedom of intimate association is assimilated to freedom of contract. Liberty is construed as freedom from external (physical or legal) constraint. To put this another way, in the liberal legal paradigm, liberty and law, personal freedom and state regulation, are placed in a zero-sum relationship: the only way to ensure personal liberty is to limit the scope of state action. Privacy analysis is construed as a way to keep the state out. It contributes to the misleading conception of privacy rights as intrinsically linked to a contractualist model of ordering intimacy.

I argue that we do indeed need the liberal form of law that construes privacy rights as "negative subjective liberties" in order to protect diverse forms of intimate association and ethical decision making involved in them. Yet this can be justified from the constructivist perspective without tying privacy rights to a reified or naturalized sphere cordoned off from state action and without essentializing acts or reifying identities. One can have constitutional protection for a basic right to privacy without construing it as a natural right.

But we have also noted that negative liberty is insufficient for protecting freedom and equality in intimate relationships. The domain of intimacy involves gender and sexual relations that are socially (and legally) constructed, pervaded by power differentials, social hierarchies, and other sorts of structural inequalities. Yet it will not do to abandon privacy rights and private ordering altogether on the assumption that they shield injustice. The alternative of bringing in the heavy hand of the state through direct top-down substantive regulatory measures justified by a rather loose "rational basis test" (the law and economics approach) or aimed at enforcing a substantive conception of "good intimacy" to which all must conform is equally problematic (and true of some feminist egalitarian approaches). If the liberal paradigm has been associated with an essentialistic conception of privacy and an overly narrow conception of negative liberty (freedom from constraint provided that contracts are not based on force or fraud), the latter two approaches fail to adequately protect personal autonomy and privacy.

Reasoning from the meta-theoretical standpoint of the reflexive paradigm of law, I maintain that the liberal legal form of constitutional privacy rights, appropriately conceptualized and justified, provides a needed protective cover for wanted consensual adult intimate association. Privacy rights, accordingly, must be understood as constituting the domain of intimacy in an institutional form suitable to the presumption of gender equality such that normatively directed processes of adjustment and self-correction are possible.[171] In other words, one should understand constitutional privacy rights as partly constitutive of the personal autonomy and ethical competence that it ascribes and protects. They foster self-regulating autonomous intimate relationships that are, hopefully, structured in ways that equalize the bargaining power, voice, and standing of the partners.

But this assumption may be overly optimistic. Thus, self-regulation must also be regulated to protect against injustice. This is not oxymoronic within the reflexive paradigm, for it is ascribed social autonomy and not "natural liberty" that is protected by constitutional privacy rights. Such protection ought not involve adaptation to alleged natural orders, and it should not take prior distributions of power and prestige as given. Rather, it should steer regulation in the direction of a just distribution of rights and competencies to the intimate associates themselves. The appropriate form of juridification of such legally constructed private intimate relations would thus have a triple task: to avoid the disintegrative effects of overlegalization and the unjust effects of nonintervention, while providing normative and institutional resources that enable secure, rewarding, autonomous, and egalitarian intimate relationships to develop.

The reflexive paradigmatic perspective allows us to see that the state and regulatory regimes are and should be involved in the domain of intimate association (protecting against harm, abuse, violence, fraud, inequity, and other injustices) even when the decisional autonomy of the individual is acknowledged. "Negative liberty" in the sense of freedom of choice regarding entry into, exit from, and the conduct of intimate associations must be predicated on nondomination and freedom from exploitation (from being treated as a means only) within these relationships. The public/private line must go right through intimate association: privacy as decisional autonomy to enter and conduct intimate relationships cannot shield them from the demands of justice and the requirements of responsibility.

Regulations protecting intimate associates may take the form of materialized or reflexive law. The meta-theoretical perspective of the reflexive paradigm indicates that a flexible approach to legal forms is required. This, as already indicated, would permit us to choose the forms most appropriate to the matter at hand, guided by the principles of equal liberty and the constructivist justification of a plurality of "purposes" of intimate association. The autonomy and agency shielded by privacy rights, properly understood, can be steered by the principles of justice.

As I argued in Chapter 1, a right to personal privacy grants decisional autonomy to the legal subject, thereby protecting and partially constituting agency in the relevant domains. It enunciates and legally constitutes a realm of personal autonomy and a personal imaginary domain, within which the individual can creatively fashion her identity. Thus, the conception of a right to personal privacy covering intimate association ascribes dispositional autonomy over personal boundaries, wherever these are drawn, to the rights holder. This means that the latter is construed as an ethically competent subject with respect to what are considered to be personal matters, and then granted a certain leeway to organize her own conduct in relation to this legally constituted, presumptively protected terrain.[172] Such rights do not imply that the decisional autonomy accorded to individuals must be exercised in a certain way or in certain circumscribed "private" places. Constituted as the rights holder, it is up to the individual to choose whether, how, and where to exercise her legally acknowledged agency.

Intimate relationships create obligations, carry expectations, and entail responsibilities. Ethical competence refers to the ability of actors to recognize these, and to deliberate about what contributes to the good of intimacy and to the well-being of the partners involved. But ethical autonomy also provides the space for individuals to weave together meaning and identity in a form that they can affirm and embrace and then present for recognition to others.

Thus, in conferring a right to personal privacy, the law constitutes and protects a structure of recognition whereby the claim to individual integrity (personal inviolability, ethical competence, agency) is acknowledged and the expectation that others will respect it is institutionalized.[173] In other words, the concept of a right to personal privacy affirms the importance of intersubjectively recognized personal boundaries and places presumptive dispositional control over practice and disclosure—within whatever is socially construed as the personal—in the hands of the individuals involved.

As such, a right to privacy is dualistic, or, rather, it faces in two directions. On the one side, the ideas of inviolability, decisional autonomy, and informational privacy bring the notion of a boundary into play. Accordingly, decisional autonomy implies control over access to the self and freedom to choose intimate associates, along with the liberty to withdraw certain concerns, motives, and personal decisions from public scrutiny and control. The latter aspect involves the negative dimension of communicative liberty implied by privacy rights: the absence of any legal obligation either to reveal or to justify the reasons for one's personal ethical choices in the same terms that everyone else would accept. When personal ethical concerns are at stake, it does not matter whether the reasons decisive for me would be the same that everyone else would articulate in similar situations. One has, as it were, the right to be different in this domain. The state may not require me to reveal my reasons for acting in the domain in which I have the right to act on my own reasons.

This is one implication of the thesis of moral (but not ethical) indifference of sex. I do, however, retain the right to discuss my reasons and to try to justify my decisions to others whose judgment or recognition matter to me. The freedom of intimate association protected by privacy rights shields the relations of trust within which we first try out, express, and offer for recognition key aspects of our self-conceptions. Facing inward from the boundary established by privacy, the right protects the psychic and physical integrity of the individual and of her most personal relationships.

But privacy rights also face outward: they are exercised in public as well as in private spaces.[174] From this optic, what is at stake is the right to decide with which socially constructed identities one will identify, and which dimensions of one's personal identity one wishes to present in different fora. A second dimension of communicative liberty is tied to this aspect of personal autonomy, namely, the right to present aspects of oneself, one's way of life, one's projects in public, as a claim for recognition. Accordingly, the state may not require that I conceal my sexual orientation, my identity, my personal choices, or the reasons I have for making them. In protecting personal autonomy, privacy rights also entail the right to speak and present who one is in public, ascribing discretionary power over how to present oneself, to the individual.[175] Thus it is only apparently paradoxical that a privacy right ensuring personal decisional autonomy over certain concerns entitles one to think and to be what one chooses and to announce it to the world, thereby ensuring a right to public expression as well.

Where and how the boundaries of personal privacy are drawn is a public and political question. Just what should come under privacy coverage and who gets such protection depends on shifting cultural understandings of gender, changing perceptions of threats to individual integrity, new interpretations of what is deemed personal, and, of course, the constellation of power and the particular context in which the issue arises. Whether acts or relationships are cast as matters of morality and criminal law or as ethical questions concerning an individual's or group's form of life, autonomy, and happiness and how law should adjudicate among the competing claims depends on the outcome of such struggles.

But this does not mean that nothing is ever settled. Simply because one cannot analytically deduce a normative conception of what privacy rights should cover does not mean one has to abandon privacy analysis on the grounds that the entire issue is political. Nor does it mean that all line-drawing and every assertion of a fundamental right is arbitrary. Rather, one must start in medias res, for the normative boundary between public and private is always already drawn. It is also contested. Indeed, privacy rights are (recursively) a condition of possibility of democratic contestation. To the degree to which they protect a minimum degree of personal security regarding sensitive issues, they enable one to be an autonomous participant in the contestation over where to draw the boundaries.

Every interpretation of a general right involves line drawing that is never neutral but always distributional (including some concerns, excluding others) and in that sense, political. Hard cases involve contested conceptions of where the boundaries should be drawn. The questions to ask are (1) What is at stake in the highly politicized struggle over which forms of intimacy to include under privacy protection? and (2) Why is this battle going on now?

It should be clear that today what is at stake is the overall conception of individualized constitutional privacy rights covering the domain of intimacy. The line of decisions beginning with *Griswold* focused on intimate relationships and sexuality as partially constitutive of intimacy. The debate ever since has been over whether this decision and its progeny are to be interpreted narrowly as protecting (and privileging) only heterosexual marital relationships—the traditional family construed as an entity—or broadly as protecting the freedom of intimate association and all that it entails irrespective of marital status or gender, as implied by the ruling in *Eisenstadt*.[176]

I choose the broad construction. The conception that I argue for in this book posits the individual as the bearer of personal privacy rights and all wanted intimate relationships between consenting adults as meriting protection from unwarranted regulation by the state or third parties with one proviso: that the demands of justice are not violated within the relationship. This approach presumes, as did Justice Blackmun in his dissent in *Hardwick*, that "in a Nation as diverse as ours, . . . there may be many 'right' ways of conducting those relationships and that much of the richness of a relationship will come from the freedom an individual has to *choose* the form and nature of these intensely personal bonds."[177] Indeed. The interpretive dispute indicates both that the old consensus on the moral privileging of reproductive sex within marriage is deeply shaken (otherwise there would be no open contest) and that sexuality is politically and ethically important. By focusing on the diversity of our nation and on the many "'right' ways" of conducting intimate relationships, Justice Blackmun understood what characterizes the historical context in which the argument for privacy protection of intimacy has emerged. The previously hegemonic form of intimate association—monogamous heterosexual, permanent, patriarchal marriage with its rigid gender norms and hierarchies and explicit homophobia—has been decentered, and a pluralization of forms of intimacy demanding equal treatment has occurred.[178] The battle is between those trying to reinstate the former model regardless of the amount of repression necessary to do so, and those defending pluralization.

But the dispute also involves a challenge to the version of the medical model of sexuality that constructs perverse sexual identities and ascribes them to the perpetrators of "abnormal" and/or "immoral" sexual acts. It is this model that informs current efforts to revitalize laws criminalizing sodomy, as the majority opinion in *Hardwick* patently demonstrates.

The destabilization of both the moral and medical models makes it seem unjust to deny privacy protection to intimate relationships merely because they deviate from old norms whose claim to legitimacy is no longer compelling (e.g., *Hardwick*). The conception of privacy (secrecy) and the related form of toleration articulated in the "don't ask, don't tell" policy is inadequate to this situation: they rest on the assumption that one kind of intimate association is morally better than all others. "Permissive," privatizing toleration is particularly inappropriate in our heterogeneous society. For justice to be served, a shift must be made to the qualitative respect model of toleration and a corresponding conception of privacy premised on the moral and civic equality of all citizens whatever their gender or sexual orientation. The latter attributes decisional autonomy, ethical competence, and communicative liberty to the rights holder. On this approach, a wide plurality of forms of intimacy can be afforded privacy protection without legally inscribing or reinforcing stigma. The reciprocity entailed in the respect model means that the majority has taken a reflexive stance regarding its own form of intimate association and understands that it cannot legitimately deny the expressive freedom or legal protection to a minority that it grants to itself. The majority acknowledges, in other words, that its preferred form of intimate association has an ethical rather than a moral status and thus cannot serve as the basis for denying rights to those who construct different forms of association merely because they are different. The majority need not admire minority forms of intimate association but it cannot deem them immoral or reprehensible and criminalize them on that basis.

Here is where one must look in order to answer the second question. The historically specific "deployment of sexuality" discussed above not only reinforced the power of normative marital heterosexuality; it also helped construct the terrain on which it could be challenged.[179] As Foucault pointed out, the appearance in psychiatry, jurisprudence, and literature of a whole series of discourses on the species and subspecies of homosexuality (and other "perversions") facilitated a strong advance of social controls into this area, "but it also made possible the formation of a 're-verse' discourse: homosexuality began to speak in its own behalf, to demand that its legitimacy . . . be acknowledged."[180]

Accordingly, new forms of sexual politics have emerged on the terrain developed historically through the deployment of sexuality, some of which challenge the very presuppositions of that deployment. In part, the political struggle has taken the form of demands for a set of rights (synthesized in the United States by appeals to a general privacy right to sexual autonomy). As Foucault argued, "The 'right' to life, to one's body, to health, to happiness . . . and beyond all the oppressions or 'alienations,' the 'right' to rediscover what one is and all that one can be, this 'right' . . . was the political response to all these new procedures of power."[181]

When such demands are articulated by those whose sexuality is considered deviant or whose sexual identity is deemed pathological, they clearly are meant to challenge such evaluations. In other words, these claims involve an effort to shift different sexualities and acts from the status of immorality and pathology to the status of personal expression and ethical choice (to be protected by privacy rights).

Certainly such demands emerge on a historically constructed cultural field in which sexuality is deemed constitutive of identity. Yet rights discourse need not carry the baggage of essentialist or liberationist "identity politics." The demand for legal ascription of ethical competence in the domain of intimacy could be construed as a challenge to the idea that sexual acts or desires determine identity. But it presupposes that intimate relationships are very important and worthy of constitutional protection. Privacy discourse provides a language for challenging policing by governmental agencies of unacceptable sexual identities or intimate relationships and/or of those deemed ethically incompetent sexual subjects.

Properly interpreted, appeals to personal privacy in the domain of intimacy involve choices regarding a range of activity and an endorsement constraint: the right not to have an identity imposed on one by the state that one cannot freely affirm and embrace. Whatever the source of one's sexual orientation or choices, the notion of personal autonomy leaves it up to the individual whether or not to construe sexual desires or acts as defining the core of one's identity.[182] The choice of affiliating with the relevant group identity should also be an individual one. Accordingly, legal imposition of an unwanted identity constitutes a real harm regardless of its social status.[183] Needless to say, the harm is especially great if the identity so imposed is a stigmatized one. The *Hardwick* opinion articulated an interpretation of homosexual identity as perverse and immoral, and construed it to be inherent a set of criminalizable sexual acts. This legal construction provided the pretext for denying a wide range of other rights to the people falling into the stigmatized identity category. The new military policy is an example. By imposing a duty of privacy regarding sexual desire and conduct selectively onto one particular category of individuals, it violated both dimensions of communicative liberty discussed above for the targeted group, thereby denying their status as moral persons. Had the privacy rights of gays and lesbians been acknowledged instead of denied in *Hardwick*, the military would have had to find some other route for accomplishing its goal—unequal treatment of a particular group.

The point is not that privacy secures gay rights or liberation. Only if voice and equal protection are secured can the low social status of a group identity be challenged, and equal dignity prevail over the shame, secrecy, and fear attached to previously disdained forms of life. But privacy serves to protect individuals from having an identity (whatever its social status) ascribed to them that they do not endorse, or with which they wish only partially and sporadically to identify, without coercion and without the risk of being "totalized" as essentially this or that. It also facilitates the development of rewarding and just intimate relationships. Were this to be acknowledged in full, it would go a long way toward undermining the epistemology of the closet.

CHAPTER THREE

Sexual Harassment Law: Equality vs. Expressive Freedom and Personal Privacy?

◆ The clash between values of liberty, privacy, and equality appears especially intense in the relatively new continent in the legal regulation of intimacy: sexual harassment law. The same cultural transformations of sexual and gender relations that triggered the new privacy jurisprudence are at issue here. Unlike the concept of a privacy right, however, the principles of equality and anti-discrimination that inform laws regulating sexual harassment are clearly present in the Constitution and in federal statute law.[1] Indeed, it seems that in this area the courts can avoid the worst difficulties of privacy analysis, for instead of having to discover unenumerated, discrete "fundamental" rights, they need only establish that discrimination on the basis of sex, outlawed by Congress and in violation of the Fourteenth Amendment, has occurred in order to grant relief.

Nevertheless, a clash between core constitutional values seems unavoidable in this domain. For it is by no means obvious which sexual expression in the workplace constitutes harassment and why any of it should be construed as gender discrimination instead of, say, as the individualized abuse of supervisory power or as a common law dignity harm, actionable as a tort.[2] Intense debates have erupted over just what the harm of harassment is, over the reasoning behind recent Court rulings that construe even same-sex harassment as discrimination on the basis of sex, and over the more general issue of equality analysis and anti-discrimination law in this area. Here, too, it seems that juridification aimed at deterring the serious gender injustices that occur in the workplace partly through the medium of sex entails the sacrifice of privacy and autonomy. Rules regulating sexual harassment often force people to submit to interrogation regarding their sexual past, to assume a schoolmarm persona to maintain credibility (if one is a woman), to risk public exposure of the most intimate details of their lives, to accept censorship of erotic expression and intrusive regulation of consensual as well as unwanted relationships. Here, too, freedom seems to get sacrificed on the altar of equality.

Sexual harassment is a pernicious form of gender discrimination and I strongly support laws aimed at preventing and punishing it. But the way sexual harassment has been juridified in the United States is flawed. This chapter has two theses: first, too much of the reasoning (feminist and juridical) in sexual harassment law is informed by a cavalier attitude toward personal privacy, a tendency to confuse sex with sexism and to view women as victims in need of protection with no sexual agency of their own. This attitude is partly responsible for the unattractive choices facing those striving for gender equality in the workplace and elsewhere. But I attempt to show, second, that these choices are dictated by a deeper problematic. I have in mind the tendency to approach the issue of regulation from within the framework of either of two competing paradigms of law—the liberal and the welfare model—that structure the possible responses in ways that are characteristically one-sided and reciprocally blind.[3] Only if this deeper level is thematized will we be able to grasp the dynamics behind the paradoxes in sexual harassment law.

I provide a brief overview of the development of sexual harassment law in the United States and a discussion of the various positions in the new debate it has triggered. Feminists now disagree about how to characterize the harm of sexual harassment. Most want to revise the hegemonic "sex-desire/subordination" model informing legal and corporate regulation, because it is imbued with the attitude just described and leads, paradoxically, both to over- and underregulation.[4] Yet neither the liberal objections to this model that inspire some feminist proposals nor the postmodern theoretical approach that informs others has led to a satisfactory alternative. Instead, the new debate has spawned a set of antinomic positions, each offering remedies to one redescription of the harm while screening out the others.

Part of the problem lies in the monistic character of each approach. But not even the most comprehensive construal of the harms of harassment will resolve the dilemmas of regulation unless the effects of particular legal forms on the relevant domain of action are also addressed. Law has its own efficacy, and the mode of legal regulation matters very much indeed. The subject before the law and even the harm being redressed are in part legally constructed. Yet few of the participants in the debate has addressed this issue.[5]

I thus shift perspective and thematize the two paradigmatic conceptions of law presupposed by the various approaches and informing much legal interpretation. The tendency to over- or underregulate, to pair autonomous subjectivity with legally unconstrained action and impaired subjectivity with legally regulated action, and thus to turn equality (secured by regulation) and liberty into a zero-sum game can be traced back to these sets of background assumptions. As in the first two chapters, I try to indicate a way out of these dilemmas by shifting to a third, "reflexive" legal paradigm as the appropriate terrain on which to repose the key issues. In this case, however, I argue that sexual harassment law is and should take the particular form of reflexive law. But I also analyze the flaws specific to the institutionalization of sexual harassment law and conclude with some suggestions for revising the current approach to regulation in this domain.

THE DEVELOPMENT OF SEXUAL HARASSMENT LAW

Sexual harassment is a relatively recent concept in law. It was first thematized in the 1970s by a grass roots women's movement that identified sexual pressure on the job as sexism, a form of gender discrimination.[6]

Title VII of the 1964 Civil Rights Act had already declared it unlawful for an employer "to discriminate against any individual with respect to . . . compensation, terms, conditions or privileges of employment, because of such individual's . . . sex."[7] Yet not until 1980 did the Equal Employment Opportunity Commission (EEOC) draw up guidelines making sexual harassment an actionable form of gender discrimination under Title VII.[8] By 1986 the Supreme Court identified two broad forms: quid pro quo harassment, the conditioning of employment benefits on submission to sexual advances; and the creation of a "hostile work environment," one so polluted by intimidation, ridicule, and insult that it discriminatorily alters the terms and conditions of employment.[9] Like harassment based on race, religion, or national origin, discriminatory harassment based on sex can constitute a civil rights violation even where the employee suffers no tangible economic loss.[10] The Court's recognition of this was a major victory for feminism.

Unlike other forms of group-based harassment, however, the status insults deployed in sex discrimination are imbricated with sex, creating a unique set of problems for definition, regulation, and adjudication. Indeed, in its 1986 decision, the Court ruled that even consensual sex could be coercive. The gravamen of a sexual harassment claim is not "consent" but whether the alleged sexual advances are unwelcome and the misconduct sufficiently "severe" or "pervasive" as to "unreasonably" interfere with and alter the conditions of the victim's employment and create an abusive working environment.[11]

Nevertheless, it was not until the aftermath of the Clarence Thomas confirmation hearings that Congress passed the 1991 Civil Rights Act expanding Title VII relief to include compensatory and punitive damages in civil suits.[12] In 1998 the Supreme Court took on a record number of sexual harassment cases and returned to the issue of employer liability in two of them.[13] It held that employers are liable if a supervisor creates a sexually hostile work environment, or if no measures were taken to prevent and correct harassing by employees. It also held that same-sex harassment in the workplace is actionable as sex discrimination under Title VII.[14]

The threat of monetary damages and these expansive interpretations of hostile environment harassment law certainly provide a strong incentive to employers to issue and enforce policies against sexual harassment. But therein lies part of the problem. To avoid costly lawsuits, many companies have developed highly repressive and intrusive rules regulating their employees' intimate expression. A quarter of American companies now have policies (many unwritten) punishing offensive expression and often simply prohibiting office romance on and off premises.[15] They employ an army of human resource managers empowered to interrogate workers about their relationships with one another, including those that are consensual and wanted. Moreover, lawyers have a new interest in civil suits because Title VII targets wealthy employers rather than poor employees, thereby raising the specter of ceaseless litigation. The stakes have become very high: one can be fired, demoted, or transferred on the say-so of an apparent harassment victim or human resource manager even in the absence of any complaint.

It should not be surprising that these developments have triggered a new debate over sexual harassment. The current controversy has shifted from disputes about standards to the deeper question of how to characterize the harm. Recent front-page publicity given to allegations of sexual misconduct by public officials invites the assumption, ambiguous from a feminist perspective, that the issue is general offensiveness, or transgression of rather traditional norms of civility regarding women, rather than gender discrimination. Given the censorious focus on sex in corporate policy and judicial interpretation, and given the astonishingly undertheorized inclusion of same-sex harassment under Title VII's ambit, the wrong of sexual harassment suddenly seems indeterminate and in need of redefinition.

Wanted consensual relationships are not within the purview of sexual harassment law. Nevertheless, its theory and legal interpretation have spawned rules regulating all forms of intimacy between co-workers. At the same time, harassment that is gender-based but not sexually abusive tends to become invisible.[16] Since the way in which the harm of harassment is construed has direct implications for the appropriate mode of legal regulation, much rides on the definition. It is this conundrum that is sparking the current controversy.

The debate is stylized as an opposition between sex equality on the one side and liberty (decisional and expressive), privacy, and happiness on the other. I present the various positions and antinomies in ideal-typical form and then turn to the deeper analytical issues.

THE HEGEMONIC FEMINIST SEX-DESIRE/ SUBORDINATION MODEL

Radical feminism provided the conceptual underpinning of sexual harassment law nearly twenty years ago—and Catharine MacKinnon's work remains the dominant influence in the field.[17] As noted above, Title VII of the 1964 Civil Rights Act forbade discrimination on the basis of sex. However, it did not mention sexual harassment. Thus feminist legal theorists had to come up with an account of where the legal harm lay and why it should be considered a form of sex discrimination.

In 1979, MacKinnon's pathbreaking *Sexual Harassment of Working Women* provided the new theoretical framework needed for claiming legal remedies.[18] Four features of her analysis merit scrutiny: the critique of privacy discourse, the social constructionist approach to sex, the consequentialist orientation of the subordination/inequality approach to gender discrimination, and the assumption that in the context of gender hierarchy, consent to intimacy cannot be construed as an autonomous choice. Together with the dual thesis of the illocutionary and silencing effects of sexually harassing speech developed in later writings, these assumptions exert great influence on the way in which the harm of sexual harassment and its remedy is defined to this day.[19]

The prevailing judicial approach in the 1970s to complaints about sexual harassment framed sexual overtures in the workplace as personal and natural. Because such overtures were thought to be motivated by desire, not sex discrimination, the women lost their cases. Courts viewed sexual advances as a private, intimate matter concerning only the parties involved.

MacKinnon developed a compelling analysis of the strategic uses of these frames.[20] The term *personal*, she argued, has at least four meanings in this context—it conjures up single expressions of individualized desire as opposed to group-based oppression; it refers to private as distinct from public and important matters; it is invoked to distinguish work-related from nonwork-related concerns (the latter being irrelevant to issues of job discrimination); and it implies that harassment by a supervisor is at most an individual abuse of authority and not the institutional policy or responsibility of the employer.[21] In short, calling sexual harassment in the workplace personal or intimate serves to individualize and privatize it, and to pathologize women's objections to it. Construing sexual harassment as private serves to shield it from public scrutiny.

The same holds for the truism that a sexually charged atmosphere is only natural when men and women come into contact. By implication, sexual overtures are based on biological attraction and the predatory male behavior this involves cannot be changed. MacKinnon counters this discourse with the argument that such behavior is predicated on contingent, potentially changeable power relations between women and men.[22] Sexual overtures and innuendo in the workplace are hardly a benign or natural expression of desire seeking reciprocity. Rather, it is under conditions of male supremacy that sexual harassment and male predation become socially constructed and condoned as natural eroticism, as expressive speech, and as a private intimate matter instead of being seen as the historically specific mechanism of subordination of women as a group that it really is. Indeed, construing men's expression of sexual desire as natural, and construing sexualization of women by men as the simple expression of desire, shields from critique both the mode of such expression as well as its purpose and effects.

But, as MacKinnon rightly argues, women's economic and social subordination throughout society are reinforced by cultural power dynamics that eroticize domination, sexualize aggression, and construct the subject position "woman" as a (provocative or passive) sexual object of male desire. Indeed, on the social construction thesis, inequality is built into all heterosexual intimate relations in societies characterized by gender hierarchy: "Women's place at work and in sexual relations can be seen as socially constructed, not naturally given; public and structural, not private and individual; separate and subordinate and not equal. . . . Gender *is* a power division and sexuality is one sphere of its expression."[23] MacKinnon insists that the effect of treating women like sex objects is dual: it keeps women sexually subordinate to men and blocks equal treatment of women as normal workers. The sexual harassment of working women occurs because as a group they have little power and occupy inferior job positions, and harassment works to keep them there. Its function is to extract sex and to reinforce women's subordination to men at work and in society at large.[24]

But sexualization of women on the job, as elsewhere, does more: it constructs women's self-understanding and their choices. It teaches them that in order to succeed, they ought to telegraph receptivity, respond supportively to male sexual overtures, and take sexual ridicule in stride, no matter how they feel about the man.[25] Even if they consent to do so out of intimidation or calculation, it is not their desires that are at play in such circumstances. Under relations of gender hierarchy, women do not have the power to define the ordinary conditions of their own consent.[26] Their preferences, or what they consent to, may be adaptive to oppression.[27]

Sexual harassment in this analysis is an institutionalized practice, not an attitude.[28] It must be analyzed in terms of group-based inequality and discrimination, not as a dignity harm, a moral injury, or an offense to a code of good conduct. It is not a matter of an individualizable tort, but a strategy specific to an inegalitarian social structure that reinforces the relegation of a social group to an inferior position of status and power.[29] Sexual harassment subordinates women by sexual means in the workplace—a consequence of male supremacy throughout society.

Accordingly, MacKinnon defined sexual harassment as "the unwanted imposition of sexual requirements in the context of a relationship of unequal power" involving quid pro quos as well and the treatment of women workers as sex objects.[30] In her subordination/inequality approach, it constitutes sex discrimination not because women are unjustly treated differently from men, but because it serves to subordinate women as a group to men as a group and hence to reproduce gender inequality.[31] Both men and women can be sexual victims. A theory of group-based inequality and a consequentialist analysis of the effects of harassment is necessary to establish sex discrimination, for it is the subordinating effect of sexual harassment, rather than a supposed error of classification, that should be the criteria and target of anti-discrimination law: "The only question for litigation is whether the policy or practice in question integrally contributes to the maintenance of . . . a deprived position because of gender status."[32] The analysis thus merges a "subordination/discrimination frame" with a "sexual desire/abuse frame."[33] It places sexualization at the heart of sexism.

Clearly in this approach, any appeal to personal privacy or freedom of (sexual) expression in the workplace is inherently suspect. Indeed, MacKinnon's more recent arguments regarding the "illocutionary" status and "silencing" effects of sexually harassing speech are meant to ensure that legal regulation in the name of equality trumps any personal or expressive liberty claims.[34] Sexually harassing speech acts are illocutionary because they have the power to immediately violate and subordinate the harassment victim. Sexual harassment (like pornography) does what it says: sex talk is a sex act.[35] Precisely because sexuality is coded as intimate, harassment that is sexual is a form of abuse, because it transgresses the boundaries of the self and imposes the feelings of sex in the body of the harassed and in the harasser, which is a large part of its purpose.

Sexualization of this sort defines and positions its target as sexually available, while effectively silencing her. The addressee is transformed into sex through sexual harassment.[36] Being sexualized, turned into sex, renders her speech unworthy and unbelievable. These effects are reproduced when women recount the abuse in court or to supervisors, with the consequence that their speech is discredited. That is why sexualization is central to gender domination and harassment.[37] Harassment that is not sexual does its harm through content; harassment that is sexual does its harm as an act of sexual abuse.[38] Thus more speech, the traditional remedy to offensive expression, cannot help here. The law has yet to find a means to challenge women's lack of credibility once they are sexualized in this way.[39]

The obvious conclusion to draw from this analysis is that so long as gender inequality exists, sex must be kept out of the workplace, particularly where there are power differentials between the workers. MacKinnon acknowledges that sexual expression must be "unwelcome" in order to trigger a lawsuit for sexual harassment.[40] But the logic of her analysis implies that under conditions of inequality, even wanted relationships can be exploitative and preferences adaptive, and employers are right to bar them. It also implies that legal intervention should be "more substantive than formal, directed toward changing unequal social relations rather than monitoring their equal positioning before the law."[41] Title VII's prohibitions regarding sex discrimination should, in short, foster intrusive, comprehensive, effective, result-oriented regulations.

LIBERAL OBJECTIONS

This stance confirms the suspicion that sexual harassment law is intrinsically illiberal. It appears to threaten important liberal values including privacy, freedom of speech, and freedom of association.

Current sexual harassment law is alarming to some liberals because civil suits lack protection of privacy for the accused and all those who come into contact with him or her.[42] The "hostile environment" claim triggers unlimited investigation of people's character and past sex lives (in order to establish a pattern), including not only that of the alleged harasser but also the harassment victim (was it unwelcome; did she fantasize or provoke it?). Forcing people to publicly disclose the most intimate details of their sexual history violates the "privacies of life." It also makes them vulnerable to all sorts of manipulation by workplace (sex) commissars, politically motivated attackers, and any co-worker who is ambitious or wants revenge.[43]

The intrusive corporate policies regulating sexual expression triggered by Title VII are also disturbing. The vague standard for deciding what creates a hostile environment together with the system of vicarious employer liability leads employers to overregulate employee speech. This concern has led to the charge that current harassment law is incompatible with First Amendment principles.

Indeed, the battle over equality-inspired speech restrictions has shifted from college campus speech codes (regulating sexist/hate speech) and the pornography controversy to workplace harassment rules. Liberal publicists have sounded the alarm.[44] Jeffrey Rosen recently declared in the *New Republic*, "The most serious threat to the First Amendment of the past decade [is] the notion that words that create an intimidating, hostile or offensive working environment without inflicting more tangible harms can be punished as harassment."[45]

This is hyperbole. Yet a serious scholarly debate over the constitutionality of sexual harassment law has emerged in the law reviews, echoing the concerns raised in the hate speech controversy. The problem is the following: in both areas, the law targets discriminatory speech on the basis of its message, thereby challenging the most central tenet of First Amendment doctrine: the requirement of content and viewpoint neutrality in regulation.[46] Accordingly, government may not prohibit expression simply because society finds its message offensive.[47] In an important 1992 decision, the Supreme Court struck down a hate speech ordinance with apparent implications for workplace harassment law on these very grounds.[48] Yet in deciding *Harris v. Forklift* the next term, the Court did not mention the First Amendment even though the case was based almost entirely on speech.[49]

The Court's silence, the proliferation of lawsuits, and the sweeping range of policies regulating offensive speech in the workplace have deepened the fears of free-speech liberals.[50] Some have concluded that Title VII's hostile environment cause of action runs afoul of the First Amendment. Accordingly, it should be abolished or limited to instances involving unwanted physical contact.[51] Others suggest that the way to make harassment law comport with the First Amendment is to prohibit only harassing speech that is intentionally directed at a particular employee.[52] On both approaches, the First Amendment trumps equality concerns and should substantially limit the reach of harassment law.

Moderates have tried to stake out a middle ground that strikes a balance between equality and speech interests. Richard Fallon points out that the norm of content neutrality has always admitted specific, well-theorized exceptions in the complex tapestry of First Amendment law.[53] He thus tries to give an account of why sexually harassing expression possesses little First Amendment value and why the workplace is a context apt for regulation. Central to this account is the claim that employees are a captive audience and that harassment often occurs within the structure of authority relationships, making it potentially costly to parry harassment with more speech, the traditional First Amendment remedy to offensiveness.[54] Adjustments to Title VII doctrine should be made only to shield political speech and workplaces where constitutionally protected sexual materials are produced.[55]

Deborah Epstein counters that the interests of equality and free speech are already balanced through the carefully calibrated procedures required by law for filing suit.[56] Only in the fallacious view propagated by First Amendment absolutists, that hostile environment harassment law prohibits all offensive speech, are the readjustments suggested above necessary to save its constitutionality. But Title VII is not meant to be a "clean language act," nor need it lead to overbroad enforcement. On the contrary, a review of the law's ten-year record shows that a small number of cases succeeded at trial, while a far greater number of women were denied relief after being subjected to substantial discriminatory abuse.[57] The main problem remains underenforcement, not overenforcement.

Epstein, however, is also concerned with protecting workers' speech. In place of the targeting requirement (which would screen out much undirected harassment that destroys workplace equality), she advocates time, place, and manner restrictions to solve the problem of overbreadth.[58] All worksites have private settings that can be avoided, and these should be free of regulation.

Nevertheless, there remains the disturbing tendency of employers to adopt a "zero-tolerance" policy suppressing all sexual speech as a defense to liability.[59] Epstein argues that if companies enact draconian and censorious policies, the law is not to blame. The problem stems from a dearth of sophisticated legal counsel.[60]

However, the incentives to censor employee speech operate prior to the bringing of suit.[61] Indeed, the rational employer will try to avoid having to go to court. It is not the bad advice of lawyers but the combined effect of the structure of Title VII law (its preventive thrust), the employer liability rules, and the vagueness of the standard for hostile environment harassment that virtually compel the employer to censoriously overregulate. The employer faces huge litigation costs and damage awards if its efforts are deemed inadequate. Rather than bothering with painstaking distinctions and complex procedures, the rational employer will simply prohibit the expression of all language and conduct that could even arguably be viewed as impermissible.[62] The effect of hostile environment law is thus to encourage repressive corporate control over workers' lives.

Speech and privacy liberals like Jeffrey Rosen, Jeffrey Toobin, and Kingsley Browne thus conclude that the proper response to all this is not to try to get sex out of the workplace (at the price of our most basic liberties), but to get the law out of the area of sex. Quid pro quo harassment should remain actionable (as a form of extortion), but the "hostile environment" cause of action should be eliminated.[63] Policies favoring one sex in hiring or promotion should be the target of Title VII, not sexual expression.

LIBERAL FEMINIST ALTERNATIVES: REDEFINING THE HARM

The idea of reorienting sexual harassment law away from sex and back to gender is resonating among feminist legal theorists, albeit for different reasons. ACLU president Nadine Strossen agrees that the false equation between sexual expression and sexual harassment violates employee's free speech rights. A danger in focusing on sex talk in the workplace is indeed overinclusiveness: benign sexual expression will tend to be prohibited.[64]

More important, this focus undermines women's equality by resurrecting the traditional and disempowering notion that sex and sexual expression are intrinsically demeaning to women. That notion is now being used, as it was in the past, to exclude women from employment opportunities, including informal networking with male colleagues or clients that are crucial to job advancement.[65]

It is also being used to exclude nonsexual conduct that is gender discriminatory from the hostile environment claim. In a widely cited recent article, Vicki Schultz echoes Strossen's criticism of the judicial emphasis on sex for diverting attention away from prevalent forms of gender harassment in the workplace that do not involve sex at all.[66] Her careful analysis of ten years of litigation shows that courts have "highlighted the harm of conduct considered sexual and motivated by sexual designs, while the larger gender-based processes once deemed the principle focus of Title VII have faded from view."[67] Consequently, they fail to provide remedies for hostile workplace environments that privilege men and masculinity while undermining women's competence to do the job. Strossen and Schultz both attribute this development to the influence of the sex-desire/subordination model.[68]

Schultz seeks to redirect interpretation of the harm of sexual harassment away from sex and back to sexism. Pace MacKinnon, Schultz insists that sexual exploitation is not the central dynamic in gender inequality: workplace harassment that is not explicitly sexual is the broader, more pervasive phenomenon.[69] Stratification of work by gender is the key dynamic in producing women's disadvantage. Under the influence of the radical feminists' sexual-desire/subordination approach, however, courts now tend to define harassment on the basis of sex exclusively as a matter of unwelcome sexual expression and to exclude nonsexual conduct from the hostile work environment claim.[70]

Indeed, the 1980 EEOC guidelines that define hostile environment harassment as "verbal and physical conduct of a sexual nature" have been interpreted as limiting the universe of gender-based harassment to sexual conduct.[71] In an effort to change that, the commission decided in 1993 to put in guideline form the rule that sexual harassment is not limited to sexual conduct but also includes harassment due to gender-based animus. Yet the commission backed down from this decision in response to criticism that the new rule would violate First Amendment rights![72]

Schultz thus argues for replacing the sex-desire/subordination model with what she calls a "competence-centered paradigm." On this approach, sexual harassment aims to undermine women's competence to do jobs formerly held by men and to maintain the most highly rewarded forms of work as male-identified turf. Accordingly, the harm of hostile-environment sexual harassment should be understood as conduct that relegates people to gendered work roles against their own aims and in ways that disadvantage them.[73]

The problem with sexualizing the harassment claim is not only that it is underinclusive of too many forms of harassment on the basis of gender.[74] It also mischaracterizes the motive for sexual harassment as men's desire to exploit women sexually rather than to preserve their economic privileges and an image of masculine gender superiority.

The danger with the focus on sex is that it shifts the understanding of the harm of harassment away from a politically motivated group-based civil rights violation to a "dignity" harm that involves the violation of a person's honor or self-respect. Moreover, the belief that sexual expression is demeaning to women invites legal protection for the wrong reasons. It positions women as a sexually pure and vulnerable victim class whose virtue or special sensibilities require protection against men, positioned as natural sexual predators. It justifies legal regulation to prevent sexual extortion construed as an abuse of supervisory power. But anyone in a superordinate position can abuse their power over subordinates: group-based discrimination and gender injustice are not necessary for this. The view that sexual harassment law is meant to protect innocent women's sexual purity or honor from the abuse of institutionally powerful male predators reinforces the harmful gender stereotypes that block equal opportunity for women—the original purpose of Title VII.

Indeed, the resulting legal paternalism allows judges to feel enlightened about protecting women from sexual offensiveness while playing into the hands of those who aim to repress women's and deviant sexuality, not to fight gender injustice. This attitude perhaps explains the astonishing unanimity of the Supreme Court in its sexual harassment rulings, as opposed to the deep divisions characterizing its privacy jurisprudence. The focus on sex, on essentialist arguments about male predators and vulnerable females, creates strange bedfellows. The hijacking of the issue of sexual harassment by social conservatives during the impeachment crisis of President Clinton is a striking example.[75]

POSTMODERN FEMINIST REFRAMINGS: CRITICIZING LEGAL NORMALIZATION

This point is at the heart of postmodern feminist critiques of sexual harassment law. As Jane Gallop recently quipped, "There are few people in the world between whom there isn't a power differential."[76] A criterion that rules out sex between such people makes all sex abusive.

Underlying many workplace sex codes is a puritanical attitude that views sex as bad and casts women as needing protection from male sexuality and their own sick desires. The ideology that women's sexuality is nonexistent or shameful accounts for why sexualization can become a means to discredit and silence them. It also deprives women of their own legitimate sexual expression.

Hence we have Judith Butler's objections to juridification in this domain.[77] Butler criticizes MacKinnon's use of Austinian speech-act theory to justify using the law to encourage censorship of sexuality in order to alter unfair gender relations. She challenges the conflation of speech and conduct undergirding MacKinnon's insistence on the illocutionary status of sexually harassing expression.[78]

As we have seen, for MacKinnon, sexually harassing utterances have the power to immediately violate and subordinate the harassment victim.[79] This is precisely what Butler disputes. Drawing on Derrida, she maintains that language is always citational, and that the speaker is never fully in control of the meaning or effect of an utterance. Hate speech, pornography, and sexually harassing speech are indeed performative: they are acts and even threats. This does not mean, however, that such speech does what it says. There is always a gap between the originating context or intention of the speaker and the effects it produces, hence the possibility of decontextualizing speech and the potential for subversive resignification.[80] Instead of being crushed by sexually harassing speech, targets may turn it around and fight it, thereby becoming empowered and exercising agency.

This means that the case for state intervention is not as sound as MacKinnon believes. She assumes that if "words wound" through their illocutionary force, there is no possibility of defusing the harmful effects of speech through counterspeech. Substantive legal controls are required to deter and redress the harms of such speech and to protect relatively powerless groups from the more powerful.

Butler resists this solution because she fears that by expanding legal and state-induced corporate regulatory power, feminists risk becoming like the sorcerer's apprentice: The increased scope of regulation can be used against the very social movements that pushed for juridification. Striking examples are the use of gender equality provisions to censor lesbian and gay pornography in Canada, homosexual and lesbian speech in the U.S. military, and offensive literature, artwork, and now sexual expression generally in the workplace and schools.[81]

Those in favor of state regulation naively assume that state power is likely to be deployed to undermine gender inequality. They ignore the law's role in constituting the gender hierarchies it regulates. Critical insight into state power and violence, especially of the law's own "discursive power," is thereby undermined.

In Butler's view, juridification of sexual expression is a form of violence that places discretionary power in the hands of the authorities.[82] The discursive productive power of the state (and not only its limiting function) lies in its active production of the domains of publicly acceptable and unacceptable (hence, punishable) sexual expression. To give the task of adjudicating sexual expression to the state or its proxies is to give these actors the task of misappropriation. Moreover, the process of seeking legal redress for a harm constituted as legally actionable reinforces this discursive state power. The power and agency of the ordinary citizen disappears.

Echoing the critique of dominance feminism by sex radicals of the 1970s, Butler refuses the image of women as passive victims of male sexuality. She insists on their agency even while acknowledging the social construction of the various "subject positions" they occupy. Nevertheless, her assumption that legal regulation undermines agency places her in the discursive field of classical liberalism. Certainly, her sophisticated understanding of the productive effects of power, of the construction by law of subjectivity (subject positions), and of the partial agency rather than full autonomy of social actors is not characteristic of liberalism. But if legalization is repressive or constructive only in the negative sense of normalization, then we are back to a conception of the subject able to act on its own only if the state stays out. Women's partial agency becomes assimilated to the wholly autonomous subject of liberalism whose self-regulable circumstances do not require legal intervention.[83] Butler does not even think it necessary to provide social actors with a legal safety net that would, for instance, protect them from reprisals if they parody or directly challenge harassment on the job.[84]

In short, to Butler, legal regulation of sexual expression is dangerous and to be avoided. Juridification entails normalization: the construal of legitimate versus deviant sexuality in the eyes of the law. Once this discursive decisional power is attributed to the state, punitive regulation of disdained forms of sexuality and gender behavior inevitably follows. That this is justified now in the name of gender equality rather than the Bible is small consolation to those rendered deviant or abject. Far better to leave it up to the citizenry and their creative forms of social contestation and counterspeech to challenge and reappropriate the injuries of harassing sexual speech.[85]

We seem to have come full circle. Although this postmodern theory has a different model of power, the state and the law than the liberal approach (constructive and productive versus simply prohibitory and repressive), both construe juridification and regulation of intimacy as standing in a zero-sum relationship with personal freedom. To both, where state sovereignty stops, individual liberty begins. Butler's analysis, like that of the liberal, suffers from the mirror weakness of MacKinnon's: if the latter forgets the repressive and non-neutral aspects of legal regulation, the former ignores the facts of social power that may render counterspeech and efforts to performatively reconfigure harassing speech ineffective and dangerous.

POSTMODERN FEMINIST REFRAMINGS, PART 2: REDESCRIBING THE ROLE OF LAW

Other postmodern feminists do see an empowering potential in the legal regulation of sexual harassment, provided that the feminine subject before the law is construed as a sexual agent. It is conceivable that the law could establish "subject-positions" that facilitate women's sexual agency. Legal regulation would still have to address sexual coercion and sexualized shaming as discrimination. But it need not proceed on the premise that sexuality per se is harmful or imposed on women. Instead, it should be guided by the understanding that women are "sexuate beings" with their own desires and with an equal right to respect, happiness, and control over their intimate associations.[86]

This approach proposes a major shift in the understanding of the harm of sexual harassment. It also suggests a strategy that is the diametrical opposite of that proposed by Vicki Schultz to remedy overinclusive legal regulation. As Drucilla Cornell argues, instead of shifting the focus from sex to gender, we ought to put women's sexuate being in the center of the analysis. Like MacKinnon, Cornell argues that the focus on gender is too limited because it makes equality analysis turn on comparison: on differential treatment of similar or similarly situated groups of people. To Cornell, however, women are different from men in a way that is denigrated and turned into the basis of unfair treatment.[87] The harm and remedy of harassment has to be posed in these terms.

Accordingly, sexual harassment is an equality harm: the denial of the social bases of self-respect to people because of their sexual difference. Cornell thus redefines the harm as the unilateral imposition of sexual requirements in the context of unequal power and/or the creation of a hostile work environment that enforces sexual shame by reducing members of a specific group to projected sexual stereotypes or objectified fantasies of their sex.[88]

This redefinition of the harm of sexual harassment is meant to secure the equality and reciprocity of sexual agency while addressing sexual coercion and the discriminatory cultural strategies that perpetuate inequality because of sex. By replacing the "unwelcomeness" standard with the concept of "unilateral imposition," Cornell hopes to avoid the danger of reencoding in law the fantasy of the asexual female victim who merits protection as opposed to the evil seductress who does not. She also hopes to render such matters as a woman's sexual history or style of dress irrelevant to any inquiry. The issue is not male desire and whether or not the woman provoked it, but whether the perpetrator acted on his desire in a unilateral way: that is, without reference to the desires or wishes of the target.

Accordingly, the law would address harassing strategies that erase women's equal chance for sexual expression by denigrating their sexuate being.[89] Its purpose would not be to protect women against sex but to diminish the disproportionate weight given to the masculine sexual imaginary at work and in the law.

Thus, like Butler, Cornell rejects the sexual puritanism that informs so much interpretation of sexual harassment law. Unlike Butler, she believes that law, appropriately reinterpreted, can foster women's sexual agency.[90] If legal regulation is poorly framed, the appropriate response is to reframe and reinterpret the law, not to abandon the field to the social powers that be.

Sexual harassment does involve sexualization of a specific sort: the imposition of an abject and subordinate sexualized identity onto women for the purposes of keeping them subordinate.[91] But it is unnecessary to conflate sexual imagination with the male sexual imaginary, or sexual expression in the workplace with harassment, as MacKinnon seems to do, in order to recognize this. As Cornell puts it: "Sexual harassment forces us to confront our deepest cultural myths . . . about how each one of us comes to have a 'sex.'"[92] It must be combated on that terrain.

This redescription of the harm of sexual harassment takes an important step away from the stark antinomy between equality and liberty plaguing legal regulation in this domain. Instead of promoting a repressive environment that denies our existence as sexuate beings and censures even benign sexual expression in the workplace—the chief flaw of MacKinnon's approach—it demands equal protection for a plurality of forms of sexuate being.

Nevertheless, it is one-sided. It leaves the impression that the harm of sexual harassment is the discriminatory denial of sexual freedom to women. Cornell's approach thus mirrors that of Schultz, and is open to a parallel critique. If Schultz's analysis downplays the significance of sexualization of women and nonconforming men in undermining their professional competence, Cornell's (like MacKinnon's, albeit for opposite reasons) tends to disregard the role of nonsexual, discriminatory sexist derogation in maintaining a workplace segregated on the basis of gender norms.

It should be apparent by now that the problem with these attempts to redescribe the harm of sexual harassment is that they are monistic. Each runs the risk of leading courts and employers to overreact to one harm while screening out other motives and modes of sexual harassment. We might do better, as Kathryn Abrams suggests, to pluralize the analysis.

It is true that the desire/subordination model diverts attention from forms of sexual harassment that do not sexualize.[93] But to correct the over-emphasis on sexual coercion by downplaying the dynamics of sexualization is to miss the comparative advantage sexualization provides in casting aspersions on women's competence.[94] Indeed, Abrams fears that rejection of a sexuality-based understanding of harassment may encourage courts to turn away from regulation of sexualized abuse altogether.[95]

A more productive approach would be to sever the subordination model from its essentialist analysis of sexuality (as intrinsically coercive) and to link it to a theory of "partial agency."[96] Women's sexuality is neither totally constructed by male desire nor a repressed imaginary waiting to burst free once legally sanctioned controls are lifted. Although shaped by social constructions, women are neither fully silenced nor fully defined by male power. They can exercise partial agency in challenging male norms, in redefining femininity and their own sexuality and identities.

Accordingly, sexual harassment should be seen as a strategy to perpetuate male control *and* to entrench masculine norms and a masculinist cultural imaginary in the workplace.[97] It takes sexualizing as well as nonsexual forms. The weight of each varies from case to case. They all must be considered in hostile environment claims.[98]

This approach allows for a richer understanding of the role of law in the construction of "the subject before the law." With few exceptions, the theorists discussed above along with many legal professionals construe the subject before the law either as wholly autonomous or wholly dependent. They thus mirror the dichotomizing tendency in the legal system that pairs autonomous subjectivity with legally unconstrained action on the one hand, and subordinated or impaired subjectivity with legally regulated action on the other.[99] This reproduces the traditional liberal contrast between autonomous self-directing legal subjects and wards of the state: a category of subjects before the law who lack the capacity for self-direction.

In the case of harassment law, such assumptions dichotomize women's agency by ascribing powerlessness to exonerated "good" victims of sexualized injury (those who conform to traditional gender roles) and full agency culpably exercised to sanctioned, nonconforming women (those who are sexually active or live unconventional lives).[100] The policing function at work here is obvious: one has to comport with the image of the proper victim as the price of legal protection.

Abrams's alternative is to view law as multifaceted: at times prohibitive, at times constructive of normalizing gender stereotypes, at times a vehicle for communicating the partial agency of the legal subject. A great deal hinges on how the subject before the law is construed by legal concepts and interpretation. The ascription of partial agency to the legal subject construes the aim of legal regulation as prevention of discrimination instead of compensating for an allegedly inherent weakness in the harassment victim. Legal relief would not be denied those who demonstrate agency or responsibility.[101] What is needed, in short, is a new conceptualization of legal subjectivity that does not ascribe incapacity in order to justify legal intervention and recovery.

Abrams is certainly on the right track here. Her redescription of the harms of sexual harassment and the agency (sexual and otherwise) of the harassed party is clearly meant to block overregulation of benign sexual expression as well as legal intrusion into the privacy and autonomy of mutually desired intimate relationships. It is also meant to remedy underregulation of harassment.

Nevertheless, even this superb redescription of the harms of sexual harassment will not on its own block the dichotomizing tendency in law. Abrams herself has noted that complex feminist analyses tend to be reduced to one-sided simplistic positions once they enter the legal system.[102] Yet neither she nor the other theorists discussed above analyze the dynamics of legal regulation from the perspective of the effects of particular legal forms on the relevant domain of action. I contend that there are such effects and that they are operative irrespective of which standard is used to understand the harms at issue. There is no dichotomizing tendency inherent in law as such: rather, this has to be attributed to the paradigmatic assumptions informing legal regulation and the specific forms it takes. It is thus necessary to pay attention not only to the appropriate understanding of the harms of harassment but also to the modes of legal regulation. Unless one shifts to this perspective, the tendency to overregulate or underregulate, to reduce the subject before the law to a dependent victim or a fully autonomous agent not in need of protection, and to turn the tension between equality and liberty into an antinomy will remain in force.

LEGAL PARADIGMS: AN EXPLANATION AND A WAY OUT?

It is my thesis that key dilemmas in harassment law are dictated in large part by anachronistic or inappropriately applied paradigmatic conceptions of law. This problematic drives the various arguments into antinomic configurations and turns even the best intentions into "regulatory paradoxes."[103] Let us thus take a closer look at the form of harassment law, at the paradigmatic assumptions on which it rests, and at the mechanisms and incentives it puts in place.

Behind the apparent clash of values (liberty versus equality) in the debates over appropriate legal responses to sexual harassment is a deep disagreement over the source of threats to liberty and equality and of the role of the state in relation to these. As I indicated in the introduction, two dominant legal paradigms are at play here—the liberal and the welfare model. A paradigm of law is not a scientific theory or a legal doctrine—it is an integrated set of cognitive and normative background assumptions about the relationship the law should establish between the state and society, and the form legal regulation must take.[104] It can harden into ideology if it is closed off from new interpretations of rights and principles.[105]

This is now the case with the two legal paradigms that inform the dominant discourses regarding sexual harassment law. As we have seen, for the sake of protecting personal privacy, expressive liberty, or the pursuit of happiness, strong arguments against the regulation of sexual expression in the workplace have been made by liberal, liberal feminist, and postmodern feminist theorists. Reasoning on the basis of the liberal paradigm of law, they locate the threat to liberty in the state and in regulation generally.

Accordingly, the state should limit itself to guaranteeing the negative liberty of each to pursue their particular conception of the good. The latter should be restricted by prohibitions or commands as little as possible.[106] On the liberal paradigm, law must be formal, rule bound, general, and concise—limited to the function of defining the abstract spheres of action (liberties) for the autonomous pursuit of personal interests. It is assumed that legal formality will ensure impartiality in the administration of justice.

None of the feminist theorists I have discussed buy into classic versions of the public/private dichotomy or simplistic views about legal neutrality. When confronted with what they take to be the stark choice between the direct regulation or nonregulation of sexuality, however, many opt for the latter. Despite their sophisticated understandings of discursive power, of the socially constructed background conditions of autonomy and conceptions of the good, and of the non-natural and inegalitarian character of the social order that the state sometimes secures through protecting negative liberty, they tend to revert to the paradigmatically liberal conception of law when it comes to sexual harassment.

The welfare paradigm of law challenges two core premises of the liberal model: that imbalances in social power can be neutralized without state help and that the universal right to equal individual liberties could be guaranteed through the juridical status of the legal subject and the formality of the law.

On the welfare paradigm, positive state action is needed to counter injustice due to inequalities of power and status between social groups. The model of society/state relations informing the liberal paradigm is misleading, for the state is always already there intervening in society even when it decides not to. There is no social domain sealed off from state action, no intelligible meaning to the idea of state inaction.[107] Accordingly for feminist theorists involved with this paradigm, the goal is to persuade the state to intervene in favor of the relatively powerless gender.[108]

Juridification in this model is directly regulatory and interventionist. Law is substantive, particularized, and goal-directed. Unlike formal law, it does not take prior distributions of power, status, or wealth as given or leave it to social actors to try to alter them on their own. Rather, substantive legal regulation means to equalize, and it does so by dictating outcomes. This mode of juridification wields a heavy hand. It is intrusive, substantive, authoritative, and meant to be so.

In both of these paradigms, privacy and equality, liberty and state action, formal and substantive law are in an antinomic relationship.[109] Defenders of the first seem unconcerned by the role of private power in producing inequality. Partisans of the second seem equally blind to the effects of substantive intervention on agency or privacy. Even theorists who are aware of the characteristic dilemmas of nonregulation and overregulation shift back and forth between these paradigms as if there were no other alternative. The development of a third, reflexive legal paradigm allows us to reframe and perhaps resolve some of these tensions.[110] Like the others, this paradigm entails a specific type of law—reflexive law—involving the application of procedures to procedures (reflexivity). Reflexive law can stimulate the establishment or transformation of institutionalized procedures of conflict resolution by creating various incentives and meta-procedures of oversight and indirect controls.

This form of law aims to foster responsible self-regulation within social institutions. It thus supports social autonomy. But unlike formal law on the liberal paradigm, it does not simply adapt to prior distributions or posit natural liberty. Instead, it aims to create regulated autonomy (generating new "subject positions"), by institutionalizing procedures in which the bargaining power, voice, and standing of the interacting parties is equalized. Provided that certain procedural norms and principles of justice are respected, social actors can strike whatever substantive agreements they wish. An example is the law regulating collective bargaining through the mediation of the NLRB in labor disputes.[111]

The reflexive paradigm assumes a differentiated model of the social structure; it rejects the fusion thesis of state and society presupposed by the welfare paradigm. But it also abandons the idea of naturally private spheres of life immune to state regulation informing the liberal paradigm. Instead, it is assumed that the differentiated subsystems of the social structure enter into relationship with each other and it is an important desiderata that state regulation respect the requirements and integrity of each sphere.[112]

Accordingly, unlike substantive law in the welfare paradigm, reflexive law does not dictate outcomes. The state regulates in this paradigm, but indirectly. The idea is to provide legal incentives for self-regulation that will lead social actors to comply with general legislative goals, norms, and constitutional principles. This is thus quite distinct from the privatization of regulatory functions: it entails the regulation of self-regulation.

The reflexive paradigm thus makes it possible to avoid some of the regulatory paradoxes plaguing substantive intervention under the welfare model.[113] Many of these are traceable to heavy-handed, detailed, substantive rules regulating social life articulated either in legislative statutes, administrative rules, or legal interpretation of these by the courts. The appropriate response to regulatory paradoxes, however, is not to abandon regulation and return to laissez-faire (the liberal paradigm), but to learn from past failures.[114] Regulation should be reformed so as to achieve salutory egalitarian purposes by institutionalizing appropriate incentives, norms, and guidelines while incorporating flexibility and respect for the autonomy and initiative of social actors.[115] This is just what reflexive law does. This mode of legal regulation "squares the circle" by providing protection for autonomy while fostering responsible and fair self-regulation. Regulating self-regulation to ensure that it is guided by the principles of justice can avoid the dilemmas plaguing the other two legal paradigms.

Reflexive law, however, is not a panacea. It too can generate regulatory paradoxes when inadequately institutionalized on the normative or instrumental level. This is precisely the problem with contemporary sexual harassment law.

The juridification of sexual harassment in the United States today is a prime if flawed example of the use of the reflexive form of law to regulate intimacy in the workplace. Neither Congress nor the Court has imposed a set of substantive regulations onto employers. Yet it is not left to employers to choose, in an unconstrained way, whether and how they will address the issue. Instead, harassment law has a reflexive regulatory structure that deploys a complex set of incentives, meta-procedures, norms, and principles meant to spur and inform employer self-regulation.

Title VII established two tracks for dealing with sexual harassment: a conciliation process mediated by the EEOC, and a private cause of action under which the harassed could obtain damages should the conciliation process fails. In order to pursue a claim of sexual harassment, an employee must first file a complaint with the EEOC.[116] If the EEOC finds the charge to have merit, it will attempt to persuade the employer to eliminate the offending practice through "informal methods of conference, conciliation and persuasion." After thirty days, if the issue remains unresolved, the harassment victim may then bring suit in federal court.[117]

To facilitate effective prevention, the EEOC has periodically issued guidelines defining the harm and suggesting appropriate procedures and grievance mechanisms for employers to adopt. Yet these guidelines do not have the force of law. Nor does the EEOC have any adjudicative power. Title VII is primarily enforced in civil suits (or the threat of suits) brought against employers. The meta-procedures established for dealing with sexual harassment were designed to protect the interests of employers charged with harassment as well as the interest of the complainant in remedying the harms of discriminatory behavior. It was assumed that by limiting the EEOC to conciliation and channeling suits to the federal court system, employers and their accusers would be placed on a level and neutral playing field.[118]

Congress has amended the act several times to ensure impartiality. In 1972 it granted the EEOC power to bring suit on behalf of aggrieved persons after it became apparent that employers ignored the conciliation process, relying on the assumption that accusers would fail to litigate their claims independently.[119] The 1991 Civil Rights Act providing for compensatory and punitive damages attempted to further redress the imbalance between accuser and accused. The statute clearly aims to spur employers to deter harassment. So do the 1998 Supreme Court rulings specifying the bases for employer liability. According to the Court, the primary objective of Title VII is to encourage employers to create anti-harassment policies and effective grievance procedures, partly linking the defense to liability to such preventive and conciliatory mechanisms.[120] Title VII's deterrent purpose is designed to lessen the need to litigate, not to ensure that harassment victims win suits.

The Court and Congress thus remain committed to the reflexive thrust of Title VII. Employers are urged to "take all steps necessary to prevent sexual harassment from occurring," or suffer the consequences: costly civil suits.[121] After all, the duty not to harass is a matter of federal civil rights law and constitutional principle. What is at stake are political relationships—group-based inequality and injustices (discrimination)—not personal individual torts or crimes. Legal development in this area has thus been guided by the effort to foster equality, and fairness by encouraging the promulgation and consistent enforcement of reasonable rules and fair procedures that minimize the need to resort to costly litigation. The reflexive legal form is meant to ensure the equal protection of the laws to everyone and to protect civil rights.

Yet many sexual harassment policies fail miserably to reach this standard. As already indicated, the incentives put in place by the reflexive form of law in this area have led to highly repressive and intrusive corporate regulations, many of which reinforce the gender stereotypes and discriminatory attitudes they are meant to undermine. They thus generate regulatory paradoxes. Why? The problem cannot be located at the level of the choice between regulating and not regulating (the wrong paradigmatic approach). Reflexive law is the way to go in this area. Rather, it is a matter of the inadequate normative and instrumental institutionalization of the type of reflexive, postregulatory regulation that has been established.

Kingsley Browne is right: in order to avoid costly lawsuits and damage awards, the rational employer has a strong incentive to play it safe and overregulate employee speech and intimate association. There is also a strong incentive to simply fire an accused harasser instead of investing resources in investigating claims or providing hearings.[122] After all, the employer's interest is not in the expressive, privacy, or associational liberties of employees but in keeping costs down.

Unfortunately, it is also true that under existing law, the employer confronts no effective counterbalancing pressure to limit overregulation or arbitrary punishment. There are two reasons for this: the assumption that the Constitution covers only relations between the individual and the state, and the background rules governing employer prerogatives in most private-sector and many public-sector workplaces.

As regards the first, it is assumed that where there is no "state action"— in the private sector—constitutional protection of speech, due process, or personal privacy do not apply. Ironically under these conditions, reflexive law can trigger controls as intrusive and even more arbitrary than direct state regulation, which is at least bound by the Constitution.

Yet congressional legislation and Supreme Court rulings have effectively charged employers with regulating the speech of their employees, thereby turning the employer into the state's agent. Some have argued that this amounts to indirect state action.[123] There thus may be grounds for invoking some constitutional controls on such state-induced regulation. Indirect state action does not transform the private workplace into a branch of the state. Regulation through reflexive law does imply, however, that there are important public purposes carried out in the workplace, suggesting the need to reconsider its status as simply private. A thorough analysis of the workplace as a special kind of institution is needed before one can make the case that it can generate constitutional arguments for and not only against speech.[124] This is not the place for such an analysis. I simply want to point to a line of inquiry.

Nevertheless, a quick look at the background rules governing the workplace will clarify some of the other regulatory paradoxes plaguing harassment law. The key background rule for our purposes is the doctrine of employment "at will." This doctrine permits most private employers to terminate the employment contract and to discipline employees for any reason at any time.[125] If the workplace is not unionized or covered by civil service law, then there are very few legal protections for the average employee against punishment or being fired. In such a context, the employer cannot lose by taking action against an at-will employee accused of harassment. Nor are harassed employees protected against retaliation by supervisors or from the chilling effect on their own speech that is inherent in fear of reprisals for complaints they lodge. The employee who believes s/he was unjustly retaliated against, penalized, fired, or silenced, either for making a harassment complaint or for alleged harassment, has no realistic legal recourse or effective remedies.

Under these conditions, the tendency to overreact to harassment complaints and the tendency to suppress them do not offset each other.[126] Arbitrariness of enforcement is the greatest danger here. Nothing prevents management from inconsistently applying its disciplinary powers by aggressively pursuing complaints against relatively powerless or troublesome workers and by ignoring complaints directed against high level supervisors or favored employees, as Cynthia Estlund argued: "In an at-will environment, the fate of both the accused and the accuser is largely in the hands of the employer who may be moved by whim, sexism, favoritism, fear of litigation, or a rational assessment of the costs and benefits of various responses."[127]

The lop-sided incentives in hostile environment harassment law that penalize only the failure to regulate and not overzealous or arbitrary regulation thus leaves at-will employees extremely vulnerable. This is the level on which to refine the incentives established by the reflexive structure of the law. Accordingly, I argue that corporate regulation in this domain can and should be better regulated—by appropriately tailored, fair procedural norms informed by an adequate understanding of the harms involved.[128]

I am not in a position to determine whether a narrowly construed First Amendment protection of workplace speech, aimed at counterbalancing Title VII's incentive to censor, is possible in current constitutional doctrine.[129] But it should not be so difficult to imagine a statutory reform of Title VII that institutionalizes procedures constraining employer discretion that are fair to both accuser and accused. Important procedural protection already exist in just-cause systems for unionized workers and government employees.[130] Perhaps similar protection could be afforded to at-will employees when they are accused of harassment.

According to one proposal, Congress should require all employers to develop and publish grievance procedures for the prompt and fair resolution of sexual harassment complaints and to abide by these in resolving all claims.[131] It could make this requirement in general terms articulating the guiding principles and overall structure that every grievance procedure must include to be considered fair. This should include investigation into the charges and an opportunity for alleged victims and alleged harassers to tell their sides of the story without fear of reprisals. EEOC guidelines should state that simply firing an alleged harasser will not insulate employers from liability. They could also indicate appropriate penalties such as mandatory counseling, formal reprimands, and suspension for recidivists. Such reforms would foster learning, communication, and cooperative solutions.[132] They could serve as a counterincentive to overregulation, if backed up by a cause of action should these procedures not be respected.

Generalized procedural requirements and norms of fairness ensure that employers harmonize their regulatory practices with the public purposes articulated by Title VII. The role of the courts should be to encourage enterprises to develop fora for discussion and collective problem-solving, and to give contextualized meaning to the abstract principles of nondiscrimination and nonharassment. Courts could foster learning across organizations about effective ways to deal with sexual harassment. They could, moreover, lead employers to apply rules more consistently to employees.[133] This would protect against both the suppression of harassment complaints (underregulation) and the inconsistent pursuit of such complaints against relatively powerless co-workers.

Changes in the rules of evidence governing the process of discovery in civil suits should also be made to rule out as irrelevant any inquiry into people's consensual, wanted intimacies on the job or elsewhere.[134] Such a change would go a long way in protecting the privacies of life without blocking needed inquiry into patterns of harassment.

CONCLUSION

The reflexive structure of harassment law under Title VII, involving federally established incentives to employer self-regulation, conciliation procedures, and a private cause of action, should certainly be retained. But the one-sided incentives toward overregulation and arbitrariness in enforcement should be counterbalanced by statutory reforms that rectify the dearth of procedural protection for at-will employees and reduce the impulse to censure and monitor nondiscriminatory sexual expression and wanted intimate associations. Better regulation of self-regulation is needed.

It is crucial that such changes be informed by an appropriate feminist understanding of the harms and effects of sexual harassment, along the lines suggested by Abrams. Group-based discrimination backed up by deeply entrenched cultural norms about gender, and not simply the individualized abuse of hierarchical power or an individual dignity harm, is the issue here.

Harassment law assumes that preferences are not static. It operates through incentives geared toward the rational actor (the employer), but its deeper goal is cultural and normative change: the elimination of gender bias in employment opportunity and in the attribution of sexual agency. Women are now in the paid workplace for good and it has become a key locale where people meet, date, and establish intimate relationships. It is absurd to try to banish or repress such interaction. Instead, Title VII should foster a learning process that leads to reciprocity, and to the recognition of the agency (sexual and other), competence, voice, moral and civic equality, and integrity of all workers. Only a nuanced redescription of the harm of harassment and the development of an appropriately reformed set of incentives and meta-norms that protect all parties fairly can avoid the regulatory paradoxes (normative backlash, over- and underregulation, invasion of privacy) I have described here. After all, the target is not sex but sexism.

CHAPTER FOUR

The Debate over the Reflexive Paradigm

◆ As indicated in the preceding chapters, I am convinced that the paradigm framework can shed a great deal of light on the dilemmas of regulating intimacy in the contemporary epoch. Many of the negative consequences and regulatory paradoxes in this domain stem from use of the wrong paradigmatic approach by courts and lawmakers. Moreover, the pluralization of the contexts and forms of intimate association and the explosion of issues requiring legal attention (ranging from contraception, abortion, surrogacy, genetic engineering, homosexuality, and nonmarital intimacy of all sorts to divorce, marital rape, and sexual harassment) have created the need for a differentiated approach to regulatory strategies. Unless serious thought is given to legal forms, the effects of regulatory choices, and the core assumptions guiding lawmakers and courts, even the best-intentioned normative discussions and political resolutions will have ambiguous or negative consequences.

I believe that the reflexive paradigm provides the most appropriate perspective for dealing with such issues. This paradigm presupposes the decentered character of contemporary society and a nuanced relationship between the state and civil institutions. It enables one to acknowledge contextual differences and ethical multiplicity in modes of intimacy, as well as the plurality of possible legal approaches. It thus allows for a reflective choice among forms of regulation and an intelligent combination among these.

We are already in the world of legal pluralism when it comes to law and intimate relationships, as even a casual perusal of the types of regulations in this domain will reveal. But theoretical clarity regarding the issues and range of choices is lacking, as is an adequate reflective awareness of the overarching paradigmatic framework with which multiplicity, plurality, and alternatives should be approached. That is why the regulation of intimacy under the new cultural and social circumstances of contemporary society seems to create intractable dilemmas. Anachronistic or ad hoc regulatory responses too often substitute for reasoned reflection regarding the underlying assumptions and effects of legal intervention in the shifting and increasingly uncharted domain of intimacy. But recognition of social and legal pluralism should not and need not entail normative or conceptual incoherence. I argue that a new paradigmatic approach involving reflexive law offers a systematic way to reframe and even resolve many of the old dichotomies and regulatory paradoxes.

As I indicated in the Introduction, however, the reflexive paradigm has itself become the target of criticism. Three charges have been raised against it: first, that reflexive law is simply a new form of privatization and/or neocorporatism involving the delegation of authority and decision making to ultimately irresponsible powers; second, that this paradigm undermines either the rule of law or democracy or both; and third, that the general theory of legal paradigms is unconvincing, because it rests on an untenable evolutionism.[1]

In this chapter I consider these charges. In order to do so I discuss the strengths and weaknesses of four attempts to develop a new legal paradigm. I argue that the reflexive form of law is a useful type of regulation in certain circumstances. However, as we have seen, a great deal depends upon how it is institutionalized. But I also argue that it is necessary to shift over to a cogent version of the reflexive legal paradigm, for this provides a perspective that allows one to reframe choices and alternatives and resolve regulatory dilemmas in the domain of intimacy. I begin by presenting the four main conceptions of the paradigm: the systems-theoretical approach; the action-theoretical approach; the sociological reflexivity model; and the theory of "responsive law." I then address the most important charges leveled against this paradigm and conclude with a summary of my own conception.

The search for a new paradigm of law was triggered by a growing awareness of the regulatory paradoxes inherent in the centralized, directly interventionist approach to steering typical of the welfare state. The welfare paradigm deploys a particular form of law: substantive, purposive, goal-oriented, and implemented through regulations, standards, and rules. This materialized law aims at achieving specific goals in concrete situations. In part it seeks to secure the equal worth of liberty (substantive in addition to formal equality) or real freedom for all. Rematerialized law revives status in order to target differences in power and resources that undermine equal liberty and social justice. The type of legal regulation it uses is thus more particularistic than classic formal law, yet often involves vague and open-ended directives. Therein lies the problem.

From the systems-theoretical perspective, the main flaw with this mode of regulation is that it leads to negative externalities and overall ungovernability.[2] From the action-theoretical perspective, the problem is that it undermines instead of fostering the liberty it seeks to equalize because it increases arbitrariness and paternalism.[3] From both perspectives, responsibility and autonomy of the regulated are threatened, although these terms have rather different meanings in the two approaches. The solution is not, however, to return to formal law cum private ordering associated with the liberal paradigm but to shift over to a new paradigmatic approach.

THE SYSTEMS-THEORETICAL MODEL OF REFLEXIVE LAW

As Gunther Teubner has argued, following Luhmann, the welfare-state model of substantive law often appears ineffective and even harmful because it assumes the impossible task of steering society from a single control center: the polity.[4] This approach derives from a misleading and anachronistic conception of state/society relations: the presumed constitutive omnipresence and omnicompetence of the political. Indeed, it operates with a "rather primitive" model of linear causality guiding purposive legal action: "Legislative goals are thought to lead to the selection of a legal program which in turn changes social behavior so as to realize the desired goals."[5] Societal institutions are construed as directly amenable to administrative channeling. Personal preferences are deemed open to molding by "environmental" incentives or disincentives.

This model is misleading because of its failure to acknowledge the specificity and internal requirements (self-referentiality) of the differentiated spheres of society. It is anachronistic because contemporary society is decentered: composed of differentiated subsystems (e.g., economy, science, politics, law) with such high degrees of internal complexity that none of them could evolve the requisite control capacity for steering the others or coordinating them coherently and compatibly.[6] Welfare state law lacks the requisite social engineering capacities to steer development in highly evolved, functionally differentiated modern societies.

Moreover, remoralized, repoliticized law would destroy the specific juridical rationality of the legal system (its own self-referentiality) without replacing it, as Weber and then Luhmann pointed out long ago.[7] Such a legal response would increase rather than mitigate the proliferation of negative externalities among subsystems. Since centralized political/legal regulators lack the requisite knowledge of the respective subsystem they target (be it the economy, scientific research, or intimate association), efforts to maximize the rationality or fairness of a subsystem through goal-oriented directives inevitably have unintended consequences that often create insoluble problems in the other subsystems. Substantive legal directives cannot anticipate or control for all possible damaging side effects.[8] The problem is how to rationalize the interplay between already differentiated and rationalized subsystems.[9]

It is not necessary to reproduce the arcane language of systems theory or to buy into the thesis of self-referentially closed, autopoietic subsystems, to grasp the main point in this argument. Teubner maintains that compensatory state intervention targeting undesirable side effects of modernization is ineffective and tends to shift legal doctrine from juridical conflict resolution to more of a legal policy orientation, turning law into a form of social technology for which it is poorly suited.[10] Indeed, this regulatory strategy inevitably ends in a trilemma: it leads either to "incongruence" of law and society or to the "over-legalization" of society or the "over-socialization of law."[11] In the first case, the regulated system reacts by not reacting because the regulation does not comport with the internal logic or relevance criteria of the regulated system. It is, in short, ineffective. In the second case, the regulations are influential but negatively so: they have disintegrative effects on internal interactions within the regulated field. This occurs when the regulatory programs obey a functional logic or follow criteria of rationality that are poorly suited to the internal social structure of the relevant sphere of life. Many of the problems of legal regulation of intimacy fall into this category. In the third case, regulatory failure involves threats not to the reproduction of the targeted subsystem but to the autonomy of law itself. The instrumentalization of law for policy purposes can involve its surrender to the regulated field, threatening its own self-production. Law becomes overpoliticized, overmoralized, overpsychologized, overtechnicized, and so on. Law risks losing its general or universalist character either by directly delegating legal and regulatory functions to private instances or by serving particularistic purposes.

In all these cases, regulatory failure can be attributed to the lack of respect for the autonomy and internal logics of the regulated subsystem. But centralized legal/political control does not only lead to dedifferentiation; it also undermines responsible decision making. Indeed, as Ulrich Beck has pointed out, if the state poses as the center of coordination it thereby assumes responsibility for the negative externalities of decisions that have actually been made elsewhere. Instead of fostering responsibility within each subsystem for the consequences of its own actions, law takes on tasks (anticipating and warding off risks) and responsibilities with which it cannot cope.[12]

It is worth reemphasizing that this critique of the welfare model of regulation is not a neoliberal plea for deregulation. Teubner argues that although strategies of reformalization would increase subsystem autonomy, deregulation and/or reprivatization (shift over to private ordering) would not resolve the problem of negative externalities.[13] Although it is true that formal law did facilitate social autonomy, its means of doing so—withdrawal from regulatory functions and retreat to sheer formality—can no longer cope with the problems generated by the autopoietic structure of social subsystems.[14] The task at hand is far too complex for such a simple solution. Indeed, juridification has three desiderata: to integrate environmental demands into the system (fostering responsibility) without undermining its conditions of self-production and reproduction and without undermining autonomy.

It is Teubner's thesis that reflexive/procedural law can accomplish these tasks. The way to counteract the negative externalities of specific institutional practices and combat the self-closure and irresponsibility of subsystems vis-à-vis their environment is to foster forms of reflection within them. This can occur through the regulation of self-regulation. Reflexive law does this by applying procedures to procedures (reflexivity): by establishing the structural premises for future decisions within the subsystems in terms of norms of procedure, organization, membership, and competencies that can make overall processes of decision making sensitive to side effects and externalities and change the weights of different parties and members.[15] Indirect and self-limiting, reflexive regulatory law respects the autonomy of the regulated subsystem while prodding it in the direction of social purposes (responsibility).[16] Restricted to stimulating appropriate forms of self-regulation, reflexive law thus preserves its own autonomy as well: "Law's role is to decide about decisions, regulate regulations. . . . Law realizes its own reflexive orientation insofar as it provides the structural premises for reflexive processes in other social subsystems."[17]

Regulation of self-regulation is necessary because the tendency toward self-closure renders subsystems insensitive to their own externalities regardless of how internally rational they are. Deregulation is thus the wrong approach. The purpose of regulated self-regulation is to foster internal reflection: to force the organization to internalize outside conflicts in its own decision structure, so as to become socially sensitive to the effects of attempts to maximize internal rationality, and to develop effective internal control structures.[18] In other words, external stimulation of internal self-regulating processes, which, in principle, cannot be controlled from the outside, is required.

The main mechanism for creating sensitivity to externalities is the establishment of discursive structures within the subsystems, according to Teubner.[19] But the purpose of this form of "democratization" is, from the system-theoretical point of view, neither the increase of participation nor the neutralization of power structures; it is, rather, to make possible the internal reflexion of external implications of future actions. Although there is some confusion about the difference in meaning between the terms *reflection* and *reflexivity*, it seems to be the case that Teubner sees postregulatory regulation as reflexive insofar as it applies procedures to procedures of self-regulation. Reflexive law tends to rely on procedural norms regulating processes, organization, and the distribution of rights and competencies. It fosters "reflection" (systemic self-consciousness) internally by the establishment of discursive structures that allow for communication and bargaining within each particular subsystem between various actors conscious of potential external effects of decisions. Reflexive law thus is a new legal form that solves the problem of governability.

Teubner uses the example of contract law to make his point. Under formal law, the only issue to resolve regarding disputed contracts is whether certain general and objective conditions were met: the absence of force or fraud, the meeting of minds. Formal law is indifferent to outcomes. By contrast, substantive regulation of contracts would involve the direct intervention of legislatures and courts in setting and altering contract terms to achieve a desired goal. Alternatively, reflexive legal regulation would attempt to subject contracting parties to mechanisms of public responsibility designed to ensure that bargaining processes take account of various externalities (reflection) while also equalizing bargaining power. Thus the law regulating collective bargaining, or co-determination practices, is reflexive: it applies procedures (stipulated by law) to procedures of conflict resolution and internal decision making. Yet Teubner is careful to note that the reduction of power discrepancies or inequalities is no more the point of reflexive law than is increased participation in decision making. Such normative concerns are studiously avoided by the systems-theoretical approach. When unavoidable (as in the goal of averting negative externalities), they are translated into systems-theoretical language.

Indeed, Teubner maintains that one can no longer hope for universal legitimation structures, for a generally applicable morality of discourse or even for a common procedure of reflexion in complex differentiated societies. He insists that reflexion processes have to differ according to the specific internal logic of the regulated subsystem. What is appropriate to the economy may differ from the forms of reflexion that suit, for example, the educational system.[20]

To be sure. As Andrew Arato and I pointed out in 1992, however, the relentless anti-normativism of this approach prevents Teubner from showing how and why internal discursive structures institutionalized in the various subsystems would actually be sensitive to environmental problems (broader societal concerns) or lead to the creation of procedures of decision and conflict resolution compatible with universal norms.[21] It is unclear why sheer reflexivity and increased subsystem autonomy would have normatively desirable consequences. If discursive structures within each subsystem speak only the language of that subsystem, as the idea of self-reference implies, neither reflection, self-reflection (self-consciousness of the subsystem's own logic and place in the environment), nor reflexivity (application of its own types of procedures and assumptions to itself) would automatically foster more social responsibility. Moreover, since nothing coordinates the internal structures of receptivity (discourses) triggered by reflexive law with general norms or societal goals, or with other subsystems, proceduralism gets reduced to particularistic subsystem reflexion. It thus cannot produce universalist, democratic legitimacy. According to Teubner, there is no superior coordination regime in contemporary decentered societies. There is only external pressure, irritation, and, in response to this, internal reflection that takes the form of translation. For example, law affects other subsystems as an external irritation that causes a response in the shape of a translation of legal requirements into the subsystem's own language. Translation is thus necessarily mistranslation: hence the creation of a new meaning. For example, legal rules get translated into cost factors in economic discourse, into power positions in political discourse, and so on. One can tell only after such translation has occurred whether it has led to a productive or a negative misunderstanding: one leading to disintegrative or other destructive consequences. The means by which subsystems influence one another are thus not through the articulation of universal principles in law or through external superior coordination mechanisms (administration/politics) but rather through collision, translation, productive, or dysfunctional misunderstanding.[22]

Accordingly, the theory of reflexive law has been subject to a range of criticisms. On the one hand, as already indicated, it has been attacked for its democratic deficit, in particular for its lack of universalism and hence of democratic legitimacy. Some have pointed to its strong neocorporatist orientation, while still others see it as a new and dangerous form of privatization.

It has also been criticized for further undermining the rule of law (legal formality) and hence for fostering arbitrariness, insofar as reflexive law seems to rely on vague indeterminate standards. On the other hand, the Teubner model has been taken to task for relying on an untenable evolutionism that masks the negative uses to which reflexive law can and is being put. From this perspective, reflexive law can turn into a new and penetrating form of juridical normalization—providing the illusion of autonomy while enforcing conformity via subtle, almost imperceptible forms of regulation. These criticisms are serious but if appropriately reframed, the idea of reflexive law and of a reflexive legal paradigm can be defended.

THE ACTION-THEORETICAL APPROACH: A PROCEDURAL PARADIGM

Habermas's recent discussion of legal paradigms can be seen as one such effort at reformulation. Proceeding from a frankly normative perspective, Habermas's theory of procedural law aims at solving the legitimation problems inherent in the welfare paradigm and left unresolved in the systems-theoretical approach to reflexive law.[23] His concern is not primarily with steering problems, issues of ungovernability, or negative externalities threatening system-integration, although he certainly is aware of these.[24] Instead, reasoning from an action-theoretical perspective, Habermas recently argued that the welfare paradigm of law poses two distinct threats: it undermines individual autonomy and harms the integrity of communicative structures necessary for reproduction and social integration of the life-world.[25] Consequently, democratic legitimacy is also at risk.

To be sure, this is not the first time he addressed the issue. In an earlier critique of welfare state juridification based on the distinction between law as institution and law as medium, Habermas focused primarily on the threat to horizontal solidarity and communication (colonization) posed by substantive legal regulation.[26] When juridification entails bureaucratic implementation in areas of life that are not formally organized, like families, this threat is particularly grave.[27] In such a context, law functions as a reifying steering medium. It substitutes nonlinguistic forms of action-coordination (administrative criteria) for natural language communications.[28] Juridification of this type is thus not only dysfunctional for social integration (prong 2 of the regulatory trilemma, i.e., the overlegalization of society); it also threatens personal autonomy.

Accordingly, in his first writings on the subject, Habermas focused on a form of postregulatory regulation that would restrict law to establishing an "external framework" (an external constitution) in sensitive areas like family or education. This framework would provide incentives to individuals to communicatively coordinate their interactions on their own, in fair and just ways, in light of the purposes of the institution in which they were operating.[29] The restriction of procedural law to "external constitution" via the institutionalization of procedures for discursive conflict resolution within certain life-world domains was primarily geared toward protecting the autonomy and integrity of communicative interaction within them. It did not, however, address the problem of rationality crises, or acknowledge the more general character of the regulatory trilemmas that arises with regard to all the social subsystems. Nor did this approach offer an adequate solution to the problem of inequity within or unfairness across regulated domains.

Habermas has abandoned this analytic approach for a variety of reasons. Yet in his more recent and more systematic discussion of legal paradigms he continues to pursue the project of a "reflective continuation of the welfare state," even if his critique seems to some to be less radical than in the past. This time, however, the main focus is on parrying the threats to private *and* public autonomy inherent in both the welfare and liberal paradigms, respectively. The negative "dialectic of legal and factual equality" that appears intractable from the perspective of both orientations cannot be avoided unless one sees that the normative key is autonomy: "In a legal community, *no one* is free as long as the freedom of one person must be purchased with another's oppression. The distribution of compensations only follows from an equal distribution of rights, which in turn results from the mutuality of recognizing all as free and equal members."[30]

Autonomy, from the action-theoretical perspective, thus cannot be interpreted as freedom from external steering or subsystemic integrity. Nor can it be construed as the unfettered exercise of choice (the liberal paradigmatic model) secured by noninterference, or assimilated to well-being (the welfare approach). The distributive aspect of equal liberty and equal treatment—the just distribution of benefits—is the result of universalist realizations of the system of rights. But, and this is crucial to Habermas's interpretation of the procedural paradigm, the latter is not possible unless public as well as private autonomy—public participation in the practice of interpreting, legislating, and exercising rights—is guaranteed.[31] Autonomy on this approach accordingly means freedom from oppression plus voice: having a say in fashioning the rules according to which one lives together with others. The two are linked because the ways in which oppression is enacted and experienced even in the private intimate domain must be publicly articulated by those affected in order to properly perceive and protect against it. Inversely, the threat to autonomy and the clash between liberty and equality in the system of rights can be avoided only if the realization of the system of rights involves public autonomy—democratic input. Democratic legitimacy, in other words, is not only intrinsically important, it is also the only way to prevent legal regulation from becoming paternalistic and normalizing.

On Habermas's understanding of the procedural legal paradigm, the key mechanism for accomplishing this is reflection. Like Teubner, he understands this paradigm to involve procedural rather than substantive regulations. However, "procedural" for Habermas does not refer to a type of law, but to the input side of lawmaking. In particular, it refers to the quality of the processes of democratic lawmaking and of the discursive interaction (voice) among the citizenry and lawmakers. Procedures are to provide for voice, for participation, for influence of the citizenry on legislation and on the formulation of the norms guiding regulation, hence providing democratic legitimacy.

Moreover, although he often uses the word "reflexivity," Habermas for the most part means reflection in the sense of conscious awareness on the part of those involved and those affected by a particular area of legal regulation. He does also speak of self-reflection (thought applied to thought), which is a form of reflexivity. But in his version of the procedural paradigm of law, the application of procedures to procedures refers to the meta-procedures of discourse ethics being applied to all discursive public spheres to foster fair and reflective participation in the democratic genesis of norms; it does not entail privileging a specific, new form of law.

Indeed, Habermas explicitly rejects such a move.[32] To be sure, he too advocates indirect rather than direct forms of administrative steering. But the point in advocating mild forms of steering (together with democratic procedures to decide on the normative direction of regulation) is to bring administrative, regulative power under control by linking it to communicative power. Neither context-sensitivity on the part of regulators, nor self-limited regulations fostering reflection of environmental consequences in decision-making processes typical of the reflexive form of law as conceived by Teubner, can yield the requisite democratic legitimacy.[33] Only society-wide public discourses through which communicative power is generated and which then influence legislation via the official circulation of power can yield the appropriate general norms and principles to guide regulation in whatever form.

The process of reflection Habermas has in mind presupposes the co-originality of citizens' private and public autonomy and aims at securing these simultaneously. As Andrew Arato has pointed out, there are two directions in which reflection determines the specificity of the procedural paradigm for Habermas.[34] The first seeks to avoid placing private and public forms of autonomy, rights and democracy, in an antagonistic relationship as in the liberal and welfare paradigms. "The process of reflection Habermas has in mind leads first and foremost to an understanding of the 'co-originality' and complementarity of public and private freedom, democracy and rights."[35] This theoretical awareness is complemented by a focus on public political action in relation to the input side of lawmaking involving publics in both the state and civil society. Reflection is thus rooted in the democratic genesis of law.

Reflection in the form of self-reflection also serves to mitigate the dialectic of legal and factual equality haunting the liberal and welfare paradigms. As we have seen, liberal legal formalism has been blind to the role that private power and privilege play in blocking the autonomy of those formally free and protected by rights. The substantive, authoritative, intrusive interventions of welfare regulations, however, tend to equalize at the cost of normalizations that restrict freedom.[36] The first secures formal civil and political rights but not equality, while the latter insists on the importance of social rights and entitlements to ensure that civil and political rights are really available to all. But this second approach often backfires because the ways in which some "social rights" or entitlements are structured undermines personal autonomy.[37] Thus in each case the system of rights is developed in a one-sided or paradoxical manner. The solution lies in institutionalizing democratic procedures of reflection and self-reflection entailing the participation of all concerned in articulating the ways in which the relevant social rights and conceptions of equality and autonomy should be understood. This, according to Habermas, would permit the adoption of precisely those social rights necessary and appropriate to the adequate functioning of all rights.[38] By focusing the legislature's attention on the conditions for mobilizing law, the procedural paradigm would simultaneously solve the problem of democratic legitimacy and avoid the antagonisms between the two dimensions of the core principle of our constitutional system: equal liberty.

It would also reconcile private and public autonomy. Habermas's point is that citizens must experience the organization of legal protection as a democratic political process. They themselves must be able to take part in the articulation of social interests. Those potentially affected must have a role in the clarification of the differences in experiences and situations that become relevant for an equal opportunity to realize equal liberty. Habermas refers to feminist critiques of both formal and instrumental law to make his point: "In women's struggle for equality, as well as the transformation of the paradigmatic understanding of the corresponding legal programs . . . the rights meant to guarantee the autonomous pursuit of a personal life project for women cannot be adequately formulated at all unless the relevant aspects for defining equal and unequal treatment are convincingly articulated and justified beforehand."[39] Indeed, it is the absence of voice, the lack of an appropriate connection between public norms and individual experience/reasoning, that accounts for the paternalism and normalizing effects of legal regulation.

In sum, the Habermasian conception of the procedural paradigm is characterized by the application of procedures of democratic reflection to the determination of the meaning of rights. This is a bottom-up process: private citizens in civil society debate and express their views in civil publics, and these generate communicative power and opinions that (ideally) influence the deliberations within the legislature. The latter legislates in light of the relevant principles and public opinion, generating norms that then guide the courts, authorize and program the administration, and inform whatever regulations emerge in the juridification process. The publicly mobilized critique of judicial decisions, in turn, intensifies justificatory obligations of activist courts.[40] No regulation, in Habermas's view, however sensitive to context, can adequately concretize the equal right to an autonomous private life unless it simultaneously strengthens the position of those affected in the political public sphere where they can clarify the relevant aspects that define equal status.[41] Thus, voice is crucial both to personal autonomy and equality. This is why on the proceduralist paradigm, the realization of basic rights is a process that secures the private autonomy of equally entitled citizens only in step with the activation of their political autonomy.[42]

Accordingly, representative democracy on the procedural paradigm is not state-centered as it is in the other two legal paradigms. Instead, it is dualistic: it focuses on forms of communication between unrestricted civil publics and decisional bodies in the polity. This circulation of opinion targeting legislation secures universalist principles and political responsibility in the interpretation of rights even if context-sensitivity and differential classifications are necessary in their application. For it ties legislation to the actual discursive genesis of norms guided by the principle of reasonable nonrejectability: only those norms, rules, and regulations are legitimate that could not be reasonably rejected by those affected. Just which these norms are can be discovered, *au fond*, only by attending to those potentially affected insofar as they exercise voice in articulating the respects in which they are affected.

What has been gained with this shift in perspective? First, it should be clear that it is possible to respect the integrity of the internal logic and requirements of subsystems without concluding that universalist principles of legitimacy and the political center (legislation for the whole of society) have no role to play, something of a non sequitur in Teubner's analysis in any case. Inclusive and universalist normative principles regulating regulation need not recenter society in the state or fall prey to the regulatory trilemma if such regulations are self-limiting, that is, aimed at general guidance, not substantive, bureaucratic steering. Democratization of legislation (in the above sense) and of the administration (see below) would, moreover, address the specter of neocorporatism haunting the reflexive paradigm. For, as Habermas and others have correctly noted, if the administration abandons its role of normative guidance regarding those subsystems whose internal complexity and social power render them inaccessible to direct legal imperatives, then legitimacy suffers. Reflexive law of the sort exemplified by the application of procedures regulating collective bargaining and management (*mitbestimmung*) discussed by Teubner is open to the charge of neocorporatism precisely because it cannot guarantee the desirable level of equality of outcomes or fairness across organizations.[43]

When faced with political decisions relevant to the whole of society, the state must be able to perceive, and if necessary assert, public interests as it has in the past. Even when it appears in the role of an intelligent adviser or supervisor who makes procedural law available, this kind of lawmaking must remain linked to legislative programs in a transparent, comprehensible, and controllable way. There is no patented recipe for this.[44] Only a mobile, alert, informed public sphere that affects parliament can secure the sources from which legitimate, universalistic law can arise.

Despite its advantages, however, this approach suffers from the mirror difficulty of the Teubner model. If Teubner fails to adequately address the problem of normative universalism, Habermas seems to purchase universalism at the price of efficacy on normative and empirical levels. It is certainly important to argue for the monitoring of administration through general laws and articulate, attentive civil publics able to generate ideas, influence, and critique. But unless these find an anchor within the subsystems themselves, the influence of the latter will be too diffuse, and the control power of the former will be too weak to get results. To be sure, Habermas also suggests the partial democratization ("constitutionalization") of the administration itself, pointing to a variety of possible forms ranging from participation of clients, ombudspersons, quasi-judicial procedures, hearings, and so forth.[45] This brief discussion of internal democratization of the administrative subsystem is reminiscent of Teubner's idea of institutionalizing internal discourses. And it proceeds from a normative perspective concerned with fostering voice, autonomy, participation, and democratic legitimacy. But Habermas does not link this proposal to any new legal form—it is a mere desiderata. Moreover, the proposal targets only one subsystem and does not address the issue of receptivity to norms and democratic input in the others. Nor does it deal with rationality problems of coordination noted by Teubner. In short, for the most part Habermas's procedural paradigm addresses primarily the official circulation of power.

Thus far the key theories of the reflexive/procedural paradigm have yielded ambiguous results: reflexivity of a subsystem may increase its autonomy and power and trigger forms of self-regulation that are compatible with the subsystem's rationality yet sensitive to its external effects. But there is nothing in the systems-theoretical approach to convince us that this would have normatively positive or legitimate results for society as a whole. Enhanced self-regulation of a subsystem must be made compatible with the enhanced self-regulation of others, raising the obvious problem of coordination. The regulation of self-regulation via reflexive law also has to occur in the name of legitimate public purposes; otherwise it could appear to fall prey to the third prong of the regulatory trilemma: the capturing and instrumentalization of law by the subsystem's own purposes (the oversocialization of law).

On the other hand, reflection in the procedural paradigm on the Habermas model would generate legitimacy by addressing the problem of the normative direction of self-regulation. It allows us to raise the evaluative and normative questions regarding which sorts of outcomes, including openness to multiple discourses, ought to be avoided or fostered by postregulatory regulation. But Teubner's suspicions against appeals to a general society-wide discourse (or democratic forum) are right in one key respect: there is no convincing indication that rationality and coordination problems can be resolved through focusing on the input side (democratic legitimacy) of legislation without attending to legal forms of regulation that could trigger subsystem responsibility. Learning and openness to multiple discourses must occur within each subsystem; otherwise both democratic publics and political philosophy become overburdened. Nor is there any indication that legislatively articulated legitimate norms would resonate for (orient the action of) actors within the various subsystems without mechanisms to provide incentives for this. In short, we come up against the problem of institutionalization regarding norms, incentives, and mechanisms of reflection and reflexivity.

Curiously, this issue has not been seriously addressed by either model of the reflexive/procedural paradigm. Part of the problem lies in the failure to adequately theorize the distinction between reflexivity and reflection. Unless this is done, one cannot see that there is an issue of institutionalization involving a choice among, and the best way to set up, reflexive mechanisms. Only once one sees, pace Luhmann and Teubner, that reflexivity is a neutral process that can have positive and/or destructive effects, depending on how it is institutionalized, can one confront the real issues: which institutional form should reflexive law take, how ought reflection to be institutionalized in the various domains, and whether one should shift over to reflexive law in a particular domain at all.

A PROPOSED SYNTHESIS: THE SOCIOLOGICAL REFLEXIVITY MODEL

Although it is not concerned with law or the forms legal regulation takes, the sociological reflexivity model developed by Ulrich Beck provides us with some very useful insights and theoretical tools in this regard.[46] Beck makes the neutrality of reflexive modernization his core premise, thereby placing institutional issues at the center of his analysis.[47] Indeed for Beck, how to institutionalize reflexive mechanisms is the key political question to be faced in contemporary "risk societies." Moreover, he zeroes in precisely on the distinction between reflexivity and reflection from a dualistic perspective: systemic and action-theoretical. Beck revisits this conceptual problematic in order to theorize the dynamics of negative externalities and political/normative deficits apparently inherent in contemporary processes of "reflexive modernization." It is from Beck's work that we can see that reflexivity is complex and neutral. Hence it cannot be advocated as a cure-all without, as it were, reflection on its implications in law and every other domain.

What Beck understands by reflexive modernization is the application of modernity to itself. If modernization involves the dissolution and disembedding of traditional social forms and their replacement by the social forms of industrial society, then reflexive modernization entails the disembedding and dissolution of modern industrial society and the potential replacement of its respective social forms by new reflexive ones characteristic of risk societies.[48] The important point about this process is that it involves the application of modernity's own dynamism to modern institutions (self-application).

Reflexive modernization, however, occurs *surreptitiously*—it involves the unplanned, unsteered, modernization of modernity. The transition from industrial society to what Beck calls "risk society" occurs in the wake of the autonomized dynamism of modernization, following the pattern of latent side effects.[49] Reflexivity—involving self-thematization and the application of a process to itself—does not necessarily involve consciousness or reflection and it is ultimately ambivalent. The enhancement of a system's ability to do its tasks when a process is applied to itself can have destructive and not only power-enhancing outcomes for the others. The application of scientific reasoning to science as an enterprise, of legal reasoning to law, would not alter the structure of risk production. Reflexively modernized social subsystems do tend to produce negative externalities (risks) for one another and for individuals, while the state is less and less able to guide or steer society as a whole.

In this, Beck agrees with Luhmann and Teubner, although unlike them he sees the nonprogressive side of reflexivity. The subsystems are indeed the locus of dynamism: important decisions are taken within the various subsystems of science, medicine, business, and so on that are very innovative and affect all of society. But without adequate forms of self-reflection, conscious debate over appropriateness of locally developed goals and norms, and the appropriate regulation of self-regulation, this dynamism can be dangerous. Uncontrolled genetic engineering, biotechnology, and production decisions having long-term effects on the environment are only the most obvious examples. Thus reflexive modernization involving the self-confrontation of modernity with its own processes (reflexivity) is an ambivalent development. It is the terrain on which to repose the problems of regulation, but it is not in itself the solution.

In short, the process of autonomized reflexive modernization is neutral: it can culminate in self-referential subsystem closure that worsens societal risks and leads ultimately to self-dissolution of the infrastructure of modernity. Or it can provide fertile grounds for focusing on interrelationships, contextual understandings, and cross-boundary communication, by triggering reflection and new forms of political action.[50] In other words, the reflexive paradigm can but need not involve the conception of a decentered society composed of autistic subsystems, following the logic of differentiation, autonomy, and self-thematization. It is not doomed to construe subsystems as hermetically closed around their own codes and rationality as does Luhmann and, to a great extent, Teubner. Reflexive modernization could become reflective, entailing cross-linking, networking, intertranslatability or fusion of codes, and other new forms of interrelatedness following a logic of mediation and self-limitation. For

Beck, unlike for Habermas, however, this would not proceed via society-wide reflection influencing the state, which then coordinates and steers society from above. Like Teubner, Beck thinks the idea of a decentered society precludes this. Rather, Beck proposes a version of the regulation of self-regulation that involves the building of reflection (in Beck's hands, democratic public spaces) into reflexive mechanisms within the various subsystems.

In order to see this, however, one must be clear that reflection (knowledge) and self-reflection (self-knowledge and thinking about thought) are different from reflexivity even if self-reflection is one form of the latter. One must also be careful in using the term *reflection* to avoid the progressivist illusion that has accompanied it since the Enlightenment. Classical reflection theory is overly optimistic, according to Beck. It involves the idea that reflection, knowledge, and self-reflection (self-consciousness) proceed with modernization such that more and more agents acquire the ability to know and think about the social conditions of their existence and to change them. Reflection theory thus relies on the ideas of subject philosophy: the knowing subject masters more and more of her environment (and herself) through reflection. Sociologically it implies that more reflection, more experts, more science, more public sphere, more self-awareness and self-criticism will open up new and better possibilities for action.[51]

Beck's theory of reflexive modernization dispenses with this happy consciousness. As indicated, reflexivity involves the problematic of unconscious unintended self-application, and self-endangerment of modernized social spheres. The point is that destructive modernization of modernity can, although it need not, occur without reflection, beyond knowledge and consciousness. But the appropriate response is not to try simply to add reflection or self-reflection, understood as conscious awareness into the mix, as if knowledge would entail mastery of formerly uncontrolled processes. Reflection as well as self-reflection can involve the illusion of rational control or autonomy and the triumph of normalization, as Adorno and Horkheimer's critique of the dialectic of enlightenment—as well as Foucault's critique of the techniques of self-interrogation, confession, and self-discipline that orient modern forms of self-reflection—so penetratingly demonstrated.[52] To introduce reflection into processes of reflexive modernization must mean neither self-thematization in Luhmann's sense nor some sort of expert overview or conscious intellectual mastery by the sovereign knowing subject(s) (elites): complexity precludes this. Rather, it must involve the creation of democratic public spaces for "reflection in concert" by all those potentially affected via discussion and debate on norms, values, and goals, in a variety of institutional forms, in each subsystem.

Beck calls this solution to the twin dangers of reflexive modernization—irresponsible decision making by the subsystems and lack of legitimacy—"subpolitics."[53] Since social subsystems increasingly rationalize their internal processes in ways that have harmful side effects for others, their decisions and decision-making processes become thematized by the public, and they become more and more dependent upon legitimation.[54] They are thereby opened up to political claims. But the politics to which they must become open ought to be "subpolitics": the creation of spaces *within* the subsystems for political participation, critique, and reflection by those potentially affected, such as lay individuals, social movements, and citizen initiatives, in addition to the experts and organized interests included in corporatist models of interest-bargaining. The participation of such groups in thematizing problems allows for self-criticism, learning, and self-limitation.

Here, of course, Beck is reasoning from an action-theoretical perspective. There are actually two steps in the process of introducing reflection into reflexive subsystems in Beck's approach. Somewhat like Habermas, Beck argues that it is only by way of nonexperts who publicly articulate their experiences and sensitize society to problems in general-public societal discussions, appealing to norms and values and opening them to reflection, that risks become perceived and recognized in the first place.[55] Nonspecialized discussion by ordinary persons in ordinary language can be informed by expertise, but in articulating experience one does not speak in the code of the relevant subsystem or as an expert; rather, one uses the ordinary language of prudential judgment.

Thus the general civil public sphere has a crucial, albeit informal, signaling role to play here. But it must be able to connect up with and influence insiders in the various subsystems: provision for normative discussions within each subsystem and for participation of all concerned is crucial to ensure openness and receptivity to self-limitation. The presence and voice of nonexperts as well as experts in institutionalized public spaces within each subsystem also requires the translation of codes into ordinary language so that there can be communication about concerns that transcend the system's own exclusionary internal code and rationality. Within each domain, ordinary persons can raise the relevant normative and political questions selected out by the subsystem's own code. Thus subpolitics solves the Teubner problem of cross-boundary communication and the opening up of subsystems to social standards of relevance and norms.

Beck's model of subpolitics comports rather well with the conception of a reflexive legal paradigm developed by Teubner, since it too renounces direct substantive regulation and steering by the state of the various subsystems. But Teubner, as we have seen, construes "democratization," or the establishment of reflection within each subsystem, exclusively in the sense of an internal reflexion of social identity involving sensitivity to the outside effects of attempts to maximize internal rationality by subsystems.[56] To Beck, on the contrary, democratization is understood from the action theoretical point of view as involving voice and participation. Reflection established within the subsystems would thus involve more than self-thematization. On the one hand it would ensure autonomy and self-regulation, while creating openness to participation and lay forms of communication and reasoning about goals and norms that translate the specific code of a subsystem into ordinary language without violating its rationality. On the other hand, Beck's conception of the institutionalization of subpolitics would open up subsystems to learning and influence of social norms in ways that elude Teubner's model.[57] Subpolitics, in short, establishes receptors for influence of public values, norms, and concerns within each subsystem. It appears to avoid the exclusiveness of neocorporatism because it includes the unorganized within the decentralized public spaces opened up within the subsystems. The advantage that the subpolitics model has over the local self-knowledge of system theory is that it can be informed by norms generated in a multiplicity of discourses and hence potentially can bring together expertise with democratic discussion on the local level, as it were.

However, by focusing exclusively on subpolitics, Beck's analysis, like that of Teubner, remains deficient from the standpoint of democratic legitimacy. The regulation of self-regulation that his model offers occurs exclusively on the subsystem level. The institutionalization of spaces for subpolitics provides for discussion, participation, and genesis of norms within but not among or across the various subsystems, for Beck neglects the universalizing aspects of politics despite his recognition of the importance of overall societal discussions. He consistently shows contempt for the official circulation of power in the representative political process and thus downplays the issue of the democratic genesis of universal principles and legal norms that should guide or orient self-regulation.[58] Yet he does not offer other mechanisms or candidates for mediating between the various subsystems, or for communicating information about successful problem-solving techniques across organizations. Consequently, Beck's model risks being construed as a form of democratized neocorporatism despite its anti-elitist thrust. It suffers from the opposite weakness of Habermas: if the latter fails to reflect on the institutional mechanisms necessary to secure influence of general public debate at the level of subsystems (Beck's forte), the former neglects the general democratic process of legislation, and the universalizing thrust of society-wide discussion influencing the legislative articulation of legal norms (representation) that must regulate self-regulation. Unless mechanisms for the influence of societal discussions and general legislation via the representative political process exist, particularism and inequalities across each organization and subsystem would be inevitable. Moreover, there will be no vehicle for the voice of those who are not participants in civic initiatives, social movements, or particular organizations.

Beck reduces the state's role to providing incentives for the establishment of (and legal protection for) institutionalized subpolitics within each domain. This is a necessary but insufficient step, in my view. He cannot draw on Habermas's insights, however, because he, like Teubner, is convinced that the impossibility of centrally steering society through the state means that the public articulation through legislation of general rules and principles is impossible or meaningless. Hence for him subpolitics replaces rather than supplements general politics.[59] But as I indicated via the example of sexual harassment, reflexive law must operate on both levels. It should trigger the establishment of reflexive mechanisms within a subsystem—institutions for conflict resolution, for participation and discussion about norms and issues, and for contextual concretization of abstract principles—but it must simultaneously involve the legislative enactment of norms and procedures regulating self-regulation oriented by general principles, actionable sanctions, clear criteria, and publicly acceptable goals.

In order to be legitimate, in other words, reflexive law must be oriented to genuine public purposes. Otherwise it risks degenerating, as indicated, into neocorporatism. Even worse, it could turn into a new form of privatization in which the state delegates its responsibilities for regulating and decision making to private elites reinforcing their power and privilege in relation to the rest of society and violating basic principles of fairness. But law must also respect the local purposes of what it regulates. From the system-theoretical point of view, the issue is the integrity of an organization's or subsystem's code. From an action-theoretical point of view, what is at stake is not only the protection of spontaneous social communication processes, not only the political participation of those affected in articulating experiences and debating norms and goals, but also the integrity of the particular local ethos and purpose of the specific subsystem or organization.

RESPONSIVE LAW

Advocating what he calls "responsive self-regulation," Philip Selznick has long maintained that public values and concerns for morally legitimate outcomes must inform the theory of reflexive law.[60] But reflexive law must also foster and respect the "internal morality" of institutions. If the key normative question is "self-regulation for what?" the key issue for institutional design is the proper form of institutionalization.[61] Accordingly, Selznick calls his version of regulated self-regulation "responsive law," meaning that regulators should be responsive to and respectful of the internal morality of that which is regulated. In addition to maintaining integrity, however, responsiveness also means dealing constructively with (openness to) new problems, demands, and expectations.[62] Indeed, whether or not it is appropriate for the state to shift over to indirect, albeit regulated self-regulation depends on whether an organization is properly institutionalized—equipped with an appropriate "internal morality" or "corporate culture."[63]

By "internal morality" Selznick means the set of standards that must be honored if the distinctive mission of an institution or practice is to be achieved. He gives us several examples: the internal morality of family life, he maintains, includes trust and shared commitment, while that of adjudication involves impartiality and the opportunity for each party to offer proofs and arguments.[64] Since each institution has special functions and values, the important thing from the point of view of external regulation is whether or not a particular organization has a well-developed internal morality and whether it or the people who make it up respect its integrity.

Thus, unlike Teubner, Selznick focuses on the normative issues raised by reflexive law. He insists that organizations must be seen both as open and closed systems and that the management of increasingly blurred boundaries constitutes the key problematic in contemporary institutional life. For example, a school may need to be a good parent, especially if parents are under stress, while parents may need to be good teachers.[65] What is required accordingly is to think of legal regulation in terms of fostering regularized (normatively structured) forms of openness within a particular system and between the system and its environment. In order for external norms to be effective, this means that internal structures for consultation, communication, and learning must be established and reinforced.[66] Thus like Teubner and Beck, Selznick focuses on forms of regulation that would foster the autonomy of the relevant subsystem to the extent to which it develops institutions that facilitate internal and external communication. He is concerned, however, with the normative level ignored by Teubner and which is secondary to Beck, whose main concern is with subpolitics rather than respecting institutional moralities.

Steering legal attention to institutional design aimed at reinforcing internal moralities and respecting the purpose of institutions is a form of reflexive law, insofar as it involves structuring of mechanisms for internal self-regulation.[67] Unlike substantive law, responsive law does not attempt to directly guide behavior, but unlike formal law, it does more than set up abstract rules of the game. Thus, responsive regulation differs from deregulation and privatization to the extent that it orients regulation toward the public interest while fostering the institutionalization of internal moralities that would justify strategies of self-regulation. Responsive law maintains autonomy but does so by being responsive to and facilitative of the intrinsic moral purpose of an institution. Somewhat along the lines of Habermas's early colonization thesis, the idea is that when such internal moralities exist, regulators should restrict themselves to external, limited rather than internal, heavy-handed, disintegrative forms of control.[68]

The idea of internal moralities thus adds another important piece to the discussion of reflexive law, especially as it pertains to the regulation of intimate association. It clarifies one aspect of the normative stakes that subpolitics must respect in order to avoid dedifferentiation and the regulatory trilemma. It tries to link general principles and local norms through the concept of an interplay between openness and closure, boundedness and interdependence, and the thesis of the genesis and institutionalization of morality from below, as it were, thereby acknowledging the problem of the sources of obligation and responsibility.

Nevertheless, Selznick's argument, like Beck's, tends to sacrifice the general to the particular, the universal to the local. Over and over again Selznick states that regulation cannot demand conformity to "eternal rules"; that the administration of justice cannot be "rule-centered"; that the shift from external to internal control is an advance.[69] His disdain for the legal articulation of general principles stems from the way in which Selznick construes the regulatory choice facing us today. Formal rule-bound law, in Selznick's view, is, in short, a thing of the past. Either we opt for heavy-handed intrusive regulation of those areas that lack appropriate institutionalization of internal moralities and impose norms from the outside, or we choose context-sensitive open-ended generalized directives (responsive law) that "encourage the formation of private regulatory institutions."[70] In the latter case, regulators should refrain from demanding conformity to external standards and rely instead on the internal morality of an institution as a resource for public policy.[71]

This, in my view, is a false choice, one that derives from Selznick's failure to analyze internal moralities from a dual perspective. Internal moralities must be respected (this is the meaning of responsiveness or context-sensitivity), but they can also function as receptors to generalized and legally articulated societal norms and principles within the local, if properly institutionalized. The choice is not between local moralities or general norms externally imposed by the state. Rather, the issue is how to set up the regulation of self-regulation such that mutual recognition and mutual influence of local and general purposes and moralities occurs.

What gets lost in Selznick's analysis, moreover, is clarity regarding the particular legal form to be used in indirect, external regulation. Indeed, it seems that Selznick believes that responsive reflexive law must operate with very vague general standards and open-ended directives, much like materialized welfare law, if it is to be sufficiently responsive to the organization it is regulating. Small wonder that this approach, like its predecessor, has provoked fears for the rule of law. This sort of "responsiveness" to the local risks brings us back into the regulatory trilemma, carrying the threat of the oversocialization of law. Selznick's rather communitarian interpretation of responsiveness, in short, tends to downplay the dimension of reflexivity and of proceduralism in favor of preserving substance (local *sittlichkeit*) blurring the differences between reflexive and materialized law.

DANGERS OF REFLEXIVE/PROCEDURAL/RESPONSIVE LAW: ARBITRARINESS AND/OR NORMALIZATION

Critics of reflexive law fear that it entails, like the welfare model preceding it, the loss of integrity of the legal medium itself.[72] It is not only the communitarian model of responsiveness that has triggered such fears. Indeed, Ingeborg Maus argued nearly fifteen years ago that Teubner's tendency to view formal law along with the classic rule of law virtues once associated with it—clarity, cogency, impartiality—as anachronistic opens his model of reflexive law to the charge of threatening the rule of law. Despite his insistence that reflexively triggered forms of self-regulation must be socially sensitive and public-regarding, Maus and more recently Bill Scheuerman have argued that unless regulations of self-regulation are themselves clear and cogent, they will be as open to manipulation by privileged social and economic interests as material law has been. Echoing older critiques of the materialization of law, Maus and Scheuerman argue that when regulation involves vague and open-ended legal norms (e.g., the best interests of the child), it will invariably become arbitrary and unfair, playing into the hands of the powerful either in the state or in the private institution. This holds equally true for procedural and organizational norms as it does for more substantive directives.[73] Indeed, the powerful may well prefer soft and open-ended legal regulation because it allows them to benefit from their existing advantages in bargaining or in private mediation processes.[74]

Nevertheless, Maus does not retreat to a position calling for the revival of formal law. She is aware of the dangers of overburdening legislatures and courts with administrative tasks of regulation (ungovernability, irrelevance, or destruction of the legal medium), yet she accepts the need to regulate and to decentralize regulatory functions. However, as Scheuerman cogently points out, "Maus underscores the fact that the legal framework of 'regulated self-regulation' nonetheless will have to respect some traditional formalistic ideals (by insisting that procedural and organizational norms are relatively clear and cogent) if reflexive law can meaningfully hope to counteract the advantages often enjoyed by the privileged within regulatory law."[75]

It is not enough to equalize the bargaining positions of those affected; to ensure voice for all affected, or to respect autonomy, one must also protect against arbitrariness and particularism. The powerful in society and in the state can be controlled only if law retains its classic virtues. In other words, legislation will retain its claim to be universalistic, and law will hold onto its normative structure (law as institution) if regulatory principles and general procedures are clearly delimited and impartial, and if law (thereby) maintains its distance from the domain whose self-regulation it is regulating.

This involves a challenge to a simplistic evolutionism regarding legal forms, however. Maus has argued that it is possible to detach classic rule-of-law virtues from the rigid doctrinal legal formalism that is characteristic of the liberal legal paradigm and to shape reflexive or procedural law according to these virtues without buying into other doctrines or methods of the earlier paradigm.[76] She thus avoids the genetic fallacy as well as a rigid evolutionism that ties legal forms, legal paradigms, legal methods, and doctrines together too closely. Scheuerman also argues that rule-of-law virtues still have a decisive role to play within reflexive law.[77] They both thus accept the idea of legal paradigms and the argument that there is indeed something new and normatively valuable in the reflexive legal form without maintaining that everything characteristic of earlier legal forms is ipso facto anachronistic and without assuming that it is impossible to create combinations of forms, methods, and doctrines within a new paradigm. I quite agree.

Some critics, however, throw down the gauntlet to the entire concept of legal paradigms, by challenging the very idea of evolution regarding legal forms. Indeed, both the systems-theoretical and the action-theoretical approach to reflexive/procedural law have been accused of a naive progressivism regarding legal evolution that is misleading in its assessment of the normative advantages and newness of reflexive or procedural legal forms. Erhard Blankenburg's is the most penetrating critique.[78] Of course he acknowledges that new legal forms emerge, but they do not supplant old ones: rather, they all coexist in complex messy ways supplementing but not replacing one another.[79] Moreover, he insists that legal development is not linear in terms of density. Law does penetrate into areas that in the past were not subjected to legal regulation; it has also retreated from some domains as a mechanism of social control. Blankenburg cites the "cross-national" tendency to deregulate sexual behavior and the sharp decrease in disputes over honor and status in Europe since the nineteenth century.[80] In other areas substantive law has changed in ways that limit the relevant legal issues in conflict resolution: for example, guilt has become irrelevant to modern no-fault divorce.[81]

Blankenburg's point is that formal, material, and procedural elements of law have long existed in different combinations and relations to each other and thus one cannot speak of evolution between legal paradigms or of a new legal rationality. There is thus nothing new in the "reflexive" approach to law. Regulating procedure and leaving substantive rules to be worked out over time has always been the technique of the "wise legislator" entering new fields of regulation, according to Blankenburg.

Moreover, the normative claims made for reflexive/procedural law are misleading. Instead of preserving horizontal ordinary social communication (Habermas's concern) or enabling self-regulation and protecting institutional autonomy (Teubner's concern), Blankenburg argues that the observed increase in the use of reflexive law multiplies the overall density of regulation via the juridification of formerly unregulated social areas (pace Habermas) and that this has the effect of normalization, expanding rather than limiting social control (pace Teubner).[82] Proceduralization and greater chances for participation in organizational decision making are not an unambiguous good. First, postbureaucratic regulations actually tend to deflect rather than facilitate protest via cooptation.[83] Even worse, reflexive legislation often results in overregulation because it delegates rule production to lower-level regulators—participatory bodies and/or supervisory agencies—who are quick to fill in the gaps of discretion left open by legislation. They tend to produce highly detailed and cumbersome rules and regulations that make those involved long for the old-fashioned hierarchical bureaucracies.[84] We have seen this in the case of sexual harassment law. Thus Blankenburg prefers resistance to the pressures to enmesh unregulated areas in legal regulations (any form of juridification), over the allegedly misleading claims of "self-limitation" made by advocates of reflexive law.

Teubner's response to these arguments is not without interest, for the critique forces him to clarify and refine the evolutionary dimension of the theory by specifying what really is new in the context and form of reflexive law. What is new about the context are the problems posed by increasing functional differentiation, internal subsystemic complexity, and self-referentiality of subsystems equipped with their own codes and purposes. This is what law must now take into consideration when issues of regulation come up. The recognition of the complexity and requisite integrity of each differentiated subsystem poses the problem of respect for their autonomy—the core problematic of reflexive law, in Teubner's view. Thus, pace Blankenburg, reflexive law cannot be identified with just any procedurally oriented type of law. Of course, procedural law has existed for centuries, but the problem of what kind of procedure the law will develop in order to cope with a high degree of social autonomy and self-referential tendencies toward closure is another, and specifically contemporary, matter.[85] The internal models of social reality and the forms of regulation that the law develops in dealing with social systems that are resistant to regulation remain important. Thus one can speak of legal paradigms, after all. Indeed, Blankenburg is the one who is naive insofar as he has the expectation that delegalization is the way to preserve the few remaining arenas of social autonomy. This approach indicates that he remains caught up in the liberal legal paradigm.

To be sure, Teubner agrees that preserving social autonomy was the core value of the liberal legal paradigm, one which it attempted to secure via a withdrawal from regulatory functions and a retreat to sheer legal formalism.[86] Formal law defines its task as guaranteeing freedom for autonomous social action. But the twentieth century has revealed the dysfunctional consequences of such a legal-political withdrawal: legal formalism cannot satisfactorily deal with the negative consequences of the self-referentiality of other social systems. It does, admittedly, preserve the autonomy of the legal system itself. But it cannot redress the disadvantages (risks) generated by autonomized subsystems for the rest of society. Thus, pace Blankenburg, a way of regulation has to be found that takes self-reference seriously, but one that does not involve direct, substantive, regulatory action. For purposive law, as we have seen, is often ill-suited to the complex structure of self-organizing social systems. The reflexive paradigm is aware of the autopoietic tendencies of its surrounding social systems (the new model of social reality) and adapts its structures accordingly. It develops reflexive law as a new way to preserve the original substantive value of social autonomy that developed with liberalism, without withdrawing from regulation and without threatening its own autonomy by heavy-handed interventions. This at least is the problematic and the desiderata of the reflexive paradigm.

We seem to be going in circles. Teubner does grasp what is new in our contemporary situation and the reflexive legal form, but he is unable to take the same distance toward reflexive law that he advocates toward the liberal paradigm; thus he invites the charge of progressivism, or naive evolutionism. Blankenburg is also right: there is indeed a coexistence of legal forms, but this does not mean that the concept of legal paradigms is mistaken or that there are no normative advantages to reflexive forms of law.

RECONCEPTUALIZING THE REFLEXIVE PARADIGM: A SYNTHETIC, PLURALIST APPROACH

In order to get beyond this vicious circle of objections and counter-objections, it is necessary to adopt a reflexive attitude toward the reflexive paradigm itself. In other words, just as it is possible to disconnect some rule of law virtues from their embeddedness in the liberal legal paradigm and their link to legal formalism, so too one can conceptualize the reflexive legal paradigm in such a way that reflexive law is one, but not the only one of the possible forms of legal regulation compatible with it. Indeed, from this perspective, one can also sever forms of material law from the welfare paradigm's simplistic model of society and its voluntaristic statist phantasm of administratively shaping preferences and controlling outcomes. It is possible, in short, to choose to use direct substantive intervention and direct prohibitions when, upon reflection, these are deemed necessary and appropriate.

One has to see, in other words, that the reflexive paradigm of law is, as Andrew Arato has argued, reflexive on the meta-level toward itself. It involves both a specific form of law as well as a new conceptual framework and a new (decentered) societal model that pluralizes our regulatory options.[87] In addition to refining the reflexive/procedural legal form itself in order to cope with problems of self-referentiality and to avoid regulatory paradoxes, Arato argues that the reflexive paradigm puts us in the position to select regulatory strategies on the basis both of context sensitivity, contextual creativity, and post-facto learning. In short, one can approach reflexivity from both an action-theoretical and a system-theoretical perspective, synthesizing, as it were, the Habermasian and Teubner perspectives: "On reflection we should see that procedural law now has a double status in the conception, unlike that of formal and materialized law. It represents not only a new form of law but also a new framework within which the choice of legal forms is to be made. For this reason it is a good idea to insist on the 'reflexivity' of procedural law."[88] The meta-theoretical reflexivity of the reflexive legal paradigm thus involves not only a more sophisticated model of society (complex, decentered, differentiated) than its predecessors but also a reflective attitude toward the legal medium itself. It allows for the thematization of a plurality of legal forms and indeed of the possibility of a choice among them.

Arato's dualistic conception of reflexivity thus theorizes what Blankenburg has noticed on the empirical level. But it also gives democratic reflection in decisional political publics (so central to the Habermasian procedural model) its proper task: namely, to reflect upon general social norms and choose among the three types of legal forms: formal, substantive, and reflexive. I would add that reflection in political publics must also be attentive to the different forms of institutionalization possible for each type of law. The normative discussions and experiential input of civil publics within each subsystem and in civil society at large must inform these decisions as should the desiderata of maintaining the integrity of what is regulated and the reciprocal autonomy of regulated and regulator (Teubner's and Selznick's concern). In other words, the regulation of self-regulation involves the democratic articulation of principles, goals, and norms as well as a choice among forms of institutionalized autonomy. On the reflexive paradigm this democratic articulation occurs at two levels. First, on the input side—that is, on the level of the official circulation of power—it involves receptivity of political bodies to the influence of civil publics, as just indicated.[89] But it also involves, second, fostering the establishment of procedures, discursive structures, and mechanisms of conflict resolution within the subsystems that render them receptive to the influence of political publics and legal principles on the one side, and that open them up to what Beck called subpolitics, and what Teubner called learning, on the other.

Accordingly, reflexive or procedural law has no intrinsic normative priority or superiority in an evolutionary sense over other legal forms. Hence it is not susceptible to the charge of naive progressivism. To be sure, in the appropriate context reflexive law does have distinct properties that render it a highly desirable option. As Arato puts it, "Reflexive law . . . represents a legal form especially suited to combine three advantages: non-intrusive, postregulatory regulation, a renewed formal structure preserving the integrity of the legal medium, and the normatively desirable combination of freedom and regulation."[90] However, this does not mean that one should always opt for the reflexive over the other legal forms. Context and the political options must be considered as well as other normative desiderata.[91] I shall give more examples pertaining to the domain of intimacy in the next chapter.

This clarification of the status of the reflexive form of law is important in another respect. The reader might think that it is paradoxical to claim simultaneously that reflexive law fosters self-regulation by leaving outcomes indeterminate and that reflexive law should be better institutionalized so that it rests on clearly defined legislative goals with real sanctions backing them up. What is at stake in this objection is the distinctiveness of reflexive law altogether, albeit from a different point of view than Blankenburg's.

The problem seems to be the following: If we take the proceduralist attributes of reflexive law seriously, view it as basically indeterminate and therefore consistent with nearly any substantive outcome, then the difference between it and privatization evaporates. To deliver an area over to "self-regulation" could in fact simply be a form of privatization that delegates far-reaching authority to those potentially affected by a particular form of regulation. A directive meant to encourage voluntary self-regulation would be an example. On the other hand, to the extent that reflexive law rests on clearly defined legislative goals, this problem is reduced but at the cost of also reducing the real significance of self-regulation. Indeed, reflexive law appears then to approximate material law.[92]

The idea of "regulated self-regulation" as a form of reflexive law should, in my view, rest on clearly defined legislative goals. But everything turns on how one understands the term *goal*. By this I mean principles, not outcomes. Thus the reforms I suggest in Chapter 3 for sexual harassment law aim at better institutionalization of the principles guiding the regulation of self-regulation. These principles—equality, anti-discrimination on the basis of race and sex, personal freedom, and protection of privacy—are articulated both on the constitutional level and in national legislation. They are broad enough to leave particular ways of conforming with them relatively open and to permit local, contextual development of the content of these norms, but they are not completely indeterminate. Indeed, in different periods they acquire a rather specific range of meanings.[93] But whatever the going interpretation, these principles should guide self-regulation.

Reflexive law does entail incentives to private institutions to "self-regulate" so that their practices and workplaces generally conform to such principles. Regulated self-regulation, however, would have to involve more than mere reliance on voluntarism—it must put in place legal sanctions of a special sort. The threat of lawsuits and monetary damages and the stipulation that companies must institutionalize grievance procedures in harassment law is a perfect example. Reformed reflexive law in this area could further articulate and institutionalize the substantive principles guiding regulation and even specify the appropriate types of procedures and procedural protection, without becoming a form of materialized law. As in the case of collective-bargaining processes that are highly institutionalized and oriented by clearly articulated principles, the outcomes would still not be determined or stipulated. Nor would administrative controls replace the communicative structures generated by appropriate forms of self-regulation. We thus have to distinguish between principles and outcomes when clarifying the term *goal*. Reflexive law does not determine specific outcomes; to that extent it is indeterminate. But it is based on liberal principles embedded in the Constitution: in the cases of collective bargaining or harassment law, these are the principles of equal liberty and anti-discrimination. Accordingly, this form of legal regulation is oriented toward ensuring that autonomous actors comport with constitutional principles. This does not guarantee outcomes, but it steers self-regulation in the right direction. Reflexive law is thus a distinct legal form.

The paradigm concept need not be linked either to a rigid structuralism, by insisting on complete historical discontinuity and normative incommensurability between epistemic formations and legal forms, nor to an evolutionary model that insists on normative progress, privileging the reflexive legal form as a panacea.[94] Instead, the paradigm concept serves to take historical transformation into account while incorporating the idea of development in the sense of building upon and expanding opportunities, allowing for continuities as well as change. The reflexive paradigm, on the meta-level, however, is superior cognitively and normatively insofar as it opens up learning, abandons anachronistic models of the social structure, reveals political choices among forms of regulation, and renders inescapable the responsibility for them on both levels.

CHAPTER FIVE

Status or Contract? Beyond the Dichotomy

◆ This book began by taking note of an important new trend in the legal regulation of intimacy: the constitutionalization and individualization of matters formerly dealt with by state legislators and local courts under the rubric of family law. The Supreme Court's discovery in the 1960s of fundamental privacy and equality rights in the domain of intimacy indicated a profound shift in the cultural meaning of gender and sexual relations. It registered the changing status of women and their claims to equal liberty and personal happiness. The transformation of intimacy and the new constitutional analysis also heralded important changes in the meaning of the privacy that attaches to intimacy, in the conception of the kind of liberty/autonomy that is at stake, and in the purpose of regulation.

Yet the debate over how to respond legally to the changes in this domain remains mired in categories and conceptions that preclude adequate responses and unnecessarily dichotomize choices and values. We have already seen that this is so in the case of sexual harassment law and privacy analysis. In the former, reflexive law has not been adequately institutionalized because the regulation of self-regulation has not been sufficiently thought through: it thus tends to regress into a form of privatization. In the latter, claims to personal privacy and liberty are unnecessarily burdened with the baggage of the liberal paradigm (such as the state action doctrine), creating unpalatable choices between autonomy and equality.

Part of the problem addressed by both neocommunitarian and feminist critics is that privacy analysis seems to invite a wholesale shift from public to private ordering, from status to contract. The old discourse about a natural private sphere off-limits to state regulation has been resurrected. This has fed fears that a contractual model of intimacy will undermine responsibility (the communication concern) and equality (the feminist concern) within intimate relationships. The market does not acknowledge mutual obligations, responsibility, or care in intimate relationships if these are not literally contracted for. Nor does the principle of formal equality on which contracts are based (no force or fraud) redress the substantive and gendered inequalities in resources and power that often obtain in such relationships, even if it does away with the previous unjust status regime. That is why certain feminist privacy critics argue that constitutional privacy and equality analysis are on a collision course: formal liberty to consent or choose (freedom of contract) in the "domain of intimacy" often conceals substantive inequality and the absence of meaningful choice or consent due to the lack of real alternatives. Indeed, contract talk, private ordering, and privacy discourse in general seem to block needed reflection on how to institutionalize a just form of public ordering.

But the problem is more general than constitutional privacy analysis. Indeed, with regard to the entire range of issues pertaining to intimacy and family, it is now assumed that we must opt for private ordering or reconstruct a status regime attuned, to be sure, to contemporary conditions, but one that nonetheless protects marriage and the family from disintegrative forces via the direct substantive public ordering of intimate association. In other words, the choice everywhere is posed as one between contract or status, private or public, deregulation or heavy-handed, intrusive state regulation. Theoretically, this is expressed in the conflict between the law and economics school (the contractualists) and the neocommunitarians (the regulators).[1]

The shift of large areas of what was once the province of state-controlled family law over to private ordering seems to indicate that the contractualists have won—hence the recent plethora of articles and books bewailing, or alternatively praising and seeking to further, the privatization of family law.[2] But the communitarian critique invited by this empirical and conceptual shift is gaining ground as the discourse of family values and pleas for the revival of status to protect marriage reveal.[3] Even feminist critics of privatization seem forced to deploy the language of status to counteract this, although of course they assume that its revival along with renewed state regulation will occur on the terrain of gender equality.[4] Their hope is that it is possible to sever status from connotations of gender hierarchy, male dominance, and moralism regarding sex. Perhaps. Yet one is rather hard put to see how it will be feasible to stuff the genies of gender equality, personal liberty, pleasure, and happiness back into the bottle of a state-imposed status regime dedicated to recentering marriage.[5]

My reflections in this book aim to shift the terms of the debate and to show that the reflexive paradigm offers a way to recast the entire problematic and to construct more appropriate responses then either approach has to offer. In this conclusion I demonstrate my thesis, briefly considering a few of the issues mentioned above, first in the terms of the contemporary debate over status and contract and then from my alternative analytical perspective. I begin with a brief description of the traditional status regime and then turn to a discussion of the implications and regulatory paradoxes involved in the recent shift over to private ordering defended by the contractualists. I briefly consider the proposed communitarian alternative of a renewed status regime, assessing the dilemmas it cannot avoid, and finally show how reposing these issues in terms of the paradigm framework serves us better. From the perspective of the reflexive paradigm, it becomes clear that constitutional privacy analysis need not entail contractualist private ordering and that the alternative to contractualism need not be an all-embracing state-imposed status regime.

THE TRADITIONAL STATUS REGIME REGULATING INTIMACY

The previously hegemonic form of intimate association—monogamous, heterosexual, permanent, patriarchal marriage—with its rigid gender norms, moralistic attitude toward sex, and explicit homophobia, was widely acknowledged to constitute a public status regime directly regulated and enforced by the state. Despite the discourse of contract and marital privacy, under nineteenth and much of twentieth century law (and in some important respects even today), marriage was not a civil contract, for it was not the contracting parties but the state that set the terms of the marital relationship.[6] As the Supreme Court stated in *Maynard v. Hill,*

> Marriage is more than a mere contract. The consent of the parties is of course essential to its existence, but when the contract to marry is executed by the marriage, a relation is created between the parties which they cannot change. Other contracts may be modified, restricted, or enlarged, or entirely released upon the consent of the parties. Not so with marriage. The relation once formed, the law steps in and holds the parties to the various obligations and liabilities.[7]

In other words, the state, rather than individual marriage partners, determined the consequences of marital status including the obligations (economic, sexual, legal) owed to each other by the spouses.

The law drew a sharp line between marriage and other intimate relationships. It established marital status as a criteria for a wide range of public benefits and burdens. By criminalizing adultery, fornication, and nonmarital cohabitation, moreover, it carved out marriage as the only legitimate arena for sexual intercourse.[8] The law not only decided who could marry whom, it also sharply distinguished between children born within marriage and those born outside of it, affording the latter group no legal status through which to make claims upon biological parents.[9] Indeed, by legally designating legitimacy and paternity (the husband was presumed by law to be the father of his wife's children), marriage was constituted as the center for both sexual activity and filiation: it defined the family and who was a family member. No legal recognition was granted to nonmarried intimate associations.[10]

Last but hardly least, the state-imposed terms of the traditional marriage contract were, as many have pointed out, both hierarchical and rigidly gender-based.[11] Compulsory gendered statuses of wife and husband and the duties entailed by each were unalterable in any binding way by those concerned.[12] The law recognized no private agreements to alter these or the economic incidents of marriage, thus explicitly restricting opportunities for private ordering.[13] It also insisted on interspousal tort immunity based on the fictitious unity of husband and wife as one rather than two separate persons, and of marriage as establishing a community with no conflicting interests extant between the spouses. Accordingly, divorce was deemed a privilege: a state-bestowed remedy for an innocent spouse against a guilty one regarding very specific harms, not a private right available to resolve controversy between private parties. The assumption was that marriage (the only legally and morally legitimate form of intimacy) is a public institution of universal concern, and its dissolution affects others and not only the husband and wife.

This traditional status regime regulated intimate association on the basis of two key premises: first, that the moral/immoral binary maps directly onto sexual relationships, and, second, that the gender identities it institutionalized are natural, unalterable, and based on the biological facts of sexual difference.[14] Consequently, all relations outside marriage are by definition immoral; all nonreproductive sexuality and deviations from traditional gender roles are unnatural. Thus an organicist discourse justified the matrimonial model enforced by state legislation and the common law in part by institutionalizing the notion of complementarity between essentially different masculine and feminine identities. It did so by superimposing what is actually a particular symbolic model of sexual difference onto historically specific gender relations on the one side, and onto historical social constructions of sexuality on the other, construing all as anthropological givens. Needless to say, the organicist discourse of complementarity was predicated on a hierarchical inegalitarian gender order also construed as natural. The law regulating intimacy installed and reinforced women's subordination and the double moral standard within marriage, while controlling extra-matrimonial sexuality, in particular women's.

Thus the discourse of privacy in relation to the traditional family unit must not be misconstrued. It neither instituted marriage on a contractual model nor delivered over marital arrangements to private ordering. What it did was construct and protect the prerogatives and power of the husband/father as the authority over everyone within the family unit and as the bearer of state-protected immunities and privileges regarding outsiders.[15] Indeed, the traditional notion of entity privacy reinforced public control over the definition and composition of families while constructing the family as the source of public norms. Concepts of individual privacy and decisional autonomy played a rather minor role in the traditional legal regime governing family relations.[16]

When in the course of the nineteenth century the legal concept of the family shifted from traditional notions of paternal sovereignty and household legal unity to a model of the family as a collection of separate legal individuals, this did not mean that women were accorded decisional autonomy, or construed as equal sovereign individuals. Rather, their new status as legal persons was mapped onto the older gendered assumptions regarding their essentially dependent character: the state through its police powers acquired the paternal authority lost by husbands. For the most part, these regulatory powers were delegated to the bench. Wives or mothers in need received individualized "rights" at the discretion of the judges in charge of domestic-relations law and at the price of embracing their dependent status.

PRIVATIZATION OF FAMILY LAW

Trends shifting modern family law toward contract as its governing principle are putting an end to the traditional status regime. Private norm creation and private decision making have indeed supplanted state-imposed rules in many areas. Moreover, a preference for private over public ordering seems to have encompassed both the substantive legal doctrines governing family relations and the preferred procedures for resolving disputes.[17] Hence we see the tendency to construe the constitutionalization and individualization of family law initiated by the Supreme Court in the 1970s as leading naturally to the private ordering of intimacy and confirming the contractual model so dear to the heart of theorists in the law and economics tradition.[18] But many others assume that the only alternative to the old unjust, hierarchically gendered status regime is to insist on formal equality and to shift the entire domain over to private ordering.

While I believe this conclusion is false, there can be no doubt that privatization has advanced in key areas of intimate association and that the importance of status has declined. I shall argue, however, that this development has been a mixed bag in both conceptual and normative terms. I shall also argue that the shift to contract does not follow automatically from the principles of gender equality or personal autonomy informing the relevant Court decisions. Private ordering is appropriate in some instances but certainly not for all the dimensions of intimate association. As we shall see, however, the point is not to resort to a revived status regime of public ordering, but to reflect upon the principles governing the appropriate regulation of private ordering and the choice among other legal forms.

It is easy to document the rise of contract and the decline of status with respect to marriage, divorce, nonmarital intimacies, and having children. As many commentators have pointed out, state regulation of entry into and exit from marriage as well as determination of the terms of the marital relationship have increasingly shifted in favor of private arrangements.[19] The Uniform Marriage and Divorce Act approved by the National Conference of Commissioners on Uniform State Laws in 1970 greatly simplified and reduced the procedural prerequisites for formal marriage, permitting couples to choose their ceremonies without traditional religious or civil trappings.[20] For the most part, entry into marriage has become simply a process of licensing and registration. Change has been in the direction of increased private control.[21]

Many of the substantive restrictions on entry into marriage have also been abandoned by the states—including those blocking the mentally retarded, prison inmates, or guilty divorcees from marrying—along with restrictions based on affinity.[22] The Supreme Court has declared marriage to be a fundamental constitutional right, invalidating racial restrictions and other regulations that unduly burden the exercise of individual choice and personal autonomy.[23] To be sure, this right is not yet extended to same-sex couples, although some municipalities and recently the state of Vermont have begun to recognize such unions.[24] It is obvious that the tension between the view that marriage is a fundamental constitutional right and its denial to a specific category of individuals on the basis of their ascribed status/identity as homosexuals will be the occasion of increasingly heated debate and challenge. Whether this restriction can be convincingly justified on moral grounds that trump claims to equal citizenship remains to be seen, although I sincerely doubt it.[25] In any case, most of the other state restrictions to marriage on the basis of status have declined.

The law has also become far more receptive to private ordering of the terms of marriage. Indeed, most of the explicitly gender-based obligations and privileges in the state-imposed marriage contract have been eliminated. The Supreme Court has explicitly abandoned gendered status as the basis for ascription of roles, disabilities, and duties.[26] States have come to accept and are willing to enforce prenuptial agreements, as well as separation agreements with respect to property division and other economic matters that do not violate public policy.[27]

Even more significant, the rise of some form of no-fault divorce statutes in all the states places control over exit decisions in the hands of the intimate associates themselves.[28] This is a major shift in the legal paradigm governing divorce and, by implication, marriage, for the privatization of divorce signals that the state has abandoned its role as moral arbiter of marital behavior. Moral categories of innocence or guilt are now deemed irrelevant, especially given the lack of a social consensus on the propriety of behavior within marriage. The decision to end a marriage is based on private judgment shifting divorce from a publicly bestowed remedy to a private transaction.[29] Property division after divorce follows from the assumption that divorcing spouses should be able to move on without being unduly encumbered by their previous relationship: hence the tendency of courts to seek to divide property equitably without regard for legal title or fault.[30] Marriage and divorce, in short, are increasingly viewed by the courts and the states as a matter of private ordering oriented to the happiness and fulfillment of individuals.

Much of the above has been analyzed in terms of the declining importance of status in determining individuals' rights and obligations in intimate life. Indeed, it is now the individual and intimate relationships rather than marital status, husbands, wives, or the family that is the referent of legal rights and obligations in intimate association. As indicated in Chapter 1, the Supreme Court's new privacy analysis accords decisional autonomy to the individual regarding a range of intimate issues, including contraception, abortion, and the decision to become a parent. The Court articulated most clearly the shift away from regarding marriage as a public institution, conferring state-defined statuses toward a private relationship between distinct individuals in *Eisenstadt v. Baird*: "The marital couple is not an independent entity with a mind and heart of its own, but an association of two individuals each with a separate intellectual and emotional makeup."[31] The individual, as we have seen, irrespective of her marital status, has become the rights-bearer in intimate association.

Accordingly, marital status has diminished in importance. The law increasingly recognizes the rights of unmarried natural fathers based on the substance of their relationship to the child.[32] It has also rendered discrimination against children of unmarried parents unconstitutional, thereby deconstructing the legal category of illegitimacy and further decentering marital status.[33] Moreover, many of the privileges accorded to married over unmarried couples have been erased and the law has become willing to enforce contracts between unmarried cohabitants, revealing increased deference to private ordering.[34] Indeed, marriage has lost its privileged legal status as the only legitimate form of intimate association and the only acceptable locus for sex and reproduction. The recognition by some municipalities of domestic partnerships—unmarried heterosexual or homosexual couples who publicly register their relationship and pay a fee—witnesses the further erosion of the line between marital status and other consensual intimate associations.[35] So does the legal recognition in many states of the rights of singles and same-sex couples to have and keep children and to adopt.[36]

Status distinctions are, of course, still made, marriage has not disappeared, and married people retain many legal privileges.[37] The point is that the changes I describe are taken as evidence that the state-constructed status hierarchy is being replaced by a contractual model of intimacy favoring private over public ordering. For contractualists who are convinced that such a shift is the only way to secure formal gender equality and personal autonomy, this means that regulation of intimate association by the state should occur only in order to prevent harm, force, or fraud. State oversight should no longer aim at substantive outcomes or try to impose norms. It should only ensure the formal equality and fidelity to voluntarily assumed obligations of the contracting intimate partners.

The problem with this analysis is that a contract does not deliver factual equality, or do justice to the specificity of intimate association as distinct from market-based contractual arrangements or business partnerships. I have already alluded to the first set of problems in the discussion of certain feminist sex-equality theorists in Chapter 1. Despite the obvious benefits of private ordering in expanding personal autonomy and control and in protecting diversity when compared to the old state-controlled status regime, it does not adequately serve these ends when one is confronted by private concentrations of power and gendered inequalities within the family.[38] The most obvious example is the deleterious effects of no-fault divorce on the economic position of women. One's autonomy and control is hardly expanded when upon divorce one's standard of living falls drastically and when one must shoulder the burden of child care alone.[39] Choice and consent can indeed become empty categories when applied, for example, to an economically dependent battered wife who fails to leave her abusive husband.[40]

I do not want to pursue this line of reasoning here. Instead, I want to focus on the second set of issues and look at the alternative that is increasingly being proposed by communitarians, including some feminists: the revival of status. To be sure, I have also already addressed the theoretical limits of the contractual model in relation to the specificity and unique importance of intimate association in my analysis of Posner's work. Communitarians have been quick to pick up on this and to make rather powerful arguments to the effect that the privatization of family law not only misconstrues and undermines the purpose of intimate association, but also places less powerful family members in jeopardy, particularly women and children. Their point, however, is allegedly not to return to the bad old days of gender hierarchy, but to develop a new status regime that uses the state and public ordering to strengthen egalitarian marriage and reinforce the family.

THE COMMUNITARIAN CRITIQUE OF PRIVATE ORDERING: TOWARD A NEW STATUS ORDER

The communitarian arguments also work with the dichotomies of contract versus status, private versus public ordering. They too equate the new constitutionalization and individualization of rights in the domain of intimacy with contract, market, privatization. Their strategy is to indict both for fostering egoism, utilitarian interest calculations, self-indulgence, and a consumer ethic at the expense of solidarity, responsibility, and mutual care: the main purpose of intimate association in their view.[41]

To the communitarian, then, the main flaw of the contractual model is that it undermines the ethos of intimate association while harming, as already stated, the most vulnerable family members. Their suit is strongest when one considers such things as the privatization of adoption together with the emergence of the surrogacy market, on the one hand, and the shift to private mediation in divorce, on the other. But the effort to return the regulation of intimacy back to a status regime using substantive public ordering is not an adequate alternative.

As is well known, one of the key functions of the traditional status regime regulating intimacy was to restrict procreation to marriage by ascribing paternity to the husband, care to the wife, and legitimacy to the progeny of the married couple. American adoption law served a corresponding public function: to promote the welfare of those children in need of parents.[42] Adoption agencies were responsible for placing the child with suitable adoptive parents, providing care in the interim, and following up after placing the child to ensure proper adjustment for the child and family. Adoption agencies, whether they were public or private, were construed as serving a public purpose. They were and still are, accordingly, heavily regulated by the state: for the most part they must be licensed and operate as nonprofit entities.[43]

Private ordering and the rise of surrogate motherhood have altered this situation. A second model of adoption has gained ground—private placement adoption—that bypasses licensed agencies and operates through contact established between prospective adoptive parents and birth mothers, either directly via advertisement or through an intermediary such as a lawyer or physician, often referred to as a facilitator.[44] In the states that allow private adoptions, they now account for 80 percent of newborn placement. Contract is thus replacing public ordering. To be sure, contract is not fully unconstrained in this domain. In order to avoid charges of illegal baby selling, payments in private adoptions to the birth mother are supposed to be limited to her medical (pregnancy-related) and legal expenses.[45] Of course, intermediaries (lawyers, physicians) are also paid for their professional services. Needless to say, there is not much clarity as to what qualifies as a compensable pregnancy-related expense or a legitimate professional service and there is a wide variety from state to state.[46]

Regulation of private adoption is minimal compared to agency regulation.[47] Advocates argue that private ordering in this domain is salutory because it allows the birth mother and the prospective adoptive parents to choose one another on the basis of information about background and health history, as well as first-hand experience. Hence, unlike agency adoptions, private ordering gives control over the adoption process to the private individuals directly concerned in the matter. It should be noted that this orientation implies a shift in the purpose of adoption: from fulfilling a public function to fulfilling the needs and desires of individuals who want children.[48]

This shift is most obvious in surrogacy contracts. Since there is no child prior to the contract, the purpose of surrogacy can hardly be construed as serving the welfare of the child. Rather, the point is to serve the interests of the individuals who desire to become parents. As Margaret J. Radin has put it, "Unlike a mother relinquishing a baby for adoption, the surrogate mother bears a baby only in response to the demand of the would-be parents: their demand is the reason for its being born."[49] In a surrogacy arrangement, private individuals contract with each other directly or through a private, for-profit intermediary to create and transfer a baby. The surrogate mother typically agrees to conceive and give birth to a child, terminate her parental rights, relinquish custody to the contracting father or couple, undergo medical and genetic tests, and have an abortion upon the father's request. In return, the prospective father provides monetary compensation to the surrogate and covers medical expenses, travel costs, and attorney fees.[50] The response of state legislators and courts to surrogacy contracts varies. Some states declare paid surrogacy contracts void or unenforceable; others authorize noncommercial surrogacy contracts, while still others permit paid surrogacy contracts under certain provisos.[51] Courts too have reached varied conclusions regarding the enforceability of surrogacy contracts. In some cases they have upheld statutory restrictions on commercial surrogacy against claims that they violate contractual rights. In others, courts have enforced such contracts against charges that they are a disguised form of baby selling. The counterargument is that surrogacy contracts do not violate the purpose of baby-selling statutes, which is to prevent financial pressure on parents to part with their children—since the children do not exist prior to the arrangement.[52] That such pressure can be exerted on poor women via financial inducements, first to produce and then to part with children, seems not to have occurred to those judges.

Thus the legal situation indicates reticence in the face of full-fledged private ordering in the case of surrogacy. Nevertheless, the trend of public opinion, especially among the young, is strongly in favor of such contracts because they apparently increase choice and control for private individuals.[53] Arguments for using market structures to govern adoption and surrogacy have received increasingly favorable academic attention in recent years. Richard Posner's original co-authored 1978 piece advocating a free market in babies initially provoked a very negative reaction, but when it reappeared in a slightly modified form in 1987 the response was much more positive.[54] To be sure, surrogacy contracts in particular have been at the center of a wide debate, with most critics concerned about the conditions surrounding the surrogate's prebirth consent to adoption and compensation. But as Jana B. Singer has pointed out, the deeper issue of whether the private transfer of parental rights and obligations is wise or appropriate has received little attention.[55] This is the focus of the communitarian critique.

Privatization has made incursions into the procedural as well as the substantive dimensions of family law. The replacement of adjudication by private mediation in the resolution of disputes over economic matters and child custody relating to divorce is an example. It is also a highly ambiguous development from the communitarian perspective. In the aftermath of the emergence of no-fault divorce, the use of mediation to solve issues relating to marital dissolution has skyrocketed. Under the old status regime private mediation was nonexistent, and court-ordered conciliation counseling was aimed at reconciliation of the marital partners.[56] Today, on the contrary, existing court conciliation services and the enormous plethora of private divorce mediators focus on resolving disputes relating to divorce's aftermath. An army of professional mediators has emerged with varying degrees of qualification.[57] Nevertheless, people are turning more and more to private paid mediation and away from public adjudication.

The key argument in favor of this shift from public to private conflict resolution is that mediation facilitates direct communication between the divorcing spouses, thus reducing hostility and generating agreements that both will be committed to fulfilling. Here it seems that contract fosters communicative coordination of interaction. The adversarial legal system, on the other hand, allegedly exacerbates conflict. Mediation, in short, produces more satisfaction and is cheaper than going to court.

The privatization of this procedural component of family law is in tune with the privatization of the substantive dimensions already discussed and has similar proclaimed advantages: it allegedly places control and responsibility in the hands of the individuals involved, increases their choices by enabling them to develop their own financial, property, and parental agreements, and hence returns decision making to the family, to the private sphere, taking it out of the hands of government.[58] Individual autonomy is enhanced while the concrete situation of the particular people involved is respected: each mediation can come up with an agreement appropriate to the unique case at hand. By freeing individuals from publicly imposed rules (public ordering, status), private mediation allows them to come up with consensual conflict resolutions that are deemed inherently superior to those that rest on external imposition. Indeed, the privacy of the mediation process (no outsider has access to it) is touted as one of its main advantages.[59] It is premised, as are the other aspects of privatization, on the assumption that the formation and dissolution of family relationships are essentially private matters regarding which the public has no legitimate interest or significant regulatory role to play.[60]

The communitarian objections to these privatization processes are substantial and not without merit. Delivering adoption and surrogacy entirely over to monetized private contractual arrangements does seem to undermine the specific nature of the family as comprising relationships that are different from the calculating self-interest of market interactions. There are indeed some things in a civilized society, as the New Jersey Supreme Court opined in the Baby M case, that money cannot buy.[61] Framing parents' relationship to children in contractual terms thus mischaracterizes the ties that bind. It also fosters the view that if it is permissible to contract in, it is okay to contract out of parental relationships, especially if something unexpected occurs, like a less-than-perfect baby being born to a surrogate. Privatization of divorce procedures and the no-fault approach also encourage the assumption that one can completely dissolve a past relationship and all obligations it once entailed, since such obligations are no longer voluntarily assumed. The contractual model of intimacy, in short, is deeply one-sided. It focuses exclusively on the interests, desires, self-realization, or personal happiness of the individual, to the exclusion of any concern for the solidarities, emotional bonds, responsibilities, and mutual obligations that are also intrinsic to intimate association.[62] It thus undermines commitment to and responsibility within marriage and family.

Indeed, under the contractual model of private ordering, marriage becomes construed as a collection of temporarily affiliated individuals pursuing their own aims and interests. But private norm creation and private dispute resolution based on this model in family law can harm vulnerable family members. Moreover, the autonomy that privatization allegedly enhances is often either illusory or purchased at the price of inequality.

Jana B. Singer documents the evidence showing the detrimental effects of private ordering of divorce. She notes, as have many others, that as a result of divorce bargaining practices in which a parent often trades financial claims for custody assurances, children and their custodial parents, usually women, often become impoverished.[63] Moreover, children are not represented in private mediation processes and could suffer emotional harm from deals that, for example, sever their connection to beloved grandparents or even a parent. The dearth of significant public controls on the private adoption process also threatens children's physical and moral welfare. They may end up in the hands of adoptive parents who are abusive or incapable of caring for them. We have already seen that private surrogacy contracts carry the risk that people will opt out if dissatisfied with the "product."

Feminist communitarians have not failed to note other disadvantages of privatization for women. Most often identified is the danger that it will exacerbate existing economic and power inequalities. Indeed, here we come up again against the tension between liberty and equality that always stalks the debate over private versus public ordering. Many have already made the case regarding the privatization of substantive areas of family law. It is obvious that surrogacy contracts, for example, trade on the gendered inequality of poor women, for whom financial pressures make their consent as problematic as any more explicit form of baby selling. The substantive outcomes of no-fault divorce have also been widely cited as producing gendered female and child poverty.[64] Moreover, the procedural privatization of divorce mediation, despite its apparent fostering of voice and communicative autonomy, seriously exacerbates existing power imbalances between the genders.[65] Private mediators tend not to address the unequal bargaining positions that often obtain between husband and wife due to the former's financial sophistication and domination during marriage. Ideals of neutrality, impartiality, and the mediator's claim to be a mere facilitator of the couple's decision-making process undermine attempts by mediators to raise the issue of power imbalances.[66] Besides, since private mediation is particularistic and individualistic, even if glaring imbalances in power are addressed in a specific case, systematic gender inequalities tend to be ignored.[67] The issue, of course, is more general: if private mediation is not publicly regulated, it cannot be made receptive to or steered by public norms.

Indeed, privatization can also block needed reforms within family law by individualizing and depoliticizing grievances while deflecting people from reflecting on the public values and principles, even if these are diverse, to which personal relations ought to aspire.[68] It thus indirectly legitimates the traditional gendered structures and inequalities that continue to exist within the domain of intimate association as well as outside it.

The communitarian's critique on the empirical level is thus in many respects quite convincing. However, the theoretical construction upon which it relies and the solution it embraces—a revived status regime—are both deeply flawed. The answer to the drawbacks of private ordering cannot, in my view, lie in a wholesale shift back to a state-imposed status regime.

As we have already seen in the cases of Michael Sandel and Mary Ann Glendon, the communitarian critique of privatization targets the acontextual self that constitutionalized rights-talk allegedly presupposes.[69] Equated with the voluntaristic contractual model of private ordering, constitutional privacy analysis is thus also rejected for its supposed atomistic assumptions.

In a recent comprehensive book on the privatization of family law, Milton C. Regan, Jr., has expanded this line of analysis, indicting the acontextual self presupposed by contract, private ordering, and privacy analysis as antithetical to intimacy, family, and commitment. He proposes that one embrace instead the model of the situated "relational self" as the basis for thinking about family.[70] On the relational model, according to Regan following Sandel, the self is not detached or focused exclusively on its interests. It is, instead, defined, partly constituted by and bound by its relationships with intimate others, especially within the family. Family nourishes the relational self by creating ties that bind, interdependencies and intimacies that carry obligations, and emotional relationships that involve responsibilities, whether or not these are voluntaristically contracted for. Conversely, the relational model of the self reaffirms and acknowledges familial ties. Regan thus mobilizes the old opposition between the discourses of family and market, construing the former as a bulwark against the atomizing, fragmenting, utilitarian orientation of private autonomous contracting selves allegedly characteristic of the latter.[71]

This analysis is the basis of the argument for the revival of a public status regime. Instead of delivering marriage and the family over to contract law, causing us to lose sight of the purposes, responsibilities, and obligations entailed by intimacy, Regan proposes that we return to status and public ordering, albeit in a new form. He is, of course, quite aware that status has historically connoted hierarchy, male dominance, and moralistic attitudes toward sex and sexual orientation. But a new public status regime need not be so encumbered. Instead of being based on hierarchy, the statuses created by public regulation could and should be based on the premise of gender equality. Public ordering of intimacy and the imposition of status obligations are indispensable, however, to ensuring that family life fulfill its communal purposes.[72] It is also needed to protect intimate association from the fragmenting and unjust consequences of privatization.

What is wrong with this analysis and this project? First, it is conceptually fuzzy. Indeed, status, the key concept of the communitarian approach, is something of a catchall term in this analysis. It seems at times to be a shorthand for all that is of value in family and intimate association that are lost in the contractual frame.[73] A contract signals that certain behavior is the business only of those who directly engage in it and involves responsibility only for that which is contracted. Status communicates the message that intimate relationships create special obligations whether or not these are intended. As such, status connotes the connection, dependencies, responsibilities, solidarity, and care that attach to the various roles adopted in intimate relationships. It thus allegedly acknowledges the ways in which intimate relationships can be constitutive of one's sense of self by presupposing a relational model of identity defined in terms of communal norms.

Status accordingly protects intimate commitment by providing the appropriate model of the self, according to Regan: "My first contention . . . is that status is sensitive to the fact that intimacy can shape identity; my second is that status is responsive to the fact that committed intimacy depends on coherent identity."[74]

Finally, status is also a legally articulated system that identifies the reciprocal obligations and duties entailed by intimate association. Indeed, status is the vehicle for regulations aimed at protecting vulnerable parties in a given relationship. Because certain relationships by their nature involve dependency and vulnerability, a regime of pure private ordering is deemed inappropriate. The law must acknowledge the relational character of obligation and ensure that the stronger party carries out responsibilities owed to the weaker whether or not they flow from express agreement.[75]

Indeed, Regan points out, in a clear reference to the welfare state, that there has been an increased willingness to regulate even commercial life on the basis of status in order to protect the weaker parties to contractual arrangements.[76] The irony of the contemporary tendency to shift family law over to private ordering in such a context does not escape him: "Family law thus seems to be moving toward contract precisely at a moment when that paradigm's influence over commercial life is waning, and when the analytical foundation of contract law itself seems to be shifting. The fact that these changes in commercial law are occurring because of the need to acknowledge dependence is of direct relevance to family law, because family relationships also feature considerable vulnerability and reliance."[77] Just as status can enhance freedom in economy, so Regan argues, it can promote intimacy and security in family life.

The conceptual fuzziness and diffuseness of the communitarian's concept of status serves a political purpose. The claim is that a new status regime will simultaneously protect the vulnerable and ensure responsibility and solidarity within intimate association, while respecting the equality of intimate associates. But this rather overburdened concept is hardly up to the task. Despite the rhetoric, the real focus of contemporary status discourse is to revive the primacy of one form of intimate association: marriage.

What are the premises and purpose of the new status model advocated by communitarians and relational feminists alike? Let's look more closely at the rhetoric. Status presupposes that the intimate association is of public relevance and hence should be subject to public ordering. The purpose of reviving status is, as Regan explicitly states, to strengthen marriage and the family by rearticulating the obligations and privileges these should entail in a regime of gender equality. This means that status should not assign family roles on the basis of gender.[78] It should, however, give expression to the enduring obligations spouses have to one another (even after divorce) and that parents have to children, and it should reinforce familial attitudes.[79]

Thus the heart and soul of the new status regime is its focus on recentering, remoralizing, and reprivileging marriage.[80] Communitarians accept that today the purpose of marriage is no longer taken to be procreation but emotional support. Accordingly, marriage entails first and foremost an ethic of relational obligation and mutual commitment. It is this that allegedly renders it superior and preferable to unmarried cohabitation. Indeed, many want to put a stop to the tendency justified by contract theory, to extend to unmarried cohabitants the legal benefits currently available only to married spouses.[81] For example, Regan supports legal acknowledgment of the duties that arise between unmarried partners due to their intimate association, on the basis of a relational as opposed to the contractual model of obligation.[82] But according to him, such couples have no legitimate claim to benefits from the government or third parties. Society does, however, have an interest in promoting marriage as the model of the constitutive relationship, and thus marital status should entail privilege. That is why Regan insists that "a new model of status would be sympathetic to the claim that the social interest in promoting marriage justifies preserving a firm distinction between the legal treatment of married and unmarried couples."[83]

Other policy implications flow from this approach aimed at correcting the flaws of the contractual model. Remoralizing marriage on the relational model would entail the reintroduction of the option of a fault-based divorce scheme.[84] If a spouse feels that the minimal standards of marriage were violated, she should have the opportunity of arguing this in court. Communitarian feminists also want greater public scrutiny of divorce, varying according to the presence or absence of young children.[85] Needless to say, the new status model would also militate against the idea that no obligations obtain after the marriage contract is dissolved.

At the same time, Regan argues that marriage and family must be redefined not only to exclude gendered roles, but also to include same-sex couples. Since the point of marriage is emotional support for spouses and children, and since same-sex couples can procreate outside of sexual relations through the use of fertilization technologies (or adoption), it would be wrong to deny them the opportunity to marry. Indeed, on the communitarian analysis, marriage would make same-sex relationships more like heterosexual ones: fostering stability, community, and responsibility between the partners.[86] Gay marriage is justified not on the grounds of freedom of contract or individual rights claims, but because recognition of their relationships through marriage would integrate them as full members into the community, making them more like everyone else. At the same time, however, the revived status regime would *not* acknowledge domestic partnerships.[87]

THE LIMITS OF STATUS

It is not necessary to probe further into the specific policy proposals that follow from the communitarian analysis. The question is whether replacing contract and constitutionalized rights with a new, allegedly egalitarian status regime and direct public ordering that privileges marriage is the appropriate response to the negative consequences of privatization. I argue that it is not.

To be sure, the critics are right about many of the negative effects of private ordering. They are also right to insist that law can and should articulate principles that constrain and influence how we construct our intimate associations.[88] Certainly preferences are not entirely exogenous to law but can be shaped by it, not only in terms of instrumental calculations of incentives but also with regard to the values that law articulates and legitimizes. When law expresses principles, it assumes an aspirational function regarding how we think individuals ought to orient their behavior. Law can thus perform an educational and inspirational role.[89] Indeed, law cannot avoid articulating standards, and it does so even vis-à-vis contract. Unlike straightforward legal rules, however, standards and legal doctrines refer to substantive objectives of the legal order, and to the consideration of ends.[90] Pace law and economics discourse, this cannot be avoided in the regulation of intimacy. Thus communicative reflection over ends, standards, and principles is indispensable.

Nevertheless, these truisms do not lead where the communitarian thinks they do. They do not, in short, justify a wholesale shift back to substantive public ordering as if the differentiation between law and morality constitutive of modern legal systems could simply be ignored.[91] Rather, they signal the need to transcend the old dichotomies for a more nuanced approach to the legal regulation of intimacy. The status regime proposed by the communitarians suffers from symmetrical flaws to the contractual model it seeks to replace.

The justification for returning to a status regime privileging marriage is that it will be based on gender equality while fostering the emotional support, responsibility, and solidarity appropriate to relational ties and dependencies intrinsic to intimate association. There will be no injustice in recentering marriage because it will be available to everyone.

But even if marriage is open to all and even if the law does not explicitly impose gendered obligations onto the statuses of wife and husband, mother and father, the fact remains that these are laden with symbolic meaning that still have a gendering effect. Moreover, if the law privileges one among the many forms of intimate association, it will certainly create a hierarchy among them. Indeed, we have already seen this in the policy proposals regarding unmarried cohabitation. Status will also undermine plurality, as the suggestion that the law refrain from acknowledging domestic partnerships witnesses. The implication of such a status system is that there is really still only one right way to conduct intimate relationships. Equal access to one core institution would be purchased at the price of assimilation and normalization. Those who will not or cannot conform to the marital model will indubitably be construed as deviant, their relationships as inferior. Au fond, the model is monistic and despite disclaimers, still based on a link between status and social hierarchy.

Moreover, remoralizing marriage would inevitably carry with it a puritanical attitude toward nonmarital and extramarital sex. The communitarian's argument for construing sexual infidelity as a breach of marital trust and hence as a basis for compensable fault in divorce cases proves my point.[92] This would once again make sex acts the business of the law, with all the obvious oppressive implications. Last but hardly least, and despite disclaimers, such a status regime would revive gender stereotypes. This can be seen in the very arguments that are mobilized to justify the regime as egalitarian in the substantive sense of rendering those with more power as responsive to and responsible for those with less. Framed as a way to change male attitudes, this approach once again positions women as caring, dependent, vulnerable, and in need of protection against the irresponsible, autonomous, philandering male.[93] Instead of addressing the reasons for gendered economic and power inequalities, the status approach presupposes them even as it offers to redress some of the grievances that they occasion. It invites the revival of a judicial patriarchy now on the national level that grants women benefits if they comport with the image of a vulnerable dependent.

CONCLUSION

Both privatization and state regulation, as we have seen, can have ambivalent effects on equality and autonomy.[94] Private ordering can deliver subordinates and dependents over to private power while fostering the illusion of greater autonomy. Public regulation that revives status and uniformity can become paternalistic and create new forms of domination and privilege and become oppressive, especially when it takes the shape of substantive, goal-oriented interventions. It can also increase arbitrariness when the legal criteria are vague and open-ended. Both alternatives can involve forms of juridification that may undermine horizontal communication and solidarity among intimate associates.[95]

Nevertheless, public ordering of some of the aspects of intimate association is clearly needed—but so are contractual arrangements as well as constitutional protection for individualized privacy rights. Only an approach
that abandons the dichotomies of status and contract, public and private,
regulation versus nonregulation, and which frankly acknowledges both
the legitimacy of diverse forms of intimacy as well as the necessity for a
context-sensitive pluralistic legal regime, has any hope of coming to grips
with the complex situation we face today. The reflexive paradigm accom-
plishes just that.

I have criticized the assumption, shared by advocates and critics of
the liberal legal paradigm, that constitutionally protected privacy rights
and the individualization of some areas of family law are intrinsically
linked to an atomist conception of the self, a contractualist model, or a
rejection of public ordering.[96] In other words, from the perspective of the
reflexive paradigm, one can see that constitutionally protected privacy and
autonomy can be dissociated from untenable dimensions of the liberal
legal paradigm.

As indicated, in my understanding the constitutionalization of individualized privacy rights ascribes to the intimate associates themselves the
competence to choose the forms in which they pursue happiness and attempt to realize their conceptions of the good of intimacy. Constitutional
privacy thus secures some of the basic dimensions of legal personhood and
equal liberty as they have come to be understood today. It also acknowledges legitimate plurality in forms of intimacy, registering the shift of
many matters from the moral to the ethical domain. It provides, in short,
the basic principles—the sine qua non—that any public ordering must
respect: equal individual liberty. The freedom/autonomy protected by
such a right should be framed not as mere choice (*willkur*) predicated on
noninterference but as freedom from normalizing judgments and constraints, freedom from domination and from arbitrary regulation. Its flip
side is the ascription of ethical competence and hence decisional autonomy
to the rights holder. Privacy on the constructivist approach thus does not
block intervention either to ensure equality of the liberty granted or to
control for the effects of relations of subordination. Since power and responsibility as well as ethical competence and decisional autonomy are at
stake in intimate association, the issue is to what purpose and how, not
whether the state should regulate intimacy. Yet this need not involve a
utilitarian calculus: as I have shown, deontological principles are at stake.

However, it is not possible to derive from the abstract principle of equal
liberty (or anti-discrimination) an answer to the question of which liberties should be ascribed to the individual or what the state purpose in regulation should be. One needs an independent argument to show why "X"
should be covered as part of one's decisional autonomy and what, if any,

interest "society" has in the matter, before the question of fair distribution of the respective liberty comes up. Although constitutional equality analysis that is focused on anti-discrimination principles is crucial to achieving gender justice in the domain of intimacy, it steers one away from such considerations. On the other hand, once naturalistic or essentialistic arguments are ruled out, privacy analysis forces one to confront the above questions directly and reflectively. Privacy is symbolic not only of personal autonomy (ethical competence) and control over access/information, but also of the uniquely personal imaginary domain that renders us incommensurate with others and that deserves protection from public scrutiny and normalizing judgments.[97] Privacy talk, in short, addresses the issue of which dimensions of life deserve a reprieve from social control, especially in its legal form.

Accordingly, I have argued for a constructivist approach to the issue of what a right to privacy/autonomy in the domain of intimacy should cover under the presumption of gender equality. Recall that this involves two steps. First we must become reflective about the alleged natural or essential character of personal privacy/liberty in the domain of intimacy and understand that these are constructed in part socially and in part legally. It then becomes possible to ask which rights we as equal citizens should grant one another and what their reach should be. The core idea is that we are construed as equal persons to be treated with respect whatever our differences, and consequently the rules imposed on us can only be those that we could reasonably be expected to accept. Reciprocity is also presupposed: we cannot impose restriction on others that we would not impose on ourselves.

This is important because the principles of gender equality and the moral indifference of sex do not herald the decline of the ethical importance of intimacy but rather shift its meaning. Indeed, today the (e)quality of intimate association is construed as deeply entwined with issues of personal identity, happiness, solidarity, and respect. Freedom to choose intimate associations and the free play of the imagination within them are as important as the obligations and responsibilities these generate. For example, the right to decide freely and responsibly on matters related to their sexuality without coercion, discrimination, or violence has become a key demand of the women's movement worldwide. No individual, it is argued, should be forced into or endure forms of intimacy that she can neither affirm nor embrace, or that violate her conception of the good, who she is or wants to be. Nor should one's sexuality be legally regulated or instrumentalized to serve community purposes without very strong arguments justifying such state action.

If the women's movement in tandem with breakthroughs in contraceptive and reproductive technology has severed sexual activity from the reproductive imperative (moral indifference), the changes in women's status have also invalidated regulations of intimacy that reinforce gendered inequality. But this does not mean that private must replace public ordering. Instead it means, as indicated, that the purpose and mode of public and private ordering have to be rethought.

As I argued in Chapter 2, the ethical standards that should guide public regulation in this domain are the principles of equality, fairness, solidarity, and relational responsibility. Personal autonomy understood as freedom from domination, exploitation, and normalization, along with the forms of privacy that are constitutive of intimacy and of chances for personal happiness, should be protected by legal regulation. A plurality of legitimate forms of intimate association should be acknowledged along with fair treatment of each of them. The public purpose of regulation thus goes beyond ensuring against force or fraud. It should provide security for personal imaginative experimentation, protect difference along with civic equality, and foster responsible ethical choice as well as public reflection on what that entails (appropriate forms of mutually given care especially but not only for children).

Thus, as the discussions in Chapters 1 and 2 show, we do need the liberal form of law that ascribes negative liberty and decisional autonomy to the legal person. This helps protect the plurality of forms of intimate association and the personal imaginary and ethical decision-making involved in them. But as already indicated, negative liberty in the sense of freedom of choice regarding entry and exit into intimate associations also must involve nondomination and freedom from exploitation (being treated as a means only) within them. Constitutional rights protecting autonomy and allowing for private ordering of key aspects of intimate association (like the decision to use contraception, to have an abortion, choice of sexual partners, and privacy of sexual acts) are indeed indispensable for personal freedom. But they do not ipso facto entail the rejection of regulation of other aspects of intimacy. The public/private line must go right through intimate association: privacy as decisional autonomy to enter and conduct intimate sexual relationships cannot shield them from the demands of justice and the requirements of responsibility.

Accordingly, I argue from the standpoint of the reflexive paradigm of law for the liberal legal form of constitutional privacy rights appropriately conceptualized and justified, as a protective cover for certain key dimensions of intimate association and personhood. But this protection must not be construed as involving adaptation to alleged natural orders, nor should it take prior distributions of power and prestige as given. Constitutional privacy rights ascribe autonomy and self-regulation to the individuals involved, protecting them against the state and third parties. They should be complemented by regulation aimed at securing a just distribution of rights and competencies, for, as we also saw from the preceding chapters, negative liberty is necessary but not sufficient for protecting freedom and equality in this domain.

Since the domain of intimacy involves socially constructed gender and sexual relations that are permeated by power differentials, social hierarchies, and other sorts of structural inequalities, direct substantive forms of regulation of intimate association are at times indispensable. This is obvious if one thinks of such things as prohibitions of marital rape, rules against polygamy, age restrictions on entry into marriage, proscriptions against marketized surrogacy, and adoption, all of which can be justified as protecting gender equality. The need for national standards and clear rules applying directly to all adoption and surrogacy transactions, backed up by strong sanctions, should be obvious. Some of these regulations, like age restrictions and rules about obligations of parental care (child support in all its senses), are clearly based on status. But this need not revive illegitimate hierarchy or privilege one form of intimate association over others. Substantive regulations based on status could also ensure equality by providing for appropriate child support upon divorce, abortion funding, child care allowances, paid parental leaves, paid leaves to care for ill family members, and so forth. Indeed, a particular ruling could combine legal forms as do the various parts of the decision in *Roe v. Wade* that ascribe the negative liberties of privacy and decisional autonomy to the individual woman in the first trimester, while permitting regulation for the health of the mother in the second and for the interests of the fetus in the third. Substantive provisions for public funding for abortion would ensure that the liberty protected in this matter is equal. Such would be a good example of autonomy-enhancing direct state regulation using substantive, materialized law.

Last but hardly least, there are, of course, areas of intimate association that should be self-regulated but which require careful regulation of self-regulation. We have already seen that sexual harassment law is an example. Simple privatization will not do in such instances because room must be made for guidance by public principles and norms. Gender equality and nondiscrimination on the basis of sex are public principles and violations of them do not involve only a personal harm or a straightforward abuse of supervisory power. That is why suggestions to shift sexual harassment law entirely over to the domain of torts would be a serious error. Sexual harassment law is not yet adequately institutionalized. Yet the discriminatory harms of harassment are far too varied and contextual for direct state regulation through detailed rules to handle. Regulation should take the form of self-regulation, for neither privatization nor direct state regulation could avoid the regulatory trilemma in this area. But self-regulation by corporations or schools has to be regulated. The point is not to establish elaborate rules but to provide incentives to organizations to correct the workplace practices and culture that lead to harassment, by initiating a learning process. The appropriate response is to thus reflect upon the universal principles and substantive ends that should orient sexual harassment law and develop the appropriate public regulation of self-regulation to facilitate local problem solving. In other words, in this domain, the reflexive form of law is most appropriate.

Surely this would also be the right way to go to alleviate the problems of private ordering in, for example, deciding upon financial settlements and mediation processes upon divorce. The recent attempts by courts and legislatures to adopt new publicly imposed standards for postdivorce financial awards—designed to recognize both spouses' investment in a marriage and to protect vulnerable spouses and children without endorsing traditional gender stereotypes pointed to by Jana B. Singer—could be seen as a move in that direction.[98] Shifting to a form of reflexive law to govern the procedural aspects of divorce would be an appropriate solution to the problems of private mediation. While the option of going to court should remain available, it is clear that the contemporary orientation of mediation processes toward the aftermath of divorce—custody and visitation questions on the one side, and financial arrangements on the other—calls for public oversight. Indeed, private divorce mediation is an obvious candidate for the regulation of self-regulation. The context and the particularities of each case matter a great deal, but public standards are indispensable. The reflexive legal form would involve the institutionalization of such processes that would, in turn, depend upon a sustained public debate over the appropriate norms that should orient both public and private procedures of mediation.

The legal recognition of domestic partnerships (both heterosexual and same-sex) and the extension to these relationships of benefits traditionally reserved to married couples would also involve a form of reflexive law. Obviously this would provide public recognition of private relationships. But, as Singer argues, it would also force legislators and policy makers to reflect upon and articulate the values once attached exclusively to marriage—provision of stability, nurturance, solidarity, mutual responsibility, commitment—as values inherent in all forms of intimate association seeking institutionalization.[99] According legal status to registered domestic partnerships should involve a form of reflexive law that makes them receptive to the influence of such publicly articulated values (that everyone can accept!) and subject to the constitutional principles of equal liberty, while leaving the details of the intimate association up to the associates themselves. It would, in short, be another example of institutionalized regulation of self-regulation.

It should by now be clear that a reflective assessment of the context and set of issues to be regulated and of the legal form most appropriate to the task is what the reflexive legal paradigm makes possible. Indeed, it also permits the choice of no regulation where this is justified, as it is, in my view, regarding consensual adult sex conducted in private. It is this perspective that allows us to transcend the dead-end dichotomous thinking that pervades so much of the reasoning (legal, political, and theoretical) about the regulation of intimate relations. The transformations of intimacy that I have discussed beg for serious theoretical reconsideration of regulatory strategies. And, indeed, we are just at the threshold of rather staggering changes and possibilities in this area: one need only think of the potential impact of burgeoning reproductive and other biotechnologies on intimate association and intimate decision making. The only way to secure freedom, equality, and the chance of happiness for everyone in this domain is to let go of unhelpful approaches, embrace the paradigm shift, and reflect together on the choices it opens up for us.

Notes

INTRODUCTION

1. I am purposely vague about the word "domain." Intimate relationships involving sex and eroticism cannot be localized in a particular "sphere" or institution such as the family. They constitute a "domain" only to the extent that they can be distinguished from other sorts of relationships, not in terms of locale or institutional setting.

2. As of 1992, three-fifths of married women with preschool-age children and half of married women with children under two were in the labor force. See Cherlin, *Public and Private Families*, 298, citing U.S. Bureau of the Census, *Statistical Abstract of the United States* (1993). The 2000 census reports that less than a quarter of U.S. households are made up of married couples with children (*New York Times*, 15 May 2001, A1). Labor force participation for single mothers with dependent children is similar. See Spain and Banchi, *Balancing Act*, 146. See also Furstenberg, "Family Change and the Welfare of Children"; Furstenberg, "Family Change and Family Diversity"; Giddens, *Transformation of Intimacy*; Fineman, *Neutered Mother*; and Beck, *Risk Society*.

3. See Sunstein, *After the Rights Revolution*, 1–46. For a different view, see Glendon, *Rights Talk*.

4. The right to marry (*Loving v. Virginia*), the right of married couples to use contraception (*Griswold v. Connecticut*), the right of the unmarried to do the same (*Eisenstadt v. Baird*), the right to abortion (*Roe v. Wade, Planned Parenthood of Southeastern Pennsylvania v. Casey*), the right to use "obscene" materials in the privacy of one's home (*Stanley v. Georgia*), and the right to work in an environment free of sexual discrimination and sexual harassment (the 1964 Civil Rights Act, backed by a series of Supreme Court decisions beginning in 1986 with *Harris v. Forklift*) have all been deemed fundamental constitutional rights by the Supreme Court. There are many more examples.

5. Richards, *Women, Gays, and the Constitution*), 233–287, 460–462; Lawrence Tribe, "Rights of Privacy and Personhood," in *American Constitutional Law*, 1302–1435; and Karst, "Freedom of Intimate Association," arguing for a right to freedom of intimate association when consensual relationships between adults are at issue.

6. For a libertarian argument along these lines see Posner, *Sex and Reason*. For a feminist argument for the dejuridification of marriage and the sexual conjugal unit, see Fineman, *Neutered Mother*.

7. Okin, *Justice, Gender, and the Family*; MacKinnon, *Toward a Feminist Theory of the State*.

8. There is a third model developed by neocommunitarians that advocates a revival of status-based regulation of intimate relationships, this time on the na-

tional level, based on "shared" substantive moral values, similar in kind to the type of morals legislation once employed on the state level. I also address this position in Chapter 5.

9. On the concept of a legal paradigm, see Habermas, *Between Facts and Norms*, 388–446; Teubner, "After Legal Instrumentalism"; and Teubner, "Substantive and Reflexive Elements." See Chapter 4 for a fuller discussion.

10. Teubner,"Substantive and Reflexive Elements."

11. Arato, "Paradigms of Law: Some Questions." See Chapter 4.

12. *Griswold v. Connecticut*, 381 U.S. 479 (1965). See Tribe, *American Constitutional Law*, 1302–1435, for a summary of this development. See also Gunther and Sullivan, *Constitutional Law*, 516–615.

13. The "domain of intimacy" has in the past been taken to refer to marriage, the family, and intimacy in the home. But intimate association and intimate personal decisions, as indicated, occur outside of marriage and take shape outside the home. The spatial metaphors of public and private and the centrality of marriage can no longer be mapped onto the "domain" of intimate relationships.

14. Fineman, *Neutered Mother*, and Grossberg, *Governing the Hearth*. See also Foucault, *History of Sexuality*, vol. 1.

15. Grossberg, *Governing the Hearth*. Thus there were and still are on the books laws against adultery, sodomy, "fornication," incest, rape, obscenity, the sale of contraceptives, abortion, and so forth.

16. See Gillman, *Constitution Besieged*, for a general and excellent discussion. See also Grossberg, *Governing the Hearth*, and Fineman, *Neutered Mother*.

17. Gillman, *Constitution Besieged*. Under the doctrine of coverture first articulated by Blackstone, women upon marriage gave up their legal personhood and their ability to sue in court and were "covered" by the head of household.

18. See the new line of privacy decisions beginning with *Griswold v. Connecticut* in 1965, running through *Planned Parenthood of Southeastern Pennsylvania v. Casey* in 1992, in Tribe, *American Constitutional Law*.

19. Gillman, *Constitution Besieged*.

20. Ibid., 204. Of course the emergence of "neo-federalism" and new arguments for state's rights over the past ten years in reaction to these developments indicate that the entire issue is still hotly contested.

21. Ibid. See also Ackerman, *We the People*, 1–33, 150–162. Just which particular liberties are to be considered "preferred" or "basic" has consequently become a much-debated issue, as has the highly visible active role of the Court in making such decisions.

22. See Habermas, *Theory of Communicative Action*, 1:1–143, 339–403; Habermas, "An Alternative Way Out of the Philosophy of the Subject," in *Philosophical Discourse of Modernity*, 294–327. See also Foucault, *Order of Things*.

23. Habermas, "Alternative Way," and Foucault, *Order of Things*.

24. The due process clause of the Fourteenth Amendment provides that "no state shall make or enforce any law which shall . . . deprive any person of life, liberty, or property without due process of law." In the period roughly from the 1890s to the New Deal, the Supreme Court gave this clause a substantive interpretation, overturning many state laws regulating the economy and the labor market as violations of property and liberty (freedom of contract). The most famous case

in this line of jurisprudence was *Lochner v. New York*, 198 U.S. 45 (1905). Substantive due process analysis, subsequently dubbed "Lochnerizing," was completely discredited after the New Deal until its revival in the new privacy jurisprudence in the 1960s. See Chapter 1.

25. See Berger, *Government by Judiciary.*

26. See Grossberg, *Governing the Hearth*, 300–302, for the concept of judicial patriarchy. The term applies to shifts in family law initiated by state-level trial and appellate courts in the second half of the nineteenth century, which resulted in the dilution of paternal sovereignty and household legal unity. Male judges attributed partial legal capacity to married women by construing them as dependents and making their rights turn on the guardianship of the judiciary rather than husbands. This enabled state judges to expand their own jurisdictional and discretionary powers. The judges resisted attempts to establish independent legal rights in statute form assertable by women themselves. In short, the gendered assumptions of republican ideology that informed the nineteenth century courts' understanding of the family and of the public/private distinction militated against full personal autonomy and full legal rights for women. Married women in need got individualized benefits at the discretion of judges in charge of domestic-relations law, at the price of having to embrace their dependent status.

It thus seems wrong to repeat this charge regarding contemporary privacy or equality jurisprudence because these are premised on the full legal personhood of women, married or single. If judges condition the enjoyment of such rights on some view of the proper comportment of women, as often happens in sexual harassment decisions, then they should be criticized for operating with an anachronistic and illegitimate understanding of gender or of what privacy and anti-discrimination rights should mean. See Chapter 3.

27. Reflexive law could "relieve" the courts as well as administrative agencies from the detailed substantive regulatory burden placed on them since the New Deal. But this is the topic of another book, perhaps my next one.

28. See two works by Hannah Arendt: *Human Condition* and *On Revolution.*

29. Classic statements of the liberal concept of the person is to be found in Kant, *Metaphysics of Morals*, and Mill, *On Liberty.* Among legal theorists, the strongest defender of this position is Tribe, *American Constitutional Law*, and Richards, *Women, Gays, and the Constitution.*

30. See Glendon, *Rights Talk.*

31. Ibid.

32. For the argument that the term privacy is imprecise and should be replaced by the concept of sexual autonomy, see Rosen, "My Child, Mine to Protect." See also McClain, "Poverty of Privacy." I argue that sexual autonomy is, of course, at issue here but that privacy in regard to the domain of intimacy encompasses much more. See Morris, "Privacy, Privation, Perversity."

33. Olsen, "Myth of State Intervention in the Family," 835, 842–844, 862, n. 73; Olsen, "Family and the Market." See Chapter 1.

34. The abortion funding controversy is the paradigmatic example of this apparent paradox.

35. Sedgwick, *Epistemology of the Closet.*

36. *Bowers v. Hardwick*, 478 U.S. 186 (1986).

37. Habermas, *Theory of Communicative Action*; Nonet and Selznick, *Law and Society in Transition*; Teubner, "Substantive and Reflexive Elements"; and Teubner, "After Legal Instrumentalism." See also Rogowski and Wilthagen, *Reflexive Labor Law*, as well as Teubner, Farmer, and Murphy, *Environmental Law and Ecological Responsibility*, and Ortes, "Reflexive Environmental Law," for a more recent series of articles on reflexive law and the environment. Dorf and Sabel, "A Constitution of Democratic Experimentalism," n. 2, apply the new reflexive form of regulation—which they call "democratic experimentalism"—to constitutional design generally. Their version of "reflexive law" is presented as a wholesale alternative to the mode of regulation and governance put in place during and after the New Deal. See also Black, "Constitutionalizing Self-Regulation."

38. See Chapter 4.

39. The systems-theoretical approach of Teubner insists on the second, arguing that the former involves an anachronistic image of central political steering. I want to thank Professor Teubner for pointing this out to me in a very generous discussion in Frankfurt. See Chapter 4.

40. See Chapter 4. I owe the insight into the role of mediators in transmitting learning across organizations to Sturm, "Second-Generation Employment Discrimination," 475, 479–488, 525–530, 555 n. 3; see below. Ranging from human resource professionals and lawyers to outside consulting organizations, intermediaries can encourage organizations to build institutional capacity to creatively respond to reflexive regulation of self-regulation oriented by general principles, and to gather and share relevant information. Local development of norms and procedures to address, for example, sexual harassment can then be transmitted to other organizations and to the courts as well, thus enabling them recursively to refine their understanding of those proactive approaches that judicial involvement is designed to trigger and of what the legal norm should involve. As Sturm correctly notes, the challenge is to institutionalize a regulatory system that fosters dynamic interaction among workplaces, nongovernmental organizations, courts, and administrative agencies and that ensures effectiveness and accountability.

41. Ibid., 555 n. 3. According to Sturm, second-generation forms of discrimination do not involve formal policies of racial or sex discrimination, nor need they entail intentional discriminatory acts by particular actors. Rather one must think in terms of more subtle patterns of discriminatory interaction that may include cognitive and often unconscious bias and/or structures of decision making that perpetuate exclusion or harassment in the aggregate in the workplace. Second-generation bias is "structural, relational, and situational" (459–460).

Sturm provides impressive research to demonstrate the use and successes of "structural approach"—reflexive law in my terminology—in three firms: Deloitte & Touche, Intel Corporation, and Home Depot. She also addresses many criticisms and makes proposals for reform, that is, for the better institutionalization of that approach. Thus her work dovetails very nicely with my own.

42. Ibid., 458–465; the author collapses the liberal and the welfare paradigms together under the concept of the "rule-based enforcement approach." This could easily be rectified without disturbing her argument for the importance of the structural (i.e., reflexive) regulatory approach to problems of second-generation discrimination.

43. Key figures in the law and economics school are Becker, *Economic Approach to Human Behavior*; Schultz, *Essays in Economics of the Family*; Posner, "Regulation of the Market in Adoption"; Posner, "Ethics and Economics of Enforcing Contracts of Surrogate Motherhood"; and Posner, *Sex and Reason*.

Among the communitarians and communitarian feminists, in addition to Sandel and Glendon, see especially Regan, *Family Law and the Pursuit of Intimacy*; Singer, "Privatization of Family Law"; West, "Jurisprudence and Gender"; and West, "Difference in Women's Hedonic Lives."

44. See Regan, *Family Law*, and Singer, *Privatization of Family Law*.

45. On the new familism, see Streunung, "Feminist Challenges to the New Familism."

46. This is true for Singer. But see Brinig, "Status, Contract and Covenant," for a critique of status discourse by a feminist communitarian who is clearly also critical of contract as well.

47. Arato, "Paradigms of Law."

CHAPTER ONE
CONSTITUTIONAL PRIVACY IN THE DOMAIN OF INTIMACY

1. See Furstenberg, "Family Change and Family Diversity," and Cohen, "Does Voluntary Association Make Democracy Work?"

2. See Taylor, *Sources of the Self*, for the concept of "strong evaluation."

3. See Introduction.

4. For the concept of "redescription" see Rorty, *Contingency, Irony, and Solidarity*, 79–80. I should add that I do not subscribe to Rorty's understanding of the public/private dichotomy. For an early feminist effort see Allen, *Uneasy Access*. More recent contributions include de Crew, *In Pursuit of Privacy*, and Boling, *Privacy and the Politics of Intimate Life*. The very best recent piece I have read on privacy is Morris, "Privacy, Privation, Perversity."

5. For an early discussion of the philosophical concept of privacy see *Philosophical Dimensions of Privacy*, ed. Ferdinand Schoeman. See also Schoeman, *Privacy and Social Freedom*. For a superb recent analysis see Morris, "Privacy, Privation, Perversity."

6. See Garrow, *Liberty and Sexuality*, for a history.

7. *Griswold v. Connecticut*, 381 U.S. 479 (1965); *Eisenstadt v. Baird*, 405 U.S. 438 (1972).

8. *Roe v. Wade*, 410 U.S. 113 (1973).

9. Ibid. The original article on which this chapter is based was prepared for the "Reproductive Rights in a Post-*Roe* World" conference at the Columbia University School of Law, New York, fall 1991. At the time, many of us feared that the decision in *Webster v. Reproductive Health Services*, 429 U.S. 490 (1989), which upheld a Missouri law whose preamble found that life begins at conception and that the unborn fetus is entitled to all the rights, privileges, and immunities of all other persons, would be used as precedent to overturn *Roe* and grant full personhood to fetuses. The more recent decision in *Planned Parenthood of Southeastern Pennsylvania v. Casey*, 505 U.S. 833 (1992), however, did not do this. Instead, it reaffirmed the "essential" holding of *Roe*—to wit, that women have a fundamental

right to decisional autonomy regarding pregnancy and that this cannot be subject to a plenary override in the name of protecting life (*Casey*, 112 S.Ct., at 4, 13–17). Moreover, the joint opinion articulated the principles of personal liberty, bodily integrity, and respect for the self-definition of every individual in its arguments upholding *Roe* (*Casey*, 112 S.Ct., at 13–17). In this Justices Stevens and Blackmun concurred, explicitly thematizing the concept of privacy as the principle that encompasses all these concerns (Justice Blackmun, 112 S.Ct., at 51; Justice Stevens, 112 S.Ct., at 68).

Nevertheless, the *Casey* ruling opened the door to ever increased state regulation of abortion by upholding regulations imposed by the Pennsylvania law on abortion from the time of conception (thereby abandoning the trimester framework of *Roe*), and by reducing the standard of review from one of strict scrutiny to the "undue burden" test. Indeed, it upheld all the restrictions in the Pennsylvania law under review except the husband notification requirement. This puts it in line with the series of abortion funding cases like *Maher v. Roe*, 432 U.S. 464 (1977), and *Harris v. McRae*, 448 U.S. 297 (1980), that denied a constitutional right to funding for abortions for poor women and included other restrictions of the rights granted in *Roe*. If we consider that *Casey* also overruled important parts of *Thornburgh v. American College of Obstetricians and Gynecologists*, 476 U.S. 758–771 (1986), regarding informed consent regulations, and *City of Akron v. Akron Center for Reproductive Health (Akron 1)*, 462 U.S. 416, 474 (1983), regarding waiting periods, then things do begin to look bad for women's reproductive freedom. It is thus well worth our effort to clarify the normative issues involved in the abortion debate in the hopes of influencing the courts and legislatures to take them more seriously.

For a pessimistic view of the meaning of *Casey* see Patricia Ireland, president of the National Organization of Women (NOW), "Abortion Angst." For a more optimistic interpretation see Ronald Dworkin, "Center Holds!"

10. For the equality argument, see the next section. For an argument that what is at stake "substantively" in the privacy and substantive due process analysis revived in *Griswold* is the freedom of intimate association and personal choice, see Karst, "Freedom of Intimate Association." Karst argued that even if calling the liberty protected in the relevant line of decisions "privacy" misleadingly implied that what was at stake is informational privacy, grounding the freedom of intimate personal choice, including associational liberty in the due process clause of the Fourteenth Amendment (*Roe v. Wade*, 410 U.S., at 169) and in a generalized "zone of privacy" created in part by the Third, Fourth, and Fifth Amendments as well (*Griswold* 381 U.S., at 484–485), indeed the general revival of "substantive due process," makes sense once one grasps the organizing principle at stake: the importance of intimate choice to one's self-understanding, self-expression, self-identity, dignity (as a person), and status as an equal citizen. In a context in which there is new appreciation for cultural diversity and a presumptive equal status of women in society, the assertion of fundamental privacy rights in the "domain of intimacy" rightly shifts burden of proof onto the state when it regulates intimate associations and intimate acts. Such a right calls for new justifications of state regulation, even when it protects the traditional family. The point is that if marriage was the typical association protected by the emergent freedom of intimate association

(protected under privacy analysis), then the principle of equality presses for the extension of that freedom to other relationships. Karst (662) cites *Eisenstadt* (the case extending that freedom to use contraception to unmarried women and persons generally—implying the equal status of women) and *Loving v. Virginia* (388 U.S. 374 [1967]), extending the right to marry to interracial couples invoking substantive due process and equal protection analysis.

For a more recent analysis that argues for shifting away from privacy and substantive due process analysis to ground the freedom of intimate association in the First Amendment, see Watson, "An Alternative to Privacy." See also Wenz, *Abortion Rights as Religious Freedom*, for a defense of abortion rights as a First Amendment issue rather than as a matter of privacy.

For the argument that abortion be dealt by the "normal" political process, see Glendon, *Abortion and Divorce in Western Law*. For a counterargument see Tribe, *Clash of Absolutes*. See also the discussion in Davis, "Abortion Debate."

11. There is a specifically feminist version of this communitarian argument: namely, that such a move from "status" to "contract" apparently frees women to shape their own lives, but at the price of buying into a possessive individualist model of the self that denies a reality women know especially well—the centrality of interdependence, of interconnectedness, and of relationships of care in constituting the self. These feminists prefer "responsibility-based" arguments to privacy analysis for justification of abortion rights. See Colker, "Feminist Liberation," and West, *Caring for Justice*. For a useful discussion see McClain, "Poverty of Privacy." For a more recent argument to that effect, with which I strongly disagree, see Boling, *Politics of Intimate Life*, 90–101.

12. For an excellent theoretical analysis and critique of both types of reductionism, see Lefort, "Politics and Human Rights."

13. For a discussion of the distinction between "entity" privacy and personal privacy, see Fineman, "Intimacy Outside of the Natural Family." See also Fineman, *Neutered Mother*, 177–198.

14. The reasons are too complex to go into here, but they have to do in part with the rise of the interventionist welfare state and the related demotion of property from a sacred principle to an economic concept. See Cohen, "Redescribing Privacy: Identity, Difference, and the Abortion Controversy," and Nedelsky, "American Constitutionalism and the Paradox of Private Property."

15. Debra Morris, drawing on Drucilla Cornell's work, provides an excellent analysis of the latter aspect of privacy. Accordingly, privacy shields the psychic space of experience, one's personal "imaginary domain" that flowers in solitude and in intimacy with others, and that is crucial to the opportunity to, as it were, creatively come into one's own: to become a unique individual and presence in the world. This deserves to be shielded from normalizing pressure, pressures to confess, pressures to act and reason as everyone else does. See Morris, "Privacy, Privation, Perversity," and Cornell, *Imaginary Domain*.

16. This is not to say there are not important struggles going on over informational privacy today. Indeed, the ability of new electronic technologies and biogenetic research to generate and spread compromising information about individuals has led to a renewed debate over access to and control over such information. This, however, is not my topic in this text.

17. Of course, control over access to oneself is not only a matter of informational privacy. It also involves control over the degrees of intimacy one wishes to have with others. For example, "going public" by reporting marital rape can be construed as an effort to secure privacy as decisional autonomy, and bodily integrity, for wives.

18. Privacy and autonomy are analytically distinct concepts, and an offense to autonomy need not always involve a compromise of privacy. For my purposes with regard to the domain of intimacy, it is important to include in the broader symbolic meaning of the concept of a privacy right the ideas of decisional autonomy as well as control over access, over reason-giving, and over the decision whether or not to communicate one's feelings and motivations. On the distinction between the concepts, see Morris, "Privacy, Privation, Perversity."

19. See ibid., 346, for the distinction between privacy as decisional autonomy that, in my view, involves ascription of the capacity to judge and to make moral and ethical decisions, and privacy as serving a form of self-relation, that holds judgment in abeyance.

20. This battle is also, of course, a battle over judicial review as well.

21. Feminists rightly point to inegalitarian gender relations, rigidly interpreted and ascribed social roles, allocation of responsibility for pregnancy and child care to women, the absence of social supports for bearing and raising children, inadequate availability of health care for women, and distributional inequalities of economic opportunity between women and men as factors structuring the social relations of reproduction in our society and conditioning our choices. See Petchesky, *Abortion and Woman's Choice*, 1–15, 326–356. For a more recent version of this argument see Davis, "Abortion Debate," 764–766, arguing for a broad view of what is at stake in abortion rights. I agree with the basic point that privacy rights are necessary but not sufficient to guarantee reproductive freedom; for this a wide array of social policies and cultural and institutional change are also necessary.

22. It was this standpoint that led some feminists (Petchesky attributes this view to Jaggar, *Abortion and Woman's Choice*, 13) to argue that if the community assumes the responsibility for the welfare of mothers and children, then the community should have a share in judging whether or not a particular abortion should be performed. Since she could neither imagine nor deem desirable a set of social conditions under which women would or should be willing to renounce control over their bodies and lives, Petchesky rejects this position. This position is reproduced in the extreme sex equality arguments below.

23. While many feminist theorists have invoked equal protection principles to protect reproductive rights, including abortion, most have presented arguments that would allow for a synthetic use of both sets of principles: privacy and equality. For a list of references see Cohen, "Redescribing Privacy," 49–50. The theorists I have in mind are those who reject privacy analysis altogether, on both normative and strategic grounds, and wish to replace, not supplement it, with some version of equal protection doctrine. See, for example, MacKinnon, "Privacy v. Equality," in *Feminism Unmodified*; Olsen, "Finger to the Devil"; Frances E. Olsen, "Unraveling Compromise"; and (with special reference to pornography, abortion, and surrogacy) Cass R. Sunstein, "Neutrality in Constitutional Law."

24. Olsen, "Finger to the Devil," 378.

25. For a summary see Olsen, "Family and the Market," and Pateman, "Feminist Critiques of the Public/Private Dichotomy."

26. See Pateman, *Sexual Contract*.

27. For a discussion of the distinction between entity privacy and personal privacy see Fineman, "Intimacy Outside," 955.

28. MacKinnon, "Privacy v. Equality"; and Sunstein, "Neutrality," 13–15.

29. Olsen, "Myth of State Intervention in the Family," 835, 842–844, 862 n. 73.

30. MacKinnon, "Privacy v. Equality," 101.

31. This is the infamous state action doctrine. Under this doctrine, the concept of privacy does not refer to a set of actions or decisions that are private as a matter of right and beyond government's ability to regulate. Rather, what is at issue is a set of actions or domains that are private in the more modest sense that they are simply not regulated by the Constitution. Government can regulate here if it chooses through legislation. However, constitutional protection can be invoked only if state action can be found. For an overview see Garvey and Aleinikoff, *Modern Constitutional Theory*, 694–738.

32. Sunstein, "Neutrality," 2.

33. See also Olsen, *Family and the Market*, and Olsen, "Myth of State Intervention in the Family," 835, 842–844, 862 n. 73. The figure of thought relied upon here is the classic Marxian one—just as Marx exploded the ideology of privacy (in this case, of private property) in the sphere of wage labor by revealing the social relations of domination and inequality within the factory, so Olsen, Sunstein, MacKinnon, and others seek to explode the ideology of privacy in the domain of intimate association by exposing the social relations of domination and inequality pervading family life and sexual interaction.

34. This is certainly true regarding marriage law that establishes legal statuses and distributes gendered benefits and burdens.

35. They each offer a revised interpretation of equal protection doctrine because, as it now stands, laws restricting abortion do not amount to sex discrimination because only women can become pregnant and hence are not "similarly situated" to men with respect to this reproductive issue. For an argument that rejects the sex equality argument along these lines while rejecting the privacy justification as well, see Ely, "Wages of Crying Wolf." For a rebuttal that defends the privacy justification see de Crew, *In Pursuit of Privacy*, 95–109. It is worth noting that the decision in *Casey* did invoke equality considerations, although the bulk of the argument rested on the liberty/privacy right protected by the due process clause of the Fourteenth Amendment (*Planned Parenthood of Southeastern Pennsylvania v. Casey*, 112 S. Ct. 2791, 2807 [1992]). See also Strauss, "Abortion, Toleration and Moral Uncertainty," noting that the Court acknowledged the effect of abortion laws on the status of women for the first time.

36. For one of the earliest versions of an equality-based theory of rights to which the notion of equal concern and respect is central, see Dworkin, *Taking Rights Seriously*, especially 184–206. Dworkin's equality arguments could be interpreted as arguments for the protection of difference and for differential treatment when warranted, in order to secure equality. Note his distinction (p. 227) between "equal treatment," defined as the right to an equal distribution of some opportu-

nity, resource or burden, and "treatment as an equal," which is the right to be treated with the same respect and concern as anyone else. The first requires the identical treatment to all others with regard to a benefit or burden; the second requires neutrality on the part of the state regarding the acknowledgment of one's identity and of one's conception of the good. "Government must treat those whom it governs with concern, that is, as human beings who are capable of suffering and frustration, and with respect, that is, as human beings who are capable of forming and acting on intelligent conceptions of how their lives should be lived. . . . It must not constrain liberty on the ground that one citizen's or one group's conception of the good life is nobler or superior to another's" (272–273). Therefore, in some cases, people may have to be treated "differently," and their differences acknowledged, if they are to be treated with equal concern and respect.

37. Sunstein, "Neutrality," 37. The equality argument for abortion rights was originally made by Thompson, "Defense of Abortion," and then by Law, "Rethinking Sex, Law, and the Constitution," 1023 n. 245.

38. Olsen, "Finger to the Devil," 380. Let me say that I also agree with this point but not with the critique of privacy analysis.

39. MacKinnon, "Privacy v. Equality," 100–101. The first major abortion funding case was *Maher v. Roe*, 403 U.S. 464 (1977), which sustained a Connecticut law that did not include nontherapeutic medically unnecessary abortions within a Medicaid-funded program. The second major case was *Harris v. McRae*, 448 U.S. 297 (1980), which rejected constitutional challenges to public funding limitations that barred payments for most medically necessary abortions. The *Harris* ruling held that the right to privacy does not compel states to pay for poor women's abortions. The separation of public and private was extended by the Court in *Webster v. Reproductive Health Services*, 492 U.S. 490 (1989), which upheld restrictions on the use of public facilities for abortion services and permitting states to prohibit the performance of abortions by public employees. See also *Rust v. Sullivan*, 111 S.Ct. 1759 (1991), which upheld restrictions on providing information about abortion in family planning clinics that receive public funding. Other decisions restricting abortion rights include *H. v. Matheson*, 450 U.S. 398 (1981), upholding parental consent provisions, and *Bellotti v. Baird*, 443 U.S. 622 (1979), upholding parental consent provisions. For a discussion of efforts to overturn *Roe* and limit abortion rights and the relevant Supreme Court decisions and the ambiguity of the "undue burden" standard in *Casey*, see Gunther and Sullivan, *Constitutional Law*, 546–584.

40. *Harris*, 448 U.S., at 316, and *Rust*, 111 S.Ct., at 1775. With respect to this argument, Sunstein's critique of the doctrine of state action and its alleged neutrality is quite on the mark, for here we have a perfect example of the Court's reliance on what I view as an anachronistic interpretation of privacy rights (Sunstein, "Neutrality," 6–8). His alternative, however, is equally problematic.

41. *Maher*, 432 U.S., at 488–489 (Justice Brennan, dissenting).

42. Ibid., at 544. Three years later, in his dissent in *Harris*, Brennan argued that the Hyde Amendment sustained by the Court's majority violates women's fundamental right to privacy, not because "the State is under an affirmative obligation to ensure access to abortions for all who may desire them; it is that the State must refrain from wielding its enormous power and influence in a manner that

might burden the pregnant woman's freedom to choose whether to have an abortion" (*Harris*, 448 U.S. 297, 330). See also the discussion in Michael J. Perry, "Abortion Funding Cases," in which he argues that if abortion is a constitutionally protected activity, the government has no right to discourage it, and that since abortions are cheaper than prenatal care and childbirth, the state could have no convincing reason for funding one and not the other apart from its attempt to impose its "majoritarian" preference for childbirth onto poor women—something explicitly prohibited by the privacy principle.

43. This is made clear in Justice Stevens's dissenting opinion in *Harris* in which he argues, "Having decided to alleviate some of the hardships of poverty by providing necessary medical care, the Government must use neutral criteria in distributing benefits. It may not deny benefits to a financially needy person simply because he is a Republican, a Catholic, or an Oriental. . . . In sum, it may not create exceptions for the sole purpose of furthering a governmental interest that is constitutionally subordinate to the individual interest that the entire program was designed to protect" (*Harris*, 448 U.S., at 356, Justice Stevens dissenting).

44. Garvey and Aleinikoff, *Modern Constitutional Theory*, 694–695.

45. The Court has thus struck down various state laws that impose such an undue burden on the exercise of the right to choose an abortion articulated in *Roe*. But it has also permitted many regulations of abortion justifying them under the state action doctrine. In a recent case, *Planned Parenthood of Southeastern Pennsylvania v. Casey*, 505 U.S. 833 (1992), which upheld the core ruling in *Roe* protecting a woman's right to choose an abortion, acknowledged that the "liberty of the woman is at stake in a sense unique to the human condition and so unique to law" (112 S.Ct., at 2807). Although refraining from invoking privacy, the undue burden standard was rather narrowly construed primarily to block husband notification regulations but little else. In other words, the majority took a relatively expansive view of the circumstances under which the state could regulate the right to choose, including requirements of parental or guardian consent for minors provided there is an adequate judicial bypass procedure.

46. Ibid.

47. The historical trajectories of these two meanings of privacy have been rather different. Indeed, the strong meaning of privacy as protecting some decisions and actions as a matter of constitutional right has been expanding, in particular in the domain of intimacy, for half a century, while the second weaker version has contracted at least since the New Deal. In other words, the courts have been willing to regulate the behavior of nonstate actors in many areas by finding state action where in the past they did not. See Garvey and Aleinikoff, *Modern Constitutional Theory*, 696.

48. For an extreme version of the argument that poverty is a legislative, not a constitutional problem, see the majority decision in *Deshaney v. Winnebago County Department of Social Services*, 489 U.S. 189 (1989). Of course, the public/private dichotomy mapped onto the state/society distinction, and the liberal paradigm of law, reinforces the resistance to social rights even on the legislative terrain. But, as already indicated, the right to personal privacy does not have to rest on the dichotomous model of the social structure.

49. There is one shining exception: the right to state-provided legal counsel for the poor in order to ensure the right to a fair trial.

50. Indeed, it would be difficult to claim affirmative obligations of the state to fund abortions on the basis of equal protection analysis, for the Court ruled in *Harris* that poor people do not constitute a suspect class and hence cannot receive heightened scrutiny under equal protection doctrine: "An indigent woman desiring an abortion does not come within the limited category of disadvantaged classes so recognized by our cases. Nor does the fact that the impact of the regulation falls upon those who cannot pay lead to a different conclusion. In a sense, every denial of welfare to an indigent creates a wealth classification as compared to non-indigent who are able to pay for the desired goods or services. But this Court has never held that financial need alone identifies a suspect class for purposes of equal protection analysis" (*Harris*, 448 U.S., at 323, quoting *Maher*, 432 U.S., at 470–471).

51. See Chapter 3.

52. Berlin, "Two Concepts of Liberty," in *Four Essays on Liberty*. See Pettit, *Republicanism*, and Skinner, *Liberty before Liberalism*, for critiques of this approach.

53. For a critique of this form of reasoning, see Jennifer Nedelsky, "Reconceiving Autonomy."

54. See below for the meaning of a constructivist interpretation of privacy rights.

55. For a different interpretation of Mill, see Urbinati, "Representation as Advocacy."

56. Recently theorists involved in the "republican revival" have developed the concept of negative liberty as nondomination in an effort to undermine the hegemony of the Hobbesian/Berlinian conception of negative liberty as noninterference. At stake is the relation between law and liberty, among other things. For the Hobbesians, these are in a zero-sum relationship, while for the republicans law is constitutive of liberty. A forerunner of this "republican view" can be found in Hayek, *Constitution of Liberty*, wherein Hayek defines law as productive of liberty and liberty as the noninstrumentalization to another's purposes. The paradigm of unfreedom is accordingly slavery, not regulation. See Pettit, *Republicanism*; Skinner, *Liberty before Liberalism*; and Hayek, *Constitution of Liberty*.

57. Urbinati, "Representation as Advocacy."

58. I am paraphrasing Singer in her excellent analysis, "Privatization of Family Law." See, for example, *Loving v. Virginia*, 388 U.S. 1 (1967); *Roe v. Wade*, 410 U.S. 113; *Cleveland Board of Education v. LaFleur*, 414 U.S. 632 (1974); and *Moore v. City of East Cleveland*, 431 U.S. 494 (1977).

59. Roberts discusses the instrumentalization of women of color for racist projects of population control in "Punishing Drug Addicts Who Have Babies."

60. "Movements in the direction of sexual equality—before, during and after conception, including after birth—unquestionably weaken the case for an abortion right by removing one of the factors that supports its existence" (Sunstein, "Neutrality," 39 n. 143).

61. MacKinnon, "Reflections on Sex Equality Under Law."

62. Sunstein, "Neutrality," 17.

63. See Karst, "Freedom of Intimate Association," for an attempt to provide a conception of the fundamental liberty that is at stake in privacy doctrine and that, under equal protection analysis, should be presumptively accorded to all intimate associations pending compelling state reasons for limiting them.

64. See Cohen, "Redescribing Privacy."

65. This is not only theoretically confused, but it would also lead to a legal nightmare since it would open the state to lawsuits regarding any private harm. See Garvey and Aleinikoff, *Modern Constitutional Theory*, 694–736.

66. Sunstein's insouciance regarding paternalism is evident in much of his work. See Sunstein, *Partial Constitution*, 162–195.

67. *Planned Parenthood of Southeastern Pennsylvania v. Casey*, 112 S.Ct., at 2827–2832. To be sure, we are not yet entirely free of the consequences of the entity privacy doctrine today: judges and police still draw a line at the threshold of the home in cases of domestic violence. And parental notification provisions regarding minor women are upheld by the Court on the extremely dubious grounds that this will foster communication between parent and child, as if this could be enforced by law.

68. For a discussion of developments in tort law toward the protection of individual privacy see Robert C. Post, "Social Foundations of Privacy: Community and Self in the Common Law Tort."

69. MacKinnon, "Privacy v. Equality," 101.

70. States regulated entry and exit into marriage, stipulating who could marry, how they must marry, determining the consequences of marital status, the appropriate obligations carried by the statuses of husband and wife, and the very strictly regulated terms of termination of marriage. Laws criminalizing the use of contraception within marriage, along with laws articulating male decisional and even punitive power within the family unit, installed the reproductive patriarchal family as the norm. Laws criminalizing adultery, fornication, and nonmarital cohabitation, and laws penalizing children born out of wedlock, carved out marriage as the only legitimate arena for sexual intercourse. See Hafen, *Family as an Entity*. See also Grossberg, *Governing the Hearth*.

71. The key case in which this doctrine was articulated is *Maynard v. Hill*, 125 U.S. 190 (1988). For an excellent discussion see Singer, "Privatization of Family Law," 1508–1515.

72. Paraphrased from Singer, "Privatization of Family Law." See *Balfour v. Balfour*, 2 K.B. 571, 579 (1919), which refused to enforce written agreement between spouses. The two key constitutional privacy decisions prior to *Griswold* are *Pierce v. Society of Sisters*, 268 U.S. 510 (1925), and *Meyer v. Nebraska*, 262 U.S. 390 (1923), which ascribed privacy and decisional autonomy to the family as a unit, not to particular individuals within the family.

73. Orren, "Officers' Rights."

74. Employers' ability to fire employers at will, husbands immunity to suits by wives, and the fact that until very recently marital rape was an oxymoron are examples. See Chapter 5 for a discussion of the shifts between status and contract.

75. The 1960s Civil Rights Acts, equal protection analysis under the Fourteenth Amendment, and the new constitutional privacy jurisprudence all can be

interpreted as shifting the balance from officers' privileges and powers of superordination to egalitarian citizenship rights (see Orren, "Officers' Rights").

76. Orren, "Officers' Rights."

77. *Griswold v. Connecticut*, 381 U.S. 479; *Eisenstadt v. Baird* 405 U.S. 438; *Stanley v. Illinois*, 405 U.S. 645 (1972); *Roe v. Wade*, 410 U.S. 113; *Cleveland Board of Education v. LaFleur*, 414 U.S. 632; *Carey v. Population Services*, 431 U.S. 678 (1977); and *Zablocki v. Redhail*, 434 U.S. 374 (1978).

78. As Singer points out, the key case exemplifying this shift is *Zablocki v. Redhail*, 434 U.S., at 374, 383–387, where the importance of marriage is invoked as the reason for insulating private marriage choices from state interference instead of, as was the case in *Maynard*, the linchpin for state regulation. In *Loving v. Virginia*, 388 U.S., at 1, 12, the Supreme Court first characterized the freedom to marry as a "vital personal right" in which it held unconstitutional a Virginia law forbidding interracial marriages (cited in Singer, "Privatization of Family Law," 5111–5112).

79. See Cohen, "Redescribing Privacy," 48–65, for a more detailed analysis of these issues.

80. Whether the effects of this jurisprudence contribute to equality is of course disputed. I argue in the conclusion to this chapter and throughout the book that autonomy can foster equality and vice versa only if it is "regulated autonomy"— that is, only if it does not simply entail a wholesale shift from public to private (contractual) ordering but involves the regulation of self-regulation complemented by a form of public ordering premised on and oriented to gender equality.

81. For a discussion of protection extended to the "traditional" family but not to other forms of intimate association, see Franklin, "Family Like Any Other."

82. As Singer points out, "If the law protects marriage primarily to safeguard the opportunities it offers for individual happiness, then it is difficult to see why the law should not also protect other consensual intimate relationships that are likely to offer these same opportunities. Similarly, to the extent that the preferred legal status of marriage derives not from the social utility of marriage, but from its importance to the individuals involved, then it no longer seems legitimate for the state to privilege the decision to marry over the decision to enter into a functionally similar intimate relationship" (Singer, "Privatization of Family Law," 1512). This does not mean that intimacy should go unregulated, rather that the form of regulation has to be rethought.

83. Indeed, by taking up the case *Troxel v. Granville*, 530 U.S. 57 (2000), in which the Washington Supreme Court in 1998 decided that a parent has a constitutionally protected right to rear his/her children without state interference, the U.S. Supreme Court will be making a constitutional ruling in the area of family privacy in which the very definition of what constitutes a family, and who can claim visiting rights and decisional autonomy over access to children, is at stake. Interests of, for example, grandparents, women, gays, the poor, and biological versus nonbiological parents all potentially enter into conflict in this area. That some conception of family privacy—involving some important range of decisional autonomy for child-rearers/parents—is worth preserving is clear. All other parameters of family "entity privacy," however, are hotly contested. Whatever the outcome, the contestation and the fact that the Court is reviewing a decision in this

area indicates that privacy no longer entrenches "traditionalism." The fact that grandparents' rights laws have been adopted in all fifty states is an indication that profound shifts in familial entity privacy are occurring. See Greenhouse, "Case on Visitation Rights Hinges on Defining Family."

84. See Karst, "Freedom of Intimate Association," 624, which argues that the principle of the freedom of intimate association is the organizing principle behind privacy analysis, informing a broad range of Court decisions in the "domain of intimacy." In *Roberts v. United States Jaycees*, 468 U.S. 609 (1984), the Court explicitly distinguished a broad right to intimate association rooted in the general concept of liberty, involving privacy principles and protected by the due process clause of the Fourteenth Amendment. This is distinct from an older expressive associational right rooted in the First Amendment and referring to association for the purpose of expressing ideas. The Court found that freedom to enter into and maintain certain intimate human relationships is at stake. Writing for the Court, Justice Brennan argued that protecting intimate relationships safeguards the ability to independently define one's identity that is central to any concept of liberty. See Gunther and Sullivan, *Constitutional Law*, 601–602, for a discussion.

85. I thus disagree with Martha Fineman's argument that privacy construed in terms of individualized constitutional rights leads to the pitting of one family member's rights against another's, thereby exposing single mothers in particular to intrusive regulation by state agencies claiming to be acting in the name of their capacity to protect the child against the mother. It certainly is the case that poor single-parent households headed by women are subject to intervention and regulation to a degree that would not be tolerated in "normal" families (Fineman, *Intimacy Outside*, 958–959, 963–964). However, surely the acquisition of individualized privacy rights by women (as well as the attribution of rights to children against battery, for example) must be considered an important gain in all families. If children's rights are invoked in order to justify unfair regulation and supervision of mothering on the part of single poor women on welfare, what we have is not strictly speaking a conflict of rights, but the demand that women on welfare relinquish rights for benefits. It can only help women to be able to invoke a privacy right against such a trade-off. The fact that women are required to undergo mandatory paternity proceedings, or reveal their sexual history as a condition of receiving benefits, means that their individual privacy rights are being violated, not that they are the cause of such tradeoffs.

Herein lies part of the solution to the third paradox of privacy articulated above. Entity privacy is not undermined by individual privacy rights—rather, the lack of a full panoply of rights is what exposes individuals to unwarranted administrative control. See Cohen, "Redescribing Privacy," 62–63 n. 57.

86. MacKinnon, "Difference and Dominance: On Sex Discrimination," in *Feminism Unmodified*, 32–45.

87. Fineman, *Neutered Mother*, 41.

88. MacKinnon, "Sex Equality: On Difference and Dominance," in *Toward a Feminist Theory of the State*, 215–236.

89. Sandel, "Moral Argument and Liberal Toleration." See also Sandel, "Religious Liberty—Freedom of Conscience or Freedom of Choice?,' and "Procedural Republic and the Unencumbered Self." Many of these arguments are reproduced

in Sandel, *Democracy's Discontent* (1996). See also Glendon, *Abortion and Divorce in Western Law* and *Rights Talk*.

These theorists are typical of the views of contemporary communitarians associated with Amitai Etzioni's journal *The Responsive Community*. Etzioni has published his own critique of privacy analysis in *Limits of Privacy*. For an extensive critique of this groups' "family values" discourse see Cohen, "Trust, Voluntary Association, and Workable Democracy."

90. They also charge that *Roe* rests on an unconvincing claim to neutrality vis-à-vis the question of the value of fetal life. Due to constraints of space, I can address only the first consideration here. For a discussion of their other objection see Cohen, "Redescribing Privacy," 69-92.

91. Sandel, "Moral Argument," 324; Glendon, *Abortion and Divorce*, 36-37.

92. *Griswold v. Connecticut*, 381 U.S. 479. There are many other objections to the right to privacy "discovered" in *Griswold*. Some argue that since a right to privacy appears nowhere in the text of the Constitution, we have no such right. On these grounds, *Griswold* is as flawed as *Roe*. For commentary, see Bork, *Tempting of America*, 112, 115-116; and Ely, "Wages of Crying Wolf."

The neocommunitarian journal edited by Etzioni, *The Responsive Community*, is full of defenses of the traditional family and attacks on the right to privacy. The main figures of this movement include Amitai Etzioni, William Galston, Mary Ann Glendon, and Michael Sandel. For a representative sample of their work see Etzioni, *Rights and the Common Good*. See also Etzioni, *Limits of Privacy*. For a critique see Cohen, "Trust, Voluntary Association," 263-291.

93. Sandel, "Moral Argument," 527. According to Glendon, what *Griswold* protected could thus be construed as some sort of family right (Glendon, *Abortion and Divorce*, 36).

94. In this sense *Griswold* could seem continuous with the traditional common law concept of "entity" privacy (in the sense discussed by Fineman, "Intimacy Outside") and thus susceptible to MacKinnon's charges. Indeed, this sort of reasoning is just what MacKinnon objects to: doctrinal privacy as rooted in traditional (patriarchal) morality aimed at keeping sex out of public life and the state out of married people's bedrooms. The problem with the intrusion of police in marital bedrooms to verify contraceptive use would be its unseemliness. Others, however, interpret *Griswold* far more broadly. See Karst, "Freedom of Intimate Association," and Ackerman, *We the People*, 150-159.

95. Cited in Glendon, *Abortion and Divorce*, 36, and Sandel, "Moral Argument," 527.

96. Sandel, "Moral Argument," 527.

97. In *Eisenstadt v. Baird*, 405 U.S., at 453, the Court stated, "It is true that in *Griswold* the right to privacy in question inhered in the marital relationship. Yet the marital couple is not an independent entity with a mind and heart of its own, but an association of two individuals each with a separate intellectual and emotional makeup."

98. "*Griswold* may no longer be read as holding only that a State may not prohibit a married couple's use of contraceptives. Read in light of its progeny, the teaching of *Griswold* is that the Constitution protects individual decisions in matters of childbearing from unjustified intrusion by the State" (431 U.S., at 687).

99. *Bowers v. Hardwick*, 478 U.S. 186 (1986). This case involved a challenge to the constitutionality of a Georgia statute criminalizing consensual sodomy. The Court's majority decision rejected the claim that the right to personal privacy applied to homosexual activity, but Justice Blackmun wrote a vigorous dissent to this decision. See the next chapter for my analysis of its implications for privacy jurisprudence.

100. For my discussion of the communitarian critique of the liberal idea of neutrality related specifically to the privacy justification for abortion rights see Cohen, "Redescribing Privacy," 69–92.

101. Glendon, *Abortion and Divorce*, 35, and Glendon, *Rights Talk*, 47–75.

102. Glendon, *Rights Talk*, 50–51.

103. Sandel, *Liberalism and the Limits of Justice*, 179–183.

104. Sandel, "Justice and the Good," 166.

105. Bellah et al., *Habits of the Heart*. This fear is echoed by other neocommunitarians, for example Galston, "New Familism, New Politics." For the opposite assessment of the new expressive individualism, see Giddens, *Transformation of Intimacy.*

106. Glendon argues that the "legalization" of American society and the saturation of political discourse with "rights talk" began with the civil rights movement and accelerated when the Warren Court decided vigorously to exercise the power of judicial review as a means of protecting individual rights (Glendon, *Rights Talk*, 1–30). For a critique see Cohen, "Trust, Voluntary Association."

107. This argument has been taken up by all the neocommunitarians. See Cohen, "Trust, Voluntary Association," 279, and Etzioni, *Limits of Privacy,* for the latest version of the argument that privacy is in essential tension with "the common good."

108. Sandel, *Democracy's Discontent*, 11–14.

109. This point is powerfully brought out in Lefort, "Politics and Human Rights." Lefort shows that what appears to be separation reinforced or created by individual rights, especially privacy rights, is actually a modality of one's relation to others, but one that escapes all corporate models of the social whole. As such, basic rights construct the conditions for interaction and communication (certain structures of interpersonal respect and mutual recognition); they do not presuppose atomism—a mistake shared by the "bourgeois" understanding of rights and by many of its critics (see especially p. 257). Lefort thus provides a solution to the second "paradox of privacy rights" mentioned in the introduction of this essay.

110. See Waldron, *Nonsense upon Stilts*, 166–190, for a cogent reply to the claims that personal rights entail an abstract or atomist conception of the individual.

111. See Larmore, *Patterns of Moral Complexity*, 40–91, and Larmore, "Political Liberalism."

112. Needless to say, what counts as a crucial personal concern changes over time and can be among the stakes of intense debate and conflict. Surely this is the case for abortion.

113. See Arendt, *Origins of Totalitarianism*, 267–302, for an excellent discussion of the protective role of the legal persona, and the principle of equality that is attached to it.

114. Sandel cites statements in a multitude of opinions in the "new" privacy cases from *Eisenstadt* through *Roe; Doe v. Bolton*, 410 U.S. 179 (1973); *Carey, Thornburgh, Bowers*, and *Casey*, that reveal the Court's shift from a focus on informational privacy to privacy as decisional autonomy. These are taken as proof of voluntarist assumptions and of a reliance on the simple value of choice on the Court's part, each of which allegedly presupposes the atomist disembedded individual. See Sandel, *Democracy's Discontent*, 97–119.

115. Nor does the discourse of choice or decisional autonomy entail a particular theory of autonomy. There is little agreement today over how to define a philosophical concept of autonomy. For a recent effort to develop a nonmetaphysical, "relational," and woman-friendly version, see Nedelsky, "Reconceiving Autonomy." For a critique of this enterprise see Di Stefano, "Rethinking Autonomy." For an attempt to develop adequate psychological conception of autonomy see Whitebook, "Reflections on the Autonomous Individual."

116. Needless to say, the abortion issue straddles this fault line.

117. For an amusing critique of what he calls "the phantom community," see Holmes, "Permanent Structure of Anti-Liberal Thought."

118. To point out that individual identities are developed through communicative interaction and require recognition by others in no way undermines this claim. See Giddens, *Transformation of Intimacy*, for a positive assessment of this contemporary context. See Beck, *Risk Society*, for the downside of this.

119. For the role that privacy rights play in protecting the capacities of individuals to maintain a coherent sense of self in highly differentiated societies see Luhmann, *Grundrechte als Institution*, 53–85.

120. Taylor, *Sources of the Self*.

121. I do hope that I shall not be accused of realism or essentialism regarding individual identity, or of reinscribing a naive modernist conception of the unitary self and the fully autonomous rational subject because of these statements. Self-reflection does not mean full self-determination or self-transparency. I acknowledge the multiple and often conflicting sources of identity, as well as the frequent contestation over the cultural codes and social practices that go into identity formation. But I also believe that the ability to develop and maintain a coherent sense of self is the *sine qua non* of successful individuation—a fragile process that needs protection. The sign that one is relatively successful in this project is one's ability to present one's sense of self through narratives that construct and reconstruct one's identity for affirmation and acknowledgment by others.

122. See Guenter, "Communicative Freedom." See also Morris, "Privacy, Privation, Perversity."

123. See Ferrara, *Reflective Authenticity*.

124. The earliest constitutional privacy cases, *Meyer v. Nebraska*, 262 U.S. 390 (1923), and *Pierce v. Society of Sisters*, 268 U.S. 510 (1925), both linked the protection of difference from state-imposed homogeneity and state efforts to standardize the up-bringing of children to the right to privacy. See the discussion in Gunther and Sullivan, *Constitutional Law*, 516–518.

125. The right to personal privacy protects the capacity of individuals to evaluate, reflect upon, and rethink received ideas and identity needs, to affirm or rede-

fine them, to think and act on reasons, and to debate or attempt to justify these to others, but it does not *impose* critical reflection or a detached stance on them.

126. This is how we should interpret the right to "inviolate personality" as protected by privacy rights. See Warren and Brandeis, "Right to Privacy," 85, for a classic statement. Most commentators have focused only on the famous "right to be let alone," also articulated by Brandeis and Warren in this article. But this has led to a one-sided interpretation of our current privacy doctrine, as evidenced by Glendon's approach.

127. See Habermas, *Between Facts and Norms*, Chapter 3. On the concept of constructivist justification, see Rawls, "Political Constructivism," in *Political Liberalism*, 89–130.

128. For various models of the constructivist approach see Rawls, *Political Liberalism*; Habermas, "Frank Michelman and 'Democracy vs Constitutionalism,'" 17–23; Habermas, *Between Facts and Norms*; Scanlon, "Contractualism and Utilitarianism"; and Forst, "Praktische Vernunft und Rechtfertigende Grunde." I follow the Habermasian line more than the Rawlsian, in particular because I do not think that the idea of the veil of ignorance is useful for ensuring that rights and their contents are determined fairly. See Barry, *Justice as Impartiality*, for a liberal alternative to Rawls's veil of ignorance.

129. Habermas, *Between Facts and Norms*.

130. Ibid., 82–131, and Habermas, "Frank Michelman."

131. Just who does the interpreting is a complicated issue. Of course in the United States, privacy jurisprudence has been developed on the basis of new interpretations of basic rights by the Supreme Court responding, in part, to societal developments and discourses and to the core principle of the equal moral worth and equal citizenship of women.

132. I cannot go into this further here. For a discussion of this originally Scanlonian principle, see Scanlon, "Contractualism and Utilitarianism"; Habermas, *Between Facts and Norms* and "Frank Michelman"; Forst, "Praktische Vernunft"; Barry, *Justice as Impartiality*; and Joshua Cohen, "Procedure and Substance in Deliberative Democracy."

133. This approach should guide judicial review of statutes that affect privacy.

134. See Habermas, "On the Pragmatic, the Ethical, and the Moral Employments of Practical Reason," in *Justification and Application*, 1–18. The criterion of "reasonable non-rejectability" was first developed in Scanlon, "Contractualism and Utilitarianism." Rawlsians like Joshua Cohen and Habermasians like Rainer Forst have adopted some version of this criterion for their analysis of political morals. The Habermasians continue to insist that the criterion be applied in actual moral discourses. See Forst, "Praktische Vernunft," for an effort to distinguish between the moral and the ethical. How to draw this distinction is a matter of dispute but what is at issue, as Forst, following Habermas, clearly argues, is the differentiation between two sorts of questions: (1) what is good for a person or a group, and (2) what is morally right for everyone. Two different forms and contexts of justification are involved. Answers to the first can be justified with reference to the strong evaluations of a person connected to ethical communities and "significant others"—the defining condition of validity being that the person can, upon reflection, identify with the answer that has been given. The second involves

a *right answer* that does not violate categorically binding norms and against which no morally valid counterarguments can be raised. A moral answer would have to be equally justifiable to every person morally affected by certain actions.

135. This is a general trend, despite alarming revivals of moralism as in the Supreme Court's majority decision in *Bowers v. Hardwick*, 478 U.S. 186. See the next chapter, as well as Singer, "Privatization of Family Law," 1527–1531.

136. Singer, "Privatization of Family Law," 1527. Singer shows that in a wide range of areas, from marital choices to extramarital relationships to no-fault divorce to child custody issues, moral discourse has been dropped from courts. But the continued presence of sex laws on the books in many states, ranging from criminalized adultery to criminalized sodomy in a context where it has become difficult to justify public ordering of intimate sexual behavior, is dangerous. It fosters arbitrariness of enforcement. Similarly, dead letter laws should be swept off the books (see Singer, 1540–1564). See also Chapters 2 and 5 for an analysis of drawbacks of certain forms of privatization of family law.

137. They may do this to protect public health and the rules of civility that are generally agreed upon. See the next chapter for an analysis of the shift of sex from the moral to the ethical.

138. I owe this formulation to Guenter, "Communicative Freedom." Regarding the abortion decision, this means that if my right to an early, safe abortion is covered by a general right to privacy, then the reasons for my decision remain my own, and I do not have to submit these to boards of doctors, judges, or any other external authority for approval.

139. It would, however, be false to interpret this as implying that the individual's needs are fixed and given, that she does not engage in ethical discourses with significant others about her personal judgments in which her decisions and self-understanding are articulated and possibly revised, or that she solipsistically opts out of any and every dialogic community when she makes personal decisions. My argument does not involve an essentialist notion of the private or a private language. Nor does it involve an idiosyncratic conception of autonomy. While her own reasons can be clarified or altered in a discussion with others from whom one seeks recognition and to whom one feels obligated to justify oneself, what counts is not that one takes on the reasons of the community at large, but that one arrives at personal reasons acceptable to oneself for one's projects, which one hopes can be acknowledged by particular significant others as appropriate *for her.* Of course, no one can stand alone or affirm an identity by herself.

140. Glendon, *Rights Talk*, 40, 52.

141. See Moore, *Privacy*, and Robert R. Murphy, "Social Distance and the Veil."

142. Post, "Social Foundations of Privacy."

143. Goffman, "Nature of Deference and Demeanor," in *Interaction Ritual: Essays on Face-to-Face Behavior.*

144. Goffman, "Territories of the Self," in *Relations in Public*, 28. Similarly, Georg Simmel speaks of "the feeling . . . that an ideal sphere lies around every human being . . . [that] cannot be penetrated, unless the personality value of the individual is thereby destroyed," in *Sociology of Georg Simmel*, ed. Kurt Wolff, 321.

145. Goffman, "Territories of the Self," in *Relations in Public*, 29–41.

146. Ibid., 60.

147. See Reiman, "Privacy, Intimacy and Personhood," 310, for a discussion of the normative coherence of the concept of privacy and of a right to privacy that rejects the possessive-individualist model of the self and challenges objectivistic interpretations.

148. The distribution of personal privacy and control has for too long been class- and gender-based in our society. For an enlightening discussion of the importance of this dimension of rights for the maintenance of an intact sense of self and self-respect to African Americans in particular, see Williams, *Alchemy of Race and Rights*. Against the critique of rights fashionable in certain legal circles, Williams argues that rights help establish boundaries that eliminate the overly personalized and contemptuous character of relationships between dominant (white) and subordinate (black) groups. Thus, personal privacy rights serve to prohibit others from acting upon the presumed transparency and utter availability of the bodies and identities of others. "But where one's experience is rooted not just in a sense of illegitimacy but in *being* illegitimate, in being raped, and in the fear of being murdered, then the black adherence to a scheme of both positive and negative rights—to the self, to the sanctity of one's own personal boundaries—makes sense" (Williams, p. 154). But see Wendy Brown's reply (with which I strongly disagree) in her book *States of Injury*, 122–128.

149. I advocate a presumption in favor of the freedom of intimate association and of the intimate choices, including sexual, that this entails. See Chapter 2 for a full discussion.

150. *Roe v. Wade*, 410 U.S. 113. For easy access to the full text of this decision see Shapiro, *Abortion*, 46–70. The majority opinion, written by Justice Blackmun, grants that the Constitution does not explicitly mention a right to privacy. But it invokes a line of previous Court decisions that indicate that such a right has long been recognized on numerous grounds drawing on the First, Fourth, Fifth, and Ninth Amendments and on the "penumbras" of the Bill of Rights in addition to the Fourteenth Amendment's due process clause. Blackmun then goes on to say that "we feel" that the Fourteenth Amendment's concept of personal liberty and restrictions on state action is sufficient basis for applying this privacy right to abortion. See *Roe v. Wade* in Shapiro, *Abortion*, 59–60. For a full analysis of the details of *Roe*, including the trimester framework, see Cohen, "Redescribing Privacy."

151. *Roe v. Wade* in Shapiro, *Abortion*, 59–60. On the concept of "ordered liberty" see *Palko v. Connecticut*, 302 U.S. 319, 325 (1937).

152. *Roe v. Wade*, in Shapiro, *Abortion*, 60.

153. It also ruled that the fetus is not a person under the law and hence does not merit Fourteenth Amendment due process protection (*Roe v. Wade*, in Shapiro, *Abortion*, 62–63). For my argument against attributing personhood to the fetus see Cohen, "Redescribing Privacy," 69–92.

154. See Cohen, "Redescribing Privacy," 81, for my handling of the claims of a right to fetal life. I follow Dworkin, *Life's Dominion*, who argues that procreative decisions are fundamental because the moral issues on which they hinge are religious in the broad sense as they touch upon the ultimate point and value of human life itself, namely the sacred. That life is sacred all can agree, but whether or not abortion is compatible with the right respect for human life is something that

different religious and ethical worldviews will disagree on. Given the personal importance of the issue, the deep disagreement in society over it, and the very great impact on the person potentially affected by it, Dworkin concludes that First Amendment principles against the establishment of religion weigh in here to supplement privacy analysis, against criminalization of abortion.

155. Recall that the Court produced the trimester framework in order to take into account the "state's interest" in potential life of the fetus as it developed to term. It also argued that the right to privacy shielding abortion is not absolute and that the woman cannot be isolated in her privacy. See *Roe* in Shapiro, *Abortion*, 64. See also Cohen, "Redescribing Privacy," 77–89.

156. The woman by the third trimester would have had ample time to exercise her decisional autonomy.

157. *Planned Parenthood of Southeastern Pennsylvania v. Casey*, 505 U.S. 803.

158. Ibid., at 2807.

159. *Casey* in Shapiro, *Abortion*, 210–212.

160. For the best discussion of this trajectory see McClain, "Poverty of Privacy."

161. "The marital couple is not an independent entity with a mind and heart of its own, but an association of two individuals each with a separate intellectual and emotional makeup. If the right to privacy means anything, it is the right of the *individual*, married or single, to be free from unwarranted governmental intrusion into matters so fundamentally affecting a person as the decision whether to bear or beget a child" (*Eisenstadt v. Baird*, 405 U.S., at 453; 92 S.Ct., at 1028 [emphasis in original]).

162. *Casey* in Shapiro, *Abortion*, 232–233.

163. Ibid., 232.

164. The Court thus acknowledged the empirical facts of gendered inequality, while reasoning from the premise of the moral equality of women and men. It is a pity the Court did not see the force of this argument against parental notification rules, even with a judicial bypass provision, for pregnant teenagers. There, too, it is obvious that if the family is functioning well, these rules would be unnecessary and if they are not, they could be harmful to the pregnant young woman.

165. There is a burgeoning literature on the body. See O'Neill, *Five Bodies* and *Communicative Body*; Turner, *Body and Society*; Merleau-Ponty, *Phenomenology of Perception*; Eisenstein, *Female Body and the Law*; Lacquer, *Making Sex*; and Scarry, *Body in Pain*.

166. See Butler, *Bodies That Matter*, for a rather extreme constructivist view on the body.

167. Goffman, "Territories of the Self," in *Relations in Public*, 38. See also Reiman, "Privacy, Intimacy and Personhood," 310–314.

168. Goffman was one of the first to study the destructive impact on the sense of self experienced by individuals in total institutions, subjected to the complete loss of privacy and bodily integrity. More recently, Scarry has focused on the destructive impact on the self when one's bodily integrity is purposefully attacked as in the experience of torture (Scarry, *Body in Pain*, 49). Building upon this analysis, Honneth has analyzed the sense of humiliation, the loss of the sense of self and

of a coherent sense of reality, when one's bodily integrity (one's control) is not recognized by others. See Honneth, "Integrity and Disrespect."

169. See Davis, "Abortion Debate," 765ff., for a discussion.

170. No right is absolute in this sense. The state may, for example, insist upon inoculation of children attending public school against certain diseases and it may take measures to protect public health that involve inoculation of adults as well. I address the question of limits to the right to abortion in terms of the stages of pregnancy in Cohen, "Redescribing Privacy," 87–92.

171. Thomas, "Beyond The Privacy Principle." However, I reject Thomas's suggestion that we drop privacy analysis altogether; his argument points to redescribing, not abandoning, privacy discourse. See Chapter 3.

172. The harm in denying a woman this right is that it denies to her the sense that her body and her self are *hers* to imagine and construct. If the woman is cast as the container for the fetus, her sexuality and her identity are reduced to the maternal function. Small wonder that the debate over abortion is very much a debate over discourses and how the issue should be framed. Whether women are to be construed as creators or as containers; whether fetuses are cast as persons with a right to life or as potential life, potential persons; whether we see abortion as continuous with contraception and as preventing a fertilized egg from becoming a baby or as killing—all this depends very much on how the issue is framed and on the definition of women and their status in society. Some advocates of abortion rights have become reflexive regarding their own position. As observers of the current debate, they acknowledge that their views are culturally, historically, and socially situated while, qua participants, they advance moral reasons for their position. See Luker, *Abortion and the Politics of Motherhood*, for what is now a classic analysis of the genesis and stakes of competing discourses of the abortion debate in the United States. See also Rothman, *Recreating Motherhood*, and Ginsburg, *Contested Lives*, for first-rate analyses of the conflicting discourses.

173. See Dworkin, *Life's Dominion*, for a discussion.

174. See Justice Blackmun's dissent arguing that the standard of strict scrutiny of state limitations on reproductive choice still offers the most secure protection of the woman's right to make her own reproductive decisions, free from state coercion. The "undue burden" principle is a lower standard of review that permits many more regulations to pass constitutional muster and is far more open to manipulation by those seeking to restrict the exercise of the right to abortion. See *Casey* in Shapiro, *Abortion*, 239.

175. For an excellent analysis critical of *Casey*'s abandonment of privacy analysis see McClain, "Poverty of Privacy."

176. In *City of Akron v. Akron Center for Reproductive Health* (Akron 1), 462 U.S. 416 (1983), the Court struck down hospitalization requirements, informed consent requirements, and waiting periods. In *Thornburgh v. American College of Obstetricians and Gynecologists*, 476 U.S. 747 (1986), the Court again struck down informed consent warnings as well as detailed record-keeping requirements and risky postviability procedures to save the fetus. For a list of other post-*Roe* decisions in which the Court struck down nearly all regulations directed at adult women, see Gunther and Sullivan, *Constitutional Law*, 80–81.

177. *Thornburgh*, 476 U.S., at 747, 766 (quoting Justice Stevens's concurrence in *Bellotti v. Baird*, 443 U.S., at 622, 655), overruled in part by *Casey*. As Linda McClain cogently points out, in *Thornburgh* the Court struck down a number of Pennsylvania's regulations about "informed consent" that were meant to intimidate women and to "wedge the Commonwealth's message discouraging abortion into the privacy of the informed consent dialogue between the woman and her physician" (*Thornburgh*, 476 U.S., at 762).

178. *Casey*, 112 S.Ct., at 2821.

179. McClain, "Poverty of Privacy," 133. It allows states to design informed choice provisions intended to persuade women to choose childbirth.

180. *Casey*, 112 S.Ct., at 2807.

181. Shapiro, *Abortion*, 1–23.

182. It is especially alarming that the most recent Supreme Court case on the subject of abortion, *Sternberg, Attorney General of Nebraska et al. v. Leroy Carhart*, 120 S.Ct. 2597 (2000), overturned a Nebraska statute outlawing "partial birth abortion" on the rather narrow grounds that it lacked any exception for the preservation of the health of the mother and imposed an undue burden on the woman's ability to choose a particular method of abortion, thereby unduly burdening the right to choose an abortion itself. No mention of privacy was evident in this decision, and it was also argued that states need not grant physicians unfettered discretion in their selection of abortion methods. The implication was that had there been a provision for the health of the mother, states could require a doctor to follow some procedure other than the one he or she believes will best protect the woman's health. It is hard to see what the state's interest could be in so doing. This is an alarming further evisceration of the right to an abortion, which, under *Roe*'s privacy analysis rather than *Casey*'s liberty analysis, would have been inconceivable.

183. See the discussion in Chapter 5.

184. No-fault divorce is the prime example: to communitarians it fosters irresponsibility and an irreverent attitude to marriage as easily exitable; to many feminists the equal treatment of marital partners at divorce in the absence of substantive equality between the genders severely disadvantages women. See Galston, "Liberal-Democratic Case for the Two-Parent Family." For a feminist position see Weitzman, *Divorce Revolution*. See Chapter 5 for a detailed discussion of these developments.

185. Glendon, *Rights Talk*, 24. Of course she is referring here to the fear on the part of the "founders" of a threat posed to property rights by popularly elected legislatures.

186. Nedelsky, *Private Property and the Limits of American Constitutionalism*.

187. Glendon, *Rights Talk*, 40 (emphasis added).

188. Warren and Brandeis, "Right to Privacy"; Glendon, *Rights Talk*, 145–158.

189. Glendon, *Rights Talk*, 51.

190. Ibid., 29.

191. For my critique of this line of argument see Cohen, "Trust, Voluntary Association," 235–236.

192. See the discussion in Chapter 5.

193. But see Poovey, "Abortion Question and the Death of Man," for a deconstructionist feminist argument indicting the language of *Roe* for this and much more.

194. *Roe v. Wade*, 410 U.S. 113, 159. This was the point behind the trimester framework.

195. Nedelsky, "American Constitutionalism," 241, 245.

196. See Gillman, *Constitution Beseiged*, 1–45, 175–206.

197. Ibid., 180–183.

198. Ibid.

199. Indeed, family law in Anglo-American legal history arose out of the relation of associational status (marriage, legitimate parentage) to the control of property. Rights of inheritance, dower, and legitimacy were at stake, as were the duties owed by husband and wife to each other. See Grossberg, *Governing the Hearth*, and Pateman, "Feminism and the Marriage Contract," in *Sexual Contract*, 154–188, for a discussion of the legal gendered obligations of husband and wife.

200. Karst, "Freedom of Intimate Association," 648–649. See also Grossberg, *Governing the Hearth*.

201. Nedelsky, "American Constitutionalism," 255.

202. Ibid., 247–253.

203. Ibid., 246.

204. Ibid., 253.

205. For an argument that Nedelsky overstates the decline of private property in American constitutional law, see Sunstein, "Constitutions and Democracies."

206. Note the striking analogy with Hannah Arendt's analysis of property and civil rights in *On Revolution*. For a discussion of this see Cohen and Arato, *Civil Society and Political Theory*, 194–200.

207. Glendon does acknowledge that in the 1950s the U.S. Supreme Court began to expand constitutional protection for a broad range of personal rights. She even states that *Griswold v. Connecticut* "pointed toward a partial liberation of privacy from the property paradigm." But Glendon interprets this case as protecting marriage and familial privacy (entity privacy), not individual liberty or autonomy. In her view, the property paradigm returns in full force with *Eisenstadt*, *Roe*, and the subsequent abortion cases, with all their individualistic and absolutist rhetoric (Glendon, *Rights Talk*, 38, 57–61).

208. See Nedelsky, "American Constitutionalism," 256. She is not alone in this view. In arguing against overruling *Roe*, the joint decision in *Casey* marked a clear distinction between personal and economic autonomy, between privacy rights protecting individual autonomy or identity, and rights protecting property and freedom of contract (*Planned Parenthood of Southeastern Pennsylvania v. Casey*, 112 S.Ct., at 2791, 2798, 2812–2817). Moreover, the plurality argued, "It is a promise of the Constitution that there is a realm of *personal liberty* which government may not enter," and which has been upheld in substantive due process cases regarding intimate personal decisions (2805). Indeed, they cited Justice Harlan's dissent in *Poe v. Ullman*, 327 U.S. 497 (1961), at 543, defending the idea that the liberty guaranteed by the Constitution is not a discrete set of particular liberties enumerated therein, but "a rational continuum which, broadly speaking, includes a freedom from all substantial arbitrary impositions and purposeless restraints . . .

and which also recognizes . . . that certain interests require particularly careful scrutiny of the state needs asserted to justify their abridgement." The concept of ordered liberty captures this in legal doctrine.

209. Ackerman, *We the People*, 3–33. I am not interested here in his defense of judicial review or informal amendments.

210. Ibid., 141. On the symbolic level Ackerman is right but his justification of judicial review as simply interpretive and "preservationist" is not convincing.

211. Ibid., 155.

212. Ibid., 159. Douglas thus engaged in a "comprehensive" reading of the founding text based on the "penumbra" argument in *Griswold v. Connecticut* 381 U.S., at 483.

213. Ackerman, *We the People*, 158–159. In 1890, Brandeis and Warren worried about the intrusiveness of the news media and the new technology of photography. Today, those concerned with protecting personal autonomy and privacy have to contend with highly sophisticated surveillance technology, developments in the field of biotechnology, and the internet. Control over medical records is the key issue here: obtaining health insurance and employment can turn on this. These concerns today are also behind the impetus to develop a normative conception of privacy as involving personal autonomy as well as control over access and information.

214. Nedelsky, "American Constitutionalism," 250.

215. Thus, the Court's role in this line of decisions is not simply "preservationist," as Ackerman would have it. Pace Ackerman, the Court has three roles to play in our society: (1) It exercises its authority to preserve past democratic achievements; (2) It also registers important cultural change that has been evidenced by broad public discussion and agitation; and (3) It can even be ahead of legislation and widespread agitation by making innovative decisions that trigger discussion and debate of new meanings and understandings of social concerns in order to bring the law into tune with changes in social status or self-understanding of the population. The Court's decision in *Griswold* was the culmination of years of agitation begun in the 1920s over birth control. *Griswold*'s articulation of a fundamental constitutional right to privacy covering intimate sexual decisions (e.g., to use contraception) is thus an example of the second role. The decision in *Roe*, which followed important change in the status of women, the revival of feminism in the 1960s, and agitation by women, doctors, and other groups for decriminalizing abortion is an example of the third: it captured an important direction of change and triggered extensive public debate over the application of the right of privacy to cover abortion. We thus have to see the Court as part of the process of public discussion and innovation, not only as playing a preservationist role. Whether or not judicial review in this broad sense is "legitimate" is a complex issue that I cannot address here. See Garrow, *Liberty and Sexuality.*

216. Gillman, *Constitution Beseiged*, 1–60, 147–205.

217. Ibid., 204.

218. Ibid., 204ff. It was also devised, of course, to secure a share of power for the courts.

219. Ibid.

220. Ibid.

221. Gunther and Sullivan, *Constitutional Law*, 13, 590.

222. See Chapter 2. I do not want to enter into the complex debate about judicial review but rather to highlight the flawed paradigmatic assumptions at work in legal line-drawing in this domain. For even if there were an explicit textual right to privacy in our Constitution, as there is, say, to freedom of speech, the issue of justification regarding its interpretation and reach would remain. Indeed, this is true of all our basic rights.

223. I cannot delve into the enormous debate over substantive due process here. It is worth noting, however, that some legal theorists argue that it is impossible to ever fully avoid natural law discourse or the claims that there simply are fundamental liberties that we should acknowledge. See Monaghan, *Professor Jones and the Constitution*, 87, 92.

224. Glendon, *Transformation of Family Law*, 126–128, 320–323, and Glendon, "Marriage and the State,' (cited in Karst, "Freedom of Intimate Association," 648 nn. 119, 120).

225. See Chapter 5 for an in-depth discussion. The rise and enormous influence of the law and economics school is the key example. See Becker, *Economic Approach to Human Behavior*; Schultz, *Economics of the Family*; and Posner, *Sex and Reason*, as the most well known exemplars. For a general discussion see Singer, "Privatization of Family Law," 1522–1526.

226. Privatization has proceeded in the areas of marriage and consensual alternatives to marriage, divorce law, adoption, and surrogate parenting, and with regard to custody disputes. See Singer, "Privatization of Family Law," for a comprehensive discussion and a nuanced assessment of its consequences for women. See Grossberg, *Governing the Hearth*, for an argument that this represents a long-term trend stretching back to the nineteenth century.

227. Singer, "Privatization of Family Law," 1532–1533. Many of the Court's early privacy decisions were directed against racist and elitist laws such as the anti-miscegenation statute in *Loving v. Virginia*, 388 U.S. 1, 1–12, which formed the basis for the subsequent decision in *Zablocki v. Redhail*, 434 U.S., at 374, recognizing a constitutionally protected individual privacy right to marry.

228. Singer, "Privatization of Family Law," 1565. See Chapter 5.

229. On the influence of public opinion on the Court see Stimson, MacKuen, and Erikson, "Dynamic Representation."

230. In Cohen, "Redescribing Privacy," 48–65, I also make the equality argument for abortion rights, arguing for a synthetic use of equal protection analysis, privacy analysis, and bodily integrity arguments.

CHAPTER TWO
IS THERE A DUTY OF PRIVACY?

1. Elshtain, *Democracy on Trial*; *Bowers v. Hardwick*, 478 U.S. 186 (1986); and "Pentagon's New Policy Guidelines on Homosexuals in the Military."

2. Arendt, *On Revolution*, 252. Arendt saw the Bill of Rights in the American Constitution as the most exhaustive legal bulwark ever contrived in modern times for the protection of the private realm against public power. Yet she viewed the decentering of property rights in the twentieth century with deep foreboding,

fearing that the boundary between public and private was thereby fatally weakened.

3. I have in mind specifically the marriage of republican with neocommunitarian discourse exemplified by the work of Sandel, *Democracy's Discontent*; Bellah et al., *Habits of the Heart*; Elshtain, *Democracy on Trial*; and Glendon, *Rights Talk*. I do not refer here to the work of other neo-republican theorists like Sunstein or Pettit, *Republicanism*, which is concerned with freedom from domination.

4. See Elshtain, *Democracy on Trial*, 50.

5. Ibid., 52.

6. Ibid., 55–57.

7. Ibid., 54–55.

8. Here Elshtain follows Arendt. Arendt accomplished this by a conceptual maneuver that mapped an analytic distinction (public and private) onto quasi-ontologized categories of action (labor, work, and action) and then onto institutional spheres of life (domestic-private sphere/political-public sphere). Here, too, the result was the construction of an essentialized and rigid *dichotomy*.

9. Beck, *Risk Society*. See Introduction. Giddens, *Transformation of Intimacy*; Karst, "Freedom of Intimate Association."

10. Forst, "Toleration, Justice and Reason." For a broad discussion of toleration, see the collection in Heyd, *Toleration*.

11. Scanlon, "Difficulty of Tolerance."

12. This seems to be Charles Taylor's position in "Politics of Recognition."

13. See the discussion in Chapter 1.

14. Forst, "Toleration," 7, 11.

15. This is the core procedure of the constructivist approach. It was first formulated by Scanlon, "Contractualism and Utilitarianism." See Forst's discussion of this conception of moral and ethical justification in Forst, "Praktische Vernunft und Rechtfertigende Grunde."

16. Madison, "Federalist #10," 43. See also Sunstein, "Enduring Legacy of Republicanism."

17. For an interesting discussion arguing that the shift has been to a focus on prevention of harm, see Hafen, "Family as Entity."

18. See Pertman, "Clinton May Provide Fusion of Politics, Policy"; Adams, "Gay Man Returns to Navy Service." Cf. Ifill, "Clinton Accepts Delay in Lifting Military Gay Ban," reporting Clinton's post-election news conference discussing his charge to the secretary of defense to formulate a new policy.

The military ban was put in place in 1943 when the military issued final regulations banning lesbians and gays from all its branches. These regulations have remained by and large unchanged until now. See Shilts, *Conduct Unbecoming*, 17.

19. Critics of the military ban noted that all NATO countries except Britain allowed gays and lesbians into the military. Canada's 1992 decision to revoke its military ban caused little controversy. Thus Clinton was not so wrong to assume that his proposal would cause little dismay, especially given the results of the Rand Corporation study of the military ban commissioned by the Pentagon in 1992. The Rand study concluded that "the ban could be dropped without damaging the order, discipline, and individual behavior necessary to maintain cohesion, and

performance" (cited in Rimmerman, "Promise Unfulfilled," 4–5). This report was released in August 1993. See also Bawer, *Place at the Table*, 50.

20. A study by the service members' Legal Defense Network in 1996 found that the new military policy in practice was "as bad, if not worse than its predecessors," and that witch hunts for gays were still common (*New York Times*, 3 March 1996, E7). Legal challenges continue to be made to the policy. Indeed, it has become something of a political football continuously challenged in the courts and linked to complex political maneuvers by various contending parties. It has certainly not, however, disappeared.

21. The mobilization was orchestrated by the religious right. See Bawer, *Place at the Table*, 60, and Rimmerman, "Promise Unfulfilled," 6.

22. Also party to the compromise was Sam Nunn, who chaired the Senate Armed Services Committee. For reports on the political process leading to the Department of Defense Directive, see Ifill, "White House Backs 2-Step Plan to End Military's Gay Ban," reporting President Clinton's suspension of the old military policy requiring investigation and discharge of anyone evincing homosexual desire or acts. See also "Excerpts From the News Conferences by Clinton and Nunn," discussing Clinton's charge to the secretary of defense to formulate a new policy acceptable to military leaders; Schmitt, "President's Policy on Gay Troops is Backed in Vote of Senate Panel"; and, more generally, Bawer, *Place at the Table*, 59–60.

23. 10 U.S.C. #654 (1994). After the brouhaha Clinton offered a compromise with his July 1993 "Don't Ask, Don't Tell" proposal. For details, see Rimmerman, "Promise Unfulfilled," 708. Rimmerman points out that it was initially Clinton's purpose to issue the new policy as an executive order to undo the old ban, which was itself enforced through an executive order. However, upon Nunn's prodding, a modified version of the Clinton proposal was codified into law by Congress, thus making it much more difficult for opponents of the ban to offer serious reforms in the future. Any policy change would now require congressional consent. Nunn's congressional maneuver enabled specifics of the Clinton plan to take effect but also codified into law a broad policy statement rejecting the notion of accepting gays without provisos in the military (Rimmerman, "Promise Unfulfilled," 8).

24. It is worth noting that military courts have been willing to state frankly that sodomy statues apply to consensual heterosexual conduct. See Halley, "Reasoning about Sodomy," citing *United States v. Henderson*, 34 M.J. 174 (1992); *United States v. Fagg*, 34 M.J. 179, 113 S.Ct. 92 (1992).

25. See Cain, "Litigating for Lesbian and Gay Rights," discussing cases of expulsion.

26. Goldstein, "Reasoning about Homosexuality," 484. The former U.S. army regulation on the books from 1981 to 1993 required exclusion of any "homosexual," defined as "a person, regardless of sex, who engages in, desires to engage in, or intends to engage in homosexual acts" (Koppelman, "Why Discrimination Against Lesbians and Gays," 265, quoting Army Regulation (AR) 635–200 #15–2(a)). The rule is status-based since it exempted those who had been involved in an isolated homosexual act they regretted. Earlier regulations apparently focused on conduct and status. See Shilts, *Conduct Unbecoming*.

27. See "Pentagon's New Policy."

28. Although the term "sexual status" usually refers to whether one is male or female, I use it here to refer to sexual orientation. It will become clear that the distinction between status and conduct is important in the legal decisions concerning homosexuals. However, as the term "sexual orientation status" is cumbersome, I have chosen to use "status" tout court to refer to orientation as distinct from conduct.

29. See "Pentagon's New Policy," A16, defining "homosexual conduct" as "a homosexual act, a statement that the member is homosexual or bisexual, or a marriage or attempted marriage to someone of the same gender." The congressional legislation states that "the presence in the armed forces of persons who demonstrate a propensity or intent to engage in homosexual acts would create an unacceptable risk to the high standards of morale, good order and discipline, and unit cohesion that are the essence of military capability" (10 U.S.C.A. #654 a (15) 1994).

30. See Goldstein, *Reasoning about Homosexuality*, 485–488.

31. Ibid.

32. Bawer, *Place at the Table*, 61, has argued that "this compromise . . . would essentially write into law the institution of the closet."

33. Reports of harassment and continued interrogation abound. See "Word for Word: Military Gay Policy." Discharges of homosexuals from the military have increased 86 percent over the last five years (*New York Times*, 11 August 1999, A1). The number of gays discharged from the military rose by 17 percent in 2000, representing the highest total since the "don't ask, don't tell" policy began in 1994 (*New York Times*, 2 June 2001, A9). Violent harassment, including the murder of a gay soldier with a baseball bat, and incidents of verbal and physical abuse have reportedly doubled from 1998 to 2000. The new policy that bans gays from openly serving in the military creates a hostile attitude, according to a recent editorial (*New York Times*, 28 March 2000).

34. *Bowers v. Hardwick*, 478 U.S. 186 (1986).

35. See Cain, *Litigating*, 1596–1600.

36. Chapter 1 addresses feminist and communitarian critiques of the privacy doctrine with respect to the abortion controversy. Here I take up a distinctive set of arguments that have been raised in the context of debates over sexual orientation and sexual autonomy.

37. Sedgwick, *Epistemology of the Closet*.

38. Ibid., 71. See also Halley, *Reasoning about Sodomy*, 1721, 1777.

39. Sedgwick, *Epistemology*, 71.

40. The reign of the telling secret expresses the epistemology of the closet in her view: "Even an out gay person deals daily with interlocutors about whom she doesn't know whether they know or not; it is equally difficult to guess for any given interlocutor whether, if they did know, the knowledge would seem very important. Nor—at the most basic level—is it unaccountable that someone who wanted a job, custody or visiting rights, insurance, protection from violence . . . from insulting scrutiny . . . could deliberately choose to remain in or to reenter the closet in some or all segments of their life. The gay closet is not a feature only of the lives of gay people. But for many gay people it is still the fundamental feature of social life" (Sedgwick, *Epistemology*, 68).

41. See Harper, "Private Affairs," quoting D. A. Miller's proposition that " 'the social function of secrecy' . . . is 'not to conceal knowledge, so much as to conceal the knowledge of the knowledge.' "

42. "Note: The Constitutional Status of Sexual Orientation"; Halley, "Politics of the Closet"; Thomas, "Beyond the Privacy Principle"; Koppelman, "Why Discrimination Against Lesbians and Gays."

43. Thomas, "Beyond the Privacy Principle."

44. Ibid., 1455–1456.

45. Thomas seems to admit the importance of privacy rights when he states, "I believe that each of the three components of privacy articulates distinctive and important dimensions of the moral conditions and consequences of sexual intimacy. . . . Efforts to identify and secure a sphere of protected places, intimate and emotional engagements, and individual autonomy generate helpful insights about the conditions without which a concrete personal sexual morality is impossible" (ibid., 1456). Nevertheless, he rejects privacy jurisprudence with regard to sodomy statues and for protecting the rights of homosexuals. See also Thomas, "Eclipse of Reason."

46. Thomas, "Beyond the Privacy Principle," 1455.

47. Ibid., 1456.

48. See Sedgwick, *Epistemology*, 71.

49. For critiques of liberal tolerance along these lines see Wolff, Moore, and Marcuse, *Critique of Pure Tolerance*. For a more recent discussion arguing that liberalism tolerates diversity through the depoliticizing and taming of difference, see McClure, "Diversity, Difference, and the Limits of Toleration." For a theory of toleration that focuses on equality analysis, see Gaolitti, "Citizenship and Equality."

50. I rely here on the reader's common sense regarding the role played by prejudice against homosexuals in much law targeting their sexuality.

51. Sedgwick, *Epistemology*, 69–70.

52. See Chapter 1.

53. Both outing and enforced concealment or seclusion would violate such a privacy right.

54. Tribe argues that regulation of sexual activity in public must be distinguished from that dealing with sexual conduct at home or in private (*American Constitutional Law*, 1424–1425; see 1425 n. 36 for citations of relevant cases).

55. Sodomy is not protected behavior, and in some states it is illegal. But surely it would be paradoxical to impose a duty through policy or statutes to be discrete about illegal conduct! Of course, I am not discussing officials guarding state secrets. The state can insist on silence and discretion on the part of officials of the CIA or FBI, for example. Moreover, private individuals can make contracts that stipulate nondisclosure. Needless to say, these examples do not undermine my general claim.

56. See *Watkins v. United States Army*, 847 F2d 1329, 1335–1340 (9th Cir. 1988); *Meinhold v. United States Department of Defense*, 808 FSupp 1455, 1458 (CD Cal 1993). For a cogent discussion of older and more recent military cases regarding homosexuals, see Cain, "Litigating," 1596–1600.

57. *Bowers v. Hardwick*, 478 U.S. 186 (1986). For discussions of the status of sodomy statutes before and after *Hardwick* on the state level, see Halley, "Reasoning about Sodomy," Appendix B, 455–461.

58. Rosin, in "Ban Plays On," reported that no heterosexuals have been interrogated by the military for consensual sodomy or for other sex crimes such as visiting prostitutes. It is certainly true that the military can justify policies that regulate conduct even if that conduct were protected by the Constitution for civilian life. It could invoke military reasons to justify its policies regarding specific groups, such as the importance of maintaining esprit de corps or military discipline in the barracks. In the past such arguments were invoked in order to keep women out of the military and to keep blacks in special units segregated from whites. This nevertheless does not undermine my point regarding the new policy, namely that its alleged focusing on conduct and discretion is a thin disguise for targeting homosexual status. In many respects the old policy was more honest.

59. Clearly it is not the acts but the status of those committing them that interests the military. If the issue really is the commitment of a criminalizable act—sodomy—and not one's sexual preference or identity, why is it that only homosexuals and lesbians are the subject of the new policy of "don't ask, don't tell, don't pursue"?

60. See Halley, "Reasoning about Sodomy,"457–458, for statistics. On her reading only five state statutes specifically target sodomy between persons of the same sex.

61. Ibid., 1722.

62. See Ortiz, "Creating Controversy."

63. Originally anti-sodomy laws did not play that role; rather, they juridified a Christian moral worldview and were intended to ensure that married couples engaged in reproductive sex. Since the late nineteenth century and what Foucault has called the "deployment of sexuality," such laws have undergone a change in function. Now they construct and stigmatize a sexual identity: the homosexual sodomite. See Foucault, *History of Sexuality,* vol. 1; Halley, "Reasoning about Sodomy," 1.

Indeed, one could follow Rubin, "Thinking Sex," and make the general point that harsh sex law creates sexual-identity hierarchies. Others add to this argument the claim that harsh sex law serves to reinforce gender hierarchies and patriarchal norms. See Law, "Homosexuality and the Social Meaning of Gender," arguing that the legal and cultural disapprobation of homosexual behavior is a reaction to the violation of gender norms and not simply to the violation of norms of sexual behavior. For a slightly different argument to the effect that sodomy statutes violate the constitutional bar on sex discrimination when they target relations between members of the same sex, see Koppelman, "Miscegenation Analogy," and Koppelman, "Why Discrimination against Lesbians and Gays."

64. This point is argued forcefully by Goldstein, "Reasoning About Homosexuality." Indeed, on 27 September 1999, the European Court of Justice ruled that Britain's longstanding ban on homosexuals in the military was a violation of the basic human right to privacy. This ban forbids openly gay men and women to be in the military. What is noteworthy is that the ECJ evoked privacy rights here. Homosexuality in Britain was legalized some thirty years ago and, in response, the

Defense Ministry forbade gay men and lesbians from serving in the armed forces. Since the ban was put into effect, at least 600 gay men and lesbians by official count have been discharged because of their sexuality. The court ruled that this policy violates Article 8 of the European Convention on Human Rights, which says that "everyone has the right to respect for his private and family life, his home and his correspondence" (*New York Times*, 28 September 1999).

65. Rubin, "Thinking Sex."

66. See Judith Butler, *Gender Trouble*, 2.

67. This seems to have been recognized by the European Court of Human Rights in Strasbourg. See n. 64 above.

68. *Bowers v. Hardwick*, 478 U.S. 186 (1986). See Tribe, *American Constitutional Law*, 1422–1435, and Thomas, "Beyond the Privacy Principle," 1437.

69. See Thomas, "Beyond the Privacy Principle," 1436–1443, and Cain, "Litigating," 1612–1515, for a discussion of the details of the case.

70. *Griswold v. Connecticut*, 381 U.S. 479, 485 (1965), upholding the right of married couples to use contraception; Thomas, "Beyond the Privacy Principle," 1444–1448; *Bowers v. Hardwick*, 478 U.S. 186, 203–204 (1986) (Justice Blackmun, dissenting, citing cases for protecting certain personal decisions and spaces); and Samar, *Right to Privacy*, 26–42, discussing the three types of privacy rights. Restrictions of choice of adult partners may continue to be legitimate, as in cases of incest, but this has to be argued for (*Loving v. Virginia*, 388 U.S. 1 [1967], invalidating a law against racial intermarriage and holding that the freedom to marry a person of one's choice is one of the vital personal rights essential to the orderly pursuit of happiness). But the Court still has not overruled *Reynolds v. United States*, 98 U.S. 145 (1878), upholding federal law against polygamy, and it has not granted the right to homosexuals to marry.

71. Georgia Code Ann. #16–6-2 (1984), quoted in *Bowers v. Hardwick*, 478 U.S., at 188, n. 1. This statute imposes a very harsh penalty for acts of sodomy: "A person convicted of the offense of sodomy shall be punished by imprisonment for not less than one, nor more than 20 years."

72. *Bowers v. Hardwick* , 478 U.S., at 190. Emphasis added.

73. Ibid., 199 (Justice Blackmun, dissenting, quoting *Olmstead v. United States*, 277 U.S. 438, 478 (1928) [Justice Blackmun, dissenting]).

74. Ibid., 200 (Justice Blackmun, dissenting).

75. See ibid., 214–215 (Justice Stevens, dissenting).

76. Ibid., 216 (Justice Stevens, dissenting).

77. Ibid., 218 (Justice Stevens, dissenting).

78. Ibid., 186, 214–215 (Justice Stevens, dissenting).

79. It helped a great deal that a lower court had denied standing to a married heterosexual couple that also wanted to challenge the Georgia law and had joined suit with Michael Hardwick. Had the couple attained standing, it is unlikely that the law would have withstood Supreme Court scrutiny. See Halley, "Reasoning about Sodomy," 425–450. I rely on her analysis a great deal in this section.

80. *Bowers v. Hardwick*, 478 U.S. 186, 190.

81. See Dworkin, "Forum of Principle," 513–514.

82. See Thomas, "Eclipse of Reason," 1829.

83. *Bowers v. Hardwick*, 478 U.S., at 191, noting that the Court's majority understands family, marriage, and legitimate intimate relationships as involving heterosexuals and monogamy.

84. Ibid., 190. Emphasis added.

85. Ibid., 195–196. But see 209 n. 4 (Justice Blackmun, dissenting), noting that the problem with adultery and incest is not the specific form of sexual touching involved but the proscribed sexual relationships with particular sorts of partners.

86. Ibid., 191.

87. Ibid., 196. This is an interpretation consistent with the letter of the law, although not with the spirit of privacy jurisprudence since *Griswold*. As Posner states, it certainly is not compelled by precedent. See Posner, *Sex and Reason*, 344.

For an early argument that the Court never intended to articulate a fundamental right of sexual freedom, but which predicted that laws criminalizing sodomy and homosexuality would eventually be overturned by the Court because they serve no rational purpose, see Grey, "Eros, Civilization, and the Burger Court." For the opposite view see Richards, "Sexual Autonomy and the Constitutional Right to Privacy."

88. *Bowers v. Hardwick*, 478 U.S., at 196. See Thomas, "Eclipse of Reason," 1814–1817.

89. *Bowers v. Hardwick*, 478 U.S., at 197 (Chief Justice Burger, concurring, quoting William Blackstone, *Commentaries*, 215).

90. Ibid.

91. Ibid., 191.

92. Justice Stevens states that "the fact that the governing majority in the State has traditionally viewed a particular practice as immoral is not sufficient reason for upholding a law prohibiting the practice; neither history nor tradition could save a law prohibiting miscegenation from constitutional attack" (ibid., 216 [Justice Stevens, dissenting, citing *Loving v. Virginia*, 388 U.S. 1 (1967), which struck down state laws criminalizing miscegenation]). Moreover, as Justice Blackmun points out, traditional reasons for outlawing sodomy depended on Roman Catholic doctrine regarding forbidden, unnatural sex acts—hardly an appropriate foundation for secular law. He, too, cites *Loving* as an "uncanny" parallel to this case. See *Bowers v. Hardwick*, 478 U.S., at 211 n. 5 (Justice Blackmun, dissenting).

93. See Posner, *Sex and Reason*, 344.

94. Ibid., 349.

95. In 1973 The American Psychiatric Association removed homosexuality from its list of psychiatric disorders and resolved that "homosexuality per se implies no impairment in judgment, stability, reliability, or general social or vocational capabilities." It stated further that "in the reasoned judgment of most American psychiatrists, homosexuality does not constitute any form of mental disease." Similar resolutions were adopted in 1970, 1973, and 1975, respectively, by the American Anthropological Association, the American Bar Association, and the American Psychological Association. See Samar, *Right to Privacy*, 144–145.

96. Posner, *Sex and Reason*, 349.

97. See Rubenfeld, "Right of Privacy," 748; Tribe, *American Constitutional Law*, 1427–1428.

98. *Bowers v. Hardwick*, 478 U.S. 186, 191 (1986).

99. See Rubenfeld, "Right of Privacy," 748, and Richards, "Constitutional Legitimacy and Constitutional Privacy," 862, insisting on the unprincipled character of Justice White's reasoning in *Bowers v. Hardwick*.

100. Tribe, *American Constitutional Law*, 1428.

101. See *Poe v. Ullman*, 367 U.S. 497, at 524–543 (Justice Harlan dissenting).

102. Sunstein, "Sexual Orientation and the Constitution," 1173–1174.

103. Tribe, *American Constitutional Law*, 1428.

104. But compare Rubenfeld, "Right of Privacy," 752–782, presenting the most comprehensive critique of the personhood thesis from a social constructivist, Foucauldian point of view.

105. Tribe, *American Constitutional Law*, 1305–1306.

106. The pathbreaking piece on the right to intimate association was Karst, "Freedom of Intimate Association." See also Michelman, "Super-Liberal," 1306–1320, arguing that intimate relationships among other group affiliations are constitutive of who an individual is.

107. This is the step in the analysis that is contested. But personhood critics do not notice that one can assert the ethical importance of intimate relationships involving sex to personal identity without reifying sexual acts or imposing ready-made identities onto individuals. See below.

108. Richards, "Sexual Autonomy," 972–1009; Grey, "Eros, Civilization and the Burger Court," 83–85; Rubenfeld, "Right of Privacy," 738.

109. Gerald Gunther called "irresponsible" and "lawless" the Court's summary affirmation of a lower court decision upholding a Virginia sodomy statute against an attack by adult homosexuals who claimed that, as applied to their private sexual acts, it violated their right to privacy (Gunther and Sullivan, *Constitutional Law*, 565).

110. *Bowers v. Hardwick*, 478 U.S. 186, 203 n. 2 (Justice Blackmun, dissenting).

111. Ibid., 211.

112. Rubenfeld, "Right of Privacy," 781.

113. Tribe, *American Constitutional Law*, 1422. After arguing at length for the personhood thesis of privacy, Tribe asserts that "these holdings thus mandated heightened scrutiny not of state restrictions on procreative sex but of restrictions on recreational or expressional sex—sex solely as a facet of associational intimacy—whether between spouses or between unmarried lovers" (Tribe, *American Constitutional Law*, 1423).

114. *Bowers v. Hardwick*, 478 U.S., at 205 (Justice Blackmun, dissenting).

115. Sandel makes such an argument but unfortunately offers it as an alternative to privacy analysis based on the right to autonomy in intimate settings (Sandel, "Moral Argument and Liberal Toleration," 533–537). But surely part of the good of intimate association is that one's autonomy for and within it is fostered rather than squelched; that one can freely affirm and embrace the intimacy at issue rather than feeling forced or alienated from it. For an argument that the right to privacy is the basis for legal protection of homosexual conduct see Richards, "Constitutional Legitimacy and Constitutional Privacy."

116. See Regan, *Family Law and the Pursuit of Intimacy*, 89–152.

117. This is not to say that we should protect gay sexual intimacy only to the extent to which it is similar to heterosexual intimacy or marriage. That seems to be the latent message of Sandel's arguments against privacy analysis that protects decisional autonomy regarding sexual intimacy, and for protecting the "goods of intimate association" at issue in stable intimate relationships. For a critique of Sandel, see Honig, *Political Theory and the Displacement of Politics*, 191–193.

118. For prominent examples of theorists in this school see Becker, *Economic Approach to Human Behavior*; Schultz, *Essays in Economics of the Family*; Posner, "Regulation of the Market in Adoption"; Posner, "Ethics and Economics of Enforcing Contracts of Surrogate Motherhood." This analysis shares the critique of the traditional notion of the family and its radical separation from the market made by egalitarian feminists such as Olsen and Sunstein. The latter, however, argue for direct state intervention (for purposes of shoring up women's equality) in the private sphere in order to bring the demands of justice to bear on family relationships, while the former assume that private ordering on a contractual model that protects primarily against force and fraud will suffice.

119. Posner, *Sex and Reason*.

120. Ibid., 324–350, expressing his views on various privacy decisions. There he argues in favor of the ruling in *Griswold v. Connecticut*, 381 U.S. 479 (1965), and against the one in *Hardwick*. However, he criticizes privacy analysis in general. Posner is opposed to current privacy analysis because it is based on the allegedly false distinction between personal liberty as a fundamental right and economic liberty (no longer deemed fundamental). Posner challenges the idea that sexual and reproductive freedom is a fundamental right while economic liberty is not: "One might have thought libertarianism indivisible; that the same arguments which show that people ought to be allowed to make their own choices in matters of sex and procreation, though with due regard for the interests of third parties, also show that they ought to be allowed to make their own choices with regard to nonsexual goods and services. . . . The curious appropriation of the word privacy to describe what is not privacy in the ordinary sense but rather freedom is an attempt by semantic legerdemain to make sexual liberty appear to occupy a different plane of social value than economic liberty. It does not" (Posner, *Sex and Reason*, 335). Posner offers utilitarian arguments for both sorts of liberty.

121. Ibid., 181–204.

122. Foucault, *History of Sexuality*, 1:77–131.

123. See Tribe, *American Constitutional Law*, 1423–1435; Richards, "Sexual Autonomy," 1003–1009.

124. Tribe, *American Constitutional Law*, 1428, states that the real question is what the police were doing in Hardwick's bedroom, not what Hardwick was doing there.

125. Richards, "Sexual Autonomy," 999; Tribe, *American Constitutional Law*, 1435.

126. Posner, *Sex and Reason*, 230–231.

127. Ibid., 181–219.

128. Ibid., 181.

129. The bio-economic account of sex is deployed to that purpose: its function is to undermine moral theories of sex and to question the metaphysical assump-

tions on which they rest and, thereby, to free us to gain accurate scientific and historical knowledge about sexual conduct, its benefits, and its harms. As such, it is meant to pave the way to dispassionate scientific study and to the model of morally indifferent sex.

130. Posner, *Sex and Reason*, 203.

131. Ibid., 182. Emphasis added.

132. Ibid., 187.

133. Ibid., 203.

134. Ibid., 45–46, 225–226.

135. Ibid., 232, 354.

136. Ibid., 232.

137. Ibid., 344.

138. Ibid., 232–233.

139. Ibid., 202–203, 233. Posner advises us to reread Chapter 4 of J. S. Mill's *On Liberty*.

140. Bork, *Tempting of America*, 123.

141. Dworkin, *Taking Rights Seriously*, 272–276.

142. The claim that sexuality (and sexual autonomy) is central to individual self-development or happiness is also a consequentialist argument. But privacy theorists' defense of permissive attitudes to sexuality is dependent upon a prior, different sort of claim, namely that that each person "should have some sphere private to himself in which he is solely responsible, answerable only to his own character, about what he does" (Dworkin, *Taking Rights Seriously*, 350).

143. Ibid., 204.

144. Ibid., 87.

145. See Thomas, "Eclipse of Reason," 1813–1815, arguing this effect on the basis of the psychoanalytic literature.

146. Posner, *Sex and Reason*, 313. Posner argues that until the effects on the young of homosexual teachers or parents are known, it is premature to overturn state law on such issues (Posner, *Sex and Reason*, 322). This is odd given his insistence on the genetic basis of homosexual desire. It is this sort of reasoning that provokes the charge that his analysis is biased. See Bartlett, "Rumpelstiltskin," pointing out Posner's insistence on the idea of a biologically given, all-powerful male sex drive and his insistence that homosexual life is less satisfying and homosexual coupling less stable then heterosexual pairings. See also Eskridge, "Social Constructionist Critique of Posner's *Sex and Reason*," 352–365. For a defense of same-sex marriage see Kaplan, *Sexual Justice*, 207–238.

147. As Martha Nussbaum correctly points out in her review of *Sex and Reason*, at times Posner includes under the rubric "moral theories" the work of those whom I have been referring to as the personhood theorists (e.g., Kant, Feinberg, Dworkin), and at times he means the moral doctrine on sex of the Christian tradition. See Nussbaum, "Only Grey Matter?," 1701.

148. Foucault, *History of Sexuality*, 1: 75–131.

149. Posner, *Sex and Reason*, 23–30, referring to Foucault and the "social constructionist" thesis regarding sexuality.

150. Ibid., 87–110.

151. Lacquer, *Making Sex*, and Foucault, *History of Sexuality*.

152. Foucault, *History of Sexuality*, 43.

153. Posner, *Sex and Reason*, 30.

154. Nussbaum, "Grey Matter," 1708. See generally Bartlett, "Rumpelstilt-skin," 473, 474, 481, for a critique of the gendered assumptions pervading Posner's analysis.

155. Nussbaum, "Grey Matter," 1701.

156. Ibid., 1699. In an otherwise excellent discussion, Nussbaum makes the error of casting Posner as a privacy theorist who attributes to individuals a fundamental liberty interest in the protection of sexual privacy. She does not realize that he rejects fundamental rights arguments and hence privacy jurisprudence, arguing instead for a consequentialist, "rational basis" constitutional approach (Nussbaum, "Grey Matter," 1733).

157. Foucault, *History of Sexuality*, 1:145–147.

158. Ibid., 98.

159. The point is not that all these battles are being won but that they are taking place in the public space. In December 1999, the Supreme Court of Vermont ruled that gay couples must be given the same benefits and protection given married couples of the opposite sex. The ruling is the first of its kind in the United States. To be sure, the Supreme Court of Hawaii slammed the door on gay marriages due to a 1998 amendment to the state constitution against such marriages. The Vermont ruling does not grant the right to marry but grants marriage-like benefits to civil unions. Similar legislation has been passed in many European countries, including the Netherlands and France, and is pending in Germany.

160. I am using the term *ethical* to refer to values and conceptions of the good.

161. On a sophisticated reading of Freud, it is precisely because sexuality is not instinctual that cultural values and societal norms, on the one side, and personal fantasies and identifications, on the other, enter into it. Given the irreducibility of the psyche and the unconscious to the social, it is absurd to argue the total social construction or rational constructibility of sexual choices. See Davidson, "How to Do the History of Psychoanalysis." See also Laplanche, *Life and Death in Psychoanalysis*. For a critique of social constructivist reductionism in regard to the psyche and the unconscious, see Castoriadis, *Imaginary Institution of Society*, 281–329. Castoriadis provides an excellent theoretical argument for a conception of individuality and individual autonomy that avoids atomism and voluntarism of subject philosophy as well as the reductionism of social constructivist approaches. He states that "society . . . must . . . allow . . . a private world, not only as a minimum circle of 'autonomous' activity . . . but also as a world of representation (and of affect and intention), in which the individual will always be his own center" (Castoriadis, *Imaginary Institution*, 320).

162. Weeks, *Sexuality and Its Discontents*, 3.

163. See Chapter 5 for a detailed analysis.

164. Kant's interpretation of marriage as a contract between two autonomous subjects is famous for the formulation that this contract regulates "the union of two persons of different sexes for lifelong possession of each other's sexual attributes" (*Metaphysics of Morals*, 96). Of course Kant's point was to argue that only the reciprocal guarantee of equal rights creates the conditions under which both partners can enjoy respect for their moral autonomy within marriage. If they con-

ceive of each other as legal subjects, both are protected against the danger of being treated as a mere means: as the mere instrument of satisfaction of the other's desire. This latter point remains true, in my view, regardless of Hegel's equally valid point that marriage cannot be reduced to a legal relation but rather entails an ethical relationship involving emotional bonds, vulnerabilities, and obligations that transcend contractual ones (Hegel, *Philosophy of Right*, 112, para. 163).

165. For an overview see Okin, *Justice, Gender, and the Family*. See also Waldron, "When Justice Replaces Affection: The Need for Rights," in *Liberal Rights*, 370–391. Contemporary neocommunitarians revive the Hegelian critique of the contractual model of the family, but fail to provide adequately for personal liberty and gender equality within and for intimate relationships. Without this, any focus on duty, responsibility, or even solidarity on the part of adult family members becomes suspect from a feminist perspective.

166. Uniform Premarital Agreement Act 3(a)(1)-(6) (West Supp. 1991). For a critique of private ordering for overburdening the private family and, in particular, mothers with social responsibilities that society should address, see Fineman, *Neutered Mother*. See Chapter 5.

167. Regan, *Family Law*, 36. See Scheuerman, "Rule of Law," for a critique of general vague clauses in law that involve deformalization and an opening to arbitrariness and too much discretion on the part of courts and the executive.

168. See Chapter 5 for a detailed analysis. Scheuerman, "Rule of Law." See also Singer, "Privatization of Family Law"; Regan, *Family Law*, 36.

169. See Sunstein, "Sexual Orientation," 1162. Recall that sexual orientation is not a "suspect classification."

170. See Chapter 4.

171. Preuss, *Constitutional Revolution*, 109.

172. For a discussion of the idea that rights such as free speech or privacy are regulatory but also personally formative, granting to those deemed competent the chance to organize their action in the relevant domains, see Hunter, Saunders, and Williamson, *On Pornography*, 206.

173. Ibid., 95–96.

174. For a perceptive discussion of my position see Dean, *Solidarity of Strangers*, 165–167.

175. For a discussion of the political relevance of privacy see Michelman, "Law's Republic," 1521–1537, arguing that privacy rights secure the autonomy of participants in public life and thus are democracy-reinforcing. See also Michelman, "Private Personal But Not Split," arguing that what ought to be considered personal is a deeply political question.

176. *Eisenstadt v. Baird*, 405 U.S. 438, 453 (1972).

177. *Bowers v. Hardwick*, 478 U.S. 186, 205 (1986) (Justice Blackmun, dissenting, citing Karst, "Freedom of Intimate Association," 637); *Eisenstadt v. Baird*, 405 U.S. 438, 453; and *Roe v. Wade*, 410 U.S. 113, 153 (1973).

178. Marriage is certainly no longer the master event that initiates sexual encounters, new households, or intimate association for one's lifetime.

179. Foucault, *History of Sexuality*.

180. Ibid., 101.

181. Ibid., 145.

182. Ortiz, "Creating Controversy," 1842. Ortiz distinguishes between two concerns in the battle over homosexual identity: the first has to do with how a person comes to fall into a particular identity category, the second with how the identity category is formed and its status determined. "How one becomes a member of a group is separate from how that group's identity is given meaning." These should not be conflated.

183. Motherhood supposedly has a high social status but it should nonetheless not be imposed.

CHAPTER THREE
SEXUAL HARASSMENT LAW

1. See Section 1 of the Fourteenth Amendment to the Constitution, which states that "No state shall deny to any person within its jurisdiction the equal protection of the law." See also Title VII of the Civil Rights Act of 1964, sec. 706(a).

2. See Ehrenreich, "Dignity and Discrimination," for an argument that sexual harassment should be viewed first and foremost as a dignity harm and, only when relevant, as an instance of group-based discrimination.

3. See Habermas, *Between Facts and Norms*, 388–446. See also Arato, "Procedural Law and Civil Society." See Chapter 4 below for an in-depth discussion of the paradigm concept.

4. Schultz, "Reconceptualizing Sexual Harassment," Parts 1 and 2, provides the best discussion of these problems. But see Mink, *Hostile Environment*, for a counterargument.

5. The exception is Abrams, "Sex Wars Redux."

6. MacKinnon, *Sexual Harassment of Working Women*, and Schultz, "Reconceptualizing, Part 1," 1683–1689.

7. Civil Rights Act of 1964, *U.S. Statutes at Large* 78 (1965): 241, 249.

8. Equal Employment Opportunity Commission, "EEOC Guidelines."

9. *Meritor Savings Bank F.S.B. v. Vinson*, 477 U.S., at 57, 65 (1986).

10. Ibid. The point of the hostile work environment cause of action is to get at discriminatory behavior that, unlike quid pro quo harassment, does not result in a tangible job detriment like less pay or being fired, yet which interferes with the individual's work performance. The loss in hostile environment harassment is in quality of the workplace atmosphere.

11. In 1993 the Court turned to hostile environment harassment issues (*Harris v. Forklift Systems, Inc.*, 510 U.S. 17, cited in Frug, *Women and the Law*, 324–328). These rulings triggered debates over the "reasonable person" standard, with many feminists arguing that unless the perspective of the "reasonable woman" or even the "reasonable victim" replaced it, hegemonic male norms of appropriate sex talk would determine outcomes of suits, to women's disadvantage. See Abrams, "New Jurisprudence of Sexual Harassment," 1169 n. 6, for references.

The "unwelcomeness" requirement has also had its share of critical commentary. See Estrich, "Sex at Work," who argues that the *Meritor* ruling that a complainant's sexually provocative speech or dress is objectively relevant to the question of welcomeness creates a "trial of the victim" analogous to what occurs in rape cases.

This standard permits interrogation of the complainant's past sexual history, thereby threatening her privacy. The prerogatives of defendants in the discovery and trial process constitute disincentives to women to raise harassment suits. For a discussion see Mink, *Hostile Environment*, 103–113.

12. Civil Rights Act of 1991, U.S. Code vol. 42, secs. 2000e-5(k) (1996). Congress wanted to communicate to women that it takes sexual harassment seriously despite the odious treatment of Anita Hill during the Senate hearings. Previously, employers could only be required to give injunctive relief and possibly back pay to employees who quit rather than endure abuse.

13. *Burlington Industries v. Ellerth*, 118 S.Ct. 2257 (1998), and *Faragher v. City of Boca Raton*, 118 S.Ct. 2275 (1998). Both cases were decided on 26 June 1998. The Court decided four cases in one year, twice as many since 1986. The other two were *Gebser v. Lago Vist. Independent School District*, 118 S.Ct. 1989 (1998), and *Oncale v. Sundowner Offshore Services*, 118 S.Ct. 998 (1998).

14. *Oncale v. Sundowner Offshore Services*, 118 S.Ct. 998 (1998).

15. Weiss, "Don't Even Think About It," 45.

16. Schultz, "Reconceptualizing, Part 2."

17. Radical feminism is known for its critique of the subordination of women in and through sexualization and heterosexual "intimate" relationships. See Schultz, "Reconceptualizing, Part 1," 1697–1703.

18. MacKinnon, *Sexual Harassment*. Others had been involved in theorizing the harm as well, but MacKinnon's remains the dominant voice in the field. The courts first adopted the radical feminist line of reasoning (that sexual harassment consisting of sexual advances driven by sexual desire is discriminatory and falls under Title VII), in *Barnes v. Costle*, 561 F2d 983 (1977). But different interpretations were available as Brodsky, *Harassed Worker*, shows. See the discussion in Schultz, "Reconceptualizing, Part 1."

19. MacKinnon, *Only Words*.

20. MacKinnon, *Sexual Harassment*.

21. Ibid., 85–87.

22. Ibid., 91.

23. Ibid., 220–221.

24. Ibid., 10, 20. What MacKinnon documented about the inferior economic and social status of women in 1979 remains true today: they are disproportionately segregated in low-paying jobs devalued as "women's work" ("pink collar" jobs); they are disproportionately excluded from supervisory and top managerial positions (the glass ceiling); their income is inferior to men's across the board (today it amounts to about 67 cents to the male dollar); and the overall structure of labor remains highly gendered, modeled on a male life cycle, and permeated by a sort of compulsory masculinity that dictates style, standards, and goals regardless of the sex of the worker.

25. Ibid., 22.

26. Ibid., 219.

27. On adaptive preferences see Cass Sunstein, "Preferences and Politics." A strong constructivist version of this thesis would leave no room for agency, autonomy, or "self-definition" to women. That is why it is hotly contested among femi-

nists. It also opens the door to paternalism: just who is to say when a woman's consent or desires are or are not autonomous or authentic? See below.

28. MacKinnon, *Sexual Harassment*, 10, 20.

29. This is why MacKinnon so strenuously rejected situating sexual harassment under the law of torts (private harms). The law of torts historically provided civil redress for sexual invasions but under assumptions of gender inequality. The price for this was the definition of a woman's virtue as constitutive of her value (to men); hence, any violation of her sexuality or honor constituted compensable damage (ibid., 164–174).

30. Ibid., 1–2. This approach influenced the EEOC's 1980 guidelines that defined actionable harassment as follows: "*Unwelcome* sexual advances, requests for sexual favors, and *other verbal or physical conduct of a sexual nature* . . . when (1) submission to such conduct is made either explicitly or implicitly a term or condition by an individual's employment, (2) submission to or rejection of such conduct by an individual is used as the basis for employment decisions affecting such an individual, or (3) such conduct has the purpose or effect of *unreasonably* interfering with an individual's work performance or creating an intimidating, hostile, or *offensive* working environment" ("EEOC Guidelines," 622).

31. For MacKinnon's critique of the difference approach to discrimination law, which she calls the "stupid theory of equality," see *Sexual Harassment*, 110–117; MacKinnon, "Difference and Dominance," in her *Feminism Unmodified*, 32–45; and MacKinnon, *Only Words*, 98. Accordingly, on the sameness/difference approach to sex discrimination, women tend to lose both ways: either they must conform to a male standard to be treated as an equal ("the same"), or their difference is acknowledged, construed as biological, and cast out of the purview of discrimination law (only likes can be compared). The "stupid theory" focuses on distinction as difference, ignoring whether subordinated groups are hurt or helped by the relevant practice.

32. MacKinnon, *Sexual Harassment*, 117; MacKinnon, *Only Words*, 98.

33. See Schultz, "Reconceptualizing, Part 1," for the discussion of the sexual desire/domination frame. On frame analysis see Gamson, *Talking Politics*.

34. She draws on J. L. Austin for the concept of the performative and constructing effect of illocutionary speech acts. See MacKinnon, *Only Words*, 21, 57–62, 98.

35. Ibid., 56.

36. Ibid., 58.

37. Ibid., 57.

38. Ibid., 68.

39. Ibid. The presumption that women fantasize or ask for sexual abuse or are "overly sensitive" is reinforced by sexualizing harassment.

40. MacKinnon, "Harassment Law Under Siege." She has never claimed that all sexual expression in the workplace constitutes harassment.

41. MacKinnon, *Only Words*, 98.

42. Rosen, "End of Privacy." For a more general statement of his position, see Rosen, *Unwanted Gaze*.

43. The investigation of President Clinton as well as Monica Lewinsky, along with their associates, is only the most recent confirmation of this alarming trend. For my views on the Clinton case see Cohen, "Hijacking of Sexual Harassment."

44. Toobin and Rosen blame MacKinnon for entrenching the view that all sexual expression in the workplace constitutes harassment (Toobin, "Trouble with Sex"; Rosen, *Unwanted Gaze*; and Rosen, "Court Watch," 1257, n. 18, for a critique of their analysis of MacKinnon.

45. Rosen, "Court Watch," 12.

46. Browne, "Title VII as Censorship," and Fallon, "Sexual Harassment."

47. Fallon, "Sexual Harassment," 8. This is considered a bedrock principle of First Amendment jurisprudence since *Police Department of Chicago v. Mosley*, 408 U.S. 92, 95–96 (1972).

48. *R.A.V. v. St. Paul*, 112 S.Ct. 2539 (1992).

49. Generally it is assumed that where there is no "state action" the Constitution does not apply. Accordingly, regulation of employee speech by private corporations cannot trigger First Amendment protection. Yet commentators argue that insofar as such regulation is itself triggered by federal law, it should come under the purview of the Constitution. See Fallon, "Sexual Harassment"; Browne, "Title VII"; Volokh, "What Speech Does 'Hostile Work Environment' Harassment Law Restrict?"; and Estlund, "Freedom of Expression."

50. Examples are extensively cited in Browne, "Title VII" and Volokh, "What Speech." But see MacKinnon, *Only Words*, and Sangree, "Title VII Prohibitions."

51. Browne, "Title VII," 544–545, and Rosen, "Court Watch," 12.

52. Volokh, "Comment: Freedom of Speech and Workplace Harassment." This was also the ACLU position until 1993 (American Civil Liberties Union, "Policy No. 316," in *Policy Guide of the American Civil Liberties Union*). Current policy does not require targeting, much to the dismay of ACLU president Nadine Strossen, the Kenneth M. Piper Lecture entitled "The Tensions Between Regulating Workplace Harassment and the First Amendment: No Trump," 701, n. 3.

53. Fallon, "Sexual Harassment."

54. Ibid., 43. See also Greenawalt, *Fighting Words*, 86, for a counterargument to the captive audience thesis.

55. Ibid., 41–51.

56. Deborah Epstein points out that under the 1990 EEOC guidelines and on the basis of court rulings, a five-part test has emerged for establishing a hostile environment claim: harassment must be gender-based, the employer or its agent must perpetrate or condone the harassment, it must be severe or pervasive, it must be unwelcome, and it must create an environment that a reasonable person would find hostile (Epstein, "Can a 'Dumb Ass Woman' Achieve Equality"). For the 1990 guidelines, see Frug, *Women and the Law*, 183–184.

57. Epstein, "Can a 'Dumb Ass Woman' Achieve Equality," 401.

58. Ibid., 451.

59. Brown, "Title VII," and Volokh, "What Speech."

60. Epstein, "Free Speech at Work." For a similar argument see Mink, *Hostile Environment*.

61. Browne, "Workplace Censorship."

62. Browne, "Title VII," 503–504. See my discussion below.

63. Rosen, "Men Behaving Badly"; Toobin, "Trouble with Sex." This is also the position of Justices Thomas and Scalia. See Justice Thomas's dissent joined by Justice Scalia in *Burlington Industries v. Ellerth*, 118 S.Ct. 2257 (1998).

64. Strossen, "Tensions Between Regulating Workplace Harassment," 1689.

65. Ibid., 720, n. 99.

66. Ibid., 719–720, and Schultz, "Reconceptualizing, Part 1."

67. Schultz, "Reconceptualizing, Part 2," 1739.

68. Strossen, "Tensions Between Regulating Workplace Harassment," 721; Schultz, "Reconceptualizing, Part 1," 1692–1705.

69. MacKinnon, *Only Words*, 56–57, and Schultz, "Reconceptualizing, Part 2," 1748.

70. Schultz, "Reconceptualizing, Part 2," 1733.

71. Strossen, "Tensions Between Regulating Workplace Harassment," 721; Schultz, "Reconceptualizing, Part 1," 1704.

72. Strossen, "Tensions Between Regulating Workplace Harassment," 720 n. 73.

73. Schultz, "Reconceptualizing, Part 1," 1688–1690.

74. Ibid., 1689, and Schultz, "Reconceptualizing, Part 2," 1713–1728, show that by reducing hostile environment claims to matters involving sexuality and restricting "disparate treatment" claims to concrete harms flowing from discriminatory treatment that do not involve sexuality, the current approach of the courts screens out far too many forms of hostile environment harassment involving gender.

75. See Cohen, "Hijacking of Sexual Harassment." But see Ehrenreich, "Dignity and Discrimination," for a different view. Ehrenreich argues that the problem lies in the construal of the harm of sexual harassment as a group harm. It is this approach that invites essentialist arguments. She argues for construing sexual harassment as an individualized dignity harm, that is, as an insult to the dignity, autonomy, and personhood of the victim. The discriminatory workplace is best construed as the context in which the harm occurs, according to Ehrenreich. She thus advocates construal of the harm as a common tort (invasion of privacy) that should be actionable when perpetrated against any human being.

I do not find this analysis convincing. Sex discrimination in the workplace is not simply the context of the harm; it is a harm in itself. While it is certainly true that the privacy interests of the victim are violated by sexual harassment because one has sexual intimacies forced upon one by the harasser, while humiliation is always part of sexual harassment, it would be misleading to reduce the harm of harassment to that alone. Sexual harassment, like racial harassment, is all too often a strategy of discrimination against a group, albeit perpetrated against an individual. I see no reason why one cannot acknowledge both aspects of the harm. I would, however, be loath to relinquish the Title VII frame for sexual harassment. The civil rights approach involves the collective ends of equality and justice, and it challenges the prerogatives of gender power and gender discrimination. This is crucial. Focusing merely on the dignity dimension and turning sexual harassment into an individualized harm (tort) would unduly privatize the issue.

76. Gallop, *Feminist Accused of Sexual Harassment*, 32, 37, 59. Gallop fears that sexual harassment law will be used to repress eroticism and sex, especially

when initiated by active and nontraditional women. For a critique of her position, see Sanger, "Erotics of Torts."

77. Butler, *Excitable Speech.*

78. Ibid., 1–41.

79. Recently Rae Langton refined MacKinnon's argument by acknowledging that illocutionary acts may misfire, as Austin well knew. For harassing speech to "work," Langton reminds us, "felicity conditions" are necessary. She believes that in societies characterized by sex inequality, such conditions obtain (Langton, "Speech Acts"; see Austin, "Lecture Two").

80. Butler, *Excitable Speech,* 157.

81. Ibid., 23–24, 103–126.

82. Ibid., 62.

83. For the concept partial agency see Abrams, "Sex Wars Redux," 304–354.

84. Ibid., 358.

85. Butler, *Excitable Speech,* 101.

86. Cornell, *Imaginary Domain,* 3–30, 167–178, 219–227.

87. Ibid., 205.

88. Ibid., 170.

89. Ibid., 170.

90. This also challenges the "power feminists" arguments against sexual harassment law exemplified by Roiphe, *Morning After.* For an excellent critique of "power feminism," see Abrams, "Sex Wars Redux."

91. Cornell, *Imaginary Domain,* 163, 174–177.

92. Ibid., 169.

93. Abrams, "New Jurisprudence," 1171 n. 7.

94. Ibid., 1216–1218 n. 240.

95. Ibid., 1169–1173.

96. Ibid., 1201–1202.

97. Ibid., 1220.

98. Ibid., 1216–1217.

99. Abrams, "Sex Wars Redux," 374–375.

100. Ibid.

101. Ibid., 356.

102. Ibid., 318–325.

103. Sunstein, "Paradoxes of the Regulatory State."

104. Teubner, "After Legal Instrumentalism." For a discussion, see Cohen and Arato, *Civil Society and Political Theory,* chap. 9, and Habermas, *Between Facts and Norms,* 388–446. See Chapter 4 below for an extensive discussion of legal paradigms.

105. Habermas, *Between Facts and Norms,* 221.

106. Ibid., 399.

107. For an excellent overview of the state action debate and its implications for the public/private distinction, see Garvey and Aleinikoff, *Modern Constitutional Theory,* 694–736.

108. Catharine MacKinnon and Frances Olsen are the best examples. See Olsen, "Family and the Market" and "Myth of State Intervention," and MacKinnon, *Only Words.*

109. Habermas, *Between Facts and Norms,* 406.

110. Teubner, "After Legal Instrumentalism." See also Niklas Luhmann, *Differentiation of Society,* 90–121, 324–362, and Teubner, "Substantive and Reflexive Elements." For a discussion of the procedural paradigm that does not include a new legal form, see Habermas, *Between Facts and Norms,* 388–446. For a synthesis of the two approaches, see Arato, "Procedural Law," 26–36.

111. Teubner, "After Legal Instrumentalism." See also Klare, "Public/Private Distinction in Labor Law."

112. See the next chapter for an explanation and discussion of this rather complex point.

113. For a discussion of regulatory dilemmas, see Teubner, "After Legal Instrumentalism," 309–313, and Sunstein, "Paradoxes of the Regulatory State," 407.

114. Teubner, "After Legal Instrumentalism," and Sunstein, "Paradoxes of the Regulatory State."

115. Sunstein, "Paradoxes of the Regulatory State." Both Sunstein and Habermas argue for increasing the voice of those affected in procedures of conflict resolution (Sunstein, *After the Rights Revolution,* and Habermas, *Between Facts and Norms,* 388–446).

116. See the discussion in Vorwerk, "Forgotten Interest Group."

117. If the EEOC's backlog of cases prevents investigation, the individual grievant may file in federal court which can impose liability even in the absence of a preliminary investigation.

118. Vorwerk, "Forgotten Interest Group."

119. Ibid.

120. In its 1998 ruling in *Faragher v. City of Boca Raton,* 118 S.Ct. 2275, the Court stated explicitly that the main objective of Title VII, "like that of any statute meant to influence primary conduct, is not to provide redress but to avoid harm."

121. Ibid., 118 S.Ct., at 15, citing EEOC 1980 guidelines.

122. Vorwerk, "Forgotten Interest Group," 2.

123. Fallon, "Sexual Harassment," and Browne, "Title VII."

124. Estlund, "Freedom of Expression."

125. Ibid., 762–767, discussing the doctrine of employment at will, just cause, and due process. See also Vorwerk, "Forgotten Interest Group," 1019, 1044.

126. Estlund, "Freedom of Expression."

127. Ibid., 764. Class and race prejudice may also play a role. For an analysis of how the "at will" rule undermines and distorts the operation of anti-discrimination and anti-retaliation doctrines see Estlund, "Wrongful Discharge Protection."

128. Obviously, better labor law would also help enormously. Were American workers afforded protection against, for example, demands for services that have nothing to do with the job, then quid pro quo harassment would certainly be easier to deal with. Such protection could take the form of direct regulations achieved either through negotiation with unions on a corporate or industry-wide level, or simply through state legislation. Such "materialized" labor law could supplement and hence unburden reflexive sexual harassment law. In the workplace, then, a plurality of legal forms are necessary to ensure that intimacy or sexual expression is neither repressed nor a medium for harassment and oppression. For an interesting comparison between the French and American legal environments vis-

à-vis the workplace in this regard see Saguy, "Employment Discrimination or Sexual Violence?"

129. See Estlund, "Freedom of Expression," 753–755, for an interesting proposal. But she sees the alleged conflict between the First Amendment and Title VII as a minor problem for harassment law. Far more important is the need to correct the effects of the background regime governing discharge and discipline on the actual state of employee freedom of expression and on the functioning of harassment law.

130. Ibid.

131. Vorwerk, "Forgotten Interest Group," 18. The Court's 1998 liability rulings move in this direction.

132. Ibid., 1054–1055.

133. Estlund, "Freedom of Expression," 667–770.

134. It is ironic that Judge Susan Webber Wright cited the 1994 law, signed by President Clinton, articulating new Federal Rules of Evidence, including Rule 415, which makes elements of a defendant's sexual history admissible in civil cases involving sexual assault. The latter, broadly defined, includes the kind of touching often found in sexual harassment cases (Federal Rules of Evidence Rule 415, 28 U.S.C.A., cited in Mink, *Hostile Environment*, 104–109). The president later had reason to regret signing this new rule into law.

For a discussion of the importance of rules of evidence to women regarding sex offense cases, rape, and sexual harassment, see Mink, *Hostile Environment*, 103–113. Mink points out that the 1994 Violence Against Women Act (*Violent Crime Control and Law Enforcement Act of 1994*, 84 F.R.E. 4129, H.R. 3355; Title IV, The Violence Against Women Act, Chapter 4, "New Evidentiary Rules," Section 40141, Codified as Amended Federal Rule of Evidence 412) passed by Congress provided relief to women against invasion of privacy by restricting the use of evidence about a plaintiff's sexual behavior, predisposition, or reputation in civil sex offense cases involving federal law. An amendment to the Federal Rule of Evidence 412, the civil shield declares evidence about a target's sex life "generally inadmissible." It is also inadmissible under the criminal rape shield (the original evidence rule 412, F.R.E. 412.a, cited in Mink, *Hostile Environment*, 104). The importance of such a shield to women is that it protects against sexist social attitudes such as the idea that good women do not get harassed, that well-adjusted women do not let it bother them, and that nice women do not complain about it (ibid., 110). Mink also argues that Rule 415 was unnecessary for plaintiffs to introduce "pattern and practice" evidence in a hostile environment claims (Mink, *Hostile Environment*, 109).

CHAPTER FOUR
THE DEBATE OVER THE REFLEXIVE PARADIGM

1. See below.

2. Teubner, "After Legal Instrumentalism"; Teubner, "Substantive and Reflexive Elements"; Wilke, "Three Types of Legal Structure"; and to a certain extent, Beck, *Risk Society*. Beck actually tries to synthesize the system- and action-theoretical perspectives, as we shall see below.

3. Habermas, *Between Facts and Norms*; Nonet and Selznick, *Law and Society in Transition*; Selznick, *Moral Commonwealth*, 463–476; and Selznick, "Self-Regulation."

4. Teubner, "Substantive and Reflexive Elements," 271, and Cohen and Arato, *Civil Society and Political Theory*, 481.

5. Teubner, "Autopoiesis in Law and Society," 298.

6. Ibid., 272. On the decentered society, see Luhmann, *Differentiation of Society*, 90–138, 324–362.

7. Luhmann, *Differentiation of Society*, and Weber, *Economy and Society*, 641–895.

8. This is the problem of rationality crises noted by Habermas, as early as his *Legitimation Crisis*. See also Beck, "The Reinvention of Politics," in *Reflexive Modernization: Politics, Tradition, and Aesthetics in the Modern Social Order*, ed. Ulrich Beck, Anthony Giddens, and Scott Lash, 1–55; and Offe, "The Utopia of the Zero Option," in his *Modernity and the State*, 3–30.

9. Offe, "Utopia of the Zero Option," 22.

10. Teubner, "After Legal Instrumentalism," 306.

11. Ibid., 308.

12. Beck, *Risk Society*, 213, and Wilke, "Legal Structure," 289.

13. Teubner, "After Legal Instrumentalism," 306–307.

14. Ibid., 297.

15. See the discussion in Cohen and Arato, *Civil Society*, 482.

16. By autonomy, Teubner means the self-referential and autopoietic organization of a system. Legal autonomy thus can be found in the circular relation between legal decisions and normative rules: decisions refer to rules and rules to decisions. A self-referential structure emerges when a decision resolving a conflict refers to another such decision and develops criteria for deciding out of the relation between them (Teubner, "Autopoiesis in Law and Society," 295).

17. Teubner, "Substantive and Reflexive Elements," 275.

18. Ibid., 278.

19. Ibid., 273.

20. Ibid., 275.

21. Cohen and Arato, *Civil Society*, 484.
Of course, Teubner denies that there are universal norms. He maintains that only particular moralities exist specific to a particular subsystem. Each of these has the tendency to pose as universal. For example, there is the tendency of the cost/benefit rationality of economics to generalize itself to all spheres of life. This particularistic universality runs into other imperialistic moralities coming from other subsystems but there are no free-floating universal moral principles. The term *morality* thus seems equivalent, in systems theory, to the logic of a subsystem.

22. Teubner has recently radicalized his position by synthesizing the Luhmannian idea of a decentered society composed of autopoietic subsystems with postmodern ideas of mutually untranslatable discourses (Lyotard, Derrida, and Lacan). This leads me to wonder whether he has implicitly abandoned the theory of reflexive law and the idea of regulated self-regulation altogether. See Teubner, "Ältera Pars Audiatur."

23. Habermas, *Between Facts and Norms*. Habermas calls the third paradigm "procedural." I seek a synthesis of the Teubner and Habermas approach and thus will refer to my conception of the third paradigm as "reflexive/procedural."

24. Habermas, *Legitimation Crisis*, 19.

25. Habermas, *Between Facts and Norms*, 392–409. For the concept of the life-world, see Habermas, *Theory of Communicative Action*, 113–153.

26. Law serves as a medium when it functions as a means for organizing media-controlled subsystems and/or as a vehicle that brings the imperatives of these subsystems to bear on the institutions of the life-world. By "law as institution" Habermas means legal norms that must be legitimated with reference not only to procedure but also to substantive principles open to communicative discussion. Law as a steering medium is relieved of the problem of justification; law as institution is not. Examples of the latter are constitutional law, the principles of criminal law, and so forth (ibid., 365ff.).

27. For Habermas's discussion of the family as an institution that is not formally organized, see ibid., 369–371. For a critique of this analysis, see Maus, *Rechtstheorie und politische Theorie*, 302–315.

28. Habermas, *Communicative Action*, 322, 363, 371, 367.

29. Ibid., 356–373.

30. Habermas, *Between Facts and Norms*, 426.

31. Ibid., 418–149.

32. Ibid., 410. See Arato, "Procedural Law," 30 n. 11.

33. Habermas, *Between Facts and Norms*, 410.

34. Arato, "Procedural Law," 28. What follows relies heavily on Arato.

35. Ibid., 28.

36. Ibid.; Habermas, *Between Facts and Norms*, 413.

37. Habermas, *Between Facts and Norms*, 413. Habermas gives examples of this problem in a cogent analysis of the dialectic as it affects women's rights.

38. Arato, "Procedural Law," 29.

39. Habermas, *Between Facts and Norms*, 425.

40. Ibid., 442.

41. Ibid., 426.

42. Ibid.

43. Arato, "Procedural Law," 30.

44. Habermas, *Between Facts and Norms*, 441.

45. Ibid., 440.

46. Beck, *Risk Society*; Beck, "Reinvention of Politics," in Beck, Giddens, and Lash, *Reflexive Modernization*.

47. Anthony Giddens and Scott Lash, together with Ulrich Beck, are the main theorists of the sociological reflexivity model. See Beck, Giddens, and Lash, eds., *Reflexive Modernization*.

48. Beck, "Reinvention of Politics," in ibid., 2.

49. Ibid., 5.

50. Ibid., 24.

51. Beck, "Self-Dissolution and Self-Endangerment," in ibid., 176–177. Beck accuses both Giddens and Lash of this confusion.

52. Adorno and Horkheimer, *Dialectic of Enlightenment*; Foucault, *History of Sexuality*.

53. Beck, "Reinvention of Politics," in Beck, Giddens, and Lash, *Reflexive Modernization*, 22.

54. See Habermas, *Legitimation Crisis*.

55. Beck, *Risk Society*, 160.

56. Teubner, "Substantive and Reflexive Elements," 273.

57. Beck, "Reinvention of Politics," in Beck, Giddens, and Lash, *Reflexive Modernization*, 29.

58. This has been nicely formulated by Rostboll, "Reflexive Law and Democracy." See also Beck, "Reinvention of Politics," in Beck, Giddens, and Lash, *Reflexive Modernization*, 38.

59. Moreover, Beck's theory tends to overstate and dilute the meaning of reflexivity to entail any autonomization of processes that operate behind our backs, thereby losing the distinctiveness of reflexive mechanisms.

60. See Nonet and Selznick, *Law and Society*; Selznick, *Moral Commonwealth*; and Selznick, "Self-Regulation."

61. Selznick, "Self-Regulation," 396, 395.

62. Ibid., 399.

63. Ibid., 400.

64. Ibid.

65. Ibid., 399, 401–402 n. 2.

66. Within the workplace this would entail the establishment of appropriate procedures and special units capable of monitoring and determining policy.

67. Teubner, "Substantive and Reflexive Elements," 250–251, describing mechanisms providing for communicative conflict resolution, negotiation, and so forth.

68. Selznick, "Self-Regulation," 401.

69. Ibid., 398–401.

70. Ibid., 401.

71. Ibid., 400.

72. Scheuerman, "Rule of Law and the Welfare State." See also Scheuerman, "Reflexive Law and the Challenges of Globalization."

73. I am paraphrasing Scheuerman, "Reflexive Law."

74. Ibid. See Neumann, "The Change in the Function of Law in Modern Society."

75. Ibid., 39.

76. Ingeborg Maus, *Sinn und Bedeutung*, cited in Scheuerman, "Reflexive Law," 36.

77. See Scheuerman, "Reflexive Law," 38 n. 54, for a critique of Teubner's evolutionism.

78. Blankenburg, "Poverty of Evolutionism."

79. Ibid., 275.

80. Ibid., 278.

81. Ibid.

82. Ibid., 275, 285.

83. Ibid., 287.

84. Ibid., 285, 288.

85. Teubner, "Autopoiesis," 289.

86. Ibid., 297.

87. Arato, "Procedural Law," 35.

88. Ibid., 35.

89. Ibid.

90. Ibid.

91. As I have shown in the first two chapters of this book, formal law and material law can be appropriate, depending on the matter at hand. Moreover, as already indicated, the form of reflexive law also constitutes a crucial political choice. If self-regulation is not appropriately regulated, it can degenerate into abusive forms of privatization covered with the mantle of political legitimacy. Careful attention must be given to the institutionalization of reflexive law in order to ensure that it does not become just another name for deregulation.

92. I thank Bill Scheuerman for pointing out this potential difficulty.

93. For example, at the beginning of the twentieth century, legally mandated segregation was deemed compatible with the equality provision of the Fourteenth Amendment, while by mid-century, the opposite became true.

94. Arato, "Procedural Law," 27.

CHAPTER FIVE
STATUS OR CONTRACT?

1. Key figures in the law and economics school are Becker, *Economic Approach to Human Behavior*; Schultz, *Economics of the Family*; Posner, "Regulation of the Market"; Posner, "Ethics and Economics of Enforcing Contracts"; and Posner, *Sex and Reason*.
Among the communitarians and the communitarian feminists, in addition to Sandel and Glendon, see especially Regan, *Family Law*; Singer, "Privatization of Family Law"; West, "Jurisprudence and Gender"; and West, "Difference in Women's Hedonic Lives."

2. See note 1 above for books criticizing and advocating privatization. See also Fineman, *Neutered Mother*, and Dailey, "Constitutional Privacy and the Just Family," for feminist critiques of legal privatization of the family that are not easily characterizable as communitarian.

3. On the new familism see the article by Streunung, "Feminist Challenges to the New Familism."

4. This is true for Singer. But see Brinig, "Status, Contract and Covenant," for a critique of status discourse by a feminist communitarian who is clearly also critical of contract as well.

5. I am paraphrasing from ibid., 1573.

6. This, of course, is after the whole matter was shifted from religious control to secular authorities. As Michael Grossberg points out in *Governing the Hearth*, the nineteenth-century family was regulated by a combination of judge-made common law and statute law produced by state legislatures. Grossberg argues that judges by far predominated in this domain even after the codification movement, and well into the twentieth century (290–307). While acknowledging that the

purpose of family law was to reproduce stable families and male governance, he documents shifts within the traditional status regime that resulted in the dilution of paternal rights. In particular, the creation of judicially dependent individualized maternal and filial legal prerogatives occurred at the expense of traditional notions of paternal sovereignty and household legal unity (304). While codification strengthened the status dimension of the family, judge-made law fostered the contractual aspect predicated on a conception of the family as involving divided authority and composed of distinct individuals. But married women attained legal standing only within specific gendered terms that cast them as dependents and made their rights turn on guardianship, now no longer of husbands but of male judges all too ready to assume the mantle of patriarch (301). In other words, alterations in judge-made law increased married women's legal abilities, but these prerogatives remained tied to judicial discretion. Thus, in their competition with state legislatures for jurisdiction and control in the context of the codification movement launched in the nineteenth century, state judges expanded their own powers while increasing the prerogatives of individual wives vis-à-vis their husbands but only on condition of a new form of gendered dependency—on the judiciary itself.

7. *Maynard v. Hill*, 125 U.S. 190, 211 (1888).

8. See Singer, "Privatization," 1447.

9. Ibid., 1448.

10. There was recognition of common-law marriage. See Grossberg, *Governing the Hearth*, 33–64.

11. Weitzman, *Marriage Contract*; Singer, "Privatization," 1456.

12. The wife was the one responsible for household services including housework, sexual services, childbearing, and care. The husband was the one responsible for financial support of wife and child. Yet claims based on public status were not really actionable. See Segal, "Rule of Love."

13. Singer, "Privatization," 1457.

14. See Regan, *Family Law*, 25–33, for an interesting discussion of role identification and Victorian assumptions about the self and sexual morality.

15. See Orren, "Officer's Rights," for an interesting analysis of the powers of husbands as private officer's rights.

16. Hafen, "Family as an Entity"; Singer, "Privatization," 1508–1509.

17. I am paraphrasing Singer, "Privatization," 1444. We should of course be wary of describing this trend as either linear or all pervasive. There is a great deal of variety and incoherence in state-level family law.

18. See the discussion in Singer, "Privatization," 1508–1518. See also Regan, *Family Law*, 37, for a discussion of the relevant Supreme Court cases articulating individualized conceptions of private autonomy. See also Chapter 1. Of course law and economics theorists like Posner reject constitutional privacy analysis while embracing private ordering of many aspects of intimate association.

19. See especially Singer, "Privatization," 1446–1527.

20. Ibid., 1469. See also Regan, *Family Law*, 37.

21. See Glendon, *Transformation of Family Law*, 35–36.

22. Singer, "Privatization," 1465. Restrictions still remain regarding incest between close relatives.

23. *Loving v. Virginia*, 388 U.S. 1 (1967), striking down Virginia's anti-miscegenation laws on due process and equal protection grounds; *Zablocki v. Redhail*, 434 U.S. 374 (1978), striking down an attempt by Wisconsin to prohibit marriage by parents who fail to support their existing children; and *Turner v. Safely*, 482 U.S. 78 (1987), invalidating regulations by Missouri requiring prison inmates to obtain the warden's permission to marry.

Establishing as fundamental the individual's right to marry, however, is no reason to assume the Court sees marriage along the lines of a business contract. Ending discrimination regarding the access to intimacy does not preclude acknowledging its specificity, its importance, or the type of bonds it establishes.

24. On 22 December 1999, Vermont ruled that gay couples must be given the same benefits and protections as couples of the opposite sex (*New York Times*, 22 December 1999). The following July the Vermont legislature passed a law establishing equality between civil unions and marriage (*New York Times*, 25 October 2000). The issue is still very contentious: thirty-three states have passed "defense of marriage acts" specifying that only marriage between a man and a woman is valid (*New York Times*, 21 October 2000). Age-based restrictions also remain, but these are no longer justified for the purpose of reinforcing family control; rather, their purpose is to avoid the risks allegedly involved in youthful marriage, especially for girls. See Singer, "Privatization," 1466.

25. Other restrictions regarding age (minors) or polygamous marriages can be justified on the basis of equality arguments. But this is hardly the case with prohibitions of gay or lesbian marriage.

26. The Court has proclaimed, "No longer is the female destined solely for the home and the rearing of the family, and only the male for the marketplace and world of ideas" (*Stanton v. Stanton*, 421 U.S., at 14–15, quoted in Regan, *Family Law*, 37). For a description of other changes see Singer, "Privatization," 1458–1460.

27. This is true but for the important exception of child support and child custody issues. Sixteen states adopted the uniform Prenuptial Agreement Act by 1992 authorizing potential spouses to contract with each other with respect to their property rights and support obligations. See Singer, "Privatization," 1460, for details. See also Regan, *Family Law*, 37–39, discussing the adoption of the Uniform Marital Property Act (1987) providing that marital property agreements would be enforceable.

28. Regan, *Family Law*, 38–39, and Singer, "Privatization," 1470–1478. In all but two states divorce is authorized on the motion of only one party. See Walker and Elrod, "Family Law in the Fifty States."

29. I am paraphrasing Singer, "Privatization," 1472.

30. Regan, *Family Law*, 39.

31. *Eisenstadt v. Baird*, 405 U.S., at 453, extending the right to use contraception to the unmarried, and hence indirectly accepting extramarital sex as legitimate.

32. This is, of course, highly contested and contestable. See Regan, *Family Law*, 40.

33. Ibid., 41.

34. For a discussion see Singer, "Privatization," 1452–1460.

35. See ibid., 1453–1454, for the list up to 1992.

36. According to Tim Fisher, executive director of the Gay and Lesbian Parents Coalition, the following twenty-one states and the District of Columbia have court precedents that allow for "second-parent adoptions" for same-sex couples: Alaska, California, Colorado, Connecticut, Illinois, Indiana, Iowa, Maryland, Massachusetts, Michigan, Minnesota, Nevada, New Jersey, New York, Ohio, Oregon, Pennsylvania, Rhode Island, Texas, Vermont, and Washington. In four states, the highest court decided in favor of second-parent adoptions, which makes them binding law. These states are Vermont, Massachusetts, New York, and New Jersey ("State Laws Regarding Adoption by Gay and Lesbian Parents," http://www.calib.com/naic/pubs/l_same.htm).

37. That *Bowers v. Hardwick*, 478 U.S. 186 (1986), has not been overruled is indicative of this.

38. Singer, "Privatization," 1537.

39. That is why some feminists like Martha Fineman argue for considering the mother/child, or more generally the care-giver/child, as the family unit and for the deprivatization of the burdens of care, that is, for the construal of that unit as serving important public purposes—the raising of the next generation—and as meriting state support (Fineman, *Neutered Mother*).

40. Ibid., 1538, citing West, "Authority, Autonomy, and Choice."

41. Of course, this is hardly a new charge. See Bellah et al., *Habits of the Heart*, and Berger and Berger, *War over the Family*.

42. Singer, "Privatization," 1478. Most of the factual information in what follows is drawn from this essay.

43. Ibid., 1480–1481.

44. On state laws, see Atwell, "Surrogacy and Adoption: A Case of Incompatibility," 12–13.

45. The majority of jurisdictions now permit private-placement adoption. Baby selling and baby brokering are currently illegal in all fifty states. See ibid., 27, 29 nn. 109, 110, listing statutes.

46. Singer, "Privatization," 1483 nn. 182, 183.

47. It also varies widely from state to state. See "At Core of Adoption Dispute is Crazy Quilt of State Laws," *New York Times*, 19 January 2001, A14.

48. Singer, "Privatization," 1478.

49. Margaret J. Radin, "Market-Inalienability."

50. Singer, "Privatization," 1491. See also Field, "Surrogate Motherhood," for a history of surrogacy. There are two kinds of surrogacy arrangements: gestational surrogacy, wherein the fertilized egg of the intended mother is placed into the uterus of the surrogate mother, and genetic surrogacy, wherein the "surrogate" mother provides the egg and carries the child through pregnancy.

51. The New Jersey Supreme Court in the infamous Baby M case invalidated a surrogate mother's contract since it included her irrevocable consent to surrender the child at birth, thus violating local adoption laws. The Court nevertheless awarded custody to the father and his wife under the "best interest of the child" standard (*Baby M. II*, 537 A2d 1227). Florida's law authorizes noncommercial surrogacy contracts so long as the gestational mother has the opportunity to rescind her relinquishment of parental rights within seven days, while New Hamp-

shire and Nevada allow paid contracts, although New Hampshire requires preapproval by a court and seventy-two hours after birth for the surrogate to rescind (Singer, "Privatization," 1494–1495).

52. Ibid., 1493.

53. Ibid., 1489.

54. Landes and Posner, "Economics of the Baby Shortage." The revised piece is Posner, "Regulation of the Market in Adoption." As Singer points out, Posner's article became the centerpiece of a major symposium entitled "Adoption and Market Theory" in 1987 (Singer, "Privatization," 1487).

55. Singer, "Privatization," 1496.

56. Ibid., 1497–1500.

57. Ibid., 1501.

58. Ibid., 1504.

59. Ibid., 1507.

60. Ibid., 1508.

61. In *Baby M, 527 A2d 1249.*

62. Regan, *Family Law*, 107.

63. Singer, "Privatization," 1550. Weitzman, *Divorce Revolution*, first pointed this out systematically.

64. Singer, "Privatization"; Weitzman, *Divorce Revolution.*

65. Singer, "Privatization," 1540–1556.

66. Ibid., 1542.

67. Ibid., 1541 n. 453, citing critiques of private mediation.

68. Ibid., 1556–1560.

69. See Chapter 1. There I argue that constitutionalized rights talk and constitutional privacy analysis does not entail such a conception of the self.

70. Regan, *Family Law*, 68–88.

71. Ibid., 106–117.

72. Ibid., 112.

73. This is a point made by Brinig, *Status*, 1573, in her review of Regan's book.

74. Regan, *Family Law*, 89.

75. Ibid., 92.

76. Ibid.

77. Ibid., 91–93.

78. Ibid., 116.

79. Ibid.

80. Ibid., 123.

81. Ibid.

82. Ibid., 126.

83. Ibid., 124–125.

84. Ibid., 137–143.

85. See Singer, "Privatization," 1554 n. 511. She cites Younger, "Marital Regimes," 90–91, and Glendon, *Abortion and Divorce in Western Law*, 94–103, as examples of other relational or communitarian feminists who make such proposals.

86. Regan, *Family Law*, 121–122.

87. Ibid., 128.

88. Singer, "Privatization," 1526, and Regan, *Family Law*, 178.

89. Singer, "Privatization," 1526.

90. Regan, *Family Law*, 178–179.

91. Habermas, *Between Facts and Norms*, chaps. 1, 3.

92. Regan, *Family Law*, 140.

93. Ibid., 165.

94. See Habermas, *Between Facts and Norms*, 420.

95. Private ordering is a mode of juridification insofar as it involves legal recognition of contracts and hence the constitution of legal, rights-bearing subjects. Welfare regulations carry the risk of opening up domains of action to bureaucratic intrusions, therapeutic interventions by "experts" from social workers to psychotherapists, and judicial control, undermining the communicative competence and life-world supports of intimate associates. See Habermas, *Theory of Communicative Action*, 363–369.

96. See Chapter 2.

97. Morris, "Privacy, Privation, Perversity," 337.

98. Singer, "Privatization," 1566. Singer does not discuss legal paradigms but does call for new legal standards and doctrines to govern the domain of intimacy.

99. Without thereby denigrating other forms that would still be protected by constitutional privacy analysis (Singer, "Privatization," 1567).

Cases Cited

Baby M., 109 N.J. 396 (1988).
Balfour v. Balfour, 2 K.B. 571, 579 (1919).
Barnes v. Costle, 561 F2d 983, (1977).
Bellotti v. Baird, 443 U.S. 622 (1979).
Bowers v. Hardwick, 478 U.S. 186 (1986).
Burlington Industries v. Ellerth, 118 S.Ct. 2257 (1998).
Carey v. Population Services, 431 U.S. 678 (1977).
City of Akron v. Akron Center for Reproductive Health (Akron 1), 462 U.S. 416 (1983).
Cleveland Board of Education v. LaFleur, 414 U.S. 632 (1974).
Deshaney v. Winnebago County Department of Social Services, 498 U.S. 189 (1989).
Doe v. Bolton, 410 U.S. 179 (1973).
Eisenstadt v. Baird, 405 U.S. 438 (1972).
Faragher v. City of Boca Raton, 118 S.Ct. 2275 (1998).
Gebser v. Lago Vist. Independent School District, 118 S.Ct. 1989 (1998).
Griswold v. Connecticut, 381 U.S. 479 (1965).
H. v. Matheson, 450 U.S. 398 (1981).
Harris v. Forklift Systems, Inc., 510 U.S. 17 (1993).
Harris v. McRae, 448 U.S. 297 (1980).
Loving v. Virginia, 388 U.S. 1 (1967).
Maher v. Roe, 432 U.S. 464 (1977).
Maynard v. Hill, 125 U.S. 190 (1988).
Meinhold v. United States Department of Defense, 808 Fsupp 1455, 1458 (CD Cal 1993).
Meritor Savings Bank F.S.B. v. Vinson, 477 U.S. 55 (1986).
Meyer v. Nebraska, 262 U.S. 390 (1923).
Moore v. City of East Cleveland, 431 U.S. 494 (1977).
Oncale v. Sundowner Offshore Services, 118 S.Ct. 998 (1998).
Palko v. Connecticut, 302 U.S. 319 (1937).
Pierce v. Society of Sisters, 268 U.S. 510 (1925).
Planned Parenthood of Southeastern Pennsylvania v. Casey, 505 U.S. 833 (1992).
Poe v. Ullman, 327 U.S. 497 (1961).
Police Department of Chicago v. Mosley, 408 U.S. 92 (1972).
R.A.V. v. St. Paul, 112 S.Ct. 2539 (1992).
Reynolds v. United States, 98 U.S. 145 (1878).
Roberts v. United States Jaycees, 468 U.S. 609 (1984).
Roe v. Wade, 410 U.S. 113 (1973).
Rust v. Sullivan, 111 S.Ct. 1759 (1991).
Stanley v. Georgia, 394 U.S. 557 (1969).
Stanley v. Illinois, 405 U.S. 645 (1972).

Stanton v. Stanton, 421 U.S. 7 (1975).

Sternberg, Attorney General of Nebraska et al. v. Leroy Carhart, 120 S.Ct. 2597 (2000).

Thornburgh v. American College of Obstetricians and Gynecologists, 476 U.S. 758 (1986).

Troxel v. Granville, 530 U.S. 57 (2000).

Turner v. Safely, 482 U.S. 78 (1987).

United States v. Fagg, 34 M.J. 179, 113 S.Ct. 92 (1992).

United States v. Henderson, 34 M.J. 174 (1992).

Watkins v. United States Army, 847 F2d 1329 (9th Cir. 1988).

Webster v. Reproductive Health Services, 429 U.S. 490 (1989).

Zablocki v. Redhail, 434 U.S. 374 (1978).

Bibliography

GOVERNMENT DOCUMENTS

Civil Rights Act of 1964. Pub. L. 88-352. *U.S. Statutes at Large* 78 (1965).
Civil Rights Act of 1991. Pub. L. 102-166. U.S. Code vol. 42, secs. 2000e-5(k) (1996).
Equal Employment Opportunity Commission. "EEOC Guidelines on Discrimination Because of Sex." *Federal Register* 63 (1980): 622.
Violent Crime Control and Law Enforcement Act of 1994. Pub. L. 103-322. 84 F.R.E. 4129, H.R. 3355.

BOOKS AND ARTICLES

Abrams, Kathryn. "The New Jurisprudence of Sexual Harassment." *Cornell Law Review* 83.6 (1998): 1169.
——. "Postscript, Spring 1998: A Response to Professors Bernstein and Franke." *Cornell Law Review* 83.18 (1998): 1257.
——. "Sex Wars Redux." *Columbia Law Review* 95 (1995): 304–374.
Ackerman, Bruce. *We the People.* Cambridge: Harvard University Press, 1991.
Adams, Jane Meredith. "Gay Man Returns to Navy Service: Clinton Stands By Opening of Military to Homosexuals." *Boston Globe,* 13 November 1992, A1.
Adorno, Theodor, and Max Horkheimer. *Dialectic of Enlightenment.* New York: Herder and Herder, 1972.
Allen, Anita. *Uneasy Access: Privacy for Women in a Free Society.* Totowa, N.J.: Rowman and Littlefield, 1988.
American Civil Liberties Union. *Policy Guide of the American Civil Liberties Union.* Rev. ed. New York: American Civil Liberties Union, 1995.
Arato, Andrew. "Procedural Law and Civil Society: Interpreting the Radical Democratic Paradigm." In *Habermas on Law and Democracy: Critical Exchanges,* ed. Michael Rosenfeld and Andrew Arato, 26–36. Berkeley: University of California Press, 1998.
Arendt, Hannah. *The Human Condition.* Chicago: University of Chicago Press, 1958.
——. *On Revolution.* New York: Penguin, 1963.
——. *The Origins of Totalitarianism.* New York: Harcourt Brace Jovanovich, 1951.
"At Core of Adoption Dispute Is Crazy Quilt of State Laws." *New York Times,* 19 January 2001, A14.
Atwell, Barbara L. "Surrogacy and Adoption: A Case of Incompatability." *Columbia Human Rights Law Review* 20 (1990): 1.

Austin, John. "Lecture II." In *How to Do Things with Words*, ed. Marina Sbisa and J. O. Urmsson, 12–24. Cambridge: Harvard University Press, 1975.

Barry, Brian. *Justice as Impartiality.* New York: Oxford University Press, 1995.

Bartlett, Katherine T. "Rumpelstiltskin." *Connecticut Law Review* 25 (1993): 473.

Bawer, Bruce. *A Place at the Table: The Gay Individual in American Society.* New York: Poseidon Press, 1993.

Beck, Ulrich. *Risk Society: Towards a New Modernity.* London: Sage, 1992.

———. "The Reinvention of Politics." In *Reflexive Modernization Politics: Tradition and Aesthetics in the Modern Social Order*, ed. Ulrich Beck, Anthony Giddens, and Scott Lash, 1–55. Stanford: Stanford University Press, 1994.

———. "Self-Dissolution and Self-Endangerment of Industrial Society: What Does This Mean?" In *Reflexive Modernization Politics: Tradition and Aesthetics in the Modern Social Order*, ed. Ulrich Beck, Anthony Giddens, and Scott Lash, 175–183. Stanford: Stanford University Press, 1994.

Beck, Ulrich, Anthony Giddens, and Scott Lash, eds. *Reflexive Modernization: Politics, Tradition, and Aesthetics in the Modern Social Order.* Stanford: Stanford University Press, 1994.

Becker, Gary S. *The Economic Approach to Human Behavior.* Chicago: University of Chicago Press, 1974.

Bellah, Robert, et al. *Habits of the Heart.* Berkeley: University of California Press, 1985.

Benn, Stanley I., and Gerald F. Gauss, ed. *Public and Private in Social Life.* New York: St. Martin's Press, 1983.

Berger, B., and P. Berger. *The War over the Family.* Garden City, N.Y.: Anchor Press/Doubleday, 1983.

Berger, Raoul. *Government by Judiciary: The Transformation of the Fourteenth Amendment.* Cambridge: Harvard University Press, 1997.

Berlin, Isaiah. *Four Essays on Liberty.* New York: Oxford University Press, 1958.

Black, Julia. "Constitutionalizing Self-Regulation." *Modern Law Review* 59 (1996): 24–55.

Blankenburg, Erhard. "The Poverty of Evolutionism: A Critique of Teubner's Case for Reflexive Law." *Law and Society Review* 18.2 (1984): 273–289.

Bohman, James, and William Rehg, eds. *Deliberative Democracy.* Cambridge: MIT Press, 1997.

Boling, Patricia. *Privacy and the Politics of Intimate Life.* Ithaca: Cornell University Press, 1996.

Bork, Robert. *The Tempting of America.* New York: Free Press, 1989.

Brinig, Margaret F. "Status, Contract, and Covenant." *Cornell Law Review* 79 (1994): 1573–1602.

Brodsky, Carol. *The Harassed Worker.* Lexington, Mass.: Lexington Books, 1976.

Brown, Wendy. *States of Injury.* Princeton: Princeton University Press, 1995.

Browne, Kingsley. "Title VII as Censorship: Hostile-Environment Harassment and the First Amendment." *Ohio State Law Journal* 52 (Spring 1991): 481.

———. "Workplace Censorship: A Response to Professor Sangree." *Rutgers Law Journal* 47 (1995): 579.

Butler, Judith. *Bodies That Matter.* New York: Routledge, 1993.

————. *Excitable Speech: A Politics of the Performative*. New York: Routledge, 1997.

————. *Gender Trouble*. New York: Routledge, 1990.

Butler, Judith, and Joan W. Scott, eds. *Feminists Theorize the Political*. Routledge: New York, 1992.

Cain, Patricia. "Litigating for Lesbian and Gay Rights: A Legal History." *Virginia Law Review* 79 (1993): 1551.

Castoriadis, Cornelius. *The Imaginary Institution of Society*. Cambridge: MIT Press, 1987.

Cherlin, Andrew. *Public and Private Families*. New York: McGraw-Hill, 1996.

Cohen, Jean L. "Democracy, Difference and the Right of Privacy." In *Democracy and Difference: Contesting the Boundaries of the Political*, ed. Seyla Benhabib, 187–217. Princeton: Princeton University Press, 1996.

————. "Does Voluntary Association Make Democracy Work?" In *Diversity and Its Discontents: Cultural Conflict and Common Ground in Contemporary American Society*, ed. Neil Smelser and Jeffrey C. Alexander, 263–293. Princeton: Princeton University Press, 1999.

————. "Harcelement sexuel: les dilemmes de la legislation americaine." *Esprit*, March/April 2001, 137–155.

————. "The Hijacking of Sexual Harassment." *Constellations* 6.2 (1992): 142–144.

————. "Is Privacy a Legal Duty?" In *Public and Private*, ed. Maurizio Passerain D'Entreves and Ursula Vogel, 117–148. London: Routledge, 2000.

————. "Is There a Duty of Privacy? Law, Sexual Orientation and the Construction of Identity." *Texas Journal of Women and the Law* 6.1 (1996): 47–128.

————. "Personal Autonomy and the Law." *Tocqueville Review* 26.2 (2000): 57–76.

————. "The Politics of Gender and Privacy." In *Public and Private in Thought and Practice*, ed. Krishan Kumar and Jeff Alexander, 133–165. Chicago: University of Chicago Press, 1997.

————. "Redescribing Privacy: Identity, Difference, and the Abortion Controversy." *Columbia Journal of Gender and Law* 3 (1992): 105–112.

————. "Trust, Voluntary Association, and Workable Democracy: The Contemporary American Discourse of Civil Society." In *Democracy and Trust*, ed. Mark Warren, 228–239. New York: Cambridge University Press, 1999.

Cohen, Jean L., and Andrew Arato. *Civil Society and Political Theory*. Cambridge: MIT Press, 1992.

Cohen, Joshua. "Procedure and Substance in Deliberative Democracy." In *Deliberative Democracy*, ed. James Bohman and William Rehg, 407–437. Cambridge: MIT Press, 1997.

Colker, Ruth. "Feminist Liberation: An Oxymoron? A Study of the Briefs Filed in William L. Webster v. Reproductive Health Services." *Harvard Women's Law Journal* 13 (1990): 137.

Cornell, Drucilla. *The Imaginary Domain: Abortion, Pornography, and Sexual Harassment*. New York: Routledge, 1995.

Dailey, Ann. "Constitutional Privacy and the Just Family." *Tulane Law Review* 67 (March 1992): 955–1030.

Davidson, Arnold I. "How to Do the History of Psychoanalysis: A Reading of Freud's *Three Essays on the Theory of Sexuality*." *Critical Inquiry* 13 (1987): 252.

Davis, Nancy Ann. "The Abortion Debate: The Search for Common Ground, Part 2." *Ethics* 103 (July 1993): 731–778.

Dean, Jodi. *Solidarity of Strangers*. Berkeley: University of California Press, 1996.

De Crew, Judith Wagner. *In Pursuit of Privacy: Law, Ethics and the Rise of Technology*. Ithaca: Cornell University Press, 1997.

Di Stefano, Christine. "Rethinking Autonomy." Paper presented at the annual meeting of the American Political Science Association, San Francisco, September 1990.

Dorf, Michael C., and Charles F. Sabel. "Constitution of Democratic Exceptionalism." 98.2 *Columbia Law Review* (1988): 267–473.

Dworkin, Ronald. "The Center Holds!" *New York Review of Books*, 13 August 1992, 29.

———. "The Forum of Principle." *A Matter of Principle*. Cambridge: Harvard University Press, 1985.

———. *Life's Dominion: An Argument about Abortion, Euthanasia, and Individual Freedom*. New York: Knopf, 1993.

———. *Taking Rights Seriously*. Cambridge: Harvard University Press, 1977.

Ehrenreich, Rosa. "Dignity and Discrimination: Toward a Pluralistic Understanding of Workplace Harassment." *Georgetown Law Journal* 88 (1999): 1–64.

Eisenstein, Zillah. *The Female Body and the Law*. Berkeley: University of California Press, 1990.

Elshtain, Jean Bethke. *Democracy on Trial*. New York: Basic Books, 1995.

Elster, Jon, and Rune Slagstad, eds. *Constitutionalism and Democracy*. New York: Cambridge University Press, 1998.

Ely, John Hart. "The Wages of Crying Wolf: A Comment on Roe v. Wade." *Yale Law Journal* 82 (1973): 920.

Epstein, Deborah. "Can a 'Dumb Ass Woman' Achieve Equality in the Workplace? Running the Gauntlet of Hostile Environment Harassing Speech." *Georgetown Law Journal* 84 (February 1996): 399–420.

———. "Free Speech at Work: Verbal Harassment as Gender Based Discriminatory (Mis) Treatment." *Georgetown Law Journal* 85 (1997): 649–664.

Eskridge, William, Jr. "A Social Constructionist Critique of Posner's *Sex and Reason*: Steps toward a Gay Legal Agenda." *Yale Law Journal* 102 (1992): 333.

Estlund, Cynthia. "Freedom of Expression in the Workplace and the Problem of Discriminatory Harassment." *Texas Law Review* 75 (1997): 687.

———. "Wrongful Discharge Protection in an At-Will World." *Texas Law Review* 74 (1996): 1658.

Estrich, Susan. "Sex at Work." *Stanford Law Review* 43 (1991): 826–834.

Etzioni, Amitai. *The Limits of Privacy*. New York: Basic Books, 1999.

———, ed. *Rights and the Common Good: The Communitarian Perspective*. New York: St. Martin's Press, 1995.

"Excerpts From the News Conferences by Clinton and Nunn." *New York Times*, 30 January 1993, A8.

Fallon, Richard, Jr. "Sexual Harassment, Content Neutrality, and the First Amendment Dog That Didn't Bark." *Supreme Court Review* 1994: 8–21.

Ferrara, Alessandro. *Reflective Authenticity.* New York: Routledge, 1998.

Field, Martha. *Surrogate Motherhood.* Cambridge: Harvard University Press, 1988.

Fineman, Martha Albertson. "Intimacy Outside of the Natural Family: The Limits of Privacy." *Connecticut Law Review* 23 (1992): 955.

―――. *The Neutered Mother, the Sexual Family, and Other Twentieth Century Tragedies.* New York: Routledge, 1995.

Forst, Ranier. "Praktische Vernunft und Rechtfertigende Grunde: Zur Begrundung der Moral." In *Motive, Grunde, Zwecke. Theorien Praktischer Rationalitat,* ed. Stefan Gosepath, 168–205. Frankfurt am Main: Fischer Verlag, 1999.

―――. "Toleration, Justice, and Reason." Unpublished manuscript.

Foucault, Michel. *History of Sexuality.* Volume 1. New York: Vintage, 1978.

―――. *The Order of Things: An Archeology of the Human Sciences.* New York: Vintage, 1970.

Franklin, Kris. "A Family Like Any Other: Alternative Methods of Defining Family in Law." *New York University Review of Law and Social Change* 18 (1990–91): 1027.

Frug, Mary Joe. *Women and the Law.* 2nd ed. New York: Foundation Press, 1998.

Furstenberg, Frank F., Jr. "Family Change and Family Diversity." In *Diversity and Its Discontents: Cultural Conflict and Common Ground in Contemporary American Society,* ed. Neil Smelser and Jeffrey C. Alexander, 147–166. Princeton: Princeton University Press, 1999.

―――. "Family Change and the Welfare of Children: What Do We Know and What Can We Do about It?." In *Gender and Family Change in Industrialized Countries,* ed. A. M. Jensen and K. O. Mason, 245–257. Oxford: Clarendon Press, 1997.

Gallop, Jane. *Feminist Accused of Sexual Harassment.* Durham, N.C.: Duke University Press, 1997.

Galston, William. "New Familism, New Politics." *Family Affairs* 5 (1992): 1–2.

―――. "A Liberal-Democratic Case for the Two-Parent Family." In *Rights and the Common Good: The Communitarian Perspective,* ed. Amitai Etzioni, 139–149. New York: St. Martin's Press, 1995.

Gamson, William A. *Talking Politics.* New York: Cambridge University Press, 1992.

Gaolitti, Elisabeta. "Citizenship and Equality: The Place of Toleration." *Political Theory* 21.4 (1993): 585–605.

Garrow, David J. *Liberty and Sexuality: The Right to Privacy and the Making of Roe v. Wade.* New York: Macmillan, 1994.

Garvey, John H., and Alexander T. Aleinikoff, eds. *Modern Constitutional Theory: A Reader.* 3rd ed. St. Paul: West Publishing, 1994.

Giddens, Anthony. *The Transformation of Intimacy.* Stanford: Stanford University Press, 1992.

Gillman, Howard. *The Constitution Besieged: The Rise and Demise of Lochner Era Police Powers Jurisprudence.* Durham, N.C.: Duke University Press, 1993.

Ginsburg, Faye. *Contested Lives: The Abortion Debate in an American Community.* Berkeley: University of California Press, 1989.

Glendon, Mary Ann. *Abortion and Divorce in Western Law.* Cambridge: Harvard University Press, 1987.

Glendon, Mary Ann. "Marriage and the State: The Withering Away of Marriage."
  Virginia Law Review 62 (1976): 663.
———. *Rights Talk*. New York: Free Press, 1991.
———. *The Transformation of Family Law: State, Law, and Family in the United
  States and Europe*. Chicago: University of Chicago Press, 1977.
Goffman, Erving. *Interaction Ritual: Essays in Face-to-Face Behavior*. New York:
  Pantheon Books, 1967.
———. *Reflections in Public*. New York: Harper and Row, 1971.
Goldstein, Anne. "Reasoning About Homosexuality: A Commentary on Janet
  Halley's 'Reasoning About Sodomy: Act and Identity in and after Bowers v.
  Hardwick.'" *Virginia Law Review* 79 (1993): 484.
Gosepath, Stefan, ed. *Motive, Grunde, Zwecke. Theorien Praktischer Rationalitat*.
  Frankfurt am Main: Fischer Verlag, 1999.
Greenawalt, Kent. *Fighting Words: Individuals, Communities, and Liberties of
  Speech*. Princeton: Princeton University Press, 1995.
Greenhouse, Linda. "Case on Visitation Rights Hinges on Defining Family." *New
  York Times*, 4 January 2000, A1.
Grey, Thomas. "Eros, Civilization, and the Burger Court." *Law and Contempo-
  rary Problems* 43.3 (1980): 83–99.
Grossberg, Michael. *Governing the Hearth: Law and Family in Nineteenth-Century
  America*. Chapel Hill: University of North Carolina Press, 1985.
Guenter, Klaus. "Communicative Freedom, Communicative Power, and Jurisgen-
  esis." In *Habermas on Law and Democracy: Critical Exchanges*, ed. Michael Ro-
  senfeld and Andrew Arato, 234–256. Berkeley: University of California Press,
  1998.
Gunther, Gerald, and Kathleen M. Sullivan, eds. *Constitutional Law*. New York:
  Foundation Press, 1997.
Gutmann, Amy, ed. *Multiculturalism: Examining the Politics of Recognition*.
  Princeton: Princeton University Press, 1992.
Habermas, Jürgen. *Between Facts and Norms*. Cambridge: MIT Press, 1996.
———. "Frank Michelman and 'Democracy vs. Constitutionalism.'" Unpub-
  lished manuscript.
———. *Justification and Application*. Cambridge: MIT Press, 1997.
———. *Legitimation Crisis*. Boston: Beacon Press, 1973.
———. *The Philosophical Discourse of Modernity*. Cambridge: MIT Press, 1987.
———. *The Theory of Communicative Action*. Volume 2. Boston: Beacon Press,
  1987.
Hafen, Bruce C. "The Family as an Entity." *University of California Davis Law
  Review* 22 (1989): 865.
Halley, Janet E. "The Politics of the Closet: Towards Equal Protection for Gay,
  Lesbian, and Bisexual Identity." *UCLA Law Review* 36 (1989): 915–976.
———. "Reasoning About Sodomy: Act and Identity in and after Bowers v. Hard-
  wick." *Virginia Law Review* 79 (October 1993): 1721.
Harper, Phillip Brian. "Private Affairs: Race, Sex, Property, and Persons." *GLQ:
  A Journal of Lesbian and Gay Studies* 1.2 (1994): 118.
Hayek, Friedrich A. *The Constitution of Liberty*. Chicago: University of Chicago
  Press, 1960.

Hegel, Georg Wilhelm Friedrich. *Philosophy of Right.* Trans. T. M. Knox. New York: Oxford University Press, 1967.

Heyd, David, ed. *Toleration: An Elusive Virtue.* Princeton: Princeton University Press, 1996.

Holmes, Stephen. "The Permanent Structure of Anti-Liberal Thought." In *Liberalism and the Moral Life,* ed. Nancy Rosenblum, 227–253. Cambridge: Harvard University Press, 1989.

Honig, Bonnie. *Political Theory and the Displacement of Politics.* Ithaca: Cornell University Press, 1993.

Honneth, Axel. "Integrity and Disrespect: Principles of a Conception of Morality Based on a Theory of Recognition." *Political Theory* 20.2 (1992): 190–193.

———. *The Struggle for Recognition.* Cambridge: Polity Press, 1992.

Hunter, Ian, David Saunders, and Dugald Williamson. *On Pornography.* New York: St. Martin's Press, 1993.

Ifill, Gwen. "Clinton Accepts Delay in Lifting Military Gay Ban." *New York Times,* 30 January 1993, A8.

———. "White House Backs 2-Step Plan to End Military's Gay Ban." *New York Times,* 27 January 1993, A1.

Ireland, Patricia. "Abortion Angst." *Newsweek,* 13 July 1992, 16.

Jaggar, Alison. *Abortion and Woman's Choice.* Boston: Northeastern University Press, 1984.

Kant, Immanuel. *The Metaphysics of Morals.* Trans. Mary Gregor. Cambridge: Cambridge University Press, 1991.

Kaplan, Morris. "Intimacy and Equality: The Question of Lesbian and Gay Marriage." *Philosophical Forum* 25 (1994): 333–360.

———. *Sexual Justice: Democratic Citizenship and the Politics of Desire.* New York: Routledge, 1997.

Karst, Kenneth L. "The Freedom of Intimate Association." *Yale Law Journal* 89 (1980): 624.

Klare, Karl. "The Public/Private Distinction in Labor Law." *University of Pennsylvania Law Review* 130 (1982): 1358.

Koppelman, Andrew. "The Miscegenation Analogy: Sodomy Laws as Sex Discrimination." *Yale Law Journal* 98 (1988): 145.

———. "Why Discrimination against Lesbians and Gays Is Sex Discrimination." *New York University Law Review* 69 (1994): 197.

Lacquer, Thomas. *Making Sex: Body and Gender from the Greeks to Freud.* Cambridge: Harvard University Press, 1990.

Landes, Elizabeth M., and Richard A. Posner. "The Economics of the Baby Shortage." *Journal of Legal Studies* 7 (1978): 323.

Langton, Rae. "Speech Acts and Unspeakable Acts." *Philosophy and Public Affairs* 22.4 (1993): 293–330.

Laplanche, Jean. *Life and Death in Psychoanalysis.* Baltimore: Johns Hopkins University Press, 1976.

Larmore, Charles. *Patterns of Moral Complexity.* New York: Cambridge University Press, 1987.

———. "Political Liberalism." *Political Theory* 18.3 (1990): 339–360.

Law, Sylvia. "Homosexuality and the Social Meaning of Gender." *Wisconsin Law Review* 1988 (1988): 187.

———. "Rethinking Sex, Law, and the Constitution." *University of Pennsylvania Law Review* 132 (1984): 955.

Lefort, Claude. "Politics and Human Rights." In *The Political Forms of Modern Society: Bureaucracy, Democracy, Totalitarianism*, ed. John B. Thompson, 239–272. Cambridge: MIT Press, 1986.

Luhmann, Niklas. *The Differentiation of Society.* New York: Columbia University Press, 1982.

———. *Grundrechte als Institution.* Berlin: Ducker und Humblot, 1965.

Luker, Kristin. *Abortion and the Politics of Motherhood.* Berkeley: University of California Press, 1984.

MacKinnon, Catharine A. *Feminism Unmodified.* Cambridge: Harvard University Press, 1987.

———. "Harassment Law Under Siege." *New York Times*, 5 March 1998.

———. *Only Words.* Cambridge: Harvard University Press, 1993.

———. "Reflections on Sex Equality under Law." *Yale Law Journal* 100 (1991): 1291.

———. *Sexual Harassment of Working Women.* New Haven: Yale University Press, 1979.

———. *Toward a Feminist Theory of the State.* Cambridge: Harvard University Press, 1989.

Madison, James. "Federalist #10." In *The Federalist Papers*, ed. Garry Wills, 42–49. New York: Bantam Books, 1982.

Maus, Ingeborg. *Rechtstheorie und politische Theorie im Industiekapitalismus.* Munich: Wilhelm Fink Verlag, 1986.

———. "Sinn und Bedeutung der Volkssouveranitaet in der modernen Gesellschaft." *Kritische Justiz* 24 (1991): 148–149.

McClain, Linda C. "The Poverty of Privacy." *Columbia Journal of Gender and Law* 3 (1992): 119–174.

McClure, Kirstie. "Diversity, Difference, and the Limits of Toleration." *Political Theory* 18.3 (1990): 361–392.

Merleau-Ponty, Maurice. *The Phenomenology of Perception.* London: Routledge and Kegan Paul, 1962.

Michelman, Frank. "Law's Republic." *Yale Law Journal* 97 (1987): 1493.

———. "Private Personal but Not Split: Radin versus Rorty." *Southern California Law Review* 63 (September 1990): 1783–1795.

———. "Super-Liberal: Romance, Community, and Tradition in William J. Brennan Jr.'s Constitutional Thought." *Virginia Law Review* 77 (1991): 1261.

Mill, John Stuart. *On Liberty.* New York: W. W. Norton, 1975.

Mink, Gwendolyn. *Hostile Environment: The Political Betrayal of Sexually Harassed Women.* Ithaca: Cornell University Press, 2000.

Monaghan, Henry. "Professor Jones and the Constitution." *Virginia Law Review* 4 (1979): 87.

Moore, Barrington. *Privacy: Studies in Social and Cultural History.* Armonk, N.Y.: M. E. Sharpe, 1984.

Morris, Debra. "Privacy, Privation, Perversity: Toward New Representations of the Personal." *Signs: Journal of Women in Culture* 25.21 (2000): 323–351.

Murphy, Robert R. "Social Distance and the Veil." In *Philosophical Dimensions of Privacy*, ed. Ferdinand Schoeman, 34–55. Cambridge: Cambridge University Press, 1984.

Nedelsky, Jennifer. "American Constitutionalism and the Paradox of Private Property." In *Constitutionalism and Democracy*, ed. Jon Elster and Rune Slagstad, 241–273. New York: Cambridge University Press, 1998.

———. *Private Property and the Limits of American Constitutionalism: The Madisonian Framework and Its Legacy*. Chicago: University of Chicago Press, 1991.

———. "Reconceiving Autonomy: Sources, Thoughts, and Possibilities." *Yale Journal of Law and Feminism* 1 (1989): 7–33.

Neumann, Franz. "The Change in the Function of Law in Modern Society." In *The Rule of Law Under Siege*, ed. William E. Scheuerman, 101–141. Berkeley: University of California Press, 1996.

Nonet, Philippe, and Philip Selznick. *Law and Society in Transition: Toward Responsive Law*. New York: Octagon Books, 1978.

Note, "The Constitutional Status of Sexual Orientation, Homosexuality as a Suspect Classification." *Harvard Law Review* 98 (1985): 1289.

Nussbaum, Martha. "Only Grey Matter? Richard Posner's Cost-Benefit Analysis of Sex." *University of Chicago Law Review* 59 (1992): 1689.

Offe, Claus. *Modernity and the State: East, West*. Cambridge: MIT Press, 1996.

Okin, Susan Moller. *Justice, Gender, and the Family*. New York: Basic Books, 1989.

Olsen, Frances E. "The Family and the Market: A Study of Ideology and Legal Reform." *Harvard Law Review* 96 (1983): 1497.

———. "A Finger to the Devil: Abortion, Privacy, and Equality." *Dissent* (Summer 1991): 337–381.

———. "The Myth of State Intervention in the Family." *University of Michigan Journal of Law* 18 (1985): 835.

———. "Unraveling Compromise." *Harvard Law Review* 103 (1989): 105.

O'Neill, John. *The Communicative Body*. Evanston: Northwestern University Press, 1989.

———. *Five Bodies: The Human Shape of Modern Society*. Ithaca: Cornell University Press, 1985.

Orren, Karen. "Officers' Rights: Toward a Unified Field Theory of American Constitutional Government." *Ms.*, January 2000.

Ortes, E. "Reflexive Environmental Law." *Northwestern University Law Review* 89 (1995).

Ortiz, Dan. "Creating Controversy: Essentialism and Constructivism and the Politics of Gay Identity." *Virginia Law Review* 79 (1993): 1833.

Pateman, Carole. "Feminist Critiques of the Public/Private Dichotomy." In *Public and Private in Social Life*, ed. Stanley I. Benn and Gerald F. Gauss, 281–303. New York: St. Martin's Press, 1983.

———. *The Sexual Contract*. Stanford: Stanford University Press, 1988.

"The Pentagon's New Policy Guidelines on Homosexuals in the Military." *New York Times*, 20 July 1993, A16.

Perry, Michael J. "The Abortion Funding Cases: A Comment on the Supreme Court's Role in American Government." *Georgetown Law Journal* 66 (1978): 1236–1245.

Pertman, Adam. "Clinton May Provide Fusion of Politics, Policy." *Boston Globe*, 30 October 1992, A1.

Petchesky, Rosalind. *Abortion and Woman's Choice.* Boston: Northeastern University Press, 1985.

Pettit, Philip. *Republicanism: A Theory of Freedom and Government.* Oxford: Clarendon Press, 1997.

Poovey, Mary. "The Abortion Question and the Death of Man." In *Feminists Theorize the Political,* ed. Judith Butler and Joan W. Scott, 239–256. New York: Routledge, 1992.

Posner, Richard. "The Ethics and Economics of Enforcing Contracts of Surrogate Motherhood." *Journal of Contemporary Health Law and Policy* 5 (1989): 21.

———. "The Regulation of the Market in Adoption." *Boston University Law Review* 67 (1987): 59.

———. *Sex and Reason.* Cambridge: Harvard University Press, 1992.

Post, Robert C. "The Social Foundations of Privacy: Community and Self in the Common Law Tort." *California Law Review* 77 (1989): 957.

Preuss, Ulrich. *Constitutional Revolution.* New York: Humanities Press, 1995.

Radin, Margaret J. "Market-Inalienability." *Harvard Law Journal* 100 (1987): 1849.

Rawls, John. *Political Liberalism.* New York: Columbia University Press, 1996.

Regan, Milton C., Jr. *Family Law and the Pursuit of Intimacy.* New York: New York University Press, 1993.

Reiman, J. "Privacy, Intimacy, and Personhood." In *Philosophical Dimensions of Privacy,* ed. Ferdinand Schoeman, 300–316. Cambridge: Cambridge University Press, 1984.

Richards, David. "Constitutional Legitimacy and Constitutional Privacy." *New York University Law Review* 61 (1986): 800.

———. "Sexual Autonomy and the Constitutional Right to Privacy: A Case Study in Human Rights and the Unwritten Constitution." *Hastings Law Journal* 30 (1979): 957–964.

———. *Women, Gays, and the Constitution.* Chicago: University of Chicago Press, 1998.

Rimmerman, Craig A. "Promise Unfulfilled: Clinton's Failure to Overturn the Military Ban on Gays and Lesbians." Paper presented at the annual meeting of the American Political Science Association, New York, 1–4 September 1994.

Roberts, Dorothy E. "Punishing Drug Addicts Who Have Babies: Women of Color, Equality, and the Right of Privacy." *Harvard Law Review* 104 (1991): 1419.

Rogowski, Ralph, and Ton Wilthagen, eds. *Reflexive Labor Law: Studies in Industrial Relations and Employment Regulation.* Dordrecht: Kluwer, 1991.

Roiphe, Katie. *The Morning After: Sex, Fear, and Feminism on Campus.* New York: Little, Brown, 1994.

Rorty, Richard. *Contingency, Irony, and Solidarity.* New York: Cambridge University Press, 1989.

Rosen, Jeffrey. "Court Watch: Reasonable Women." *New Republic*, 1 November 1993, 12.

———. "The End of Privacy." *New Republic*, 16 February 1998, 21–23.

———. "Men Behaving Badly." *New Republic*, 29 December 1997, 19.

———. "My Child, Mine to Protect." *New York Times*, 7 June 2000.

———. *The Unwanted Gaze*. New York: Random House, 2000.

Rosenblum, Nancy, ed. *Liberalism and the Moral Life*. Cambridge: Harvard University Press, 1989.

Rosenfeld, Michael, and Andrew Arato, eds. *Habermas on Law and Democracy: Critical Exchanges*. Berkeley: University of California Press, 1998.

Rosin, Hanna. "The Ban Plays On." *New Republic*, 2 May 1994, 11–13.

Rostboll, Christian. "Reflexive Law and Democracy." Unpublished manuscript.

Rothman, Barbara Katz. *Recreating Motherhood: Ideology and Technology in a Patriarchy*. New York: W. W. Norton, 1989.

Rubenfeld, Jed. "The Right of Privacy." *Harvard Law Review* 102 (1989): 737.

Rubin, Gayle. "Thinking Sex: Notes for a Radical Theory of the Politics of Sexuality." In *Pleasure and Danger*, ed. Carol S. Vance, 267–319. London: Routledge and Kegan Paul, 1984.

Saguy, Abigail Cope. "Employment Discrimination or Sexual Violence? Defining Sexual Harassment in French and American Law." *Law and Society Review* 34.4 (2001): 301–338.

Samar, Vincent. *The Right to Privacy: Gays, Lesbians, and the Constitution*. Philadelphia: Temple University Press, 1991.

Sandel, Michael J. *Democracy's Discontent*. Cambridge: Harvard University Press, 1996.

———. "Justice and the Good." In *Liberalism and Its Critics*, ed. Michael J. Sandel, 159–176. New York: New York University Press, 1984.

———. *Liberalism and the Limits of Justice*. Cambridge: Cambridge University Press, 1982.

———. "Moral Argument and Liberal Toleration: Abortion and Homosexuality." *California Law Review* 77 (May 1989): 521–538.

———. "The Procedural Republic and the Unencumbered Self." *Political Theory* 12.1 (1984): 81–96.

———. "Religious Liberty—Freedom of Conscience or Freedom of Choice?" *Utah Law Review* 3 (1989): 597–615.

———, ed. *Liberalism and Its Critics*. New York: New York University Press, 1984.

Sanger, Carol. "The Erotics of Torts." *Michigan Law Review* 96 (May 1998): 1852.

Sangree, Susan. "Title VII Provisions against Hostile Environment Sexual Harassment and the First Amendment: No Collision in Sight." *Rutgers Law Review* 47 (1995): 461.

Scanlon, Thomas. "Contractualism and Utilitarianism." In *Utilitarianism and Beyond*, ed. Amartya Sen and Bernard Williams, 103–128. Cambridge: Cambridge University Press, 1982.

———. "The Difficulty of Tolerance." In *Toleration: An Elusive Virtue*, ed. David Heyd, 226–239. Princeton: Princeton University Press, 1996.

Scarry, Elaine. *The Body in Pain: The Making and Unmaking of the World.* New York: Oxford University Press, 1985.

Schmitt, Eric. "President's Policy on Gay Troops Is Backed in Vote of Senate Panel." *New York Times,* 24 July 1993, A7.

Scheuerman, Bill. "Reflexive Law and the Challenges of Globalization." *Journal of Political Philosophy* 9.1 (2001): 81–102.

———. "The Rule of Law and the Welfare State: Toward a New Synthesis." *Politics and Society* 22.2 (1994): 195–213.

Schultz, Theodore W., ed. *Economics of the Family: Marriage, Children, and Human Capital.* Chicago: University of Chicago Press, 1947.

Schultz, Vicki. "Reconceptualizing Sexual Harassment, Part 1." *Yale Law Journal* 107 (1998): 1683.

———. "Reconceptualizing Sexual Harassment, Part 2." *Yale Law Journal* 107 (1998): 1733.

Sedgwick, Eve Kosofsky. *Epistemology of the Closet.* Berkeley: University of California Press, 1990.

Segal, Riva. "Rule of Love: Wife Beating as Prerogative and Privacy." *Yale Law Journal* 105 (June 1996): 2117.

Selznick, Philip. *The Moral Commonwealth.* Berkeley: University of California Press, 1992.

———. "Self-Regulation and the Theory of Institutions." In *Environmental Law and Ecological Responsibility: The Concept and Practice of Ecological Self-Organization,* ed. Gunther Teubner, Lindsay Farmer, and Declan Murphy, 395–402. New York: John Wiley, 1994.

Sen, Amartya, and Bernard Williams, eds. *Utilitarianism and Beyond.* Cambridge: Cambridge University Press, 1982.

Shapiro, Ian, ed. *Abortion: The Supreme Court Decisions.* Indianapolis: Hackett, 1995.

Shilts, Randy. *Conduct Unbecoming: Gays and Lesbians in the U.S. Military.* New York: St. Martin's Press, 1993.

Schoeman, Ferdinand, ed. *Philosophical Dimensions of Privacy.* Cambridge: Cambridge University Press, 1984.

———. *Privacy and Social Freedom.* Cambridge: Cambridge University Press, 1992.

Singer, Jana B. "The Privatization of Family Law." *Wisconsin Law Review* 1992 (1992): 1442–1567.

Skinner, Quentin. *Liberty before Liberalism.* Cambridge: Cambridge University Press, 1998.

Smelser, Neil, and Jeffrey C. Alexander, eds. *Diversity and Its Discontents: Cultural Conflict and Common Ground in Contemporary American Society.* Princeton: Princeton University Press, 1999.

Spain, Daphne, and Suzanne Banchi. *Balancing Act: Motherhood, Marriage and Employment among American Workers.* New York: Russell Sage Foundation, 1996.

Stimson, James A., Michael B. MacKuen, and Robert S. Erikson. "Dynamic Representation." *American Political Science Review* 89.3 (1995): 543–565.

Strauss, David A. "Abortion, Toleration, and Moral Uncertainty." *Supreme Court Review* 1 (1993): 1–28.

Streunung, Karen. "Feminist Challenges to the New Familism: Lifestyle Experimentation and the Freedom of Intimate Association." *Hypatia* 11 (Winter 1996): 135–154.

Strossen, Nadine. "The Tensions between Regulating Workplace Harassment and the First Amendment: No Trump." *Chicago-Kent Law Review* 71.3 (1995): 701.

Sturm, Susan. "Second-Generation Employment Discrimination: A Structural Approach." *Columbia Law Review* 101.3 (2001): 458–568.

Sunstein, Cass R. *After the Rights Revolution.* Cambridge: Harvard University Press, 1990.

———. "Constitutions and Democracies." In *Constitutionalism and Democracy,* ed. Jon Elster and Rune Slagstad, 344–348. New York: Cambridge University Press, 1988.

———. "The Enduring Legacy of Republicanism." In *A New Constitutionalism: Designing Political Institutions for a Good Society,* ed. S. E. Elkin and K. E. Soltan. Chicago: University of Chicago Press, 1993.

———. "Neutrality in Constitutional Law." *Columbia Law Review* 92 (1992): 1.

———. "Paradoxes of the Regulatory State." *University of Chicago Law Review* 57 (Spring 1990): 407.

———. *The Partial Constitution.* Cambridge: Harvard University Press, 1993.

———. "Preferences and Politics." *Philosophy and Public Affairs* 20.1 (1991): 3–34.

———. "Sexual Orientation and the Constitution: A Note on the Relationship between Due Process and Equal Protection." *University of Chicago Law Review* 55 (1988): 1161.

Taylor, Charles. "The Politics of Recognition." In *Multiculturalism: Examining the Politics of Recognition,* ed. Amy Gutmann, 25–74. Princeton: Princeton University Press, 1992.

———. *Sources of the Self.* Cambridge: Harvard University Press, 1989.

Teubner, Gunther. "After Legal Instrumentalism? Strategic Models of Post-Regulatory Law." In *Dilemmas of Law in the Welfare State,* 299–326. New York: Walter de Gruyter, 1986.

———. "Ältera Pars Audiatur: Law in the Collision of Discourses." In *Law, Society, and Economy,* ed. Richard Rawlings, 149–176. Oxford: Clarendon Press, 1997.

———. "Autopoiesis in Law and Society: A Rejoinder to Blankenburg." *Law and Society Review* 18.2 (1984): 298.

———. "Contracting Worlds: The Many Autonomies of Private Law." In *Social and Legal Studies* 9.3 (2000): 399–417.

———. "Substantive and Reflexive Elements in Modern Law." *Law and Society Review* 17.2 (1993): 239–285.

———, ed. *Dilemmas of Law in the Welfare State.* Berlin: Walter de Gruyter, 1986.

Teubner, Guenter, Lindsay Farmer, and Declan Murphy, eds. *Environmental Law and Ecological Responsibility: The Concept and Practice of Ecological Self-Organization.* New York: John Wiley and Sons, 1994.

Thomas, Kendall. "Beyond the Privacy Principle." *Columbia Law Review* 92 (1992): 1431.

―――. "The Eclipse of Reason: A Rhetorical Reading of Bowers v. Hardwick." *Virginia Law Review* 79 (1994): 1805.

Thompson, J. J. "A Defense of Abortion." *Philosophy and Public Affairs* 1 (Fall 1971): 47–66.

Toobin, Jeffrey. "The Trouble with Sex: Why the Law of Harassment Has Never Worked." *New Yorker*, 9 February 1998, 48.

Tribe, Lawrence. *American Constitutional Law.* 2nd ed. New York: Foundation Press, 1988.

―――. *The Clash of Absolutes.* New York: W. W. Norton, 1990.

Turner, Bryan. *The Body and Society.* New York: Blackwell, 1984.

Urbinati, Nadia. "Representation as Advocacy: A Study of Democratic Deliberation." *Political Theory* 28.6 (2000): 758–786.

Vance, Carol S., ed. *Pleasure and Danger.* London: Routledge and Kegan Paul, 1984.

Volokh, Eugene. "Comment: Freedom of Speech and Workplace Harassment." *UCLA Law Review* 39 (1992): 1791.

―――. "What Speech Does 'Hostile Work Environment' Harassment Law Restrict?" *Georgetown Law Journal* 85 (1997): 627–648.

Vorwerk, Hannah Katherine. "The Forgotten Interest Group: Reforming Title VII to Address the Concerns of Workers While Eliminating Sexual Harassment." *Vanderbilt Law Review* 4 (May 1995): 1019.

Waldron, Jeremy. *Liberal Rights: Collected Papers, 1981–1991.* Cambridge: Cambridge University Press, 1993.

―――, ed. *Nonsense upon Stilts.* New York: Methuen, 1987.

Walker, Timothy B., and Linda D. Elrod. "Family Law in the Fifty States: An Overview." *Family Law Quarterly* 25 (1992): 417.

Warren, Mark, ed. *Democracy and Trust.* New York: Cambridge University Press, 1999.

Warren, Samuel D., and Louis D. Brandeis. "The Right to Privacy." *Harvard Law Review* 4 (1890): 193–220. Reprinted in *Philosophical Dimensions of Privacy*, ed. Ferdinand Schoeman, 75–103. Cambridge: Cambridge University Press, 1984.

Watson, Katie. "An Alternative to Privacy: The First Amendment Right of Intimate Association." *Review of Law and Social Change* 19 (1992): 891–931.

Weber, Max. *Economy and Society, Volume 2.* Berkeley: University of California Press, 1978.

Weeks, Jeffrey. *Sexuality and Its Discontents: Meaning, Myths, and Modern Sexualities.* New York: Routledge, 1993.

Weiss, Phillip. "Don't Even Think about It." *New York Times Magazine*, 3 May 1998.

Weitzman, Lenore. *The Divorce Revolution: The Unexpected Social and Economic Consequences for Women and Children in America.* New York: Macmillan, 1985.

―――. *The Marriage Contract.* New York: Free Press, 1981.

Wenz, Peter S. *Abortion Rights as Religious Freedom.* Philadelphia: Temple University Press, 1992.

West, Robin. "Authority, Autonomy, and Choice: The Role of Consent in the Moral and Political Visions of Franz Kafka and Richard Posner." *Harvard Law Review* 99 (1985): 384.

———. *Caring for Justice.* New York: New York University Press, 1997.

———. "The Difference in Women's Hedonic Lives: A Phenomenological Critique of Feminist Legal Theory." *Wisconsin Women's Law Journal* 3 (1987): 81.

———. "Jurisprudence and Gender." *University of Chicago Law Review* 55 (1988): 1.

Whitebook, Joel. "Reflections on the Autonomous Individual and the Decentered Subject." *Am Imago* 49 (1992): 97.

Wilke, Helmut. "Three Types of Legal Structure: The Conditional, the Purposive, and the Relational Program." In *Dilemmas of Law in the Welfare State*, ed. Gunther Teubner, 280–298. New York: Walter de Gruyter, 1988.

Williams, Pat. *The Alchemy of Race and Rights.* Cambridge: Harvard University Press, 1991.

Wolff, Kurt, ed. *The Sociology of Georg Simmel.* Glencoe, Ill.: Free Press, 1964.

Wolff, Robert Paul, Barrington Moore, Jr., and Herbert Marcuse, eds. *A Critique of Pure Tolerance.* Boston: Beacon Press, 1965.

"Word for Word: Military Gay Policy; When 'Don't Ask, Don't Tell' Means Do Ask and Do Tell All." *New York Times*, 3 March 1996, E7.

Younger, Judith. "Marital Regimes: A Story of Compromise and Demoralization, Together with Criticism and Suggestions for Reform." *Cornell Law Review* 67 (1981): 45.

Index